Frankl.
Experienc   ᴊophy

*A Personal Record of Transformation
and a Discussion of Transcendental Consciousness*

Franklin Merrell-Wolff's Experience and Philosophy

*A Personal Record of Transformation
and a Discussion of Transcendental Consciousness*

Containing His
Philosophy of Consciousness Without an Object
and His
Pathways Through to Space

FRANKLIN MERRELL-WOLFF

STATE UNIVERSITY OF NEW YORK PRESS

Published by
State University of New York Press, Albany

©1994 Doroethy Leonard and Robert Briggs

All rights reserved

Printed in the United States of America

No part of this book may be used or reproduced
in any manner whatsoever without written permission
except in the case of brief quotations embodied in
critical articles and reviews.

For information, address:
  State University of New York Press
  State University Plaza
  Albany, N.Y. 12246

Production by Cathleen Collins
Marketing by Nancy Farrell

Library of Congress Cataloging in Publication Data

Merrell-Wolff, Franklin.
    Franklin Merrell-Wolff's experience and philosophy : a personal
record of transformation and a discussion of transcendental
consciousness : containing his Philosophy of consciousness without
an object, and his Pathways through to space / Franklin Merrell-Wolff.
    p.   cm.
    Includes bibliographical references and index.
    ISBN 0-7914-1963-0. — ISBN 0-7914-1964-9 (pbk.)
    1. Altered states of consciousness.   2. Self-realization—
Religious aspects.   I. Merrell-Wolff, Franklin. Philosophy of
consciousness without an object. 1994. II. Merrell-Wolff,
Franklin, Pathways through to space. 1994. III. Title.
IV. Title: Experience and philosophy.
BF1045.A48M477   1994
126—dc20   93-30880
                                                              CIP

10 9 8 7 6 5

Contents

PREFACE *ix*

PATHWAYS THROUGH TO SPACE
1 The Light Breaks Forth *3*
2 Concerning Meditative Technique *11*
3 Cosmic and Transcendent Consciousness *12*
4 The Record Continued *15*
5 Evolution and Cosmic Consciousness *16*
6 Myself *17*
7 Jesus and the Way *18*
8 The Ineffable Current of Bliss *19*
9 Concerning the Spontaneity of the Self *22*
10 Seek Me First *22*
11 Expression from Different Levels *23*
12 The Record Continued *25*
13 Nirvanic Bliss *27*
14 The Record Continued *28*
15 The Grand Adventure *30*
16 Alternative Roads to Recognition *31*
17 Being Born Again *34*
18 An Experience with the Fire *36*
19 The Drama of the Triune Man *38*
20 The Meaning of Omniscience *38*
21 The Record Continued *41*
22 The Celestial Virgin *41*
23 Beauty *42*

24 The Record Continued   43
25 Both by Thought and Feeling   45
26 The Sea of Consciousness   46
27 I Who Speak   49
28 How to Understand Mystic Writings   49
29 Concerning Opposition Aroused by Sages   51
30 The Record Continued   51
31 The Level of Real Equality   53
32 The Greatness of Man   53
33 The Moral Problem   54
34 Solar and Planetary Recognition   56
35 Recognition and the Physical Body   57
36 Concerning Occult Powers   59
37 The Underlying Force in Religion   63
38 Knowledge Through Identity   64
39 The Meaning of Substance   68
40 Communion in the Company of the Realized   69
41 Recognition and Egoism   70
42 By Many Paths   72
43 The Record Continued   72
44 The Relation of Karma to Recognition   73
45 The "Awakening," The End of All Religion   78
46 The Conditions that Favor Recognition   79
47 The Nature of the Higher Knowledge   85
48 The Record Continued   90
49 Sleep and Death   93
50 The Well of Ignorance   98
51 Beyond Genius   98
52 The High Indifference   99
53 The Evidence for the Higher Consciousness   107
54 A Poetic Interlude   118
55 The Real and the Unreal   119

Contents

56 Integration   *121*
57 The Gold Mine   *124*
58 The Power of Illumination   *124*
59 Expression and Transcendent Consciousness   *127*
60 The Symbol of the Fourth Dimension   *128*
61 The Nature of Ponderable Matter   *133*
62 Real Equality   *139*
63 The Predicament of Buddha   *140*
64 The Adept World   *142*
65 Manifestation without Evil   *144*
66 The One Element   *144*
67 The Current of Numberless Dimensions   *145*
68 Concerning Duty   *145*
69 Philosophic Reconciliations   *148*
70 Recognition as an Act of Transcendence   *150*
71 The Record Continued   *151*
72 The Problem of Government   *153*
73 Compassion   *156*
74 The Symbolism of the Butterfly   *157*
75 Concerning Asceticism   *160*
76 Poverty and Obedience   *164*
77 The Higher Consciousness and the Mind   *166*
78 The Atlantean Sage   *171*
79 The Barriers to Recognition   *173*
80 The Nameless   *182*
81 The Record Continued   *183*
82 The Point-I and the Space-I   *186*
83 Sangsara   *189*
84 Nirvana   *190*
85 Conceiving and Perceiving   *191*
86 A New Word   *194*
87 The Conflict between Space and Time   *197*

88 The Final Record *208*
89 The Supreme Adventure *213*
90 Addendum to the High Indifference *218*
91 Conclusion: Two Years Later *222*

THE PHILOSOPHY OF CONSCIOUSNESS WITHOUT AN OBJECT

Part I: The Ground of Knowledge
1 The Idea and Its Reference *241*
2 A Mystical Unfoldment *251*

Part II: The Aphorisms on Consciousness Without an Object
3 The Levels of Thought *305*
4 Aphorisms on Consciousness Without an Object *309*
5 General Discussion of Consciousness Without an Object *315*
6 Commentaries on the Aphorisms *354*

GLOSSARY *415*
INDEX *427*

Preface

Some years now have passed since the precipitation of the inner events that led to the writing of this book. It may be said now that the value of this unfoldment remains as high as it ever was. It is true that I would place this treasure far above anything which may be obtained in the ordinary world field, in whatever domain, such as achievement in government, in business, in science, philosophy, mathematics or the arts. All these stand as values far inferior to these greater values which come from Fundamental Realization.

It remains true to my present state of consciousness that I would say that no accomplishment, in the world field, can be effective in solving the wrongness which is so evident in that field, without the insight and resources which are derived from Fundamental Realization. Therefore, it follows that all the efforts of man to solve his own problems, make life richer, and free it from the manifest evils which we see all about, is ineffective in the sense of achieving an effective resolution. As we look at the report recorded in the pages of history, we see the evils which were there in the past are still here today, and even find that those evils have become, if anything, greater than they were before.

As we advance in our scientific knowledge, we not only implement the powers of good that may be in the world but we also implement the powers of evil, with the result that the old difficulties, the old wrongnesses, return again, if anything, in amplified form. Therefore, if we are to resolve in any durable way these difficulties that call for the function of Redemption it is necessary that more and more of this human whole should attain the perspective and the resources that come from Enlightenment.

The traditional solution to the wrongness has been in the form of a retreat from the world field, but it is here suggested that this is not the only possible way. There may be such a thing as transforming the very field of outer action to such an extent that that field itself becomes redeemed and transformed with the result that noble purpose is not distorted into ignoble effects. The task before us is religious in the deepest meaning of that word. But as we look upon the record of traditional religion it must be judged that traditional forms of religion have failed egregiously. This applies to all the religions that we know, less to some than to others, but so far the record of traditionalistic religion is one of essential failure. As it appears to me, that which is needed is a seeking for the ultimate Attainment on the part of as many people as possible—Attainment which is the very Essence of the religious search.

Furthermore, the seeking of this Attainment is not simply for the sake of one's own individual Redemption but for the sake of the Redemption of humanity as a whole and, in addition, of all creatures whatsoever, however humble they may be. He who forgets his own Attainment and his own Redemption in seeking for the Attainment and Redemption of all creatures, is following the Path which is most certain to involve that very Attainment and Redemption for himself. The motive should always be the good of all creatures, not one's own private good.

★ ★ ★

Pathways through to Space is a record of transformation in consciousness written down during the actual process itself, and thus, while it supplies a peculiarly intimate view, yet it loses thereby something of the objective valuation that only distance can contribute. In *Philosophy of Consciousness without an Object* a recapitulation of the record, written after the fact, forms the second chapter.

The perspective in this case is naturally more complete. As a result, the interpretative thought, which follows as the implication of the transformation, possesses a more explicit logical unity. The earlier writing was, of necessity, more in the form of a stream of ideas, composed as they welled up into the foreground of consciousness, rather than a systematic development. The writing was true to the thought of the day or the moment and synoptic in form in so far as it was related to the development of conceptions. Many problems were left incompletely handled, and this was done knowingly, with the intention subsequently to develop the thought more fully. The present book was planned to fill the gaps left in the earlier work.

However, despite my intention to write a logically organized system, I found, somewhat to my embarrassment, the thought persisted in growing in directions I had not foreseen. Formal systematic organization broke down again and again as the flow burst over the dams of preconceived structure. As a result, the present work is only somewhat more systematic than the *Pathways*, but falls short of the requirements of a completed system. Clearly the time is not yet ripe for the rounding out of all parts. Some problems have received a clearer elucidation, but in the process others have arisen that remain unfinished.

He who knows the Awakening becomes something of a poet, no matter how little he was a poet before. No longer may thought remain purely formal. The poet pioneers, while the intellect systematizes. The one opens the Door, while the other organizes command. The functions are complementary. But in this combination there are difficulties as well as advantages. The thought that seeks the rounded system, which shall stand guarded on all sides, ever finds new Doors opening in unexpected places, and then, reorganization becomes necessary. The vistas appearing through each new Opening are far too valuable to be ignored, and besides, Truth cannot be honestly denied. So the system is never closed. I beg the critic to indulge this flaw, if flaw it is.

In the present volume I have found it even logically impossible to disregard the personal factor. By preference I would have written as Spinoza wrote, but in this day we are no longer free to disregard the epistemological problem. No longer can we take conceptions at their face value as carriers of Knowledge. Since the work of Kant we must ever question the authority of all conceptions. Always it is asked, what do the conceptions mean? And in general, they mean a somewhat which is not itself a conception. How, then, is the acquaintance with this somewhat, itself, attained? When the reference is to ordinary experience, the problem is simple enough and may often be assumed, but the Way of Consciousness that becomes available through the transformation is far from the beaten track, so it cannot be taken implicitly, if one would do the reader justice. For that reason a review of the process of transformation is introduced to provide the ground on which the more systematic discussion rests.

Today it is not necessary to prove that there are states of mystical consciousness possessing positive individual and social value. Too many writers of proven intellectual and scientific competency have given serious attention to the subject and have not only demonstrated the actuality of mystical states of consciousness but have found the results for feeling and character development excellent, at least in many instances. I can list the names of men like William James, John Dewey, Bertrand Russell, James H. Leuba, and Alexis Carrel, to say nothing of the great German Idealists who have either written directly from the awakened mystical sense, or at least, know full well its actuality. But with the exception of

William James and the German Idealists, there is a general tendency among such students to claim that no true knowledge of reality, of the "thing-in-itself," can come from the mystical experience. As a result, the primary problem of the present work is the demonstration, as far as may be, of the actuality of noetic value springing from mystical or gnostic roots. I was forced, therefore, to give serious attention to philosophical and psychological criticism and to develop my thesis with an eye to the pitfalls indicated by such criticism. Much of this criticism is distinctly challenging and may not be lightly brushed aside. To him who has the poet's insight or the intuitive feeling of the unfettered religious nature, much of the critical part of the discussion will appear unnecessary and many modes of formulation unduly devious and recondite. To such I would say: "Be patient, and remember I am not writing only for those who believe easily. Know you not that there are men of intellectual power and honesty in this world who view you patronizingly as little, well-meaning, but credulous children? I would command for you respectful attention even though there may be much honest disagreement."

Franklin Merrell-Wolff

PATHWAYS THROUGH
TO SPACE

1
The Light Breaks Forth

August 17

The ineffable transition came, about ten days ago.

We had just returned to our Southern California home after a few weeks' stay in a small town in the Mother Lode country in the northern part of the State, and I was resting from the fatigue induced by the all-night driving of the automobile. At the time, I was engaged in the reading of portions of "The System of the Vedanta" by Paul Deussen, as I had been doing more or less systematically during the preceding three weeks. This work is an interpretation in western philosophic form of the Vedanta as it is developed in the commentaries of Shankara on the Brahmasutras. I had been led to this specific program of reading through the realization that Shankara's words had peculiar power, at least in my own experience. For some time I had spontaneously looked to him as to a Guru* with whom I was in complete sympathetic accord. I had found him always clear and convincing, at least in all matters relative to the analysis of consciousness, while with the other Sages I either found obscurities or emphases with which I could not feel complete sympathy. For some months I had resolved to delve more deeply into the thought of Shankara, in so far as it was available in translated form. It was in pursuance of this purpose that I was slowly reading and meditating upon "The System of the Vedanta."

I had been following this course while completing a cross-cut in a gold-prospect near the small town of Michigan Bluff. Much of this time I was completely alone and was more than usually successful in penetrating the meaning and following the logic of what I was reading. One day, after the evening meal and while still sitting at the table, I found that, by gradual transition, I had passed into a very delightful state of contemplation. The actual content of the thought of that period is forgotten, but as I made careful note of the state I was in and submitted it to close scrutiny, the quality of the state was well impressed upon my memory. My breath had changed, but not in the sense of stopping or becoming extremely

---
*'Guru' is a Sanskrit term carrying the meaning of spiritual Teacher.

slow or rapid. It was, perhaps, just a little slower than normal. The notable change was in a subtle quality associated with the air breathed. Over and above the physical gases of the air there seemed to be an impalpable substance of indescribable sweetness which, in turn, was associated with a general sense of well-being, embracing even the physical man. It was like happiness or joy, but these words are inadequate. It was of a very gentle quality, yet far transcended the value of any of the more familiar forms of happiness. It was quite independent of the beauty or comfort of the environment. At that time the latter was, to say the least, austere and not in any sense attractive. This quality, associated with the air, I had, in a smaller measure, previously experienced at high altitudes in the mountains, but in the present instance the altitude was only 1800 feet and the air was far from invigorating, due to the period being exceptionally warm. However, introspective analysis revealed the fact that the elixir-like quality was most marked during the exhalation, thus indicating that it was not derived from the surrounding air. Further, the exhaled breath was not simply air expelled into the outer atmosphere, but seemed to penetrate down through the whole organism like a gentle caress, leaving throughout a quiet sense of delight. It seemed to me like a nectar. Since that time I have learned that it is the true Ambrosia.

It is, perhaps, pertinent to note in passing that a few days previously, as a result of thought stimulated by my readings, I had developed an interpretation of the nature of ponderable matter that seemed to me to clear away certain logical difficulties which always have seemed to persist in the efforts to reconcile Transcendent Being with the physical universe. The idea is that ponderable matter—meaning by that term all things sensed whether gross or subtle—is, in fact, a relative absence of substance, a sort of partial vacuum. At the present time I shall not develop the evidence and logic supporting this idea, though this was outlined in my consciousness during the days following the origin of it. The significant point in connection with the present record is the effect this idea had upon my own consciousness. It seems to have had a vital part in clearing the way for the Illumination that came later. This effect was produced in the following manner: Habitually we regard the material filling of sensation as being substantial. To offset this, we may have been theoretically convinced that so-called empty space is not only filled, but actually more substantial than the portions of it occupied by ponderable matter. This idea is not new to metaphysics, and much in the literature of modern physics is not incompatible with it. But I have found that ideas received from outer sources, even though in convincing form, lack the power over consciousness possessed by an original idea.* *The effect of this idea with me was a far more effective acceptance of substantial reality where the senses reported emptiness, and a greater capacity to realize unreality—or merely dependent and derivative reality—in the material given through the senses.*

There are further prior pertinent factors which, it seems, should be noted. About eighteen months ago there began a series of conversations with one whom I recognized as a Sage. I checked the validity of my recognition of this One in every way that I could and proved His genuineness to my complete satisfaction. I acted on His word when I could not see clearly and found that clarity gradually unfolded. Acting upon His suggestions, Sherifa—my wife—and I undertook a phase of public work not hitherto attempted. Both of us found as we progressed in the work a gradual growth of understanding that has steadily brought Light where there had been obscurity. Among other things this Sage suggested my correlation with a previous incarnation of special importance. He advised me that He was not, and could not be, my personal Guru, as that relationship was dependent upon alignments that are not arbitrary.

In the past, two important Recognitions have come to me. First, nearly fourteen years ago, in a setting which it is not necessary to delineate, I suddenly recognized "I am Atman." This effected important changes of outlook that persisted. Second, less than one year ago, while engaged in the public work mentioned above, and while deeply interested in a book giving a report of a living Indian Sage, I also suddenly recognized that Nirvana is not a field, or space, or world which one entered and that contained one as space might contain an external object, but rather that "I am identical with Nirvana, and always have been and always will be so." This Recognition likewise had its persistent effects upon the personal consciousness.

We are now ready to return to the Recognition of ten days ago. I say "Recognition" rather than "experience" for a very definite reason. Properly it was not a case of experiential knowledge, which is knowledge from the senses whether gross or subtle, nor knowledge from deduction, though both forms, particularly the latter, have helped in a subsidiary sense. It was an Awakening to a Knowledge which I can best

---

*By 'original' I do not mean an idea that has never been thought before, but one which, for the individual, has been produced with a creative effort from himself.

represent by calling it Knowledge through Identity and thus the process—in so far as we can speak of process in this connection at all—is best expressed by the word "Recognition."

I had been sitting in a porch swing, reading as previously stated. Ahead of the sequence in the book, I turned to the section devoted to "Liberation," as I seemed to feel an especial hunger for this. I covered the material quickly and it all seemed very clear and satisfactory. Then, as I sat afterward dwelling in thought upon the subject just read, suddenly it dawned upon me that a common mistake made in the higher meditation—i.e., meditation for Liberation—is the seeking for a subtle object of Recognition, in other words, something that could be experienced. Of course, I had long known the falseness of this position theoretically, yet had failed to recognize it. (Here is a subtle but very important distinction.) At once, I dropped expectation of having anything happen. Then, with eyes open and no sense stopped in functioning—hence no trance—I abstracted the subjective moment—the "I AM" or "Atman" element—from the totality of the objective consciousness manifold. Upon this I focused. Naturally, I found what, from the relative point of view, is Darkness and Emptiness. *But I Realized It as Absolute Light and Fullness and that I was That.* Of course, I cannot tell what IT was in Its own nature. The relative forms of consciousness inevitably distort non-relative Consciousness. Not only can I not tell this to others, I cannot even contain it within my own relative consciousness, whether of sensation, feeling, or thought. Every metaphysical thinker will see this impossibility at once. I was even prepared not to have the personal consciousness share in this Recognition in any way. But in this I was happily disappointed. Presently I felt the Ambrosia-quality in the breath with the purifying benediction that it casts over the whole personality, even including the physical body. I found myself above the universe, not in the sense of leaving the physical body and being taken out in space, but in the sense of being above space, time, and causality. My karma seemed to drop away from me as an individual responsibility. I felt intangibly, yet wonderfully, free. I sustained this universe and was not bound by it. Desires and ambitions grew perceptibly more and more shadowy. All worldly honors were without power to exalt me. Physical life seemed undesirable. Repeatedly, through the days that followed, I was in a state of deep brooding, thinking thoughts that were so abstract that there were no concepts to represent them. I seemed to comprehend a veritable library of Knowledge, all less concrete than the most abstract mathematics. The personality rested in a gentle glow of happiness, but while it was very gentle, yet it was so potent as to dull the keenest sensuous delight. Likewise the sense of world-pain was absorbed. I looked, as it were, over the world, asking: "What is there of interest here? What is there worth doing?" I found but one interest: the desire that other souls should also realize this that I had realized, for in it lay the one effective key for the solving of their problems. The little tragedies of men left me indifferent. I saw one great Tragedy, the cause of all the rest, the failure of man to realize his own Divinity. I saw but one solution, the Realization of this Divinity.

Since that day I have been repeatedly in the Current of Ambrosia. Often I turn to It with the ease of a subtle movement of thought. Sometimes It breaks out spontaneously. Thought and bodily action can be continued in It, provided a subtle kind of inner concentration is not broken. But consciousness focused in action, whether intellectual or physical, stops the Current. The presence of some people affects It adversely, while that of others does not. The effect on the body is interesting. The after-effect of this surprisingly gentle Current, with all Its exquisite delight, is a feeling of intangible tiredness in the body, somewhat like that which would be experienced after a period of protracted pain. Physical effort is difficult. The reason for this seems to be evident. One effect of the Current is clearly purifying, and this action upon the matter of the body is something of an ordeal. There is no emotional nor intellectual discomfort, save that without the Current the world seems barren.

I am studying the effect of the Current upon others. Sherifa is immediately responsive to It and recognizes Its presence, at times even before I do. It will grip an audience, but those who have heretofore given recognition to a consciousness of substantially lower quality do not seem to be aware of the Ambrosia.* Perhaps It is too subtle.

August 20

On the evening of the 17th we attended a musical concert at the Hollywood Bowl. The audience was extremely large. During the early part of the program I had a sense of the crowd as an enormous weight upon

---

*At the present date, almost two and one-half years after writing the above, this statement must be strongly modified. After two intervening seasons on the lecture platform combined with several personal contacts, it has been clearly determined that a surprising number of individuals are susceptible to the Current. In some natures it is quite readily induced.

consciousness. It was so heavy I could not pierce through it. Later, during the performance of certain Bach selections there was a distinct easing up of the weight and a mild tingling along the spine. Consciousness did rise in some measure, but not to the level of the Current.

On the 19th we returned home. I felt deeply tired and was unable to rise in consciousness. It seems that the inward penetration does make some demand upon the body. Life without the Elixir has become more empty than it was before the Current was first experienced. Mere external affairs utterly fail to hold my interest.

The conditions of town life seem definitely adverse to holding consciousness within the Current of Bliss. Driving an automobile in traffic is particularly inimical. The reason seems quite clearly to be that under these conditions it is much more difficult to hold the inner concentration unbroken. To steer a way through the outer confusion requires objective concentration. I, at least, cannot yet move through these conditions with safety by giving only a peripheral attention to them. Perhaps it may be possible to establish the correlation so that it will hold under these adverse conditions, but the demand upon the vital strength is severe.

August 22

Late yesterday afternoon I awakened again to the deeper Consciousness, though not so profoundly as upon the first occasion. The immediate inducing cause was the reading of a portion of Shankara's "Direct Realization." The inciting occasion each time seems to be a new turn in Recognition, combined with a certain creative act of the relative consciousness. The moment of creative discovery is the crucial one. There is then a deepening of consciousness, a sort of retreat of the relative world, in a subtle sense, and then the quality of Bliss flows over the personality. From a profound level thought is stimulated, or, perhaps more correctly, fed.

Throughout this whole period I am engaged in thought of a degree of profundity unprecedented in my previous experience. While, in one sense, the "I AM" is the uttermost of simplicity, yet there is invoked along with the direct presence of It a new view of the universe that requires to be thought through and the elaborations in this thought are greater than those that I have known heretofore. There is so much to be made clear in thought that there is hardly time to give it expression. There is also a difference in the thought-level. In the past, I seemed, in general, to reach deeper when putting forth the effort to express myself, particularly in writing. Now expression seems more a reaching downward into forms that are inadequate. My inward thought seems clearer in its relative formlessness than when I give it formulation, yet formerly it seemed to me that I could express myself almost beyond my genuine understanding. I have to resist a certain boredom in the effort to give expression. I can understand why the plans of learned men to compose systems sometimes fail to materialize when they break through to Liberation. The objective effort seems too poor in its results. However, the expression is needed, and it is necessary that the work be done.

I find that there is a decided intellectual enrichment, but the outer sensuous life is poorer, at the present time. Does this latter fact constitute a danger to the body? The tide of physical life does run perceptibly lower. How is physical interest, never strong with me, to be cultivated so that the body will take on more virility? Disgust with the external world does help toward Liberation, but it is a barrier to the assertion of the continued will-to-live. Yet this is necessary if one is to carry on among men. I foresee the possibility that will without desire may prove to be an overly severe asceticism.

* * *

We have been practicing meditation each evening. I have aimed at the segregation of the subjective factor in consciousness. I have allowed meditation with the eyes closed. S. reported heavy sleepiness and L. nodded in her chair. I think we will have to work with the eyes open. The reason for this is becoming clear. The sensory field of the eye is stronger than that of any of the other senses. With the eyes open, waking consciousness continues stronger than otherwise. Permitting the objective consciousness to continue through its own automatism, the point will be to concentrate on the subjective moment. It would seem that this should correlate Realization more effectively with the personal consciousness. It is not enough to reach the Self in sleep.

* * *

I seem to be dreaming more than I have in a long time. Much of this dreaming seems to be a reviewing of events connected with the past, although the scenes and the events are transformed so that they are not photographic reproductions of the physical originals. There also seems to be a continuation of the trains of thought that were started during the waking state. The dreams are quite lacking in sensual intriguery, but are more the nature of a dispassionate reviewing of events, scenes, and ideas.

Night before last the outline of a plan for another book or two developed in my consciousness. The principal one* of these would be on the subject of "Recognition," the plan to be a development of the process of knowledge, tied in with the present philosophic thought, and then to have the emphasis placed upon the extraction of the subjective moment in consciousness. The theoretical part would not be new, but along with this there would be a new value afforded by reason of its being written from the perspective of an actual Recognition. It would aim to show that "Recognition" is the practical end implicit in our own best philosophy. It could be shown that to *Realize* the "pure apperception" of Kant is to attain Recognition and Liberation.

August 26

The force of physical life is running higher today, but it is far from being really vigorous.

I am exploring a new world. There is so much which requires to be thought into clarity that there seems not to be time enough for the writing, setting aside all more external activities. But it is necessary that a record should be kept as far as the inner events and ideas can be captured. My thought is extraordinarily clear. An increasing amount of it is now within the range of formulation, but my actual thought is in the form of a sort of shorthand which takes much less time than the completed expression on paper or the spoken word. The writing process seems so slow! I shall place down what I can in this record as the material comes to the foreground, leaving systematic formulation to the future.

---

* Several ideas that are properly a part of such a proposed work subsequently became incorporated in this volume. They are introduced here in the sequence in which they were actually born into formulation.

2
Concerning Meditative Technique

The form of meditation that I have found effective differs substantially from that generally given in the manuals on meditation.* Repeatedly I have tried stopping thought and closing out the senses, but the artificial state thus effected was barren of results. Heretofore, the rich values have come to me through or while thinking. I finally took this fact as a key and abandoned all effort to stop thought or to interfere with the reports of sensation. In any case, the distraction caused by the latter I have found to be too weak to be of real importance. Through the larger part of my life the thought-world has naturally dominated the sensation-world so that sensation had come to mean little more than do small waves to an ocean liner. The issue thus lay between thought-consciousness and Transcendent-Consciousness while the rest, I found, could be neglected. Now, within a process or manifold, a given phase or aspect may be isolated for special attention without stopping the process or eliminating the balance of the manifold. This is a familiar technique in scientific and philosophic thinking. When I recalled this fact and applied it, I found at once a really effective method of meditation. In fact, I realize, I have done this for many years without regarding it as a meditative technique. It was by applying this method of isolation of the essential element in the midst of a complex, without trying to restrain the other components, that the Transition was effected during the early part of this month.

I think that there is an important principle involved in this method that may be of fundamental importance, especially as it accords with certain experiences that have developed in western psychological research. Following the methods that proved so successful in physics, i.e., the isolation in high degree of a single causal factor in a given phenomenon for the purposes of special study, the psychologists sought to achieve something of the same research-efficiency in the psychical domain. Thus, for studying the effects of particular stimuli dark and silent rooms were

---

*Subsequent to the completion of these writings I came into possession of *Tibetan Yoga and Secret Doctrines*, edited by Walter Y. Evans-Wentz. In the discussion of meditative practice given in one of the Yoga manuals contained therein, I was surprised and gratified to find that my seemingly independent discovery of a meditative method was actually a re-discovery of a well-established and ancient principle of true meditation.

invented. In this respect some of these rooms were so well designed that perfection was very nearly achieved. Subjects were placed in them and then studies were made in a supposedly undistracted field. It was found, however, that a subjective distraction was introduced that interfered more than ordinary external diversion. The unusual darkness and silence placed the subject under abnormal states, and the result was an aggravated psychical complex instead of the psychical simplicity that was sought. This corresponds exactly with my experience in trying to close out sensation and, particularly, thought in meditative penetration.

But by ignoring the thought it does tend to weaken in force and there is an increasing degree of inner calmness. As the inward Life takes hold, the thought becomes something like a subdued harmonic accompaniment to a strongly accentuated inner melody. Further, this accompaniment has a positive value. It is possible that an individual could penetrate the transcendental or subjective world and make no correlation with relative consciousness. But if the thought-current remains active it can reflect, in some measure, the inner Reality, and thus the personal man has a share in the Awakening. In addition, this correlation is necessary if any of the value of the Illumination is to be conveyed to the intelligence of other individuals.

3
Cosmic and Transcendent Consciousness

Yesterday I started delving into "Cosmic Consciousness" by Dr. R. M. Bucke. This is a very valuable work. It is an analysis of the states and experiences of certain men and women who have realized, in greater or lesser degree, a kind of mystical consciousness which places them at once on a different level from other men. The common characteristics of these individuals and of their inward experiences—in so far as the word "experience" can be correctly employed in this connection—have been isolated by Dr. Bucke. At the same time, the hardly less important differences have been noted. This study constitutes a real clarification of the problem of the relationship between ordinary consciousness and the kind of consciousness commonly called mystical.

Bucke's "self-consciousness" is really equivalent to "egoism" as this term is employed by Buddha and a number of other writers on mystical subjects. It must be carefully distinguished from "Self-consciousness" as when used to designate consciousness of the SELF. As a number of writers have employed this term in the latter sense, it has seemed to me less confusing to avoid Dr. Bucke's usage but to substitute such words as "egoism," "egoistic consciousness," "subject-object consciousness," etc., and accordingly I will follow such a course. The "self-consciousness" of Dr. Bucke is an advance beyond the "simple consciousness" of the typical animal but, in its turn, something of a barrier to "Cosmic Consciousness." The latter term I find only partly satisfactory. This is a point that requires some elucidation.

Recognition of the SELF in its purity is Realization of Identity with absolute Emptiness, Darkness, and Silence, when viewed from the standpoint of relative consciousness. In point of fact this Emptiness is Absolute Fullness but, as such, never can be comprehended from the perspective of egoistic consciousness. In one sense it is the "thing-in-itself" of Kant. Relative consciousness deals with phenomena alone and can never reach beyond phenomena. But the phenomenal world rests upon the Real or Noumenal World. Thus it is that the Consciousness of the SELF or "pure apperceptive consciousness" sustains the whole universe or cosmos. But the latter is an outward projection. Behind the cosmos is the formless or Transcendental World. Within the cosmos is the domain of relative consciousness. From the latter standpoint the SELF appears as formless. Hence the approach—for from the relative point of view it seems like an approach—to the SELF from consciousness posited within the cosmos takes on the form of progressive negation of all identity with form until finally Identity in the Formless breaks forth as Recognition. At this stage Recognition may well take the form of "I am Formlessness." But this is really an incomplete Recognition, as Shankara has shown by his acute logic. The final Recognition is "I am not form and I am not formless." This standpoint is neutral with respect to the cosmos and the truly Transcendental or Formless. What this really means is that beyond Nirvana there is a Paranirvana which is a position of metaphysical indifference with respect to the states of manifestation or non-manifestation. At the same time, the individual soul may have a tendency or natural gravitation either toward the manifested or the non-manifested. Thus Buddha, being drawn toward the non-manifested, was tempted not to put forth the effort to establish His Message among men. On the other hand, Jesus, being drawn toward the manifested, faced the temptation in the form of worldly power. Both men conquered the temptation. But the form of the temptation marks what really is the individual bent or tendency of these supremely great Men. Thus we may say that the sublimated Consciousness of Jesus was predominantly "Cosmic Consciousness," while that of Buddha was "Transcendental" or "Noumenal Consciousness." The common basis of both is Identity in the SELF.

Dr. Bucke does show a considerable understanding of "Cosmic Consciousness" but seems to miss completely "Transcendental" or "Noumenal Consciousness." Hence, he very largely fails to understand the significance of Buddha and gives to Walt Whitman a rather too exalted place. But doubtless Dr. Bucke speaks with the natural bent in valuation characteristic of the West, and very likely the form of Recognition proper to the West is more in accord with that of Whitman than that of Buddha. The very genus of the West seems to be foreign to "Nirvikalpa Samadhi."

For my own part, I cannot conceive of anyone who has glimpsed the beauty of the Transcendent Formlessness ever preferring cosmic beauty. He may choose to move in the world of form from a consideration of Compassion, but not because of the intriguery of the beauty of form as compared to that other Beauty.

Today, I find that in a deep sense I understand Walt Whitman, for I, too, have Awakened. But heretofore Whitman was not at all clear to me, and his words have not helped me to the Awakening. In contrast, the writings of Shankara have proved of the highest potency, while among Western writers it is Immanuel Kant who did most to prepare the Way for me. This is clearly a matter related to individual temperament. Whitman's Recognition is unquestionably genuine, but for me his words did not clarify but served, rather, to obscure the Way. Of Mohammed's expression this would have been even truer had I tried to make serious use of it. Yet Mohammed did attain some degree of mystical insight. It seems clear that no man can effectively illumine the Way for all men. There is more than one main Road and a great number of sub-roads. On all these, men who can serve as beacons are needed.

4
The Record Continued

Sunday and Monday were spent in Los Angeles. The fatigue induced by the city was considerable and made sleep imperative.

I am practicing the holding of consciousness on the objective or relative side deliberately so as not to drive the physical organism too hard. I find that turning the one way or the other is considerably within my control, but to remain on the objective side requires rather the greater effort. Inclination draws toward the Inward. Without the Current the objective world is like a desert in the invidious sense of the term. How is it possible for humanity to be so attached to this outer life?

Yesterday I deliberately turned Inward and invoked the Current with the accompanying deepening of Consciousness, but in this Case in a modified form. Always there is the gentle Joy.

Saturday evening we had the usual meditation. I suggested the technique of not trying to stop thought or the reports of the senses, but to focus upon the Emptiness with the intellectual recognition: "I am this Emptiness." S. entered into a level of peace and joy wherein she found herself one with the stars and all things. There was none of the effect of drowsiness previously experienced. Afterwards I called attention to the point that one should aim at the Emptiness as the highest, but that the consequence in relative consciousness is a new richness developing along the lines of the natural bent of the individual consciousness. On the other hand, if one aimed at a conceivable goal, he sets that goal as an arbitrary limit. The advantage of aiming beyond all possible limits lies in rendering more nearly realizable the fullest possibilities of the individual. The Emptiness is thus the real Philosopher's Stone which transforms all things to new richnesses; It is the Alkahest that transmutes the base metal of inferior consciousness into the Gold of Higher Consciousness.

★ ★ ★

There is a growing compulsion to write. At first I did not care to bother with writing or with any other form of expression. Even the world of thought, hitherto always a rich one with me, became inferior to the Consciousness induced by the Recognition wherein I found Myself sustaining the universe. But I have accepted duty in the relative world and that duty has become, first, thought, and then as complete an exposition of it as its racing current will permit. At first I made myself write, but now there is a growing compulsion that sends me to the typewriter.

★ ★ ★

Sherifa tells me that I should write of a little incident that I would have let pass as many, many others have already passed. We were at the table partaking of the noonday meal. I had just left my writing and was still active in the current of thought. I happened to glance out of the door where a small yellow kitten was playing on a broad cement platform. It ran across the platform and I felt a thrill of delight. It was as though a tiny melody from out the Cosmic Symphony had trilled joyously into my mind—a little sketch born forth from the Grand Harmony. And from this a wave of Joy was distilled and pulsated through me.

It is not that the physical or photographic fact became different, but surrounding the incident was an enveloping matrix of meaning. It was this matrix that sublimated the ordinary so that it became joyous.

★ ★ ★

In glancing over what I have written heretofore I find that I have failed to note the sense of Power that permeates Consciousness when in the Transcendental State. When I was enveloped with the sense that I sustained the universe, there also came a feeling of unlimited Power. It seemed that I could command in whatever direction I might choose and that that which stood below me must obey in accordance with the causal sequences which are My own Self-Imposed forms. At the same time there was no wish to will things to be different from what they are.

5
Evolution and Cosmic Consciousness

"I am indeed Brahman, without difference, without change, and of the nature of Reality, Knowledge and Bliss."* Dr. Bucke in his discussion of Cosmic Consciousness speaks of an evolution of that kind of Consciousness, just as there is a development of "self-consciousness."

---

*Shankara: "Direct Realization," Sloka 24.

Hence, after the Awakening to the former, while this act involves definite transcendence of "self-consciousness" in every case, yet there are degrees and levels within the field of Cosmic Consciousness. Consider this statement in connection with the above quotation from Shankara. Clearly there can be no evolution where there can be no difference or change. Yet Dr. Bucke is right, provided we give to "Cosmic Consciousness" the interpretation given above.* Shankara is speaking of that which is neither formed nor formless and, therefore, that which transcends Cosmic Consciousness. But the Realization of the Brahman, partial or complete, is the basis of Awakening to Cosmic Consciousness. The latter does not, therefore, transcend the relative in the strict sense of the word, though it does transcend consciousness grounded in the subject-object relationship. Thus, in Cosmic Consciousness we are dealing with an intermediate World. In this domain Ignorance (avidya) has been destroyed, yet the Cosmos in a fundamental sense has not been annihilated. Thus unfoldment or evolution remains possible.

In this connection it is interesting to note the statement of a certain Sage who, speaking of unfolded Consciousness above the level of the highest human Adepts, said: "We attain glimpses of Consciousness so Transcendent, rising level upon level, that the senses fairly reel before the awe-inspiring Grandeur."

Here, certainly, is space for evolution far beyond the highest possibility of man as man.

6
Myself

What greater thing is there than this Mystery that is Myself? All things else I am able to comprehend, if not at this moment, then in time I can do so, and that is why I am able to give them names. And that which I have named is in thralldom to Me. So all creatures serve Me from the most elemental up to the highest Gods. But the SELF that I AM has no name, for no word that points toward Me comprehends Me. Names mean forms, whether gross or subtle, but I AM without form and, therefore, eternally nameless.

---

*See Chapter No. 3, page 12.

I comprehend all, but am comprehended by none.

I sustain all, yet need no support.

All creatures are but revelations of Me; for in Me abides their very existence, yet though they were not, I AM.

This space I produce that My Glory may be revealed; yet I alone Realize that Revelation.

Upon this space I cast My Shadow in numberless variations, yet ever remain, One—apart.

I AM the theme of all melodies and reveal portions of My endless Richness in symphonic elaborations.

I lead all scientists to Me as they seek for the Truth, which is none other than Myself.

The devotee seeks Me through the raiment of My Being, yet I abide in that devotee.

He who does violence but seeks Me in ignorance.

I AM the Love of all lovers, and I also am the Lover and the Beloved. Beside Me there is none other.

Note: In the foregoing a new form of expression broke forth sponaneously. Heretofore, I have never written in a poetic form. In fact, I have been unusually lacking in poetic interest and only regarded expository writing seriously. At the time of beginning this composition I had in mind another exposition but in the midst of the writing a new impulse in expression was born. The shift between the two forms is manifest in a comparison of the first and latter parts. I have left the writing unaltered so that it forms part of the record of the psychological transformation as well as being a vehicle of Meaning in its own right.

7
Jesus and the Way

"No man cometh unto the Father but by Me." Thus spake Jesus. But many heard, though few understood, and so they sought the Father through belief in a *man* who dwelt for a short time upon this earth. But no *man* is "I," since "man" is an object while I AM always the subject. Hence, to translate the above quotation as meaning, "no man cometh unto the Father but by Jesus," is completely to change its meaning. The Father is Divinity, God, Brahman, the ultimate Transcendent Reality. Now this Reality is Consciousness wherein subject and object are no longer divided but together form a united Sea of Consciousness. The general tendency of mankind is to seek God as an object, that is, God is worshiped as an object which stands as other than the worshiper. What Jesus meant is that success cannot be attained by this road. It is only through the "I" that the Father can be reached.

While both the subjective and objective factors are blended in Absolute Consciousness, yet the unitary quality is carried in the subjective moment. There is but one "I" or subject. Again, this is the most immediate and intimate of all facts. Hence, only through the "I" is Identity realized. Approached in any other way, God is ever something other than the seeker and, therefore, is at a distance. To come to the Father is to be one with the Father, and this can be achieved only through the pure Subject or the SELF.

With the more current interpretation of the above quotation there is a distinct clash between the teaching of Jesus and that of the other leading spiritual Lights of the world. But with the interpretation here offered nearly, if not quite, complete reconciliation is afforded, not alone with the teachings of the other great Founders of religions, but also with the spontaneous sayings of nearly all spiritually illumined souls. It fits perfectly with the "I AM that I AM" of the Old Testament. It is identical in meaning with the central doctrine of Buddhism and Brahmanism, where we find the clearest and most complete formulation of all. The "Christ" of St. Paul is a mystic Christ and not a distinct person. It is a level of Consciousness of which Jesus Christ was the symbol for him. This level of Consciousness is identical with that from which Jesus spoke. This agreement can further be noted by reading the works of a number of God-Realized Men, such as Jacob Boehme, Spinoza, Whitman, Hegel, Rama Tirtha, and Inayat Khan. It is unnecessary to elaborate further here.

8
The Ineffable Current of Bliss

August 27

At this very moment I am again within the Current which, also, is Myself. Speaking from the standpoint of the individual consciousness, I shall write of It, as much as I can convey in words.

I had been doing a little manual work and, at the moment, was stooping and looking at some gravel that had been carried from a distant valley. While doing so I sank into a brooding state and seemed to retreat to a distance where there was a profound, palpable, and pregnant Silence. I attended to This as to a Voice and received the value of a Communion.

There were no words, no ideas, nor any other form, yet, one might say, It was the very essence of Sound or Meaning. It was utterly satisfactory and filling. It was the very Power that makes all things to become clear. Again there flowed the Current of gentle Joy that penetrates through and through.

I shall attempt an analysis of this Current of Joy as it affects the outer consciousness including the physiological man. To the sensuous consciousness, It appears as of the nature of a fluid, for there is a sense of "flowing through." It penetrates all tensions with the effect of physical release. Spots that are not so well feel both rested and stronger. All over and through and through there is a quality that may well be described as physiological happiness. The organism feels no craving for sensuous distraction in order to find enjoyment. The external life of the individual could appear highly ascetic and austere to others, but all the while it would be profoundly happy. The fact is that the real Sage is anything but ascetic, however much He may appear to be so to the sensual man. For example, from the standpoint of a young animal, a man who sits quietly for two hours listening to a concert given by a virtuoso might well seem to be submitting himself to a rigorous discipline of ascetic self-control. But the man himself, provided he was a real lover of music, would flatly deny that such was the case. He would claim that he was keenly enjoying himself and doing just what he would prefer to do. Likewise, the Sage in his withdrawn life is not imposing hardship upon himself. Actually He faces more hardship moving in public places, administering large affairs, attending the ordinary amusements of men, etc., for in all this there is a distraction that makes the deeper enjoyment difficult and, for many, practically impossible. It is entirely natural for men to prefer gold to base metal, and He who has Realized the Spiritual Gold enjoys more, not less.

I wish, by every means possible, to make the point clear that in the Current lies the highest possible value which, from the relative standpoint, we call enjoyment.* In principle there is no need of denying any phase of external action, save as a temporary discipline, so that the necessary inward concentration may be effected. The Man who has made the

---

*I am not forgetting what the East Indians have said about the transcendence of enjoyment. They are correct in the sense in which they use the term. But at the present moment I am not speaking to the metaphysician. I am addressing myself to consciousness polarized to the objective.

Ineffable Transition is Free. Outwardly He lives the life that He chooses, but it is utterly foreign to His innermost Nature to choose evil. Just as the man who is naturally cleanly has to Impose no restraint upon himself to prevent himself from jumping into a mud puddle to wallow with the hogs, so the Realized Man is not tempted by evil. Evil is foreign to His real Nature and there is no question of an effort to make Himself good. This places Him in a position where He can, if necessary, work with the instrument of evil and do no evil.

Life in the Current of Joy is not the special prerogative of a small handful of men and women in the world. There are many living who now could Realize themselves as one with this Current, and ultimately all can do so in some Day of Time. Actually the Transition is not so difficult. Yet a lot of hard work has been put forth in the wrong direction through defining the Search in terms of complexity. It is as simple as turning from the object of, to the subject to, all relative consciousness, *plus the spontaneity of the SELF.*

Probably the most important difficulty which has made Recognition a rare event is a characteristic in our type of consciousness. The focus is placed upon the objective content of knowledge. Development in this sense involves an ever greater and greater growth in complexity. Hence, when man learns of a Transcendental Consciousness and he seeks to Realize This, his first effort, rather naturally, is in the direction of a more complex ideology. The greater the intellectual evolution of an individual, the more likely is this to be the case. And this explains why it is so often just the able men who have most difficulty in effecting the Transition. Now, the effective focusing of consciousness is precisely in the diametrically opposite direction. It is toward the subjective moment in the subject-object manifold, and this possesses the simplicity of a point. It is easily overlooked just because of its extreme simplicity. Yet it remains true that if the able man can succeed in finding this, he can reap a richer harvest, both for himself, individually, and for others, than is true in the case of those of inferior ability.

9
Concerning the Spontaneity of the Self

As the lower cannot command the Higher, the individual ego is not lord over the Universal SELF. Hence, from the individual standpoint, the Realization is spontaneous and thus is often called an act of Grace. The SELF, which it must be remembered is Identical with Divinity, does not stand within the causal sequence. Consequently, strictly considered, Realization of the SELF is never an effect of causes set up by the individual man acting in space and time. The latter through his effort prepares the candle, as it were, but the Flame is lighted through a spontaneous act of Spirit. But here is where Love enters in the highest sense, and Love is not constrained by the causal law which governs within space and time. Yet Love never fails the beloved. This Love excludes none, for—

> *I, Spirit, deny none of My children.*
> *Such is not My Nature.*
> *Ever waiting, above forgiveness,*
> *I pour Myself in through the opened doors.*

Practically, the spontaneity of the SELF works through Man to man, though it cannot be said that It manifests in no other way. In the "Gita," Krishna says: "I am in all men, but not all men are in ME." The implied meaning is, "Some men are in ME," i.e., Those who attained the Realization. Such Men are the Divine Presence Itself. Thus the Guru, if He is in fact a Guru in the true spiritual sense, is Divinity. Such a Man can light the Flame. The aspirant should seek his Guru in his inner consciousness and turn to Him as to Divinity Itself.

10
Seek Me First

The joy is not the end-in-itself to be sought.
Seek Me first, and then My Knowledge and My Joy will also be thine.
Seek Me for My own sake and not for any ulterior motive.
I and I alone am the worthy end of all endeavor.

So lay down all for Me, and My Wealth will be thy wealth, My Power thy power, My Joy thy joy, My Wisdom thy wisdom.

This universe is but a part of My Treasure, and it, with vastly greater Riches, shall be the portion of the Inheritance of all those who come to Me.

Long have ye lingered in the desert of Ignorance.

I desire not thy continued suffering.

Come unto Me. The Way is not so hard.

11
Expression from Different Levels

What is written here is given variously from the standpoint of the Self and from that of the ego—the "self-consciousness" of Dr. Bucke. It is most important to establish a cross-understanding, in so far as may be possible. Language is the creation and vehicle of egoistic consciousness. It is imbedded in the subject-object relationship. Speech or writing as from the perspective of the SELF involves unavoidable obscurity, analogous to that which would be found in attempting to express abstract thought in the very concrete language of a primitive people, but in the former case the difficulty is very much greater. Only in the Silence can the SELF be Known as It is, and this is not "knowing" in the subject-object sense. Now, from the egoistic or "self-conscious" standpoint language can be used correctly. But in this case the expression is *about* the event or reality as seen from the outside; it is not the event or reality itself. Expression as from the SELF, which is expression in the Current, IS the Reality. Necessarily there is a mystical quality in the latter, but not implying irrationality in the sense of anti-rationality. In fact the SELF is REASON, while all external reasoning is but a reflection of that REASON and, in most cases a very poor reflection indeed.

What the SELF, together with Transcendent and Cosmic Consciousness, actually is can be known only through Recognition or "Knowledge through Identity." He who Knows can speak and be understood by another who Knows; but others, at best, will feel something or sense a Light which attracts them. They may find induced in them something of the great Joy and Peace. All of this becomes strong evidence that the Kingly Knowledge is, and thus builds a presumption of the reality of the

Goal to be sought. Then one here and one there and, We hope, many may be stirred to a desire to Know in the Inner sense. And that desire must be planted in the soul before the Awakening can take place.

Strongly developed egoistic consciousness is a barrier, but at the same time it is a power. The barrier can be mastered and the power retained. Highly developed capacity in relative knowledge is not to be scorned. Many genuinely Illumined Men have not seen clearly with respect to this point. The result is that while such Men have made the Crossing for Themselves, They have left poor bridges for others. It is this bridge-building that is the really important work. The Realized Man qua Realized has no need to write either for Himself or for other Realized Men. But he may need notes for himself as egoistic man, and others do require the landmarks such a One can leave. There is also another important point. If the Recognition of the SELF is not to entail permanent immersion in the Silence, but is to be combined with active manifestation, relative powers are necessary. Egoistic consciousness and even the "simple consciousness" are, in high degree, an eclipse of Real Consciousness. But this eclipse serves a useful purpose for the invoking of relative powers. Otherwise the long journey in the Cycle of Necessity would be a vain travail. Egoistic consciousness does, therefore, forge instruments of value which the truly Wise Man will not discard, although He may very largely transform them. The more perfectly forged instruments of egoistic consciousness have greater potentiality than the less perfect. But the men who have built such instruments naturally have a stronger egoistic force than others, with correspondingly greater barriers to overcome. But having mastered these barriers and having Realized the SELF, They also transcend others in the capacity to make manifest from out of the endless Fullness of the Silence. We do not scorn but, on the contrary, desire such men, and will do all that can and may be done to demonstrate the fact of the Inner Reality and clarify the rationale of the Way whereby that Reality may be Realized.

There is a shifting of standpoint in the use of "I"—the SELF—the egoistic or individual man—and the "We," employed at times. Metaphysically, I am the One without a second or, more strictly, "I am not-one and not not-one, and there is no second." Yet while this remains eternally true, I am, in a reflected sense, the egoistic, one among others. Strictly the egoistic "I" is "I am I and none other." (It is the "none other" that makes the barrier noted above.) Now, there is between this and the highest metaphysical level another level or state, in one sense intermediate and yet also beyond, since it involves real Mastery, where I realize Myself as "I am I and yet also others." It is in this sense the "We" is employed, spelled with a capital "W."

The rules of literary form will have to be sacrificed when they interfere with the main purpose. At times I write in the midst of the Current, yet at other times more or less out of It. The Current carries Authority, and in the face of this literary rules must be discarded when they act as barriers to Meaning.

12
The Record Continued

August 28

As already stated, I can distinguish three distinct Recognitions that produced lasting effects. As I look back I can discern a progressive quality in the three which, it seems, should be noted. About fourteen years ago an old college friend called upon Sherifa and me and the time was devoted to the discussion of Theosophical subjects. (My friend was an earnest student of the Theosophia.) At one stage in the conversation he outlined the various steps of a very old discriminative technique in which it is shown, progressively, that the Self is not the body nor the various other principles of man, but that it can be only that final principle— which, strictly, is not one principle among others—i.e., the Atman or pure subjectivity. I was familiar with the method, was already convinced of the soundness of the logic and had previously employed it myself. But in this case I suddenly seemed to Realize, with certainty, that, in fact, "I am Identical with the Atman." There was a sense of a new Light which made clear much that had been obscure, but this was not a light seen in the form of a subtle sensuous perception. The effect upon the relative consciousness persisted. There was a definite enrichment, but I was not aware of the Current of Joy.

The most significant consequence, within the individual consciousness, was a certain change in the base of thought. As an example, it may be noted that, whereas, prior to that date I had read the "Bhagavadgita" because it was one of the important Theosophic books, I did not like it, and it seemed to inculcate a veritable repression of the life-interest I then cared for; on the other hand, immediately after the Recognition of my

Identity with the Atman, I found myself spontaneously thinking, as my own thought, many of the ideas contained in the "Gita." I Realized them as obviously true, and, instead of their carrying a repressive value, they were a source of Light and expansion. I have never forgotten this Recognition and have never felt disposed to question the fact I then saw so clearly. In the intellectual sense that Recognition was, and is, persistent. But other aspects of the personal nature were not included or were not sufficiently included. So, in the intervening years I have often *felt* and *acted* contrary to that Recognition.

The second occasion occurred somewhat less than a year ago. I had been reading with deep interest a book by Paul Brunton* in which, among other experiences, he told of his contact with a certain Sage in Southern India. I felt a sympathetic rapport with this Sage and repeatedly read His words with profound attention. Once, while thus engaged, it suddenly dawned upon me that Nirvana is not a field or place where man enters and is enclosed, as in a space which envelops bodies, but I Recognized that "I am Nirvana." In other words, the Real Self is not other than Nirvana, never has been other, and never will be other. All that the individual man achieves is Recognition of this eternal fact. With this Transition in consciousness, Joy was realized. Even at that time I sensed It as a Current, though in modified form as compared with the more recent Recognition. I once spent a whole day immersed within It; and, for a period, within certain limits, I could invoke It. At the time, I was engaged in lecturing and class-work concerned with metaphysical subjects. A greater Light came into this work. While previously I had employed a considerable degree of formal organization in lecturing and classwork, I then began to relax the formal aspect so that it stood more in the background as something automatic in its action. I dared to leave a larger room for spontaneity on the platform, and found by repeated experimenting that I could trust that spontaneity, provided I could secure a certain attitude in the audience. Lacking that attitude, I could rebound to the more formal preparation. Since then I have continued to be able to operate between these two modes. I found that a conceptual coordination, produced while one stood or sat before an audience, released, concomitantly, a current-like quality that had, among other features, the effect of holding the audience in a kind of stillness which I would describe as possessed of depth. The attention of the individual member of the audience was held even though he did not understand

---

*A Search in Secret India (New York: E.P. Dutton and Co., 1935).

the ideas developed, as was often found to be the case in subsequent conversation. A simple repetition of the same conceptual coordination did not have the same power in the same degree. I thus found a definite correlation between the Current and creativeness. From the relative standpoint, the Current requires a progressive disintegration and reintegration of forms. Once a form becomes relatively fixed, the Current subsides. And yet, in a very curious way, this disintegration and reintegration leaves a certain subtle master-form unaltered. The result is essential consistency between all formal integrations produced in the Current, provided the individual understands the use of language. And, even if he does not understand the art of language, that consistency still remains, though in a deeper sense which is not so easily recognized.

13
Nirvanic Bliss

In the Current, we stand in the presence of the Ceaseless Motion which, at the same time, can be characterized as Changelessness. In one sense, we may say that the Key to Immortality is to be ceaselessly creative, while remaining eternally Identical. Nirvana is pure creativeness and, consequently, cannot be captured within fixed definition. On the other hand, genuine objects of consciousness can be defined, since they are forms. Nirvana is inconceivable but It is ceaseless Conceiving. Herein is a partial explanation of the Nirvanic Bliss that can fall within the understanding of the more common consciousness. Creative activity, even on the lower levels, such as begetting, does awaken a degree of bliss, though of progressively inferior and grosser quality as we approach the physiological. Usually such minor blisses last but for a moment, or, at best, for brief periods with subsequent depression and exhaustion. Conceive of the intensity of the bliss raised beyond all relative imagination, and far beyond the power of any physiological organism to endure, and then regard it as not lasting merely for a moment or a brief period, but extending with unbroken continuity indefinitely; then something of the Bliss-aspect of Nirvana may be apprehended. Is it so surprising that many become "God-intoxicated" and fail to go on to the winning of real Mastery?

14
The Record Continued

Returning to the record, it is now to be noted that the second Recognition had produced a change that is persistent, yet, at the same time, certain aspects of my relative nature, principally below the intellectual, were not taken up. There were outer desires that still had strength, although they had become perceptibly weakened. After the period of lectures and class-work, there was a sort of partial "clouding of the sky." At the time, I could not invoke the Current, though the force of the Knowledge remained unbroken, as far as attained. Subsequently, lectures and class-work were continued in the Middle West. For the first three weeks of this work in Chicago, I had what, for me, was a most unusual experience. I felt the consciousness of the city as an almost insupportable weight which enveloped my mind with a sort of lethargy so that I could not really think. Prior to this experience, nothing had ever been able so to suffocate the power of thought that I could not, fairly readily, will my way to thought-action. I was on the platform nearly every day throughout this period, although during the greater part of the twenty-four hours of each day my consciousness was so gripped with heaviness that I desired to sleep all the time. I spoke, as it were, with the momentum of past thought, but it seems my state was not realized, at least not generally, by others. After three weeks I broke through with a deep sense of elation and victory. Once again, I found myself moving in a stream of genuine thought and, finally, gave a lecture on the "Crest Jewel" of Shankara which represented the highest point I had attained on the platform up to that time. In subsequent work in the smaller cities, I had no further experience of the obscuration.

By the time the work was drawing to a close, I had a feeling as of being emptied, and the desire grew strong to return to the West and live for a time under conditions where I could have complete solitude. This condition was met in July on one of the tributaries of the American River near Michigan Bluff. Two purposes conjoined at this time. It was desirable that some cross-cut work should be done on a gold-prospect for further sampling and, in addition, I found a curious value in underground activity in association with inward penetration toward depth. So, during the latter half of July, I had some days of solitude combined with underground physical work, plus meditative readings in the "System of the Vedanta," as noted previously. Much clarification was achieved in my consciousness during this period, but two facts,* one a correlating idea and the other an experience, stand out above the rest. The experience was a spontaneous development in the Current, but this time in a form that was more sensuously evident than on any prior occasion. Here, for the first time, I submitted It to analysis, in so far as It was reflected in the organism.

The Current is clearly a subtle, fluid-like substance which brings the sense of well-being already described. Along with It, a more than earthly Joy suffuses the whole nature. To myself, I called It a Nectar. Now, I recognize It under several names. It is also the "Soma," the "Ambrosia of the Gods," the "Elixir of Life," the "Water of Life" of Jesus, and the "Baptism of the Spirit" of St. Paul. It is more than *related* to Immortality; in fact, It is *Identical* with Immortality.

During the first week of August we returned to San Fernando and, on or about the 7th of the month, the Glorious Transition came. This third Recognition was much profounder than the others. The Recognitions as expressed in the forms, "I am Atman" and "I am Nirvana," were not devoid of an objective element. Each of these forms is a complete judgment or proposition involving, therefore, a subject and a predicate. In the use of relative language such a form is unavoidable, if the statement is to be correct according to the laws of language. But in my own consciousness, in addition to this fact, I also actually retained a degree of the objective element. Hence, the Recognition, in each case, fell short of genuine identification. In the third instance, I isolated the subjective moment from the relative manifold of consciousness, as already stated, and the result was Emptiness, Darkness, and Silence, i.e., Consciousness with no object. It should be borne in mind, however, that relative consciousness by its own momentum continued to function all this time, so that I never for one moment lost sight of my environment or the ceaseless train of thoughts. It was simply a discriminative abstraction of the pure subjective moment and Recognizing myself as That. At this moment, I found Myself above space, time, and causality, and actually sustaining the whole universe by the Light of Consciousness which I AM. Almost at once, there followed the Nectar-like Current and the gentle, yet so powerful Joy. Now, always heretofore with me, as a practical working principle, thought was life, even though theoretically I had

---

*Both of these have been recorded in the opening section of this book. The idea will be developed more fully later.

for some time recognized that thought itself, no matter how abstract, required a matrix. But with the third Recognition I found myself more than content in a World above thought, since It comprehended thought with all else. I was tempted to abandon thought and draw Inward. All the outer effort and work seemed so useless. But on this point I had been already warned by literature, such as the "Voice of the Silence"; and, further, it did not seem like good sportsmanship to have received an inward aid making possible the Attainment of the most precious Value of all and fail to carry It on to others. So I looked over the world, as it were, to find what value there remained to hold my interest. It seemed to me that I had garnered, at least in seed-form, enough relative knowledge. I had no real interest in the grosser constructions, such as the tangible forms, institutions, societies, governments, and arts. But there was one thing that did remain: a humanity, also part of Myself, that was almost famished for that saving Knowledge and the Divine Nectar that I had found so precious. So, for me, there was a commission to be fulfilled, to "carry on" in the objective effort so that these others might be brought nearer to the Goal. But then the question arose: How was this to be done? I placed this question before One who has given me much excellent advice and asked for a formula of action. He said, in effect: "None of Us knows such a formula. All other compartments of nature under the sun We can, and have, penetrated and know the laws and, knowing them, We can act with and mold nature according to Our wills. But the human soul is a mystery, and its inner depths lie beyond Our penetrations. We try many ways to reach these human souls, often disappointed where We expect much, and yet surprised at times beyond Our expectations. Find your own way and try."—Well, this book is such an attempt.

15
The Grand Adventure

I have a sense of a Grand Adventure, the most glorious of all.

A veritable World looms before my inner gaze unfolding hour by hour, and day by day, so that I cannot begin to record on paper what is being unfolded within the mind by the shorthand of thought.

Such Joy and Freedom shed their luster about that even this remaining bondage of action is losing, progressively, the sense of restriction.

Within the Grand Abstraction, which is the one Concrete Reality, there is a silent Communion, wordless, thoughtless, utterly formless; yet within it I barely discern, like the dim paling that heralds a new dawn, the silent Voices of Others, separated here by both space and time—even distant time.

There are other Communities beyond this.

There are far more satisfying Companionships than are possible within the veil of gross matter.

The Silence is Full and Pregnant, and out of It flows the Stream of all formations in endless variety: symphonies, philosophies, governments, sciences, arts, societies, and so on and on and on.

16
Alternative Roads to Recognition

While the book "Cosmic Consciousness" is a valuable compilation and analysis of the objectively discernible characteristics which mark Those who have Awakened to the "Cosmic Sense," as the author calls it, yet Dr. Bucke has covered only a part of the subject and misses entirely a phase of Recognition that does not possess certain of the signs he has noted. Not all Recognition carries in Its train the profound and, sometimes, intense Joy. There are Recognitions in which the element of Joy is not conspicuous and, though present, may be too hidden to be revealed to the gaze of the observer, unless the latter is unusually acute in his perceptions.

There is a science of Recognition, though in large part it remains esoteric. But some of the science may be uncovered by the uninitiated student if he seeks in the right place. Among the various races, the East Indians form the chief repository of this science, and the language employed, the Sanskrit, involves terms corresponding to concepts for which there are no real equivalents in our current western languages. It will be necessary to turn to a small portion of this science to show how Recognition may be of more than one type.

The ultimate Reality is Nameless, though word-signs have been devised that point toward but do not define It. Among these is the word SAT, designating, but not defining, THAT which is neither Being nor non-Being. This is the One Reality or, rather, THAT which is neither

One nor not-One. I, the Atman, am identical with THAT; hence, the statement, "The Atman is identical with the Brahman." This One Reality is Absolute Consciousness and Absolute Motion. Its highest representation is, therefore, a triad and this has been called in Sanskrit "SAT-CHIT-ANANDA." CHIT is Consciousness or Knowledge in the highest sense. ANANDA is Bliss or Love, again in the highest sense. But, as already shown, pure Bliss is pure Creativeness, and, as creativeness is motion in the ultimate sense of disintegrating and reintegrating form ceaselessly, we can see how Ananda becomes identical with Ceaseless Motion. Below this highest Triad there is a lower reflection, though still on a metaphysical level. This reflection abides in man as his highest aspect. It is known as Atman-Buddhi-Manas; "Atman" corresponding to "SAT," "Buddhi" to "ANANDA," and "Manas" to "CHIT." Each of these sets of three is often represented as an equilateral triangle with the Atman or SAT at the higher apex, the base being parallel to the surface of the earth—or, rather, tangent—with Buddhi and Manas or ANANDA and CHIT at the other vertices, as follows:

The equilateral form of the triangles indicates a symmetrical relationship while the position at the upper vertex of SAT or Atman signifies that here, with respect to each triangle, is the ultimate. As a consequence it follows that Atman is as accessible through Manas as through Buddhi and, likewise, SAT through CHIT as well as through ANANDA.* All of this is well above the personal man. Now, below the triad, Atman-Buddhi-Manas, there are innumerable roads leading toward Recognition; but at the level of Buddhi and Manas there are two contrasting routes, and a third which is a combination of the two. If a man reaches first to Buddhi and then to Atman—the I AM—but has attained little unfoldment of Manas—Intellectual Principle—the Recognition will manifest predominantly through Joy and Love. All such tend to see the Supreme as Love and this, apparently, is the more frequent development. But, on the other hand, he who reaches to

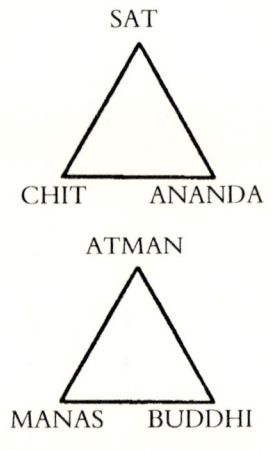

---

*This fact has been strangely neglected by many students, yet the very figures reveal it.

Atman through Manas, and with but minor development of the Love Principle, will be Illumined in terms of Knowledge, but will know relatively little of the Joy. For such a one the Supreme is seen as Knowledge or Wisdom. The third, or combined Road, is through Manas, thence through Buddhi to full Recognition in the Atman. The Supreme then stands forth equally as Wisdom-Knowledge and Love-Bliss. The latter is, of course, the most completely balanced Road. But if the Atman is reached through Manas, then Buddhi can be Awakened quite readily, or vice versa, if the appropriate effort is put forth. Thus, finally, the culminating completeness is also attained. Buddha is the outstanding example of the balanced Recognition within historic times, and thus He is One equally great in Knowledge and Compassion.

Immanuel Kant is a great example, among western peoples, of a man who attained something of Recognition through Manas. As a result, his philosophy clears the Way in the West in a sense analogous to that achieved by the thought of Shankara in the Orient but, unlike the latter, it is incomplete on the metaphysical side. Hegel partially completed this structure, but the whole of this falls short of the completeness of the pure Advaita Vedanta. Still, within this idealistic structure is to be found the best of genuinely spiritual Knowledge-Wisdom indigenous to the West. Kant's Light is very clarifying, but there is lacking in it the Substance which is Joy. This fact is revealed in his features and his writings. Yet there is a very great and clear beauty in Kant. I, for one, am profoundly indebted to him and realize that debt more clearly than ever at the present time. Without him I might have *experienced*, but I could not have understood nearly so well the Meaning unfolded through the Transition, being born, as I am, in a western body and nurtured in a western current of thought. I take this opportunity to make my acknowledgment to this great philosopher who could recognize, and so well name, the pure subjective moment of Consciousness, i.e., Pure Apperception. Is there any greater phrase in all philosophy than this: "The synthetic, transcendental unity of pure apperception?" He who penetrates this phrase and extracts from it its ultimate Meaning will have attained the Recognition.

Among the earmarks of Illumination that Dr. Bucke has noted, Kant does not reveal, at least not conspicuously, the Joy and the "subjective Light," but on the other hand the moral elevation is marked. In fact, Kant has made one of the most important contributions, if not the most important, to the theory of ethics of any thinker in our present culture. And his primary ethical principle is one of the most lofty ever formulated by man. The intellectual illumination is stupendous. Few men, if any, in history have ever surpassed the intellectual altitude attained by Immanuel Kant.

17
Being Born Again

August 29

No doubt a price is exacted from the personal man. An extraordinary demand is made upon the nervous organism and so a counter activity is helpful, perhaps necessary. But, as even the personal man is much more than the physical body, the price goes deeper than the body. There is here a kind of dying, proceeding in the midst of continued bodily existence. Doubtless it is but natural that the personal nature should dread all this and, in a measure, grieve. For here we have the real meaning of the crucifixion. The personal life is centered upon the world-field; though it is a doomed life in any case, since, inevitably, Death reaps all here. Still, the personality never quite believes this and strives in its feebleness to will its continuance in the outer world, until in ripe old age it craves rest, even though it be at the price of extinction. But when this hour of tiredness has come, it is already too late to achieve the Awakening in that body, for this Awakening calls for a profound, though possibly subtle, virility. To die in the midst of virility—the mystic thirty-three years of age—is not easy. Jesus, now in the sense of the personal man, sweat the drops of blood drawn forth by the agony of Gethsemane. He shrank from the piercing of the crown of thorns and the nails of the cross. But all this is only one side of the shield. Beyond the seemingly forsaken man of this world is the Glory of Exaltation. He who realizes the obverse of the Crucifixion of Jesus forgets the latter in the presence of that Majestic Glory which sheds a Light so potent as to consume all darkness within Its range. The "Eli, Eli, lama sabachthani," seen from one side as "My God, My God, why hast Thou forsaken me" becomes, "My God, My God, how greatly hast Thou exalted me!"

A Fire descends and consumes the personal man. For a time, short or long, this Fire continues. The personal man is the fuel, and the fuel, in greater or less measure, does suffer. But fire does not destroy; it simply transforms. This fact can be realized by an analysis of what takes place through the action of ordinary fire. If a log is burning, the fuel is principally, if not wholly, in the form of carbohydrates, and the fire transforms these into carbon dioxide and water vapor. There remains a small amount of ashes, the persistently earthy portion of the log. The carbohydrate in the log was a fixed form, partaking, for a time, of the earthy solidity of the mineral associates in the log. But as the carbohydrates become carbon dioxide and water vapor, they take on new form in the freer world of the air. So too, does the Fire which descends and consumes the personal man but Transform him. Only the ash of the personal nature is left behind, while the rest, the best of the personality, is taken up to be conscious in airy spaces. The ultimate state is one of a far, far greater Joy.

It is possible for the man passing through the ordeal so to shift his center of self-identity that the pain, instead of being strong, becomes but a shadowy undertone of a Melody that is all Joy. He who identifies himself with the fuel predominantly suffers much and keenly, but if, on the other hand, he unites himself with the Fire, all is changed. The Flame of the Fire is a dance of Joy. There is no pain on this level of Consciousness. The transforming man does not then wait until after the Burning to Know the Joy, but feels It through and through while in the midst of the ordeal, which now has almost completely ceased to be an ordeal at all.

In the days immediately following the Transition, I clearly felt the Fire; and, because I did identify myself mostly with this Fire, those were grand days, despite the fact that there were brief periods of reaction when life seemed low in the physical body and it was difficult to assert the will-to-live. But now, these periods of reaction are growing less, both in that they are shorter in duration and are less intense. Also I do employ more judgment in invoking the Current which is Bliss. There exists a throttle, command of which gives to man the power to control this Current. It is but a due exercise of wisdom so to adjust the flow of the Current that Its action is balanced to meet the strength of the personal man.

In the old days when I read of this Fire, I supposed that It had but a figurative meaning. But while the Fire is figurative, in a sense, yet It is also a quite real and even a sensuously felt and manifested fact. Not only have I felt this Fire, but It has been induced in those who live near me. They report feeling It as genuinely as the heat of the sun and manifest some of the effects of the sun's heat as it acts upon the human body. The

Inner Fire does reach down to the outermost of the man. This does imply that, looked at aright, the metaphysical is not utterly divorced from the physical.

18
An Experience with the Fire

A few years ago I experienced the Fire in another form. On that occasion I had been collecting the material for a lecture on the Akasha and the Astral Light. Such knowledge, as is externally available on this subject, is largely descended from the ancients and is expressed in archaic and often deliberately veiled form. I found it peculiarly difficult to grasp the meaning within the medium of our present concepts. I drove into the subject with an especially heavy effort of the will, with the result that some of the facts were forced into organization, but very soon I became aware that Mystery surrounded what we could, at present, comprehend intellectually. But one effect of the intense concentration was a kind of breaking through the personal mental shell and, briefly, I seemed to possess a veritable universe of Knowledge. It seemed that then I knew all things that were to be known in this world. I simply could not contain this Knowledge within my personal mind. Presently, that Knowledge would have burned up and destroyed this brain and nervous system, had I remained in rapport with It for any appreciable period of time. So, before I could assimilate any of this Knowledge concretely, I had to withdraw the concentration. Still, I retained enough to know that *I* Knew behind the Veil. Now, from that experience there were after-effects to overcome which required some years. One day, soon after this event, I was walking along a street in Los Angeles, and had stopped for a moment at a corner, when a streetcar close by started from a standing position. I was evidently within the range of the electro-magnetic field* connected with the action of the motor. Suddenly something seemed to shift, either in the consciousness or in the brain or both. For a moment I lost orientation with the body. I cannot describe the feeling quite cor-

---

*This field must have been the inciting cause as there were later similar, though less intense, experiences of the same sort when electric cars passed near me.

rectly for I know of no other experiences that are analogous. But it seemed to me to be an incipient leaving of the body. I gripped myself and the physical organism intensely with the will and walked slowly up a side street. But I had a bad time of it. The intense effort of will to hold myself tended further to induce the very condition I was trying to master. I had both to hold firmly and relax that hold. It was a kind of tightrope walking, for either too much relaxation or too much concentration had the same effect of tending to dislodge me from the rope, which in this case represented walking in the body in this world. After a time I succeeded in re-establishing the balance sufficiently so that the crisis was past. But it was as though the rope had merely widened to a narrow path which only slowly became a broad plane wherein I was free to move without careful circumspection as formerly. The completion of this correction required years. For a long time I had to be careful in the vicinity of streetcars and also had to abandon reading metaphysical literature. For I found that the reading of *Tibetan Yoga and Secret Doctrines* or the *Crest-Jewel* of Shankara had the same effect.

Now, from the foregoing an important lesson was learned. It is not safe to direct the will with full intensity into the intellect, for here we are dealing with a sort of dynamite. It can be done with safety only when the proper guarding controls are employed, but this is a problem of technique not easily learned. When one concentrates in that way he invokes an Inner Fire and that Fire can easily be too much for the organism. The fact is that the Fire of Knowledge is too intense a Flame for the human organism to endure if it is not sheathed in the Water of Life, the Current which is Bliss. At present I am approaching a level comparable with that earlier moment, but I am fundamentally at ease. The nervous organism is gathering strength. Thought moves more freely than ever before, and while there is present and active a genuinely intense will, it does not manifest as a strong personal effort. *I* do invoke the will, truly, but *I* am not this seen man. There is an enormous difference in the action of the will in these two senses. A very high order of will may be exercised while the personal organism remains relaxed and, in that case, there is none of the tension which acts like resistance to an electric Current. There is, then, an effect of flowing through with little or no resistance and, as a consequence, the organism is not strained to the point of danger.

19
The Drama of the Triune Man

PERSONALITY:

This Space is too large. Where are the comforting bars of my cage? I would like to return to the world that I know so well. I would like to move, inconspicuous, in the domain where I know my way. Release me from the Fire.

INTELLECTUAL MAN:

Be still, thou foolish one. Those pastures and encircling walls thou cravest are barren and small before this Largeness. Be not like the canary bird that refuses the offered freedom, but come on with Me.

REAL MAN:

Be patient, child, thou shalt be guarded and shalt find again all thou dost love. For this small travail, thou, too, shalt drink of the Waters of Immortality, which I AM. The limits of thy strength will not be forgotten.

And as for Thee, MY mediator to the world and all things that stand below, let not Thy restlessness and greater power lead Thee to forget the limited strength of the child. Once, Thou too wert a child and had to be aided over the difficult places. Extend, therefore, Thy aid to those who are weaker than Thou art.

20
The Meaning of Omniscience

What is Omniscience? Those who have familiarized themselves to any extent with mystical or quasi-occult literature will have found it stated that there are levels or states where a man becomes Omniscient, and yet, at the same time, it will be emphasized that no man is infallible. From the relative standpoint these two statements seem incompatible and the result is mystification, to say the least. But when properly understood both statements can be true. The fact is, no man is omniscient on the relative level; and though the knowledge of such a one may be very great, transcending even the relative knowledge of any figure that has appeared upon the screen of history, yet beyond his attainment, whatever it may be, there lie further mysteries awaiting his resolution. In other words, We find no conceivable end to evolution. But while all this is true, there is another sense in which a man may Awaken to Omniscience, and may do so instantaneously. In fact, such an Awakening cannot be a matter of gradual attainment, for the Infinite is never Realized by progressive additions of finite manifolds. It is all a question of level or state. The SELF is All Knowledge and, as It incloses, but is not inclosed or restrained by, space, time, and causality, there is no question of development on this level, in the sense of progression by finite steps. He who has Realized himself as the SELF is at once Omniscient. But it should be remembered that the SELF is absolute Emptiness, Darkness, and Silence, *from the relative standpoint*. The SELF is the Knowledge whence all proceeds, but this Knowledge is not of the subject-object type nor anything that could be conceived within the cognitive framework of the latter. The Silence *is* All-Knowledge, while knowledge in the field of the subjective-objective *becomes*, and of this it is impossible to predicate infallibility.

There is a way in which we may secure an adumbration of what All-Knowledge or the "Voice of the Silence" is. Language is composed of words, designating objects in some sense, and sentences. Words or terms, we may say, represent simple apprehensions and are analogous to simple consciousness. The sentences are representations of judgments, which are of the nature of recognition on the level of polarized consciousness, or that which Dr. Bucke has called "self-consciousness." Here all is posited in a world where an "I," considered as distinct from other selves, is conceived as conscious of an object in some sense. Here, also, we have meaning in a form that is definable, i.e., capable of representation in the form of other terms and propositions and, in the strictest usage, meaning just those terms and propositions. But this is only formal meaning and, by itself, it is barren. Now, over and above this manifold of formal knowledge there is another Meaning, or Significance which, while It may be *aroused* by words and sentences, is not *contained* in words and sentences. This higher Meaning, when Realized, is a veritable food for the soul and, thence, for the whole man. In general, men, by arousing momentary and partial recognitions, proceed to this Meaning from below by the use of formal and empiric knowledge, employed with the appropriate skill. These momentary recognitions are adumbrations, though generally in a very minor degree, of that Higher Knowledge which is identical with Divinity Itself. This is the process when man bases himself in the external, the relative world. But for him who has made the Ineffable Transition there is a radical difference. The man has then found his base in the SELF. The Knowledge from which He now starts is the Silence, and this is Significance devoid of any words or ideas. Here, Communion is on the level of Significance Itself, unfettered by any form. This is exhaustless Refreshment, and there is no waste. Now, from this level there can be a projection outward through ideas and, perchance, ultimately reaching the relatively frozen state on the most objective plane of all, i.e., the field of the visible universe. From this higher standpoint, Meaning is the base and not the apex, as It is usually conceived. The universe is the final effect, but it is utterly dependent for its existence upon this base or foundation of Meaning. That is why, from the standpoint of the SELF, the universe is unreal.

Now, on the level of Meaning, a man may Know with absolute certainty and yet express himself incorrectly when trying to fit his ideas within the already existing forms of expression. In this case, he shows himself to be quite fallible and yet Knows *what* he is talking about, however incorrect his expression may be. If careful discrimination is not employed, it is easy for the outer man, even though he has Awakened to Realization, to fall into confusion at this point. Knowing the certainty that applies on the level where He really IS, then, as outer man he attaches this certainty to his formal expressions and thus falls into error. Outer correctness, or approximation to correctness, must be acquired by effort, even though the man has attained to a high order of Realization. In formal knowledge, including all knowledge of things, whether gross or subtle, and all knowledge of relationships, processes, etc., technique is essential, including all possible methods of checking and control. Naturally, some men have gained more capacity in this than others and so, in matters falling in their respective fields, have relative authority not possessed by others. Thus, in a matter of formal or empiric knowledge, it may often happen that a man who has not reached beyond the egoistic or "self-conscious" level can very easily correct another who is genuinely emplanted in the Silence. The latter does have, however, decisive advantages when seeking mastery in any relative field. He can acquire knowledge in the relative sense in but a fraction of the time required by others, for He has the advantage of commanding perspective. But in any case, even for Him, some effort and time are required. Transcendent

Knowledge, or Knowledge on the level of Meaning, is acquired instantaneously and with certainty, but the attainment of relative knowledge always demands some time and effort, and never gives certainty.

21
The Record Continued

I find that the Current is consumed, at least apparently so, in the expression of thought. I feel It less after casting It into form. It seems to have gone forth in a kind of new birth. Yet I am happy that this should be so. The Fount is exhaustless, and there remains—enough.

22
The Celestial Virgin

Traditional woman has been the custodian of pleasure, and the dispensing of pleasure has been a large part of her glory and power. Too often, in these later days, womankind has been disposed to discredit her own natural glories and powers by becoming an imitator of man. This is really giving to man-power and man-function a greater tribute than they deserve. That essence the outer embodiment of which is woman in a peculiar sense constitutes a need of this world today that is especially poignant. There is too great an over-balance of harsh willfulness abroad in the world. Consequently, there is a need for the counter-balancing forces, and these woman, alone, is really competent to exercise. Among these essentially feminine qualities the following stand out: Beauty, Mercy, Tenderness, Charm, Ecstasy, preservation of proven values, etc. It is a grave mistake to regard these powers as inferior to the Creative Will, the Will to Power, the Daring of the Unknown, and the Judgment that peculiarly mark the masculine principle. The latter powers are unquestionably indispensable both in the world-field and for Inward Penetration, but by themselves they are unbalanced and can easily drop from a constructive to a destructive level. The isolated masculine principle cannot check this tendency and, so, right here is where the feminine quality is grievously needed. The feminine powers are just as strong as the masculine, although they function in a more subtle way. We greatly need more women who justly appreciate the ancient and natural feminine powers and arts.

Man is Siva, the formless Light; woman is Shakti, the Current which opposes and embodies the Light. Without embodiment, the Light of Consciousness remains void of self-consciousness. Since self-consciousness is the one great achieved value, it is easy to see how vitally important the Shakti principle is.

In Her highest aspect, Woman is the Celestial Virgin, and this is none other than the Current of Bliss. The Current is a Virgin, because of the quality of ever-becoming-new. Though impregnated by the Fire of Wisdom, yet She remains a Virgin because She is ever-changing within Her own Self-identity. The union of Wisdom and the Virgin gives birth to the Christ, and this is the real Immaculate Conception. This union is the untellable Joy of which all lesser ecstasies are but faint shadows. So, deep and lasting Joy is the true sign of the genuine and noble religiosity. Austere gloom in the name of religion is a sacrilege and sign of failure. Only false religion is dreary. The Holy is Free and Joyful.

23
Beauty

August 31

Upon the neutral world of things I cast a sheath of Beauty, which is Myself, and all things whatsoever stand exalted in that Beauty. Plato is right; beyond the beauty that is predicated of various forms and relationships, there is a pure Transcendent Beauty, and this is a mode of the very Being of the SELF. This Beauty is not *something* that is beautiful. It is Self-existent and casts Its luster upon all things for Him who has found Himself identical with that Beauty. When a man reports that he has found beauty in some department of nature, in a combination of sounds, a blending of colors or in the proportions of forms, he has not merely discovered an external existence. He has had, at least, a momentary, penumbral glimpse of Himself, but has interpreted it as something externally apprehended. The failure of many, while in the full possession and exercise of their senses, to see the beauty realized by others, shows that beauty is not something external. A man may gaze upon a drab and somber landscape and, taking merely the photographic record of that view, find no beauty; but let him place over his eyes appropriately chosen light filters and the scene will take on a new quality that is far more pleasing. The light filter acts like a sheath which changes the whole quality of the experience. Somewhat similarly, man projects Beauty upon the phenomenal world and, in most cases, thinks that he simply experiences it. But He who has made the ineffable Transition may say: "I am Beauty and make all things to become beautiful." But the real Beauty is entirely apart from the object, however subtle. Ecstasy is pure Beauty, as well as pure Joy and Knowledge. Beauty is one of the many facets of THAT which is the Fullness appearing as Emptiness. Another facet is Significance, and these two are One.

24
The Record Continued

I find it more difficult to write today. Yesterday we were in the city and, again, I found it acutely painful. Something of the experience may be judged by a familiar phenomenon connected with radio reception and amplification. Sometimes a receiving set is so adjusted by the dial controls that the faint impulses from distant sources may become manifest. At the limits of the receptive power of the set one may just barely discern the impulses coming from a great distance. Now, if without changing the degree of amplification the station dial is turned to a powerful broadcasting station nearby, the resultant effect of violent noise is highly distressing. I find the jazz-like discordance of the city has an analogous effect, intensified to a degree that is positively destructive. Not only does the maze of lights, sounds, and motions have this force, but, in even larger measure, the non-integrated mass of thoughts, feelings, and desires produces the same result. It is, in a measure, dangerous. This makes clear one of the reasons for the call to solitude, characteristically reported by those who are in the midst of the Transition. It is possible to build protecting shields, but this takes time and can hardly be done during the period that the inward rooting is being consolidated, since all the resources that the outer man has are required for this task. It is not easy to bridge the gulf between the worlds.

There are subtle violences and injuries that are very difficult to describe, since their symptoms are of quite different quality from the familiar sensations of the gross body. There is a place of fine-edged balance in the mind that once destroyed the whole structure crashes. There are phases of organization beyond the knowledge of the modern psychologist and the understanding of the psychiatrist. The complete organized being that man is may not be observed by the use of the external senses alone, for man has a metaphysical as well as a physical organization. Essentially, it is only the shell of man that lends itself to observation by methods adapted from the physical laboratory. Behind the shell is another organization where more primary causes operate. As a consequence, in order to trace the causes which manifest as objective effects to their root sources, both subtle senses and something of metaphysical understanding are requisite. As a general principle, this rule applies to the whole objective world, but while a fair degree of valid knowledge relative to so-called inorganic nature may be reached through the external senses, this ceases to be true in progressive degree as the field of study advances through the range of life-manifestations from its lowest forms up to its more exalted developments. The real roots of consciousness and mind, together with subtler phases of organization, are beyond the range of external observation. Unquestionably, many effects and secondary causes may be observed by this means, but these do not supply a sufficient ground for unfolding the laws involved and, consequently, do not afford an adequate basis for therapeutic control and correction.

There are domains in the inner constitution of man where the intelligent exercise of a strong will is far more effective than any external agency whatsoever. There is a hidden, as well as an obvious, meaning behind the "lever of Archimedes." There is both a lever and a fulcrum, mastery of which gives power to move the world. But these forces act solely at a point of very fine balance, which is attained only with very great difficulty, and which is also not easily maintained after having been achieved. The violent wind of world-consciousness affords a most serious obstacle to the realization of such a balance, and right here lies part of the reason why humanity enjoys so restrained a portion of the benefits that might accrue to it from the great Hidden Powers of Man.

25
Both by Thought and Feeling

I heard a man say: "Not by thought but by feeling we enter the Kingdom of Heaven." The evidence is that this is true of the majority, but it is not universally true. It is a mistake for anyone to attempt to measure the limits of the possible by his own limitations and capacities. There are instances of Realization in which thought played a part not inferior to feeling. Gautama Buddha and Shankara are examples and, certainly, in the latter case thought predominated. Further, in the instance of Immanuel Kant we have a genuine, if not complete, Realization, and, if there ever was a man who was a veritable incarnation of cognition, that man was Kant. For my own part, I have always found that cognition, when highly purified, could fly higher than feeling. It is perfectly true that Transcendental Knowledge is beyond thought, but, at the same time, it is equally beyond feeling and sensation. None of these three can be more than accessory instruments, and all of them are left behind at the final Transition. Still, it remains unquestionably true that the preponderant bulk of the instruction pointing out the Way emphasizes the silencing of thought while feeling may still continue. But this is merely a pragmatic rule designed to meet the needs of the greater number. Doubtless, with most men the greater power of soaring is in the principle of feeling, and naturally the greater opportunity for success lies along the course of the most developed power. If, in a given case, the evolution of thought has not reached beyond the lower levels, then this thought may well serve to hobble the free-roving feeling. In such a case, the shorter road normally will be through an Emancipated Feeling. But all this is only a general rule and should not be universalized into a Law.

This leads us to the practical question as to which sub-path a given individual should follow. It is determined by the quality which actually is most potent in the inner life of the individual. A man may be exceptionally skillful in the exercise of the power of thought and yet, in his inner nature, be genuinely grounded in feeling. Representatives of this class are not rare. Intellectually brilliant men, who genuinely love to attend symbolic religious services, are very apt to be instances. I do not mean men who attend or participate in such services as an example to others—a perfectly valid reason—but those who attend for their own sakes. In this they reveal what they really are, rather than what they seem to be because of an exercised skill. But in the case of the man for whom thought is the really decisive power, it is quite different. He may be more or less brilliant than the former example. The important differentia is that his life is implanted in his thought rather than his feelings. For him, the concept, and not the symbol, is the "open sesame" that discloses Value.

Thought and feeling constitute the bases of two distinct subpaths or disciplines, although these two fuse and become One at the end. It is difficult, if not quite impossible, for a man to succeed through a discipline foreign to his essential nature. It is good practice, therefore, for an aspirant, at an early stage, to acquire some familiarity with several disciplines.* He will find himself more in sympathy with one course of self-training than with others, and this will be indicative of what, for him, is the Way.

26
The Sea of Consciousness

The grand Sea of Consciousness unfolds before me on five levels. At the top is a Sea of Illimitable Depth and utter Calmness. Below This, and fusing into It, is another of mighty sweep, but not so vast in extent. Here there flow great waves in sonorous rhythm. Beneath this is a gulf and then a third sea possessed of boundaries, though its range is expanding. Here there are many sequences of waves flowing in numerous directions. There are harmonies in parts and blendings, but also there are clashings and some upheavals. Now and then, from out of this sea there arises, with a mighty whirling, a column that penetrates through the gulf and, occasionally, reaches the Sea above. Below the third sea, and contiguous to it, there is a fourth sea filled with much agitation. Waves are flowing without harmony or definiteness of direction. There is turmoil everywhere. Finally, at the bottom of all, there is a sluggish sea of no depth with low-powered waves having little meaning or purpose.

At the top is the Grand Sea of Infinite Consciousness, inexhaustible and without bounds. This is the seeming Emptiness that actually is the Fullness of the SELF—Pure Divinity, the Base of all else and the Final

---

*These are forms of Yoga, for which, see my book on *Yoga, its Technique and Practice*.

Resolution of all things. The next is the plane of Cosmic and Transcendent Consciousness. Here the One is also a Brotherhood. Likewise, permanence stands united with evolution. Below there is a gulf, not easy to cross; a gulf that mankind, in its folly, has widened while the Few, dedicated through Love to that mankind, strive ceaselessly to bridge the chasm. The third sea is the level of egoistic, or subject-object, consciousness in its highest state of development, the genuine upper-class of egoistic humanity. Here is the consciousness of those who move on the higher levels of love and intellect, but still within the limits of subject-object consciousness. These form the real "Chosen Race." Without them, the gulf would be impassable for the great human mass, and then, ultimately, all would sink down and out through the sluggish sea of ignorance. Of the human whole, only a handful, relatively, abides in the third sea, yet they are the immediate sustainers of all civilizations, the *real* burden-bearers of this outer life. From among them also come the recruits that, now and then, succeed in crossing the gulf. The fourth sea is of narrow limits, but heavily crowded with a large proportion of humanity. These are the quasi-intellectual, the semicultured, the mass that has become conceited with a little knowledge and does not know the saving humility of much knowledge. On this level are the senseless disputations fraught with emotion and passion. This is where the surgings arise that cause the turmoil of nations and classes. Yet there is some Light here, and the energy generated by Desire, the latter, to be sure, untrained and poorly directed, but still affording a force that eventually may be harnessed and guided. There still remains much hope for these despite their great folly. The fifth sea, shallow and very constricted, is densely crowded with the greatest mass of all. These are the sodden ones, drugged from drinking the final dregs of passion, those who bear little of the burden, but who are themselves the great burden. This sea is murky with the stirred-up mud of the depths, so there is only a dim twilight of the self-conscious light here. Yet there is a degree of self-consciousness, and so this lower realm does stand above the animal, even though sinking, in many respects, deep into the animal consciousness, and, by this illicit union, producing something lower than the animal. Often it seems that the passing of the cycles will not give time enough for these to rise again out of the depths into which they have sunk. For nothing is more hopeless than the task of revitalizing the sodden leaf that has sunk to the bottom of the stream. And, with respect to those leaves that have not quite sunk to the bottom, the task is of immense difficulty. It is far easier to transmute active and powerful evil than to arouse consciousness out of the dreamlike trance of soddenness. Yet much may be salvaged, and so long as the Spark is not completely extinguished, it is always possible that the Flame may be awakened anew.

Those of the lowest sea scarcely know that the third sea exists and are utterly ignorant of the realms beyond the gulf. Hence the denizens of this region frequently turn upon their own leaders and, in their ignorance, often destroy the very ones who are their hope. It is better to be the slave of an unkind master, provided the latter is superior, than to be left helplessly alone in the deeps. For a superior man, even though not so great as to have transcended selfishness, when he makes use of an inferior man, however selfish his motive, does raise the latter by the action of an inviolable law. For, inasmuch as it is true, that when a bird consumes a butterfly it raises the latter to its own level, so does the superior man raise the inferior by making use of him. Thoroughgoing and intelligent selfishness would never exploit inferiors. But as selfishness nearly always does so exploit, it is, therefore, made to serve the Great End despite itself, but does not share the Joy of that service. For any attention given by a superior to an inferior tends to raise the latter toward superiority in some measure. The law invoked here is as inevitable in its action as that related one in physics whereby an electric field tends to electrify objects in its vicinity. If ever the effort to remove really superior classes in this world should succeed, then there would soon be left only the lowest or fifth sea, with inevitable extinction as its ultimate doom. Who, then, are the real friends of mankind, the levelers or the exalters?

A simile comes to mind that, quite fairly, represents what the leveling process would really mean if successful. Suppose the lithosphere of the earth were all leveled to a common mean. Then there would be no dry land anywhere, but only an ocean of water, rolling over all. This would mean no sub-aerial life on dry land anywhere. There would be no plateaus—and all continents are plateaus—and no mountain peaks. Now all cultures that we know have developed with dry land as the physical basis of life. So, under our supposition, there could be no development of these. Thus there could be none of the grand procession of the scaled existences we know, leading up to the exalted Consciousness symbolized by the Mountain Top. And without the ascending ladder of Life, there would be no help anywhere to lead on and guide the water-bound existences.

27
I Who Speak

SOMETIMES AS I WRITE, the I becomes We and yet remains I.

There is a Consciousness which, while It remains One, is a symphony of harmoniously blended parts.

I write, and *I* watch myself writing.

I Know, and yet I wonder at the knowing.

I am the student and, at the same time, *I* am the Teacher.

As Teacher, *I* stand in Majesty looking upon the world below.

As student, I look up, humbly and amazed.

I speak and, presently, there blends with my voice the melodious Voices of Others.

One Meaning in many tones is unfolded.

So the tones of the seven-stringed Lyre are all sounded; one here, another there, in groups and, finally, all together.

And before this Melody I sit entranced, filled to the brim and more.

I who Speak none ever will know until, on that final Day he finds Himself, when *I* will appear in all My Glory.

28
How to Understand Mystic Writings

As I look back upon these writings, I note the curious fact that, at times, there is an impulse to write essentially poetic ideas. In these cases, admittedly, the form is not poetical in the conventional sense, but the essence is. Now, heretofore, throughout my life I have not been a lover of poetry and, much of the time, I had a decided distaste for it. Much less was I ever a writer of poetry. Yet now there comes a thought which requires poetry for its expression!

As I run through the pages of Bucke's *Cosmic Consciousness* I find a notable tendency, in the instances that he gives of what he calls the "Cosmic Sense," to give expression in poetry, though generally in the free form. The reason is becoming clear to me. Consciousness, descending from above the field of subject-object knowledge, is distorted just as soon as it is forced into the relative form of expression. In the latter field, discursive formulation has finished its task when it has finally shown what non-relative Knowledge is not. It clears the ground so that no obstruction remains for entering the Darkness and Silence. But when the "Voice of the Silence" speaks into the relative world, the Meaning lies between the words, as it were, rather than in the direct content of the words themselves. The result is that the external meaning of the words, in a greater or less degree, seems like "foolishness," as St. Paul said. Such writings, read in the ordinary subject-object sense of meaning, are often quite unintelligible and, in cases where they do convey a connected meaning, it is not quite this meaning, but something else, that is the real Meaning intended. We may say that the sequence of words is like the obverse side of an embroidered design. One must turn to the other side of the cloth to see the real figure. But the threads on the obverse side are continuous with those that actually display the design and, thus, there is a correlation. So it is with the words of the poet who is Awakened to the Cosmic or Transcendent. They become threads by which the intuitive consciousness may be stirred to a Recognition of an inexpressible Reality. The obverse may be quite lacking in pattern and, in that case, the writings are wholly unintelligible to the ordinary egoistic consciousness. On the other hand, they may be woven into a secondary pattern that is intelligible, which, therefore, more effectively holds the attention of the subject-object consciousness.

The foregoing indicates how to read poetry or other forms of expression of this type. The reading should be done without strained effort in the intellectual sense. The reader should let a sort of current flow into and through him, and not feel troubled as to whether he has understood anything or not, at the time. He may feel, or deeply cognize, something, though he may be unable to say what it is. If he is responsive, he will presently feel filled in a very curious but satisfying sense. He will return to the same Fount again and again, and presently, from out of Inner Meaning, understanding will begin to blossom in him. Perhaps he will find a degree of Recognition induced. Then, for him, the mystic writers will become progressively less and less obscure. He will enter into Communion on the level of a new kind of Language. On the new Level he will find the Living Presence of Those who have gone before him by the same Route. There is no death There, the possession or non-possession of physical bodies being of no moment.

29
Concerning Opposition Aroused by Sages

Why do the words of a Mystic or a Sage so often arouse such severe antagonism? Take, for instance, poems like the "Leaves of Grass" by Walt Whitman. They have aroused storms of criticism as well as enthusiastic admiration. Yet, on the other hand, readers of all sorts generally are not troubled by the weird meanderings of the written words of an insane mind. This reveals the fact that it is not simply the unconventionality of the form that stirs the antagonism. Now these storms of criticism are really tributes. They indicate, at least, an unconscious recognition of Power in the words of the Mystic or the Sage. The complacency of the forces of Mara—to employ a Buddhist term—has been struck a vital blow, and this arouses resistance. But in all such engagements, Mara is doomed to defeat, for the Power that has burst forth is united with the inexhaustible Fount. The only effective defense for Mara would be complete indifference. For if Mara causes any man to fight the Light, that man, sooner or later, is conquered by the Light and then becomes One with It. St. Paul affords us the classic example. He fought earnestly and sincerely so that quickly the Light conquered him and claimed him for Its own. From the standpoint of Mara, there is nothing more dangerous than an effort to slay a Sage or Mystic. The latter, in Their real Natures are invulnerable and, in the end, win to Themselves their would-be slayers.

30
The Record Continued

September 1

Again, last evening, I was in the state of contemplative Joy. In a growing degree, I feel It as something Sacred. Spontaneously, I tend to tread gently in Its Presence. I mean this, principally, in the sense of the treading of thought and feeling, but the physical action must be gentle also. Given a slow and passionless movement with respect to all actions, from thought downward,—the state persists. With rapid shifts, the state tends to break off. Precisely that which is required in the driving of an automobile in traffic is peculiarly unfavorable to this kind of consciousness.

Traffic driving requires a rapid noting of impressions and the forming of judgments as to whether those impressions are relevant to action and, if so, then the forming of the appropriate judgment of action. Often a new impression, such as another car entering into an intersection close in front, forces a sudden interruption in the execution of a previously formed judgment. This tends to produce an effect almost, if not quite, like a shock. Clearly there is some danger in this. Steady rhythm in the whole process becomes difficult. Consciousness is forced violently to the surface, and the inner state is broken, also violently.

There is a serious conflict between the requirements of a mechanical age and the conditions essential to inward penetration. I do not refer to the state of consciousness of the mechanical engineer, but to the kind of life the machine forces upon men. Keen alertness on the surface is essential in order to survive in this kind of life. The resultant effect is superficiality, even though an increase of keenness is forced. Profundity is quite compatible with keenness, but it is antagonistic to superficiality. It does seem that it is going to be difficult for man to achieve real happiness in the midst of this mechanical age.

This morning I awoke with a feeling of deflation in the physical body, but a little later I entered the contemplative state while tracing out a line of thought. At once there was happiness and comfort in the body, combined with the sense of well-being that penetrates through and through. What a wonderful power lies in a simple turn of thought! I recall the old materialistic outlook wherein we regarded the objects given through the senses as being substantial external existences, subsisting by themselves independently of consciousness. How inexplicable would be all this which I now experience from that standpoint! However, there is naturally in this inward Life a great mystery when It is viewed from the perspective of consciousness grounded in the physical world. We know the enormous energetic effort required to move even a relatively small portion of this world. It seems as though here must be something substantial and massive that is quite too much for anything, seemingly so delicate as a thought or a state of consciousness, to master and transform. Yet such is the case!

31
The Level of Real Equality

In the Inward Communion, there is an Equality not known out here. However, it is not equality in the geometrical sense of the agreement of superimposed configurations. Equality does not exist within the space-time manifold. But the basis of the Communion, There is not within the complex of space, time, and causality. Evolved degrees or states exist and, in this sense, every man, be he God-Realized or not, is different from and, therefore, not equal to, any other man. Thus the real Equality is equality with differences, and the range of differences exceeds the range of relative imagination. In the evolved sense, greater and less persist, but in the inmost sense, there is Equality.

Within the field of the egoistic consciousness, there is no equality, save in the one respect that all on this level are grounded on the egoistic base. To attempt to impose equality upon men in any other sense is to submit them to the torture of the Procrustean bed. There is no other folly more destructive than that. Equality, in this lower sense, if successfully imposed, would require the absolute destruction of all freedom. For freedom implies, among other things, the right to grow differently and to grow rapidly or slowly. Man has a right to choose to become wise, but the inescapable corollary of this is the right to choose the path of folly, but without hope of escaping the price of folly. Now, it is not wise to try to save men from the price of folly, for it is a necessary teacher. However, it is always true Compassion to seek to arouse in men a desire for Wisdom.

32
The Greatness of Man

There is a greatness within every human soul.

I sense this greatness in growing degree.

Something there is in every man to which I offer the gesture of respect.

As men become truly sane they reveal to Me new facets of Myself, and I feel a kind of wonder before these.

These Brothers enrich Me by revealing Myself to Myself and myself.

33
The Moral Problem

The Preponderant Portion of the literature outlining the conditions favorable to the Awakening lays heavy stress upon the cultivation of the moral qualities. The central emphasis is placed upon the elimination of a selfish point of view, i.e., a base of action, thought, motivation, valuation, etc., grounded in a self regarded as distinct from other selves. Now the Awakened Consciousness tends to manifest on the ethical level outlined in the above literature. It does this, not as a matter of forcing upon the individual an externally formulated and imposed code, but as a spontaneous expression growing out of the very Consciousness Itself. The egoistic perspective is completely submerged in fully Awakened Consciousness and, in progressive degree, this is so as the Consciousness unfolds from the Twilight stage to full Glory. For the Awakened Man, the moral problem ceases to exist in the usual sense. There may remain the technical problem of what in action is the wisest course, but there no longer exists for Him the task of mastering egoistic consciousness. There are higher fields of moral choice within the Awakened Consciousness, but they lie beyond the range of apprehension of purely egoistic consciousness.

Now the rationale behind the ethical discipline is clear. He who causes himself to act, think, feel, etc., in a form that is, in fact, the natural expression of the Awakened Consciousness, sets up a condition that tends to induce that consciousness. It is simply another illustration of the familiar relationship manifested between electricity and magnetism. An electric current always produces a magnetic field, but, likewise through the appropriate employment of a magnetic field, we can induce an electric current.

In spite of the practical importance of the moral discipline, however, it remains true that the Awakening can, and has, taken place in the midst of a life even less moral, in the *objective sense*, than the average. To be sure, the Awakening, in such cases, effects at once a moral revolution and a radical change of character. This simply shows that the preliminary moral discipline, while of the highest desirability, is not a *sine qua non* of Recognition of, at least a minor order. Some other contributory external circumstance or, perhaps, pure and unaided spontaneity may effect the Transition.

The moral discipline may be regarded as an approach toward the Goal through emphasis of the negation of evil. But that, which from one standpoint appears as evil, in other aspects, appears as ignorance, hate, and ugliness. We may call that which appears in such multiform negative aspects by the name "Mara." Now Mara may be destroyed through any of its facets and the destruction of the other facets follows sooner or later. There are thus disciplines of Beauty, Love, and Knowledge which effect the same consummation as the moral discipline. He who becomes identical with Beauty is incapable of producing ugliness, including moral ugliness. During the intermediate stages of aesthetic consciousness, there may be a considerable association with immorality, but in the end the devotion to Beauty must destroy the latter, because of its essential ugliness. The man whose nature is Beauty cannot help but be a good man, once he has become identical with that Beauty. Love achieves the same end by another road. The negation of Love is hate. He who identifies himself with Love drowns the capacity to hate and, therefore, does not act along the lines that are the normal expression of hate. Thus spontaneously he tends to act, feel, think, etc., in accordance with the code of selflessness. Love, too, in its intermediate stages may violate the code, but if the devotion to Love remains unabated, gradually or rapidly it becomes purified. Then unlovely conduct becomes impossible.

There remains the Path of Knowledge. From the perspective of the highest Knowledge, all evil is ignorance. My own conviction accords with the teaching of Shankara, in holding that there is no such thing as an essentially evil will. Definitely I take exception to St. Paul on this point, and challenge all of that phase of so-called Christian orthodoxy that is built upon the doctrine of the existence of an autonomously evil will. In fact, Will is neither good nor evil but an entirely neutral power. The Will directed by ignorance becomes evil in its manifestation, but if directed by Knowledge, it either becomes good or manifests on a level where the duality of good and evil is not relevant. Thus, from the standpoint of the Path of Knowledge, the only problem is the destruction of Ignorance. With the destruction of Ignorance, Mara is destroyed automatically with all Its works. But this Knowledge is not to be confused with information. A man may have Realized his identity with Knowledge and yet be poorly informed; likewise, a well informed man may be quite blind to this Knowledge. Now, let us say, that through Knowledge a given man has attained Recognition of his identity with the SELF. At that moment he has placed himself knowingly outside the reach of all powers inferior to the SELF, and that means he is beyond all relative powers, including evil. For him the selfless code becomes spontaneously his mode of expression, and then progressively the personal nature becomes freed from old habits. It has been my personal conviction that Knowledge is the greatest Power of all and in this I seem to be in accord with the preponderant judgment of the Indian Sages. But if the Path of Knowledge is the one of greatest Power, it is also one that is least available. Thus practically all other disciplines have the greater pragmatic availability.

We are not here concerned with the problem of the origin of evil, but only with that practical one of its destruction. Evil causes suffering; Knowledge destroys evil; seek, therefore, for that Knowledge and, having attained It, all evil and all suffering will vanish as has the forgotten dream of long ago.

34
Solar and Planetary Recognition

The man who has awakened to Cosmic Consciousness may become a Planet, but likewise, He may become a Sun. I do not mean that, at once, He becomes enrobed in those great bodies known to astronomers as planets and stars. But I do mean something that, in the essential sense, is the same thing, although there is a wide rang of difference in degree. The point is that whereas the earmark of the common consciousness of humanity is egoism, the Cosmic Consciousness is planetary or stellar in the *primary* sense. He who becomes a Sun is grounded directly in the SUPREME and thus is in high degree a Self-luminous and independent body. A planet is a body of minor luminosity which moves in an orbit around some sun. Thus a man may attain Recognition, but be so drawn by sympathetic attraction to another Liberated Soul as to revolve in the orbit of the latter. As one reads through the record of Those who have awakened Cosmic Consciousness, it is not difficult to recognize these two tendencies. Many place themselves in very humble relationship to a transcendent Greatness that has burst out within them; and, while they may say, "I am this Greatness," in practice they identify themselves with the outer man and bow humbly before a transcendent Otherness. Or, again, there may be an attitude of subservience to another God-Realized

Man who may have been the inspiration that aroused the Awakening. Here is revealed the planetary tendency. Shankara has warned that no man should regard any Realization as greater than his own. Each Realized Man should hold this thought, if he can, "There can be nothing greater than the Supreme Realization which I have." If this attitude is held unshaken, then that Man becomes a Sun. The following point should be borne clearly in consciousness: "However true it may be that there are greater Suns and greater evolutionary unfoldments, my own Inner Realization is the highest." Any other view involves duality and, hence, a planetary state in the Cosmic Life. But if a man cannot become a Sun, let him, by all means, become a Planet and play his part in the Grand Symphony—the Communion of Free Souls.

35
Recognition and the Physical Body

September 2

It is necessary that the Current be attuned to the resources of the body and particularly to the nervous system. While in the Current, I feel exaltation and a sense of well-being that reaches well down into the outer organism, yet this does not change the fact that the Current is a powerful energy and does tax certain powers of endurance. In the deflated state, there is a feeling of fatigue, not unlike that which accompanies a conflict with illness. At such times it is necessary to resist a psychological depression. The physical body is clearly the weakest link, and there is a temptation to retreat from this in the periods of deflation. I can suggest the feeling, if the body is thought of as something like a ten ampere fuse, while from the transformer, just beyond, there is being delivered a current on the order of one hundred amperes at a high potential. One is constantly under a pressure to use more than ten amperes and thus strain the fuse close to the point of burning out. Yet, if that fuse is burned out, correlation with this plane is broken and the expression here will remain unfinished.

Ecstatic states, experienced after placing the body in complete trance, do not involve the same problem. But in that case very little of the Inner Consciousness is likely to be carried down through the physical brain and the nervous organism, thus resulting in a corresponding limitation of outer expression. So from the standpoint of expression in this world, the physical brain and nervous system are the critical links.

From the standpoint of Recognition, the gross body is valuable only as an instrument, primarily for the reaching of other embodied consciousnesses. It is no longer of vital importance for its own sake or as a means of experience, since, for him who has once reached the Source of Joy and Knowledge, all of the delights and information which may be derived from experience become mere shadows for which he tends to feel a certain disgust. But the gross body still remains valuable as an instrument of action and requires the attention which a good artisan would give a useful tool, but no more. Here we come face to face with one of the higher temptations, i.e., the neglecting or letting go of an instrument which is a brake upon the play of the Higher Consciousness, whether in the sense of Knowledge or Ecstasy. An instance which illustrates this point is found in the case of a certain Oriental who, in the early part of his life, had become a college professor. He attained Illumination, and then naturally his center of interest shifted to the Higher World. He did not forget this physical world, however, and did leave it considerable benefit from his new insight. According to his own account, he finally planned a systematic philosophic statement, but the inward attraction had now become so strong that the desire to give expression to his Recognition withered. He moved more and more into the life of meditation, and finally, when bathing in a stream, was drowned, owing to his having entered an inward state while in the water. The world lost something this man could have left, for he had the power of expression in high degree. From His own standpoint, to be sure, He had merely dropped a fetter, but the present is not a time when, in general, such men may rightly feel themselves free to disregard the needs of others while satisfying Their own inner convenience.

It is difficult for the average individual, caught in the hypnotic glamour of embodied consciousness, to understand the attitude toward physical embodiment which Recognition, at least above a certain level, induces in the Realized Man. Let me assure the reader that this position is not artificial, nor forced, nor due to pessimism. It is just as natural as the distaste the normal man would feel for life in a front-line trench during a modern war. Cheerfully he may choose to accept his tour of duty in the front lines because he feels that his country needs his service there, but wholeheartedly he abominates the life. He will not feel it a hardship when circumstances so change that he will not be needed at the front.

Well, let me assure anyone who doubts, that the Inward Life is so immeasurably richer than outer life that the keenest sensual enjoyment is relatively pain. Hence, a tour of duty in gross physical embodiment is relatively like a period of life at the front during warfare. In addition to the inmost and grandest State of all, there are other Worlds, more subtle than this outer field of life, where Consciousness is also embodied, and the Life There is immeasurably richer than all life here below. Therefore, why cling to the false glamour of life cast in the dregs?

Upon the stagnant water of a swamp, filled with rotting vegetation and sewage, there is often seen an oily film, reflecting iridescent colors. In this there is a small measure of beauty, but so poor when compared with other and greater beauties. This oil-film is a fit symbol of the keener delights of the unillumined sensuous life. Is it other than natural that a man who has found greater and richer beauties should wish to turn his back upon the oil-film of the swamp?

36
Concerning Occult Powers

In the broad sense, the occult means all that is hidden to the given level of consciousness which is taken as the base of reference. Thus, to the simple consciousness of the animal, the egoistic consciousness which underlies our familiar culture and civilization is occult. A few of the higher animals, such as some dogs, do show signs indicating adumbrations of values characteristic of egoistic consciousness, and thus they are reaching to the morning twilight of the latter level. But this happens because these few individuals have come close to man, who plays for them an analogous part to that of the Guru to the Chela at a still higher level. Relative to the consciousness of the vast majority of animals, these few favored individuals occupy a position similar to that of a partial initiation into an occult domain. In these cases, we have simply instances of devoted aspiration, on the part of the individuals with the less evolved consciousness, and induction from him of the superior consciousness.

Within the egoistic field, there is a relatively wide range from those individuals who have just sufficiently established their base here to be called men—such as the Bushmen of Australia—, up to the highest evolved consciousness which yet falls short of the higher Awakened Consciousness. In a secondary sense, we may say that the higher cultures are occult for primitive man. But, in time, evolution will cross this range without an act of radical transcendence. For this is development within the field of a given type of consciousness, in this case, egoistic or subject-object consciousness. When the term "occult" is applied in this connection, it is not employed in the strict sense, for the latter implies a radical shift of base.

With reference to the preponderant portion of humanity, the "Occult" means that Consciousness which is realized when the Awakening has come. None of the Knowledge which is the common possession of this Higher Level can be understood by the purely egoistic man. Efforts at cross-translation do enrich the egoistic consciousness and tend to arouse the Awakening in those who are still sleeping, but whatever is understood within the egoistic range is essentially different from the Awakened Consciousness, as such. There is an irreducible incommensurability which forever makes correct cross-translation impossible. Even though a man is functioning on both levels, he cannot effect the really correct cross-translation in his own consciousness. He is, in a sense, both the circle and the square. He has, or is, Knowledge in both senses simultaneously, yet the essential nature of the higher type remains inexpressible in terms of the lower. Still there is such a thing as approximation to cross-translation in much the sense that a mathematician can give an approximate rational evaluation of an irrational number, such as $\sqrt{2}$. But though this approximation may be carried to any number of decimal places—the greater number of decimal places corresponding to the greater skill in cross-translation—and a value be attained which serves all the practical requirements of applied mathematics, yet, from the standpoint of the values absolutely essential to pure mathematics,* the effort has been a complete failure. For the Man who has Awakened in the higher sense and who still continues to function within the egoistic level, neither domain is any longer occult in the strict sense, however much remains occult in the sense of not having yet been mastered. So, to Awake is to Know the Occult or, rather, to become identical with Occult Knowledge.

In certain respects it is perfectly proper to attempt a cross-translation of the higher Occultism into the egoistic level, by as skillful means as may be devised. This applies to the more highly spiritual phase of the

---

*The relationship between the two levels of consciousness is represented, in the form of analogy, very beautifully by just the difference which separates pure from applied mathematics.

Occult, and that phase actually is the most important, for it affords the Key which ultimately renders possible the unlocking of the rest. This is the Occultism of Self-Recognition. He who has become well rooted in the SELF is superior to all the lesser powers, and thus stands, in principle, in a position where it is safe for Him to acquire the technique requisite for their manipulation. But even in this cross-translation, there is such a thing as "spiritual dynamite." However, in general, the individual not qualified for use of this is protected by a lack of interest, or a deficiency of understanding, so that such literature seems either uninteresting or meaningless to him.

There are, however, other domains of the Occult where enough of real power could be conveyed in cross-translation so that a dangerous misuse would become possible. There are powers, sufficiently within the range of egoistic control that, if they are viciously employed or, through inadequate understanding or control, misapplied, would effect far worse results than the simple destruction of physical life. It is clear that such powers must be artificially veiled and guarded, if the human race is not to suffer incalculable injury. Naturally, only men of proved character and capacity can be safely admitted into the knowledge of such arcana.

It by no means follows that because a man has Awakened and therefore crossed the Gulf, thus becoming essentially a citizen of the Inner World, He consequently enters into possession at once of all Powers subject to that level of Consciousness. Some Powers He has, by reason of the simple fact of Awakening, and these are reflected automatically in his life, his writings, etc. He does influence others in certain respects quite beyond the range of other men who, however skillful and able they may be, yet remain centered within the egoistic consciousness. But there are innumerable specific Powers affecting all departments of nature, both in the sense of knowledge-penetration and of capacity for active manipulation, that can be aroused and mastered. Probably few, if any, Proficients in this field actually have unfolded all possible Powers that fall within the range or level of evolution on which They stand. We have here a natural analogue with a familiar fact that obtains among men on the egoistic level. Some have capacities in one direction, others in still other directions, and no one man in one embodiment is equally proficient in all. Specific powers are awakened by the appropriate effort and evolution. The Inner World is not poorer, but richer, in the range of variety It unfolds; and, save in the very highest sense, there is in this Domain that which corresponds to "time" on the objective levels. It is another kind of "time," to be sure, but, at least, there is that which is analogous to that which is called "progress," in this inferior world. So there is much to be done, and while Proficients move within a totally different base of reference, still They are Men and not strange Beings wholly beyond the limits of all relativity. The Awakening is one fact, the most important of all, the list of developed powers quite another; and the forms of development are distinctly variable from individual to individual.

The primary principle whereby these Higher Powers are possible is simple, once the essential nature of Reality is apprehended. If the primary assumptions of the naturalists or the materialistic realists were correct, these Powers would be quite unthinkable. But the Real is Consciousness, and the development of the universe is a projection from pure subjectivity outward. At least it is so, when conceived from the relative standpoint. I produce, therefore, this world through My Power of Ideation, Will, etc. Hence, within the limits of the Law, which is also Myself, I can mold and transform that world by the same Power which produced it. The Adept Man is identical with the Divinity, which I AM, hence through Him, I act in the manipulation of My universe. This, of course, does not give the technical details, which can be learned more or less quickly, but it does give the principle whereby the whole idea of Occult Powers can be apprehended as rational, and not involving the supernatural, however much the Powers may be super-normal so far as the common experience of humanity is concerned.

The question is often asked: "Why, if there are Men who have such Powers, is the manifestation of them so rare?" It has, in fact, seemed to many that the demonstration of Powers would go far in convincing men of their own erroneous ideas in such matters, and thus serve to stimulate research in the right direction. In answer, it may be pointed out first, that there have been a few, well-attested demonstrations; and, second, ancient traditions are full of reference to them. Signs are not wanting, though admittedly they are not numerous and generally have to be searched out. But there are reasons why care is always exercised in the demonstration of Powers. The most important of these is based upon a consideration of the effect the manifestation of Powers has upon men whose understanding is not sufficiently prepared. The average man regards such Powers as supernatural or miraculous. Note, for example, the predominant attitude that has obtained throughout Christendom during the last 1900 years with respect to the works of Jesus. Now, if men regard a Power as supernatural, the result is growth of superstitions, instead of progress toward the essentially rational outlook which is so vitally important to real Mastery. In such cases, the demonstration of Powers produces just the reverse effect of that desired. Superstition is a fatal barrier to God-Realization. Divinity, for the superstitious, is either an object on which to place irrational confidence, or one to be feared. The result is a widening, not a closing, of the gap between man and his God. Few effects could be worse than that. So it remains a rule that before a man may witness a demonstration, he must first become well familiarized with the philosophy that will enable him to comprehend it within a rational outlook. He must come to see the Power, as in principle, at least, within the range of his own latent capacities, once they are unfolded. When this is the case, demonstrations may be helpful.

We do not tamper with the growth of men in such a way that they cease to be self-determined. No man is endowed with Powers as a free gift. They must all be acquired, and while We may exercise a directing hand, the impulse to effort must spring up spontaneously from within the consciousness of each individual. A Power, once achieved, is a possession of the man who has mastered It and can be lost only through his own unwise action, although temporarily We may suppress It when its premature exercise would do injury to larger issues, either within the individual himself, or to the larger whole.

37
The Underlying Force in Religion

In a fundamental sense, sometimes in a highly exalted form, but often not so exalted, the underlying force in religion is the same one that draws men and women together. When there is genuine religious ecstasy, some phase of the creative principle is manifesting, occasionally on an exceedingly lofty level, but more often on levels of progressive inferiority until, in the depths, we find the Voodoo and similar practices. A study of religious history shows a recurring tendency for religious practice to assume a phallic form, sometimes quite gross, at other times more or less hidden.

In the higher sense, the Creative Principle is sacred and is properly a part of pure religiosity. In the Christian religion, it is veiled under the word "Holy Ghost." This should make clear why the sin against the Holy Ghost is regarded as so serious. Now the sin consists in dragging the Creative Principle into a gross and impure consciousness. Here is a realm where only the Pure in Heart may enter with safety. Let others beware!

The physiological aspect of this Principle is only one of its more inferior modes. Real creativeness is conscious. Now, while there is no sin in the normal manifestation of the physiological aspect, as such, the quality of consciousness associated therewith does determine whether the effects shall be good or evil. Impure human consciousness has its most serious effect when it is brought into correlation with the action of the Creative Principle on any level, but the higher the level the worse the effect. This is one way in which evil can be inoculated into Life. This is a very serious matter, for right here is where humanity has produced its own worst curse.

The higher aspects of the Creative Principle, of which there are several levels, become progressively more potent and more sacred until, at the top, we come into Recognition of the Celestial Virgin. He who fuses his consciousness with this Virgin no longer simply believes in or seeks Immortality, but Knows himself to be Immortal, nay more, He is Immortality. This should help to make clear what Supreme Value is veiled in the words "Holy Ghost."

But, however great the benediction of the Current of Bliss may be, he who would be Master must not abandon himself even to this Glory. There is such a thing as Divine Intoxication, and while many look upon the implied abandonment as a kind of virtue, they are only partly right. The true Priest must never permit himself to lose command, even in the presence of the highest exaltation, else for him the Supreme Enlightenment will remain unknown.

38
Knowledge Through Identity

September 3

It is becoming clear that there is a radical difference between formal and empirical knowledge on the one hand and Knowledge from the standpoint of the Awakened Consciousness. Unless this difference is understood, the speech and writings of the Sages and Mystics will remain fundamentally incomprehensible for all those who remain confined within the egoistic consciousness. Formal and empirical knowledge—and here I mean all knowledge for which language is an adequate vehicle—is a knowledge of relationships. Thus, a word stands for an object which is, in some sense, other than the word. The objects, in this case, are not simply those represented by substantives, but also objects in the sense of actions, relations, qualities, etc. These objects may be gross or subtle, but, in any case, an otherness is implied. "Truth" becomes defined as some sort of relation between the verbal ideas and the objects for which they stand. All of this knowledge is thus essentially external and stands out as something other than, or counter to, the egoistic self.* But Knowledge in this sense is of instrumental value only. Hence, through this knowledge, the "Thing-in-itself" is never realized, for it imposes upon consciousness the seeming of distance. The result is that intellectuality, *if not consciously or unconsciously united to Real Knowledge*, has the effect of emptiness or "thinness" which so impressed William James. Here we have the reason for the failure of the attempts to prove, formally, the existence of God. Formal demonstration cannot rise above its fount, but can make explicit all that is contained in the latter. Thus, a demonstration which starts from a fount that is less than Divinity can never prove the existence of Divinity. *God is either Known directly through Identity, or He is not known at all.*

In contrast to formal and empirical knowledge, Real Knowledge is essentially wordless, for It does not deal with objects. This is Knowledge through Identity. Hence, It does not *represent* Substance, but *is* Substance Itself. So, it is true that "I"—the self or Atman—am not different from that Knowledge. The speech and writings of the God-Realized Men are not representations of external existences, but are the actual embodiments of the SELF. The Sage and the Mystic live in the words that They utter as truly as in Their fleshly encasements, and sometimes even more fully. Hence, to the reader or hearer these Words carry the very Presence Itself. Such Words, therefore, have magical power to transform the man who attends to Them. Real Knowledge is not instrumental but is an End-in-Itself. It may be clothed in highly organized intellectual form and, in that case, we have true Philosophy, which also is an end-in-itself.

---

*It is the external quality of this knowledge that makes the development of materialism possible.

The way to reconcile William James and Hegel now becomes clear. Both men had a high degree of insight; and, if for them the Sun had not risen to shine with the clearest brilliance, then It was either near the horizon and about to rise, or had done so already and was merely obscured. If it had been shining clearly for James, he could hardly have failed to recognize Hegel. Now with Hegel, the individual man, the principal development was in the intellect, while in the case of James, it was in sensation and feeling, and this remains true in spite of the high development of intellectual skill which he possessed. With him, intellect was foreign to the essential man, but not so with Hegel. Now Real Knowledge is most successfully expressed through and to a man in the phases most highly developed in his personal and individual nature. Not all Embodiments of the Word are equally accessible to all men. Even a God-Realized Man who lacked a given faculty could not Realize a manifestation of Real Knowledge through that faculty in an effective sense. On the levels of only partial Realization, a greater or less degree of Recognition may be given through the most highly developed doors, and yet fail through other avenues which are less developed. Hegel's philosophy is genuine and is grounded in Real Knowledge, however much, as a matter of logic, he may have failed to prove his Knowledge so that all rational men must agree.* Hegel's intellectuality does incarnate Substantiality and carries the Light, although James was unable to see It in that embodiment. Yet James did see the Light, else he could not have had so much sympathy with the essence of religion and responded so enthusiastically as he did to mystical writings, such as those of Gustav Theodor Fechner. But he was so constituted that he could not see that Light through the Door that Hegel opened.

It follows, that from the standpoint of James' vision, he was quite correct in regarding the intellect as only instrumental. He was wrong in universalizing his own standpoint. Intellectuality may be an embodiment of Substantiality, no less completely than may be the sensations and the affections; and, in that case, it enrobes Ends, and not merely means. As will be shown more fully later, all three modes of relative consciousness, cognition, affection and sensation, taken by themselves, equally fail to give substantial actuality. It is only when they are united to Knowledge through Identity that they actually embody Substantiality.

---

*The logically perfect formulation of Real Knowledge has not yet been written. Not even Shankara was wholly successful, for in the light of our, at present, greater understanding of logic, it is possible to show inadequacy in Shankara, so far as formal demonstration is concerned.

In the case we have just discussed, we come face to face with an example of a very common error among men who have at least a degree of genuine insight and may, in fact, have had their Suns rise to a considerable height. Such an individual often sees his way as the only Way and says, in effect, "By this road alone may you enter." It is not so. Any route which egoistic man may devise, in principle, can become a Way. It is a mistake to take one's own individual limitations and predicate them as being of Spirit. Always He who has Arrived may say: "This Way that I have traveled is a possible Way, for I have proven It; come and try It, for It may be a Way for you also." But for a given human soul that particular Route may be impractical, while some other Route may be the "Open Sesame."

The understanding of the place of logic is also becoming clear. There is no doubt that logic wields the final authority within the kind of knowledge that belongs to the subject-object manifold, in so far as logic has applicability. The law of contradiction is absolute in this domain. Every logical dichotomy divides the whole of the relative universe into two parts, so that of that universe we may always say: "It is either X or not-X." ("X" in this case standing for any concept whatsoever.) But from the standpoint of Real Knowledge such a dichotomy is neither true nor false, but simply irrelevant. It involves even more fundamental irrelevance than that contained in questions such as the following: "Is a lion organized according to the principles of a fugue or a symphony?" Likewise, from the perspective of Knowledge through Identity, there is no meaning in applying the logical criterion of contradiction. Here, within this subject-object, time-space manifold, there is no principle more fundamental than that "A cannot be both A and not-A at the same time and in the same sense." But what bearing could that possibly have upon a Consciousness which transcends both space and time, as well as the subject-object field? For all possible spaces and all possible times and every sense in which an idea may be employed are at once comprehended in the pure apperception of the SELF.

Still, it remains true that every expression within the subject-object manifold may be tried very properly by the canons of logic and, if found wanting, that expression must be judged incorrect. And this remains true of expressions cross-translated from Real Knowledge as well as others. But, despite all this and however incorrect the expression may be, if it is a cross-translation from Real Knowledge, it is True in the fundamental sense, for it carries Meaning. It is merely the vehicle that is inadequate.

None the less, I am convinced that the Way is made clearer as the vehicle of expression is made more highly perfect, and that He who speaks from out of the Fount should try to make himself as clear as possible.

39
The Meaning of Substance

For the first time, tho word substance has become really intelligible to me. I turn again to Spinoza's "Ethics" and read the third definition of the first part: "I understand SUBSTANCE to be that which is in itself and is conceived through itself." Many times I have struggled to give this definition an intelligible meaning, but never quite successfully. But now it stands out clearly and I know just exactly what it means. Heretofore, I tried to relate the notion of "substance" to objects, even though in a subtle sense. But this is an error. No object, whatsoever, is "in itself and conceived through itself." I am that SELF and Recognize that I am that SELF, and now I Realize what Substance is. Substance is not other than Myself.* But this Substance is just precisely that which cannot be predicated of ponderable matter, or of objects of the senses or of thought.

Spinoza's thought takes on a new clarity. There is difficulty in his mode of expression, for he uses words in a different way from that current now, but the real thought becomes clear without much effort. And why is this? It is simply that I now cognize his thought from the same standpoint from which he wrote. Take, for example, a chance sentence to which I turn in his "Short Treatise." It happens to be a sentence from Albert Schwegler's introductory summary of Spinoza's philosophy, but it very clearly carries Spinoza's meaning. "Felicity, then, is not the reward of virtue—it is virtue itself." In other words, real Happiness is virtue, and not merely an effect of virtuous living. This is quite clear. Happiness is the only praise or glorification of God. Happiness is the only worthy prayer. Happiness is virtue and gloom is sin. Now I arbitrarily shift myself back into the old egoistic consciousness, and all this sounds like nonsense. This is all due to the difference in the kind of knowledge, the Real Knowledge standing in incommensurable relationship to egoistic knowledge. But the Real Knowledge saves man, while the egoistic kind, by itself, cannot.

---

*It is a very interesting fact, that in the experience of the Current which is Bliss on the 7th of last month, spontaneously I thought of It as Substance.

Which of these two kinds of knowledge is rational and which irrational? I should certainly say that the Real Knowledge is rational and commensurable—the latter term being interpreted in the sense of "intelligible" rather than of measurable. But the subject-object standpoint would reverse this view. It is all a question of level or standpoint. But in the profounder sense, my view is right.

40
Communion in the Company of the Realized

The vista ahead grows more interesting.
There is coming a new and more intimate companionship with the new and old philosophic masters: Spinoza, Kant, Hegel, Plato, among others.
What names of real charm are these!
What artificers of great Beauty are these Men!
With rare skill do They reflect the Glory of My Eternal Thought.
How greatly do They reveal to Me how much I Know!

★   ★   ★

I Recognize, in ever increasing numbers, signs of the Supreme Light. While there are Few for Whom the Sun has risen in Its full Glory, the number who have known the Twilight before the Sun appears above the horizon, or have perhaps just glimpsed the Sun as Its rays barely surmount the barrier, is much greater than I had thought. There is also another and more mysterious class of which the members were born with the Sun above the horizon, but the Rays were obscured by a cloud-filled sky. For These, the Sun first rose in other lives, but for one reason or another They have taken incarnation under obscuration. The clouds may or may not break for Them during the current life-time. It depends primarily upon the original purpose. It is sometimes necessary to drive through from below in order to force new Doors and, in such cases, the Pioneer is very apt to be one who first broke through in some other life. Sometimes the obscuration may serve the purpose of rest, for the Inner Life, if the Final Rest is refused, is considerably more intense than life within the egoistic consciousness. Emerson is one of the known examples of such an obscuration. Dr. Bucke was not able definitely to class him as an instance of the Awakened Consciousness because certain familiar earmarks were lacking. The trace of the Ancient and Eternal Wisdom is to be found strongly marked in several of Emerson's works, and the obscuration easily accounts for the atypical features in his case.

41
Recognition and Egoism

I note a form in some of these writings that certainly has much of the appearance of egotism. I have also noted that form in the writings of others who have written from the same point of view. In the past I have even resented this as being a kind of pretension without due perspective. The fact is, however, that from the standpoint of Awakened Consciousness, the egoistic element is really lacking, or only remains as a residue in the as yet incompletely transformed egoistic consciousness of the individual who has Awakened. Egotism is one of the effects of the subject-object consciousness, for here the individual ego seems to be distinct from other egos and to have interests that are in conflict. Furthermore, egotism does not manifest solely in the form of conceit. It can also be traced in most humility, for the inferiority complex is as much a phase of egotism as is the superiority complex. But the Fire of REAL Knowledge burns all this away sooner or later.

In the record of personal and decidedly interior events, the use of the first personal pronoun is difficult to avoid, and its avoidance would hardly give a scientifically accurate record. Such events are always the "my experience" of some individual. But it is not in the "record" that the seeming egotism appears. Over and over again, I do speak from the standpoint of certainty, and not hypothetically or tentatively. I do not hide assurance under a form that merely suggests a possibility or probability.

Now assurance is categorical and not hypothetical. But, if I say at times, in effect, "thus I Know," this Knowledge should not be confused with knowledge in the field of the hypothetical, this latter being concerned with the possible rather than the actual. In the domain of the hypothetical, discussion can be silenced only by complete logical demonstration. Without such demonstration, hypothetical knowledge is only opinion. Further, I do not assert categorical assurance with respect to objective empiric knowledge, such as that which constitutes the field of physical science. Here, trained skill in observation is the best authority, and the results in any case are only relatively accurate. Higher development in skill may change them. Writing in such fields is sound only when there is, expressly or implied, a tentative presentation. Genuine scientists, for the greater part, are really quite careful in this respect, particularly when offering working hypotheses. Finally, I do not predicate Supreme Power, such as is implied in the statement, "I sustain this universe," as an attribute of the personal or relative man. All powers in their objective manifestation in space and time are relative to the capacity of the instrument, and this capacity may be great or small, but in any case it is a matter of relative degree.

I Know with categorical assurance with respect to Meaning alone. I do not know that my formal expression is the most correct possible; nay more, I can find faults in that formal expression myself, but fail to see how it may be substantially improved. In most that I write here, I start from the standpoint of Meaning, where I Know and have now Recognized that I Know. I find, in progressive degree, this same Meaning expressed, often in quite diverse form, by Others who, also, have Recognized Their own Identity. I am One and, at the same time, all others, but, in an especial sense, those Others who have Recognized Themselves. This higher "I" is spelt the same as the egoistic "I," but it means something essentially different. And further, it is only from the egoistic point of view that the Transcendent Consciousness appears as an "I" Consciousness. On the highest level, both the "I" and the "thou" disappear. The egoistic "I" is a bare point, having what might be called social position, but no magnitude. It is like the zero in analytics. But the Transcendent "I" is as much all Space as the Point. Its mathematical symbol would be both 0 (zero) and ∞ (infinity). Theoretically, it is conceivable that the Transcendent Consciousness may be approached through a diffusion, spread everywhere, as well as through concentration in the point or the "I," but the practicability of this is doubtful. It should be clear from all this that the Transcendent "I" is anything but egotistical.

Propriety might suggest a more modest form of expression. But to follow such a course would be to fall into the essence of the denial of St. Peter. For, fearing his public, Peter said, "I know Him not," and so failed in his test. Peter knew his Lord but refused to identify himself with Him at the time in question. This was not honoring the Lord, but quite the reverse. I have recognized My Lord, which is Myself and, at the same time, the REAL SELF of all creatures, and I have chosen to acknowledge that SELF before men, for I am not ashamed of THAT. Perhaps this

Recognition may help to arouse the Light of the SELF in others. At any rate, the hope that it may do so is the only reason for composing this expression at all.

42
By Many Paths

By many paths they come to Me.
I care not what the Path may be, just so they come.
I am in all, but not yet are all within Me.
I desire that none shall linger in the outer darkness.
I desire that no man should suffer this travail he himself has produced.

There are Ways to Me that are short and direct; others long and painful.

Is it not well to choose the shorter Route, rather than the Way that is long and weary?

Yet, until the last is gathered in, I shall wait.

43
The Record Continued

September 4

Now I perceive the progress of effects upon the physiological level. There is a perceptible increase of vigor in the gross body. Also there is a changing preference with respect to food. The desire and taste for meat is declining. Meat is not yet distasteful, but with continuation along this line, it will soon become so. I am becoming rather indifferent to concentrated sweets and, in general, I care less for the prepared foods. There is a mild increase of desire for fruits. But the predominant attitude toward food is one that is rather well filled with indifference and some distaste. However, on the other hand, I feel rather less need for gross nourishment.

Some years ago I had become completely disgusted with the doctrinaire dietetics, and have since taken a purely pragmatic view toward this subject. The latter course I have found practically the most satisfactory, and am continuing it at the present time. The changes of inclination, noted above, are quite free from pressure due to theoretical considerations.

44
The Relation of Karma to Recognition

The GREAT authoritative sources on Recognition, such as the Teachings of Buddha, the Writings of Shankara, the "Bhagavadgita," and the "Voice of the Silence" all state that the Realized Man is freed from the karma of past actions, save the karma that has already "sprouted" and is the causal power which maintains the continuance of the current gross body. I have already testified to the sense of feeling free from the action of karma at the time of the Transition. Further, it is a very common testimony found in the records of those who have attained Recognition; only, in many instances, the report is in the form of a statement affirming a feeling of freedom from sin. There is a very important principle involved here that should be made clear.

In its broadest sense, "karma" means the concatenation of cause and effect that produces and sustains the existence of the universe, as a whole, as well as every unit within it. Everything in the universe exists in its present state or form as the result of past causes and, in its turn, is the cause of future states of the universe. Because of the interdependence of parts, it is impossible to know completely the karma of any part without knowing all that is to be known of the universe. But within the whole, there are integrations about centers which have become individualized and thus are transformed into microcosms within the macrocosm. Whenever such a microcosm is integrated, it comes within a karmic stream that is its own in a peculiar sense, in addition to the general karma that involves all. Most generally, the term "karma" is employed as restricted to the narrower meaning, but there is no sharp demarcation between the two kinds of karma, and the lesser aspect can never be satisfactorily understood if it is taken in complete abstraction from the larger.

Necessarily, karma is limited to the field of space, time, and causality. Accordingly, the Man who has Recognized His Identity with the Supreme SELF, which abides beyond space, time, and causality, and then completely withdraws within that SELF, will have destroyed all karma related to him as an individual. The objective elements, gross or subtle, that have been associated with his various embodiments, continue in the karmic stream in the Cosmic sense, but the microcosmic field of that individual is dissolved.

Since the dissolution of the microcosm is the negative equivalent of Liberation, the idea has been suggested by some that by the complete balancing of karma, thus effecting microcosmic dissolution, Liberation could be won without prior Recognition of the SELF. Shankara has pointed out the fallacy of this view and answered it at length. While such a course may not be strictly a theoretical impossibility, it is quite impractical for several reasons. We may regard the microcosm as something like a vortex in the universal plenum. It is produced by an impulse that tends to disturb the universal balance. But as the most primary law is Equilibrium—the noumenon of all other laws—karma is at once invoked as a counter-action. Further self-induced reactions to this opposed-action complicate the sequence until finally the microcosm is involved in a very elaborate bondage. Every action brings its fruits, and the experiencing of these fruits is what is technically called "enjoyment," whether pleasant, painful, or indifferent. A cause must be exhausted as effect or *balanced by just the right amount of appropriate counter-action*. Thus, an evil action can be exhausted by experiencing the corresponding suffering or by a good action which would balance it. But a surplus of good actions brings its effects, which must likewise be exhausted, and so on. It would require a superhuman wisdom to achieve just the perfect balance requisite, and all the while the individual would have to live a life so perfect that no shade of additional action was initiated that, in its turn, would require further balancing. Further, it would be rare indeed that all the seeds of past karma would sprout in any one life, since other conditions than those afforded by that given life may be required for their germination. So not one, but a series of perfect lives, without one flaw in the balancing of counter causes, would be required. All this must be done by a man who, by hypothesis, is not Illumined and therefore is bound within the subject-object manifold—a condition which makes superhuman wisdom impossible. So, it seems the unavoidable conclusion that there is no hope of "breaking-through" in this way.

But by Recognition, man destroys his identification with the microcosm and Realizes himself as identical with the SELF of all. This destroys the microcosm so far as he, himself, is concerned. This microcosm continues, for a time, as an appearance in the space-time world, because of the karma that has already sprouted, but the Real Man is no longer incarnated there, in the usual sense, and sooner or later dissolution will finally liquidate the apparent embodiment. This temporary continuation is like the continued revolving of the flywheel of an engine from which the power has been shut off. The engine is stopped in the essential sense, and will become fully stopped shortly.

One of the consequences of the nature of the Law is that good works bind men as much as evil works. Thus, unfinished "good" karma is as truly a source of bondage as unfinished "bad" karma. Also, in principle, Recognition frees a man whose residual karma is predominantly "bad" as truly as in the case of the man where the residue is mostly "good." But the former condition is the more unfavorable one, and so the practice of positive virtue is of distinct importance. The really vital point to note is that it is not action, whether "good" or "bad," that frees, but an attitude of detachment with respect to all action. Thus, a self-righteous man, by which is meant one who is attached to his good works and is overly self-conscious of them, is further from the Recognition than the man who, while doing much evil, has really freed himself from interest in and attachment to his evil works.

In the case of the Man for whom the Sun of Recognition has risen sufficiently so that during life in the body He has entered the fringe of Nirvana, it is possible, after the dissolution of the physical organism, to enter Nirvana, or the Kingdom of Heaven, completely. He has now fully severed himself from his former microcosmic karma. In choosing such a course, in general, He invokes a higher Law which has Its effects upon another level, but that may be ages hence so far as relative time is concerned. The question now arises: What becomes of his former karmic seeds that had not yet sprouted when He became fully one with Nirvana? The answer to this question introduces a principle of the Higher Knowledge which is considerably at variance with an important working hypothesis of physical science. Accordingly, this point will require some discussion.

The term "universe," as employed in this discussion, is restricted to manifested existences, whether in a gross or subtle sense. Behind the universe is the unmanifested actuality, called here "Transcendental Consciousness" or "Absolute Consciousness." To enter the Nirvanic state is to leave the universe in this respect, that is, the whole field of space, time, and causality, in the usual sense. But this Higher World is to the lower as the Infinite is to a finite manifold, and the whole universe depends upon the former as its sustaining principle. What becomes energy and ultimately matter here is derived from the Substance of that higher level.

The interplay between these two domains, speaking now from the relative standpoint, is not an event which took place once for all in the historic past, but one which continues, either intermittently or continuously, throughout the present. Thus there is such a thing as the total supply of energy and matter in the universe increasing at times and, at others, decreasing. This does imply the ultimate falseness of the hypothesis of physical science to the effect that the total supply of matter-energy in the universe remains constant. It is true that such matter and energy do not come from nothing and do not, in turn, become nothing, but these modes do come into and leave the universe. This fact, among other things, affords a totally new statement of the problem of perpetual motion. Another important consequence is that we will have to forego the hope of setting up an energetic equation between the universe as it is at any given time and that universe at some other time. In fact, the recognition of this principle would in time utterly change the form of science, including even sociology and economics. For, if an infinite resource, covering all departments of life, actually is and may be tapped, then the human problem in all these departments takes on quite a different form from that where a finite or limited supply is assumed.

Now when a man enters Nirvana, He closes His karmic accounts, as it were, not by becoming inaccessible to his creditors, but, on the contrary, by paying all His debts in another and immeasurably better coin. It is as though a man had contracted debts in terms of the various base metals and then finally paid those debts in an equal or greater weight of pure gold. Thus none of the creditors are cheated, but quite otherwise they are enriched as never before. The method involved in this process is, in one sense, simple, yet at the same time quite mysterious. When, through Recognition, a Man pierces into the Nirvanic Level, He becomes consciously One with an Infinite Sea of Consciousness and Energy. From this inexhaustible supply, at once and automatically, He pours forth values to all those with whom He has karmic obligations, and this act leads all such forward, in some degree, toward their own Recognition. There is no debt that such a service would not repay abundantly. Thus no Man enters Nirvana without in some measure blessing the world in that very achievement.

The difference between the Man who enters fully and finally into Nirvana and the Man who refuses this Bliss consists in part in the fact that the blessing left by the former is restricted to those with whom He, as an individual, has karmic obligations, while in the case of the latter, in addition to this service, He also volunteers to continue to lift, as far as may be, the general load of the human whole. The latter, having squared His accounts, is free to choose future Bliss, but He reveals a Heart of Compassion in refusing to do so while other creatures are still suffering. These Men really occupy a station in the Gulf between the Higher and lower worlds, and are in a position to employ the resources of Wisdom and Power of that Higher World to lead on the weaker and more ignorant human beings.

Those who have made the choice of the Compassionate heart are often pictured as making the Great Renunciation, but this is only one side of the picture. They have entered an evolution toward a superior Greatness and some Day will stand on a Cosmic or Transcendental Level far beyond Those who accepted Bliss at the earliest opportunity. Essentially They dwell in a domain intermediate between Nirvanic and egoistic consciousness. Thus within Themselves, They unite the two worlds. Furthermore the primary reason for making this choice is a great Love or Compassion, and sacrifice made for Love ceases to mean sacrifice to the individual making it. For, in large measure, such a One lives in and for the Beloved. In this case, however, the Beloved, instead of being the Transcendent Divinity, is that Divinity as manifested in the Child, Humanity.

The Man who has made this higher choice does have a subtle kind of embodiment which, since the Law acts without exception on all levels, does imply a kind of karma. But this is karma under quite a different aspect from that which operates upon the crystallized, egoistic level. He may *choose* to take objective embodiment in the subject-object domain for a definite purpose, but in this case the incarnation is distinctly different from the ordinary type. In the first place, it is voluntary, whereas the ordinary individual is reborn whether he will or no, because of the causes he, himself, has invoked, usually quite blindly. In the second place, inasmuch as His former microcosmic vortex has been dissipated, and as He has mastered the glamour of matter, He incarnates in quite a different way. In fact, it is not properly an incarnation at all, if we are to understand the term in the strict sense. It is simply a mode of correlation with this plane so that something of His Consciousness may be united with this lower level. In all this, there is considerable mystery for those who have not yet understood the fundamental unity underlying the apparently multiple and diverse forms of outer life.

I cannot too strongly emphasize the fact that Liberation is no more the end of life than is a college commencement the end of the young man or woman who graduates. It is simply the end of one stage and the beginning of another. The really worth-while Life begins after Liberation. When this new Freedom is attained, a Man may return Home, as it were, and spend a long period enjoying the warmth and comfort of that Home. On the other hand, He may return and continue with his chosen profession in a larger field. Some, who have been highly exhausted by their labors at college, may need a long rest, but obviously Those who are strong should occupy Themselves with the activities of Real Life.

45
The "Awakening," The End of All Religion

The real end of all the higher religion and philosophy is the attainment of the Awakened Consciousness. Call It what you will, Cosmic Consciousness, Specialism, Liberation, Nirvana, Enlightenment, the Kingdom of Heaven, Moksha, Transcendentalism, Christ Consciousness, Seraphita, Beatrice, or any other name, these all point to one and the same fact, be it well or poorly understood. From one point of view, It may be regarded as the Awakening of a new Sense but, if so, the difference is at least as radical as the shift from sensation to conceptual thought. The change is so great as to form an entirely new Man within the frame of the old. He may apparently still live here, yet in the essential sense He is not here. For Him the great and baffling questions of reflective consciousness are solved; the problems that underlie the great antinomies are resolved. His deep soul-yearning is satisfied, and the tragedy which dogs the steps of this life here below is gone forever. With the Awakening, the end of religion is attained. The man, at last, is born again, and a new "Twice-born" steps into a New World.

The Awakening is a Death and a Birth. Then Real Life for the tired man begins. And what is that Life like? No words can really convey It as It is. Art in language, or in other forms, conveys adumbrations, but these are easily misunderstood and have often been grossly misinterpreted. There is but one way to Know and that is by Awakening. We report the Glory, the Joy, the Freedom, and some of the wonderful possibilities. We demonstrate, from time to time, the Powers beyond the command of the merely egoistic consciousness. All These are signs of the Beyond. We give testimony as to what We have found and move for seasons among men, awakening foretastes here and there, both when the latter are in ordinary waking consciousness and when asleep. But We cannot carry to the egoistic consciousness this other Reality. Man must Awake to Know and thus to solve his really great problems. Without Awakening, there is no solution of these problems. Brother fights brother for the crumbs that have fallen from the Feast, seeing not enough for all. Yet, if but for a single moment, man would look up, he would see on the Table an endless supply, a limitless abundance for all. So We are not much concerned with vain social plans and programs, with the changes of governments and economic reforms, for We Know that all organizations, all institutions, all systems are sterile if they do not incarnate the Light. We use all possible means to bring that Light nearer and to arouse in men the desire for It. But We cannot do that part which each individual man must do. We urge him to turn his back upon the trivial pleasures, combined with real bondage, so that he may Know a real and enduring Joy and may live a Life that is full. The Crossing to the Promised Land has its difficulties, but these are small beside the new Values that There will be Realized. Arise, men, and come into your ancient Inheritance! All old pleasures and activities have their higher correspondences in that Beyond, but with an inconceivably greater richness of Value.

46
The Conditions that Favor Recognition

September 5

What are the conditions, both essential and favorable, for a man to Realize the Glorious Transition? Now we are face to face with the practical question, it being granted that the Illumined Consciousness carries the Supreme Value. In spite of the fact that the record of the western cases of Illumination shows a preponderance of apparently spontaneous Awakening, there are conditions, both essential and contributory, that prepare the way for the Awakening. These we will now consider.

First of all, the individual must desire the Liberation. This desire may not be intelligently formulated, it may not be well understood, and it may take any one of a number of forms, but it must exist. If the desires are centered in the external world and there is a strong resistance to the inward development, a definite, if not insurmountable, barrier exists so long as that attitude persists. Yet it must be noted that superficially a man may seem, even to himself to care most for external things while deep within him he has the inward desire, and this latter may ultimately prove to be the triumphant one. This may be the case where the Illumination breaks forth suddenly and spontaneously, without the personal consciousness being prepared for It. The moment of Transition, in that case, effects a radical revolution in the visible outer life. The man may be utterly "floored" and personally have no idea of what has happened to him, perhaps even imagining that he has become mentally unbalanced, as some have testified. But if the outer personal desire cooperates with the deeper inner desire, a much more favorable condition is produced and the Illumination will tend to come with less of a shock and will be more quickly recognized for what It is. St. Paul is the classical example of Illumination involving great shock. The personal man, in this case, was even actively persecuting the followers of a great God-Realized Man and trying to destroy His influence, and it was while in the very midst of this activity that he suddenly received the Light in the most dramatically intense form of which we have record. It is said he was even physically blinded. But he was transformed, at once, from Saul of Tarsus to St. Paul, a God-Realized Man in His own right, and became from that time on the greatest single power in the Christian Current since Jesus.

The desire for Illumination, even though weak, does produce favorable effects, but these are much slower in their action and less far-reaching than when the desire is strong. When the desire becomes the dominant force in the man, and finally consumes his whole being, other factors being equal, the Illumination is not far away. There is an East Indian story that is illustrative of this point. One day, so the story goes, a Guru with his Chela or disciple was in a boat on a body of water, when the Chela asked, "How greatly must a man desire God to Realize Him?" The Guru then threw the Chela out of the boat into the water and held him, head and all, beneath the surface until the latter was close to the point of inhaling water. Then, drawing the Chela into the boat, the Guru asked him, "What was it that you desired while under the water?" The Chela answered, "Air, air, air." Then said the Guru, "When you desire God as intensely as you just now desired air, then you will find Him." This simply illustrates the importance that attaches to desire, the other conditions being satisfied.

Now, before a thing or goal can be desired it must be known, felt, or sensed as desirable, either dearly or dimly. The example of Those who already have attained the Recognition, together with Their testimony as to what They have found, supplies the basis whereby the man who still is engulfed in the subject-object consciousness—Sangsara—may see or feel that there is something Beyond, the Realizing of which will mean for him the possession of the Value beyond all other values. So We raise visibly before men, not one, but many Witnesses of the Truth that makes man Free, that they may know that Others, who once were men like themselves, have found the Way and Know that the Value attained is beyond price, and also may know that the Awakening is a latent possibility in every man.

The second requirement is a spiritual Guru. The Guru performs the part which is beyond the power of the as yet unawakened individual man. The highest authority has always promised that when the pupil is ready, the Teacher will appear. So it is not a question of the students seeking far and wide in distant lands for some one to take him under direction. The Guru can, and does, appear in an inward sense, often without the personal consciousness of the pupil being aware of the fact. Sometimes He appears outwardly and, again, may or may not be recognized. But let all aspirants remember that effort put forth in the right direction will draw the attention of Those who watch, and, when the time is ripe, They will do Their part. Thus, while the student cannot command the Guru, yet all may trust Him, for His is a service of Love. So, in effect, the student by doing his part does invoke the aid he needs.

The importance of the Guru lies in the fact that the Recognition is not the effect of any causes set up in the space-time or subject-object manifold. This must be so, for THAT which transcends causality cannot be Itself an effect of something else. Recognition actually is a spontaneous induction out of Spirit Itself. Man's personal effort merely removes barriers in his nature that inhibit this spontaneous induction. So there is a real, though greatly misunderstood, truth in the statement that man is saved through the Love of God. But this Love manifests to men through the Sons of God, i.e., through Those who have attained God-Realization. The Guru is the embodiment of Divinity to the disciple and, through Him in general, the spontaneous "act" of Spirit manifests in the individual disciple.

So long as the pupil has not established a personal relationship with his Guru such that direct outer instruction is possible, then the Guru-current may be entered by the personal man through attending the words and works of the God-Realized Men who either are now living in physical bodies or have lived in the past and have left Their visible signs. Remember that the Illumined Man is actually present in His works, in

His speech and His writings. Walt Whitman truly said, when speaking of his "Leaves of Grass," "Who touches this book touches a man." Such writings are not merely symbols or concepts. They are the embodiments of a living Presence which is actually God as manifested through the particular God-Realized Man who wrote them. Jesus is the best known instance in Christendom, but He is not the only one. It is well to become familiar with the writings and sayings of as many Such as possible. For not all Aspects of the Divine Manifestation are equally accessible to all men. The "Open Sesame" for one is not necessarily the "Open Sesame" for another. When the student has found One with Whose Words and Consciousness he stands in particularly close rapport, he should then delve deeply into that One's writings and sayings. In such cases there is a magnetic harmony that is most favorable to success. Further, Realization manifests in a vast range of forms, some *seemingly* the opposite of others, and so for all men there is somewhere the easiest and most direct Way.

In connection with the foregoing, it may be well to remark that the writer, for a definite reason, does not lay especial stress upon the Illumined Men who are best known within the Christian world. These Men are best known to the West and do not, therefore, need to be introduced. Further, the real meaning of these Men is obscured by the overgrowth of theological teaching, produced by men who have not understood the Higher Consciousness. In addition, these Illumined Men tend to be so largely taken for granted and placed in grooves, even in the consciousness of childhood, that They have become practically hidden and inaccessible for vast numbers of human beings. The result is that the man who is trained within the Christian complex from childhood is actually more apt to find his genuine guiding Light in other God-Realized Men whom he finds free from theological preconception. The unintelligent and more or less automatic repetition of phrases, even though they may be correct formulations of the Truth, often serves to hide Meaning instead of making it clear. For it is the active cooperation of intelligence, rather than the mere sound of words, that is the vital power for awakening Recognition of Significance in the Consciousness of the individual. Thus the fresh discovery of the same Truth in another form where the intelligence of the individual is active is far more likely to be effective in arousing this Recognition.

An illustration of this point is afforded in the case of Mahatma Gandhi. Jesus, according to Gandhi's testimony, played a very vital part in bringing the Light to him. Yet Gandhi came from India, the very

Fount of Spiritual Wisdom, so far as It is embodied more in one race than another. But Jesus could come to him as a fresh discovery, for there was no background of merely taking Jesus for granted, nor in this discovery was there any need of clearing away theological rubbish or overlying superstition.

The present writer can also testify that, although he was born in the very sphere of one of the evangelical branches of the Christian Church and in his early youth was trained in that Current of thought and imagined that he had accepted it, yet he actually found and appreciated the real Jesus only after passing through a period of atheism and, later, discovering Buddha. Only then, and in the Light of the Wisdom of the Tathagata, did he realize that Jesus carried the same Light. It was only by reaching beneath the imposed crust of Christian Theology, and then, by taking Jesus out of the peculiar Hebraic stream and seeing Him as more truly one with the Buddhist spirit, did it become possible for him to see Jesus directly for what He was and is. Since that time he has had far greater love for Him than ever before, for now Jesus is, for him, a symbol of Freedom, whereas Christian theology had made Him a symbol of bondage. It is the old, old, story of the followers of a Great Light mutilating and obscuring that Light through misunderstanding. It is, indeed, a question whether the great corporate religious organizations have not been more of a curse than a blessing with respect to the mission of the very Saviours in whose Names they are formed. There is no great religion that has not effected such damage in greater or less degree. So there is an ever-recurrent need for new Lights and new Saviours to arise who reafffirm the ancient and unchanging Truth, but who, first, must needs tear down the extraneous and weedy growth which chokes the real Message of earlier Saviours and Sages. Then the Message must be dressed in a new Garment and sent forth to leaven the hearts of men until, in time, It also suffers the old fate and is obscured in Its turn.

If the student has found a Guru, it is essential that devoted attention should be given to the sayings of the latter. If he has not found such a Teacher—and the greater number have not—then the same devotion should be given to the sayings of the Incarnations of Spiritual Light that he has found somewhere in history. It is not merely the conceptual value of the words of such Men that is important. The formulations may well be not the best possible. But surrounding and within the words is the real Message which has the transforming power. It is this more or less veiled Message that should be accepted without resistance. But while such fundamental acceptance is of high importance, it does not follow that the concepts which clothe the Message are to be taken blindly. It is the Meaning that is vital, and it often happens the true Meaning is clothed in incorrect concepts. So the requisite attitude of mind on the part of the student is a combination of discrimination with a profound pliability in an inward sense.

Besides the foregoing there are other subsidiary aids which, however, vary in their form in the different types of training. Some systems of training are intensely ascetic, while others are not. All of this meets the variable needs and possibilities of differing individualities. For that which helps to open the Way for one may not be appropriate for another. If the individual is so fortunate as to have a personal Guru, then the appropriate help can be given most effectively in directing the specific personal practices.

There is one factor that is always highly helpful that has been variously called "leavening," "contagion," and "induction." To be in the presence of a Man who has become identified with the Light is to be in a field of Consciousness which tends to arouse within the individual some degree of the corresponding kind of Consciousness. It should always be borne in mind that from a certain standpoint Consciousness may be regarded as an Energy and that in this domain we have events or tendencies that are more than analogous to certain properties of electricity. Thus, the "induction" of Consciousness is closely related to induction in electricity. The meaning of "induction," in this connection, is analogous to that of the "leavening" of Jesus, but has the added advantage of affording greater intelligibility, given our present state of scientific knowledge. The induced Consciousness in the receiving individual may be slight or of any degree up to one of high intensity. After the removal of the presence of the inducing Consciousness, the glow of the induced Consciousness may persist for a longer or shorter time. But repeated inductions tend, finally, to produce a condition such that the latent and indigenous Inner Light of the individual is aroused sympathetically into pulsation and thus, ultimately, "catches on," as it were, for Itself. When this happens, the individual has for the first time become established in his own Center in the higher sense. He becomes One grounded in the Higher Knowledge, instead of being merely a student.

In the principle of induction we have an enormous instrument for effecting the Awakening of the Higher Consciousness, in some measure at least, in individuals who, for some reason or other, fail to put forth the requisite degree of self-directed effort to be effective in their own strength. Those who aspire toward the Awakening would do well to seize every opportunity available to come within the sphere of Those who can serve as such Centers of induction. The presence of these Centers spells opportunity for all men who are near them. At the same time, to realize the best results it is not sufficient to be merely passively present. In addition, there should be thought, study, and active aspiration in the direction of the Light. All of this is analogous to the cultivation and watering of a seed that has been sown by a Sower and thus produces a condition that prevents the sowing from having been done in vain.

47
The Nature of the Higher Knowledge

September 7

I find a steady progress in the consolidation of my Inward and outward consciousness. The Recognition is fruiting for me as a definite purpose, which is steadily becoming clearer. Since I have chosen not to abandon the world of subject-object consciousness, there has developed with growing insistence an outline of work to be done.

Notwithstanding all that has been accomplished by others, there still remains a need for further clarification. While the subject-object consciousness never can contain Transcendent or Cosmic Consciousness, yet it is possible, through a due consideration of the nature of the former with a recognition of its limits, to suggest the Beyondness. This is why, for the intellectually developed aspirant, there is no more practical nor important study than that of epistemology, the science of the nature and possibilities of knowledge. An important fruit of such study is the recognition that subject-object consciousness supplies only a certain kind of knowledge; and that while this knowledge may develop in its own direction without limits, it is, none the less, confined within restricting bounds. Yet, from out the deeps of human feeling and yearning, there do arise insistent questionings which have never been successfully answered within the limits of relative knowledge. These questionings cannot be ignored, for, until satisfactory answers are found or the problem disappears, the man cannot find real happiness. At this point two choices stand before man, either he may accept the outlook of real pessimism, or he may break through to another kind of Knowledge, where the effective solutions can be found and real Happiness attained. Since I, for my own part, have come along the latter road, have found a Way to reach the Knowledge that satisfies and since I can, therefore, testify to Its reality and efficacy, I am enabled to offer real aid to those who naturally travel along the same course.

The analysis of external relationships, the field in which men like Bertrand Russell so greatly excel, is invaluable for the development of intellectual powers. This kind of work is not to be despised, even by the God-Conscious Man, unless He proposes to withdraw completely from the subject-object world. If He remains to function within that world, understanding the science of external relations will simply serve to make Him more efficient and more intelligible. But it is useless to pretend that external relations give ultimates. The knowledge of them is powerless to solve the soul-problems. If a man has no more than this science, he is doomed to pessimistic despair, once having finished the work of becoming proficient in it. Immanuel Kant must remain the most profound western philosopher, so far, for he has opened the door in a way that is intelligible and of great profundity. Somewhere, if I remember correctly, Bertrand Russell has said that in his introspective effort he was never able to find such a thing as the Self. Doubtless he looked for an object, but admittedly the Self is no object and thus can never be found as such. However this failure on Russell's part simply explains a certain barrenness in his philosophy, despite all its many real values in several respects. Kant is right in his main thesis, however much of error in detail there may be, for Kant knew the Self, else he could never have conceived of pure apperceptive Consciousness.

It is quite useless to challenge the certainty of a Man who has attained Self-Recognition. The correctness of His expression may be challenged, but not the Root-Knowledge that has become His or, rather, with which He is identical, once He has Awakened to the higher Level. It is not impossible that Bertrand Russell has attained as high a level as any man confined within the subject-object manifold, and is thus peculiarly adept in that kind of knowledge. His criticism of correctness cannot be disregarded, but none the less it remains utterly useless to challenge the basic Knowledge of a man who has awakened to a new level. A simple illustration can be taken from within the range of familiar experience. We may suppose that a man has been born blind, or that there was a race of people who had never developed the sense of sight. For these, the seen world simply would not exist. Now let us suppose that such a man or people had developed, along with their other senses, a keen intelligence, and that they are brought into contact with equally intelligent people who have the power of sight. Assume, further, that they attempted to deny to the latter the actuality of the visible world. What chance would they have of convincing the latter? Even the least intelligent man who sees knows beyond all doubt that there is, in some sense, a seen world. He may not correctly interpret it nor understand it, but he certainly knows that it is, in some sense. To this degree, he is definitely on a superior level as compared to those who have never had the organ of sight. The non-seeing entity cannot successfully challenge the fact of a seen world for those who see. Now, suppose that the relationship is changed and that those who see try to convey the actuality of their world of sight to the non-seeing. Certain interpretations, such as those of the type employed in physics, would be capable of cross-translation and could be understood, at least by the intelligent members of the non-seeing group. The latter might be convinced that those with functioning eyes had some peculiar power, because of capacities to act and to know in the domain common to both that the non-seeing did not possess. But the immediate value given through sight, such as the direct experience of color, could not be cross-translated. For instance, all of the beauty-values dependent upon sight for their recognition would remain beyond the comprehension of the non-seeing.

The foregoing affords a very good illustration of the gulf which separates the Awakened from the subject-object type of consciousness. Some aspects are capable of cross-translation, but the essential quality of the Higher Consciousness can never be realized within the framework of the lower.

Man can Awaken to the Higher, because of latent capacities within himself. He never can comprehend the Higher within the narrower and totally different kind of consciousness. Thus man must rise, or rather be born again, if he would Know.

We now come to a very important necessity. It is sometimes called the "unlearning of that which has been learned." I have found this to be the severest of all genuinely necessary austerities, but not everyone finds it so. Still, in every case it is unavoidable, and this is so for reasons that are not difficult to understand. A mind that is filled with ideas based upon an inadequate or false point of view must first be emptied of those ideas before it can be filled with others that are more correct. This principle applies, not alone in the Transition from subject-object to the Awakened Consciousness, but, as well, frequently within the subject-object field itself. Thus, part of the training involved in becoming a competent physical scientist consists of the development of the capacity to be so detached with respect to pre-conceptions that they may be readily abandoned when proved to be no longer adequate. The development in physics during the last forty years has required in unusual degree the replacement of old by new conceptions. If physicists, as a class, had been incapable of unlearning the older physical notions when the facts proved the inadequacy of the latter, we never would have acquired our present knowledge of the radiant and subatomic state of matter. Now when we come to the Transition to Transcendent or Cosmic Consciousness, the necessity for this unlearning is far greater and the method is applied in a far more sweeping sense. A too rigid holding of preconceptions is a barrier to Recognition. By such holding, the mind is bound in a vise that prevents its turning about to a new base. So it is necessary that ideas of the subject-object type should be held in a detached way.

However, the intelligent use of the process of unlearning does not imply that the aspirant should begin systematically to discard all knowledge that he has, in every sense. It means, rather, entertaining that knowledge in such a way that it is free to fly away just as soon as a greater insight proves its inadequacy. In other words, we may say that the principle is to remove all chains from the Bird of Truth and let sympathetic attraction be the only bond. Truth naturally makes Its nest within the receptive mind and does not have to be held. Further, Truth is invulnerable and therefore needs no defense. It requires only demonstration so that It may become clear. Thus it is always proper to seek the Truth and to be receptive to It, but not to try to bind It by a fixed preconception of what It is. Earlier conceptions serve a valuable function in preparing the way for more adequate understanding, but, having served their function, should, like scaffolding that has facilitated the construction of a building, be torn away.

The Transition to the Awakened Consciousness is a Copernican change which not only transforms the essential level of the individual involved, but alters his whole relationship to the subject-object world as well. When Copernicus demonstrated the superior power unfolded by regarding the sun, rather than the earth, as the center of the solar system, the world was not destroyed as an empiric fact, but its relationship and significance within the whole was radically changed. This transformation, while affecting astronomy most immediately, produced secondary effects with ramifications reaching far into different phases of social life.

This change has brought enormous clarification with respect to many vitally important problems that had formerly been quite obscure. The Awakening involves such a change, only in a much more radical sense. When It has come, the whole life of the individual is affected, and part of the effect is a profound clarification and simplification of a vast number of obscurities. So much is this the case that if the Awakened Man chooses to direct His force within the subject-object field, then in whatever compartment He may focus His attention He has superior capacity as compared to others who have not the advantage of His perspective. He now looks down on things in their relationships, rather than being involved in those relationships. The highest excellence in government, business, engineering, science, religion, art, etc., are at His command, restricted only by the limitations of his personal vehicle. But before a man can operate upon relationships from Above, he must first break his bondage within those relationships, and in part this is represented by unlearning what has been previously learned.

It does not follow that all previously acquired knowledge will be found false. To a greater or lesser extent, the Realized Man may still be able to judge it correct. Its Significance, however, will be radically changed, and He will be enabled to tie together parts that formerly had seemed irreconcilable. He stands outside and above the "game," as it were, and so is enabled to play with a master's hand.

Even though from the highest standpoint relative or subject-object knowledge has been completely Transcended and no longer affords a field of function, it does not therefore follow that it has not served a useful purpose in its time. Man builds a certain integration while in the subject-object field without which Recognition, as a self-conscious achievement, is impossible. The training in subject-object knowledge serves something of the function of a scaffold in the construction of a building. When the building is ready, the scaffolding may be and should be abandoned, for it ceases to be, in general, any longer valuable. The man may now enter the building which, in this case, represents the Transcendent or Cosmic Consciousness. However, a scaffolding should not be wrecked while workmen are still standing upon it. So the Compassionate Man who has found the Building to be ready and then enters into It will also leave the scaffold standing until all others have likewise left it and Entered In.

48
The Record Continued

September 8

A radical change in the whole relationship toward life is developing within me as time goes on. Throughout the larger portion of my life my focus of consciousness was centered in inward-penetration, with the primary emphasis placed upon understanding. I entered college, having a general idea of preparation for a professional life in the legal field, but planning to take a cultural course for the first four years. I chose pure mathematics as my major subject, for in this field lay my greatest intellectual love. Now prior to and during all this period, the search for the adequate religious value was continuing *pari passu*. I had been through the orthodox church and found it utterly barren, so far as cognitive values were concerned, and puny in what it offered for feeling. As I later realized, I somehow chose a course of study that was very nearly ideal for my individual purposes. It consisted of mathematics as a central interest, supplemented by philosophy and psychology. Here I found the values the church was wholly incapable of supplying. I discovered in mathematics what religion usually gives to men. I realized in this the presence of reality in a form of extraordinary purity, and the point of inward penetration that I reached in those days, though I lacked adequate understanding and appreciation of what it was at that time, was not surpassed at any time since, prior to the 7th of last month. I soon lost interest in the legal profession, while the natural sciences held my attention in only a subsidiary sense, but I drove on, choosing, if need be, to sacrifice financial and professional interests. Time after time I abandoned an effort just as I reached a point where I was nearly arriving at a position of outer recognition which would have given me employment. Actually, I abandoned an effort in a given direction when I had extracted the essential value from it and something else was needed to "carry on" to the main goal. When this happened, there seemed to be no energy or ambition left to finish the structure of previous partial accomplishments. By the end of five years of mathematical concentration, the center of interest had shifted to philosophy. What I had attained through mathematics in terms of symbols—and it was a rare level of consciousness—had to be supplemented by philosophy so that it could become clear to the understanding. Philosophy added reflecting and focusing power to the pure light of mathematics. By the end of seven years, I found myself in sight of the limits to which our present egoistic consciousness has reached, and also had found adumbrations of another kind of Consciousness where alone, it seemed, solution of the antinomies of the subject-object consciousness could be found. This made necessary a new kind of search. My focus was withdrawn from the academic world and I renounced a profession, not fully understanding that I was doing so. This new search required, or seemed to require, descent from a point well up on a noble mountain range and a long passage through valleys, including some minor and briefly experienced mountain peaks. But after many years I reached the foot of a far more majestic range, the heights of which were ever hidden above enveloping clouds. Here I climbed anew, finally mounting close to the clouds and glimpsing through their rifts now and then something of the Beyond. Then, no longer painfully climbing, but as though lifted instantaneously by a power of inward levitation, I pierced through the clouds to an unmeasurable height and found their seeming darkness transformed into a new kind of Light. THE SEARCH WAS ENDED.

But now, from the standpoint of the new perspective, the clouds again intervened between the World above and the world below, causing the lower field to take on obscurity. A new problem presented itself in the form—"How may those clouds be pierced again, this time from Above?" It is not enough to be There, and then again here, with a blind spot in between. Individually, I am quite satisfied to be wholly There, but a work remains to be done in the clearing away or making thinner the intervening obscuration between the Above and the below. For so long as I am only There individually, I am not wholly There, since these other parts of Me—the rest of sentient life—still move in consciousness below the clouds.

This view is not merely altruism in the usual meaning of the word, for in the latter sense, altruism involves a difference between one's own self and others. In contrast, that view implies that in striving for the Realization of others, I but complete my own Recognition. I attain more in every man's attainment. I Recognize more in every man's Recognition. I am delayed by every man's failure. Every new facet opened by another individual man breaking through is a new facet awakened in My understanding. Thus, from this standpoint, the duality of selfishness and altruism is destroyed. In serving others, I but serve Myself, and in serving Myself I serve others. So, I am beyond all sacrifices and choose only My greatest pleasure. Personally, I only fail in my duty when I fall short of choosing perfectly My own supreme delight. If any one would help Me, let him progress toward his own highest Glory. That is the only aid from out of the world that can reach Me.

The thing that requires the greatest amount of courage on the personal level I find is the employing of a form of expression which seems, superficially, to be a sort of monstrous egotism. It is not such in fact, but simply a positive reflection within the egoistic or subject-object manifold of the genuinely Selfless Consciousness; and this unavoidably takes on a form that seems egotistical. The same expression, if grounded wholly within the subject-object consciousness, would be thoroughly egotistical and indefensible. But *I* who speak am not different from the "I" in every self-conscious creature.* The form in which, and the facet through which, the words come are individual and personal, but the Meaning is universal. Use this facet if it helps you; use *some* other facet if it opens the Door; but use some facet until you have found that One which is indigenous to yourself.

★ ★ ★

I have need of the other facets of Myself, both Those already Awakened and those who have not yet Awakened. Until all have arrived the Communion is incomplete.

★ ★ ★

Such a wonderful inward delight do I feel at this moment! I apperceive clearly. But what is it I apperceive? Part of It, I, the personal man, know and express, Much more, I, the intellectual man, apprehend. But beyond this, *I*, the REAL SELF, Know all and AM all. And of this All-Knowledge the glow descends to me, the personal man, and even here I know that I Know and AM beyond all doubt.

---

*Let the reader repeat My words given in the last sentence as coming from Himself, and he will find a key to their real significance.

49
Sleep and Death

It is a common experience among Those who have attained the Realization to find that the fear of death passes. In my own case for some time, death has possessed more the value of an interesting adventure than of something to be feared, save in the sense of dreading physical pain that might be connected with the process. In fact, heretofore I have had to put forth an effort to resist a desire for death in the physical sense, not because of a great personal pain in this life, but for the reason that I sensed very clearly that physical embodiment acts like a brake on Consciousness, so that death is in some measure a kind of liberation for all men, save in the case of some very low types. But Recognition has brought to me a reconciliation with life in the world-field; or, in other words, It has brought me to a point where I can willingly accept a brake, since I see that it serves a useful purpose. In addition, I know that release will come in its own time when the particular work here is finished, and thus all that is required is to be faithful to a duty which will not be of unreasonable duration. So actually I am more concerned now with the well-being of the physical personality than at any time previously. But my concern for it is like the artisan's care for a useful tool, plus a certain feeling that it is meet to do justice to the child—the personality. But so far as death itself is concerned, I find it quite devoid of grave dramatic significance. For I realize clearly that what we commonly call death is but a shifting in the modes of life or consciousness, and most emphatically not a terminus. I cannot say that I feel any personal yearning for immortality, as I am attracted rather by the Bliss of pure impersonal Consciousness. However, I do accept the responsibilities of indefinitely continued individuality, as I realize that there are very important reasons for doing so. Thus, today, I stand in this position: I know that, in the real sense, there is no death or birth; that, in the individual sense, I can maintain continuation indefinitely; and, finally, that physical death is merely a passing incident which effects but a transformation in the mode under which Consciousness manifests. In all this there is no room for any real fear.

In a profound sense, I have already died, though the body still persists, and I did not have a hard time in the essential dying. The organism very soon acquired more from the Transition than it lost, and it is now clearly becoming stronger. But it is a fact that I cannot too strongly emphasize that the essence of dying is not the dissolution of the physical body. Fundamentally, it is a change of level of percipience and appercipience. Now, we come to a point of the very highest practical importance. If a man, while embodied, has not learned to integrate consciously the embodied with the disembodied levels of percipience, then so far as the personal consciousness is concerned, death involves entering a state like dreamless sleep. In the higher sense, it is not an unconscious state, but it is unconscious for the personal man, except that he may experience a sort of dreaming consciousness apparently constructed along the formal lines of his embodied experience. Let the reader keep it well in mind that this is not a matter of an arbitrary or imaginative eschatology but, rather, of a necessity that must be clear from purely epistemological considerations. The point is simply this: If a conscious being has integrated self-consciousness in a given kind of complex mode, such as the "five-sense" perceptive consciousness of man, and if it is familiar with no other mode of consciousness, then if it is suddenly severed from that mode and thrust into one utterly different, no matter how bright the Light of the latter may be, it will seem to this being as unconsciousness. After a time self-consciousness may awaken to function in the new mode, but there will be no basis for recognizing the new entity as being the same individual who experienced in terms of the former mode. This is a radical interruption of the continuity of self-consciousness, and, while in the Higher or Spiritual sense, Consciousness *per se* has not ceased, yet the individual, as individual, has proved to be no more than a mortal being. Actually, nature guarantees man no more than this. But he may by his own self-induced effort and by the aid of Awakened Men achieve continuity of self-conscious or individualized consciousness. This is acquired or conditional immortality and constitutes an important part of the significance of Cosmic Consciousness.

The crux of the whole problem in achieving individualized immortality is the learning to integrate while still embodied the outer and inner levels of percipience. This is, in fact, the mystic process symbolized by the squaring of the circle. The relationship between the square and the circle is incommensurable, and this means that "circular" relationships or values are not comprehensible in "square" terms. Embodied man is a square while the Inner Man is a circle. The mass of human beings shift from level to level through unconsciousness, and thus in these cases the one level is to the other like dreamless sleep. The two states are discrete instead of continuous, and, therefore, we are faced with a condition where we have, as it were, two distinct men instead of one self-conscious Being. The circle is birthless and deathless and consequently immortal, but the square is generated in time and in the course of time subject to dissolution. But by "squaring" the circle, or more correctly by "circularizing" the square, the latter kind of consciousness is taken up and blended with the immortal Consciousness of the circle. This gives to the individual consciousness immortality. It should be clear that the cross-transference in sleep or during the trance state is not enough. Man must win the power to be awake here and There at the same time. Once he has done this, even though the cross-correlation were achieved for but one moment in a given lifetime, he has mastered death and is immortal in the acquired sense. Now, when a man has succeeded in "circularizing" the square, he has shifted his center of self-identity to the circle and thus has really died while remaining in the physical body. Consequently, while moving in the world he has become One who is not *of* the world.

There is a field of tensions, or a "gulf," between the domain of the circle and the square. This is sometimes spoken of as a zone of clouds or an intervening sea. Some in crossing this field of tensions with a partial holding of self-consciousness report a sense of whirling which may produce an effect like dizziness. It is possible to hold the correlation steady without the whirling effect, but for my part I do find a tension that tends toward something like dizziness, which however may be controlled. But this does require the effort of a close, though subtle, concentration. I would say, that the effort required of the individual parallels very closely certain demands made upon the imagination in higher mathematics. In fact, the man who has been able to comprehend "rational," "irrational," and "imaginary" numbers as one integrated and real manifold, and not merely as an arbitrary creation of pragmatic value alone, has mastered the knack of conscious cross-correlation between the domain of the circle and that of the square. However, this is not the only way, but simply the one with which I, personally, am most familiar. As previously noted, the Transition may be greatly facilitated by the process of induction.

Those men who have not mastered cross-correlation while still embodied go into a state of essential sleep after death. Sooner or later they have a kind of experience in a dream-like consciousness, and these states constitute the ordinary heaven worlds, when they are of the better sort. The dream is a continuation of consciousness in the subject-object sense, but in the heavenly worlds the quality is entirely blissful. There is practically no opportunity for the exercise of discrimination in such states. It is the contrast of pain and joy, united with their appropriate causes, that tends to shock the dreaming consciousness into wakefulness. This contrasting condition is found in ordinary earth-life, and thus constitutes an important part of the reason why the vital or determinative steps can be taken only here. Dreaminess is the great barrier. But most of human consciousness even in this world is in a sort of waking-dreaming or somnambulistic state. However, we have here the instruments that can shock to wakefulness, while such is not the case in the after-death states of the ordinary individual. Unquestionably, pain is one of the very greatest of these instruments, and thus is much less an evil than a beneficent agent. The more I have studied the problem, the more I have become convinced that it has been a great mistake to concentrate so much attention upon evil. The real difficulty is the almost universal somnambulism in which men pass the bulk of their lives, some spending many lives without leaving that state at all. It is, in effect, an hypnotic sleep, and the real problem of religion is not the saving of human souls from evil but a dehypnotising of the mind.

An excellent opportunity for studying the fundamental nature of ordinary death is afforded in the phenomena of familiar waking and sleeping states. A man goes to sleep to be active in dreams, or occasionally to enter the dreamless state. Ordinarily, while dreaming the man does not know that he has gone to sleep. That means that he has not mastered the cross-correlation self-consciously, and in this case he has a foretaste of what happens in ordinary death. But it is possible to dream and know that one is dreaming at the same time, holding in the mind a memory of the waking state. In this case, self-consciousness has made the cross-correlation. Now to have done this once in a lifetime is sufficient to supply a means whereby the after-death state of dream can be broken by the man who has departed from his physical body. It is most certainly a definite step toward Recognition. So the student would do well to study carefully all of the phenomena connected with sleeping and waking.

It is even possible to go to sleep and later wake up without there having been a break in the continuity of self-consciousness. In such an instance the body does go to sleep and consciousness ceases to function on the physical plane, but it remains active on other levels with the continuity of self-consciousness remaining unbroken. It is, in addition, possible to correlate at least some measure of the inner state with the brain-mind so that the outer memory will retain something. But this memory is not the essential mark of the continuity of the self-consciousness.

The dream-state is so important that something more should be said concerning its nature. Just as it is true that man can be essentially dreaming while active in the physical body—and most life here is in this state—

it is likewise true that some of the states entered while the body sleeps are far more truly waking-states than any which are possible while in the physical body. The experiencing of these states with most men is very rare, but they do occur more or less frequently with some individuals. They have certain noble earmarks. The most important of these is the effect they have on the waking life. They may enrich, deepen, or give new direction to the outer life. They tend toward an increase of genuine rationality. These are adumbrations of the Real Life.

In contrast, the dream-state casts a glamour, which may be painful or pleasant, but in any case tends to produce a drug-like effect both upon the will and the reason. In addition to drugs, the light of the moon often produces a somewhat similar effect. The hypnotic state is a dream-state par excellence. This consciousness has the property of possessing a man, instead of the individual possessing and commanding it. It tends to lead him away from the decisions made in the light of clear and discriminating judgment. It is very characteristic of the consciousness found in psychological crowds and affords the reason why the control of crowd-consciousness is effected most successfully by psychological devices rather than by appeal to rational judgment.*

Dream-consciousness, characteristically, has a quality which may be called "blurred" or "smudged." It is quite lacking in crystalline sharpness or the quality of precision. The logical capacity is weak in the dreaming states. There is also a lack of firmness of will. The dreamer floats along in his consciousness, instead of being an achiever in it. He may dream in terms of ideality and beauty and be highly freed from the gross and the sensual, but the dreamer, as such, lacks character and strength. On the whole, his equipment is peculiarly poor for breaking from bondage to subject-object consciousness. He may be a good man and earn long periods of dreamlike bliss, but all this is less than the Liberated State. So, all in all, it should be quite obvious that for him who would attain the Higher Consciousness, one of the first necessities is the mastering of dreaming tendencies. To effect this mastery, there are several useful disciplines that can be devised, all of which cultivate the qualities that are the opposite of the dream-like consciousness. Thus, all activities that require

---

*Incidentally, this affords an explanation of the fatal defect in all popular governments. Democracy can succeed in an effective sense when, and only when, the mass of the electorate have become awakened in the real sense. Otherwise, folly has the advantage with respect to wisdom in casting the glamour that appeals to mass-consciousness.

a strong, positive, and incisive use of the mind, and all will-directed efforts, particularly if in directions that are more or less distasteful, are highly helpful.

Strong intellectuality affords one of the best resistances to the dreamlike state. Its danger is that it may develop egoism to such a degree that it becomes a serious barrier. But my judgment would be that it is easier to master an overly developed egoism—for here we have strength to work with—than it is to build the necessary strength in the too dreamy consciousness. So I should place somnambulism, rather than egoism and evil, as the first among the problems that must be mastered in this humanity if it is to progress toward Liberation.

50
The Well of Ignorance

I dip into the well of Ignorance and pull forth toads, slugs, and blind fish.

I offer them Light, and quickly they slither back into the slimy darkness.

I pour acid into the pool and hold tempting baits above its rim.

Goaded, they come forth and glimpse the bait.

I lead them to a cleaner pool and a darkness not quite so dense;

And then on to a greater cleanliness and a clearer Light.

In time, slowly they build the strength to endure the Light and a desire for cleaner waters.

Finally, one here and one there ventures out of the pool into the Brilliance.

It is a long and slow labor, but in the end I will win.

51
Beyond Genius

The power of genius is a partial Ray descending out of the grand Sun of Cosmic Wisdom, and It drives the men It engulfs like passive instruments. But the Man who has penetrated to the core of Recognition moves consciously and in command, where mere genius is moved helplessly. I do not pretend to measure to what Deeps in the inmost core of the SELF I may have penetrated. Other witnesses may measure; I admit to Myself no limit. I permit Myself no bounds There and acknowledge no inferiority. From out the Deeps, which are the Heights, I descend immeasurable distances and find the thought of abstraction so vast that I barely discern Its Presence. I think Thoughts, the "sentences" of which are volumes here, and the Volumes whole libraries of formation. Yet below This there is a Consciousness of more distinct, and yet far from distinct, delineation; and here, too, is the ineffable Communion, the Grand Love. Still, I descend and I grasp in half-forms values that are thinkable but not yet writable. And, below this, a level where I form slowly and painfully in the words of this outer consciousness a small fraction of a fraction of a fraction of a Grand Formless Thought. And that Grand Formless Thought: How may I suggest it? Pure Significance packed tight. Stripped protons and neutrons in close consolidation. (A thimble-full of neutrons is a million tons.) So there are DEEPS beyond Deeps beyond deeps, and, on the surface, this little culture of egoistic man to which he clings like a beggar to a crust.

52
*The High Indifference**

September 9

How shall I ever describe what transpired last night? It is utterly baffling to language as such. At best, what I say may suggest something, but can never communicate the Reality. It was neither an experience, in the proper sense of the word, nor a logical penetration, for both cognition and perception are hopelessly inadequate either to represent or contain it. As the Infinite is to the finite, so was that Consciousness of last night to the relative consciousness of the subject-object manifold. I penetrated a State wholly beyond the relative field, and also well beyond that Realized by me heretofore. Truly, within the Infinite there are Mysteries within Mysteries, Deeps beyond Deeps, Grandeurs beyond Grandeurs. Just as in mathematics there are infinitudes of higher orders infinitely transcending lower infinities, so is it in the Transcendent World. Is there

---

*See also Chapter 90, "Addendum to the High Indifference," on p. 216.

no end to possible Awakening? Is there no end to the progression of infinities? It may be so. I Know that I have found an Infinite World, and then another Infinite consuming the first. I can say these Worlds are, but I can place no limits upon the Beyond. Mystery of Mysteries, reaching inward and outward, but ever Beyond! And from that Beyond ever there come new whisperings of other imponderable Glories. Ah! How little is this world at the beginning of the Trail, barely a point in a Space of unlimited dimensions!

Let us try and see what may be said. After retiring last night, I lay awake for some time. My mind, instead of being calm, as has been its dominant quality during the last month, was rather agitated. In general, outer calmness of the mind is one of the prerequisites of inward penetration; but last night the mode of Consciousness which was unfolded, or was superimposed, or burst forth—none of these expressions is quite right—was so strong that the state of the mind was seemingly quite irrelevant. The agitation of the mind meant no more than the dance of the atoms in a bar of steel that quickly align themselves in regular and steady form when introduced into a strong magnetic field. Last night I was taken up into such an all-encompassing and potent Field. Enveloped with this greater Power, the activities of the outer mind were but puny, insignificant, and irrelevant. They were utterly devoid of any power to interfere. In fact, it may well be that the mind needed its strength in active and positive form to be enabled to stand by throughout the stages of the deepening Transcendent Consciousness. Otherwise, it is likely that all I could report would be a sort of inchoate Thatness. This Consciousness had no marked quality that I would call Joy in a differentiated sense, but, rather, It was a Higher Integration wherein the Joy was but an incidental moment.

I first became aware of being enveloped in an extraordinary State of Consciousness when I found myself seemingly surrounded by, and interpenetrated through and through with, a quality for which there is no adequate word but which is most nearly represented by calling it "Satisfaction." I do not simply mean that the State was satisfactory. It was Satisfaction. The difference in the significance of these two modes of expression is of fundamental importance. To say that a state is satisfactory implies the idea of relationship or qualification. All this is quite valid in the field of relative experience, but it radically falsifies the essential nature of these inward States of Recognition. The mark of these inward States is "Identification" and not "relationship." Despite the fact that my personal prejudice, fortified by academic training, would naturally lead me to employ the relative and qualifying form of expression, yet I am absolutely forced by the actuality of the Consciousness invoked by inward Recognition to employ the language expressing Identity. Further, when I employ the term "Satisfaction," I do not mean merely an abstraction, such as a state of being satisfied, but, rather, a substantial Actuality. It is not satisfaction considered as a state derived from a concrete and external experience or object. It must on the contrary be regarded as a pure self-existence, a somewhat which could be bestowed like a blessing upon objective and concrete experiences but that is not a derivative from the latter. He who is enveloped in this Satisfaction is in need of nothing whatsoever to satisfy him. The Satisfaction I realized is a real and substantial Existence prior to all experiencing. I experimented with this Satisfaction and found that I could even effect the equivalent of swallowing It, and then felt, specifically as in the stomach, the state of satisfaction something like a nutritive value without the use of a material food. I have never experienced any gross or material food that could even approximate the sense of nutritive well-being that this pure essence of Satisfaction actually did give me. But this nutritive phase was only one minor aspect of the full Satisfaction. It was the essence of aesthetic, emotional, moral, and intellectual satisfaction at the same time. There was nothing more required, so far as desire for myself was concerned, for at that time I had the full value of everything that could possibly be desired. It might be called the culminating point, the highest to which desire, individually centered, could reach. Only in one sense did I find a desire that could take me away from that State, and that was the desire to convey this new value to others. The memory of the others, as yet left out, was the one unsatisfactory element. This factor was enough to awaken the will to withdraw and to remain, as long as necessary, outside the immediate Realization of the State. I must confess that I know of no other consideration adequate to awaken the will to forego it, once an individual has Known the immediate Presence of the High Satisfaction.

Throughout this whole experience and the following more profound state, the egoistic or subject-object consciousness was actively present. It was present, however, as a witness on the sidelines, while all about and through and through there was an immeasurably vaster Consciousness. Could I have asserted the egoistic will and withdrawn from the State? I cannot give this question any certain answer. I certainly had no wish to try to do so. The greater Consciousness was more powerful than the egoistic energy, but on the other hand I had no feeling of a will in It that would have been asserted against my individual will to retreat from the

State. It was as though, all the time, the Higher Consciousness dominated the individual energy, with my individual permission. Of course, I was more than glad to give that permission, but I believe I could have withdrawn if I had so chosen. There is one sense in which it may be said that I, individually, made use of this Higher Consciousness but could have, had I so chosen, abandoned myself to It completely and forever. Not so to abandon myself was an act of sheer austerity.

Through the continued presence of the egoistic consciousness and its activity in recording in the form of thought as much as could be comprehended from the State, it has been possible to carry much of Its value into my ordinary reflective consciousness. Among other effects, this had made possible the expression that is now being written down. Through the presence of this value in the reflective consciousness I am enabled to recognize in the expression of some others a reflection of a comparable form of Recognition. Also, I am enabled to understand the Meaning behind the expression of such writers. Further, I retain at all times in my personal consciousness a memory and understanding relative to the Higher State that is substantially more than a sense of a mere inchoate Thatness. One who entered the Higher State with the relative consciousness completely paralyzed either would be unable to return, or, if he did so, could carry into his outer consciousness only a dim adumbration of a something Other.

How long the state of complete Satisfaction continued I do not know, save that it was for a protracted interval as measured in terms of objective consciousness. But as time went on, there was a gradual dimming, or fusing, or being enveloped, on the part of the Satisfaction, by another and considerably more profound State. The only expression that reasonably well represents this higher State is the term "High Indifference." Along with this was a sense of simply tremendous Authority. It was an Authority of such stupendous Majesty as to reduce the power of all Caesars relatively to the level of insects. The Caesars may destroy cultures and whole peoples, but they are utterly powerless with respect to the Inner Springs of Consciousness, and in the domains beyond the river Styx they are as impotent as most other men. But the Authority of the High Indifference has supreme dominion over all this, as well as being the Power which permits the Caesars to play their little games for brief seasons. The Caesars, as well as many who are greater than they, are capable of reaching only to some goal well within the limits of Satisfaction. They certainly do not know the Powers lying beyond the utmost sweep of individual desire. But there is such a region of Authority, supreme over all below It, and this is the High Indifference.

In this State, I was not enveloped with satisfaction, but there was no feeling, in connection with that fact, of something having been lost. Literally, I now had no need of Satisfaction. This state or quality rested, as it were, below Me, and I could have invoked it if I had so chosen. But the important point is that on the level of the High Indifference, there is no need of comfort or of Bliss, in the sense of an active Joy or Happiness. If one were to predicate Bliss in connection with the High Indifference, it would be correct only in the sense that there was an absence of misery or pain. But relative to this State, even pleasurable enjoyment is misery. I am well aware that in this we have a State of Consciousness which falls quite outside the range of ordinary human imagination. Heretofore I have for my own part never been able really to imagine a state of so superior an excellence that it was actually more than desirable. And here I mean "more" in the best possible sense. Within the limits of my old motivation, there was nothing that craved anything like this, and I do not find anything in man as man that would make such a craving possible. Yet now, deep within me, I feel that I am centered in a Level from which I look down upon all objects of all possible human desire, even the most lofty. It is a strange, almost a weird, Consciousness when viewed from the perspective of relative levels. Yet, on Its own Level, It is the one State that is really complete or adequate. What there may be still Beyond, I do not Know, but this State I do know consumes all others of which I have had any glimpse whatsoever.

The word "Indifference" is not altogether satisfactory, but I know of no other that serves as well. It is not at all indifference in the negative or *tamasic* sense. The latter is a dull, passive, and inert quality, close to the soddenness of real Death. The High Indifference is to be taken in the sense of an utter Fullness that is even more than a bare Infinity. To borrow a figure from mathematics, It is an Infinity of some higher order, that is, an INFINITY which comprehends lesser Infinities.

What is it that leads one on into this Level? As already shown, it is clearly not desire. Further, the State certainly seems to be beyond the limits of human imagination. Here we are in the presence of real Mystery. Is it Nirvana? There are excellent reasons for believing that It is something more than Nirvana in the simplest sense. Let us consider this.

Nirvana, in the simplest and most customary sense, is not so far beyond imagination as generally supposed. To be sure, Nirvanic Consciousness cannot be expressed in subject-object terms and thus must be approached largely through negative definition. But It does have some marks that are partly understandable. It is a State somewhat qualified by the terms "blown out," "Bliss," and "Rest." Most certainly, It is a desirable Goal for him who is weary from the burden of egoism and the misery of world-consciousness. There is a stage in spiritual progress such that the step of entering Nirvanic Consciousness finally appears as a sort of temptation. I do not say that every man who has reached the point where he may enter this State in a relatively final sense necessarily fails of his best in so entering. With some, the state of soul-fatigue is so great that no other course is reasonably possible. So no blame attaches to those who do so enter. But there are some Men who reach this point with such a reserve of strength that They can choose another course, and there are alternative courses of superior dignity. But even for Them, Nirvanic Consciousness is naturally highly attractive. But if They do enter Nirvana, They may no longer aid suffering mankind, whereas by following a certain alternative course, They may be of the very greatest assistance, and thus it follows that for Them Nirvana appears as a temptation. All of this implies that here we are still within the field of conceivable desire. Whatever course may be chosen, desire in some sense is active, even though it is that lofty kind of desire that is born out of pure Compassion.

This choice, induced by consideration of pure Compassion, is everywhere in literature, so far as I know, designated as utter Renunciation, and there is nothing said relative to any alleviating compensation. I have for some time suspected a blind here, for the Law of Equilibrium is universal in Its scope. Thus there can be no exception in the matter of Compensation even on the higher Levels where still, in some sense, differentiation remains. And there certainly is differentiation so long as it is possible to speak of Nirmanakayas* in the plural number. What, then, is this superior Compensation?

The answer to the foregoing question is at last clear. Nirvana is complete Satisfaction and the highest possible object of desire, except that purely selfless Desire aroused by Compassion. Because the characteristically human thought is of such a nature that desire, in some sense, is

---

*The embodiments of Those who have made the Great Renunciation.

absolutely essential to define an object for it, it is impossible to place before mankind any Goal of aspiration higher than that of selfless Compassion. Further, it is only the very best among men, in the moral or spiritual sense, who are capable of being aroused to emulation of the Compassionate Ones. Hence, the few words written on this subject are dedicated to the Few. Compassion is the absolutely final word of human goodness; in fact, It is a sort of God-like goodness. There is nothing beyond that mere man can imagine as either desirable or worthy of emulation. Beyond this the Sages have been silent.

But now We will speak further.*

He, who can turn his back upon the utmost limit of individual desire, comes within the sweep of a Current of Consciousness wholly beyond the action or lead of Desire. Human vocabularies afford no terms for representing what governs or leads to movement or transformation Here. But beyond the Great Renunciation is a Compensation that places Man where He is Lord, even over the first Nirvana. It emplants Him on a Level that is beyond Rest as well as beyond action; beyond Formlessness as well as beyond Form; and this is the High Indifference. He who abides on the Plane of the High Indifference may enter Rest or Action at will, but He remains essentially superior to both, since from that Level both these are derived. There is a Completeness, superior to that of Satisfaction, from which Satisfaction may be employed as an instrument and not merely stand as a final Goal. So Rest can be blended with action and the Balance remain unbroken. But the High Indifference unites much more, for in It are blended, at once, all qualities, all dualities. It is the End and the Beginning and all between. It is the physical as well as that beyond the physical; It is Form as well as the Formless; It spreads over and through all, not excluding time and space. It is the Desire and the desire fulfilled, at this moment and forever. It transcends all Renunciation, even the highest. Thus, the balancing Compensation is fulfilled. Here, Knowing and Being are at once the same. Literally, Here is the utter Fullness, beyond the highest reach of the imagination.

★ ★ ★

---

*Note these words. They came with that strange authority of which I have spoken. With them there was the cool, tingling and electric thrill up the spine. At such moments I dare to speak far beyond myself, in the personal sense, with a deep Knowing that it is authorized. Right here is one of the Mysteries of the Inner Consciousness.

How long I continued in the state of the High Indifference I do not know. I was long awake that night—well beyond the midnight hour—and the state continued to deepen. Throughout the whole period, the relative consciousness remained present as a witness. The personality, with the physical form, seemed to shrink toward a pointlike insignificance. The "I" spread out indefinitely like space, enveloping and piercing through all form, so far as my personal consciousness took note. So far as my thought could reach, there were no limits. I was quite indifferent whether the body passed into the state commonly called death or continued to live. Either outcome was equally unimportant. The evils, strifes, tragedies, and problems of this world shrank to an insignificance that was actually amusing. I saw that human catastrophes, even the most terrific, were relatively all less than "tempests in a teapot." There did not seem to be any need sufficiently important to require the service of Compassion. But, on the other hand, there was absolutely no reason why one should not choose to be active among and for men. From the standpoint of that State, it seemed utterly impossible to choose any course that was a mistake, or one that was better than another. There was no reason for choosing to continue to live in the physical sense, but likewise there was no good reason for choosing to abandon the body. The State was too completely non-relative and too utterly absolute for any kind of particular choice to have any significance. So, in the subject-object sense, I was quite free to choose as I saw fit. I chose to continue with the job, but from the standpoint of High Indifference, there was neither merit nor demerit in this. For There, both wrongness and rightness, as well as all other dualities, are completely absorbed in the non-relative.

I moved about in a kind of Space that was not other than Myself, and found Myself surrounded by pure Divinity, even on the physical level when I moved there. There is a sense in which God is physical Presence as well as metaphysical. But this Presence is everywhere and everything, and, at the same time, the negation of all this. Again, neither I nor God were There; only BEING remained. I vanished and the object of consciousness vanished, in the highest, as well as inferior, senses. I was no more and God was no more, but only the ETERNAL which sustains all Gods and all Selves.

Is it any wonder that SILENCE is the usual answer to the question: What is the High Indifference?

53
The Evidence for the Higher Consciousness

September 10

For many years I have worked with the hope that more than a presumption favoring the actuality of the Higher Consciousness could be found, such that every rationally alert mind within the subject-object manifold would be satisfied in the same way that mathematical demonstration convinces. I must admit that so far, at any rate, no such conclusive demonstration has been produced. For instance, there is no question about the breadth of information or the intellectual keenness of a mind such as that of Bertrand Russell. Russell is a master logician, and yet as revealed in his philosophical writings, he is not convinced of the actuality of the Higher Consciousness. The fact that this is true of him and of many others, who are in this respect similar to him, is very nearly conclusive evidence that coercive demonstration of the actuality of the Higher Consciousness has not been formulated, at least not within the range of available literature. I must confess that with all his elaborate carefulness and unquestionably great intellectual power even Shankara failed to produce proof in this sense. In places he even falls into what we would now regard as rather obvious logical errors, such as the undistributed middle. Even more clearly, Plato failed in his effort at demonstration. In our present culture we have witnessed the greatest systematic effort of all, i.e., the development that commenced with Immanuel Kant, attained its crown in Hegel, and was given detailed finishing by the hands of Hegel's disciples. Yet again I must say, though I do this regretfully, that this effort has failed in the logical sense no less truly than the others. There are two considerations that seem to be conclusive evidence of this failure. In the first place, the Hegelians sought to demonstrate the essential unreality of the subject-object consciousness by showing that it necessarily involved self-contradiction. But since the time of Hegel, there has been an enormous growth in the understanding of logic through an analysis of the foundations of mathematics and the isolation of the logical principles involved. It was soon found that the principles of rigorous deduction could not be reduced to Aristotle's logic of identity. There are other principles employed in the logic of relatives that are equally conclusive in their results. So today, under the general title of symbolic logic, we have a more powerful logical instrument than ever before. In the light of this greater power it seems clear that the apparent contradictions which both Kant and Hegel thought they had found can be resolved. This fact, by itself, destroys much of the coercive power of Hegel's philosophy, though by no means challenging the validity of his fundamental insight. The second consideration is brought to light in the development through Karl Marx. Marx took the dialectic logic of Hegel and employed it to develop a philosophy which actually contradicts the central core of the Hegelian insight. This reveals, again, that as a matter of pure logic alone, Hegel failed in his fundamental objective.

But is this failure in all existent efforts to produce a coercive demonstration merely due to insufficient skill? Or does it reveal a fundamental inadequacy in formal logic, taken by itself? Almost up to the present day, I have held the former view, but now I see no way out save to admit that the task is beyond the power of logic, taken in the purely formal sense. Now, unquestionably, pure mathematics does afford a genuine road to Recognition, but it is not the kind of mathematics that remains after men like Bertrand Russell are through defining it. Mathematics in that sense becomes merely a formal definition of possibility, but it is stripped of all spiritual actuality. Mathematics is a spiritual power just because of that element in it that is stripped away in Russell's "Principles of Mathematics." Thinkers of this type do not see it because, however great their intellectual powers may be, yet in one dimension of themselves they are blind. They see the skeleton but do not Realize the soul of mathematics. And right here is the key to the failure of the coercive method. Without the Recognition of the Soul, in some sense, such as the soul of mathematics or of logic or in some other form, formal demonstration proves merely possibility or the hypothetical imperative, but never arrives at a categorical imperative. The only Knowledge that can possibly Liberate man is categorical, i.e., certain knowledge of actuality and not merely of possibility alone. Recognition transforms the hypothetical into the categorical and is the only power that can do so. Experience cannot accomplish this, for experience can give only the material filling of subject-object knowledge, and never by itself can it lift the individual out of that field. Further, It never gives categorical certainty, for all too obviously growth in skill in observation changes the determination of what is experienced. Recognition is neither experience nor demonstration in the formal sense. The result is that the Key to the Higher Knowledge inheres in a kind of Knowing that does not fall within the subject-object field. Thus demonstration of the Higher Knowledge, in terms that are coercive strictly within the limits of the subject-object field, is impossible. Consequently, the final word relative to these higher concerns must remain absolute agnosticism for pure subject-object consciousness, as David Hume showed so clearly long ago.

The ultimate word of *pure* subject-object consciousness to those who yearn or are soul-sick is: "There is no hope. If a man would ease the deeper pain, let him play backgammon, as Hume did, and thus through concentration upon the detail of activity forget the pain." And there are many now who are doing just this, though the "game of backgammon" takes many forms. It may be a concentration upon business, upon profession, upon sports, politics, the army, the various arts and sciences, etc., etc. Some commit suicide, and they are probably the most logically consistent of all, though frightfully unwise. For the fact is that *pure* subject-object consciousness is absolutely barren of any real or soul-sustaining Value, and in the end it is as useless and purposeless as running a treadmill that does no work. It is a life of pure misery without any real hope whatsoever. The average materialistic physician or psychiatrist regards this kind of life as the measure of sanity. We regard it as the acme of insanity.

It is perfectly true that Kant did reveal the Way to escape the agnosticism of Hume and opened the door so that the soul might at least hope and not despair. But buried deep in Kant's thought lies the Recognition; so here, as ever, That remains the magic Touchstone.

For him who penetrates deeply into the roots of logic itself, the Recognition can be aroused. It lies in those very logical constants upon which the validity of all logic depends but which can never be themselves demonstrated by logic. There seem to be but a small number of such constants, perhaps ten or twelve, yet upon their recognition all the compulsive power of logic depends. Nearly all men who have understood what these constants are find it impossible not to believe them, but no man can prove them since they form the ground on which all proof rests. Now whence comes the compelling assurance that these constants are necessarily true? Experience gives probable knowledge at best, but never compelling assurance; so the source is not in pure experience. The answer for me is perfectly clear. The power of these constants is due to the fact that they constitute a veiled Recognition that the race has never completely lost, and they are probably the principal agent that has kept this humanity from becoming wholly insane. Let a man unveil this Recognition and make It immediately and consciously his own, and then he will find in logic a power which, if followed with a single eye, will take him through to the Higher Consciousness. Once given that original Recognition, logic does supply unanswerable demonstration, and thus breaks through the closed vortex of subject-object consciousness.

So finally I must conclude that the only hope for man, taken individually or as a whole, rests upon a process of Awakening which I, together with some others, have called "Recognition." This is neither pure experience nor pure formal demonstration, but a totally different kind of Knowledge. I have called It "Knowledge through Identity." It is Intuition, in the highest sense, but the word "intuition" covers other meanings; so the former term is less ambiguous. Genuine Knowledge through Identity is infallible and absolute. It is substantial and not relative. It does not merely mean something other than Itself, but is absolutely Its own Meaning. Knowledge through Identity is not possessed by any self but IS the SELF. It is not "knowledge about," not even in the sense of "about God," but is Divinity Itself. Thus we have these six primary propositions which, when exalted to Recognition, reclaim man unequivocally:

1. "I am not other than God."
2. "God is not other than I."
3. "I am not other than Knowledge."
4. "Knowledge is not other than I."
5. "God is not other than Knowledge."
6. "Knowledge is not other than God."

Let a man repeat these affirmations, but not as mere propositions. Let him add to those repetitions some measure of that indefinable quality We call "Recognition," and they will at once become magical agents with some measure of potency, ranging from a faint stirring of a bare sense of a Beyondness up to a Power so great that the whole universe is, as it were, dislodged from its commanding position. I Know this to be true, but how can I transfer this certainty?

★ ★ ★

But if conclusive demonstration of the Beyond is impossible save for one who has in some measure, however small, glimpsed It, yet it remains true that much evidence exists which builds a presumption that there is an Otherness quite outside the comprehension of mere subject-object

---

*The relationship between the two levels of consciousness is represented, in the form of analogy, very beautifully by just the difference which separates pure from applied mathematics.

knowledge. This presumption can be made stronger, and We will not cease in Our endeavor to make it so. But We do ask, nay demand, in the name of that spirit of open-mindedness and willingness to let evidence outweigh prejudice (which has been the secret of the greatness of science), that the evidence which builds a presumption that the Beyond is actual should be given the fair valuation and consideration it deserves. We ask no more than that man should dare, upon the showing of a probability that is certainly much greater than that which led men to gamble upon far less worthy enterprises. Now let us examine the case for the presumption that there is a Beyond.

First of all, there is the evidence growing out of the lives and works of all the genuine Mystics or God-Realized Men. At the core of every great and enduring religion, such Men are to be found. Thus there are Buddha, Krishna, Shankara, Lao-tzu, Moses, Christ, St. Paul, Mohammed, among others. Judge these Men by Their enormous influence with hundreds of millions of human beings, extending over periods of the order of many centuries and even millennia, and bear in mind that this influence strikes at the very core of human motivation, and then the conclusion seems unavoidable that before these Men we stand in the Presence of a mysterious and tremendous Power. Then penetrating surface differences, go to the core of these Men's Teachings and Their general relationship to Life, and a fundamental similarity is to be found. In every case, They place the Source of Their Messages and Power in something that cannot be reached when standing solely within the subject-object manifold. They, with Others of Their own kind, are indubitably the greatest moral force in the world. But They are not solely a moral force. Some of Those named, together with some others, stand on the highest level of intellectual influence. There are, to be sure, men of great intellectual power who have not attained Recognition, but the more powerful and the more lasting any intellectual current, the greater the probability that at its fount are to be found Men of Recognition. This is a notable fact in Hindu philosophy, but it is also an outstanding fact in Greek philosophy and science. The earmarks of Recognition are very strong among the pre-Socratics. Of the great triumvirate of Greece, Socrates, Plato, and Aristotle, two have It. At the fountainhead of our own science and philosophy stand men like Francis Bacon, Descartes, and Spinoza. The lives or writings of two of these, Bacon and Spinoza, reveal unmistakable evidences of Recognition of, if not the highest, at least a high, order. And as for Descartes: What were the words with which he began his constructive reflection and at the same time ushered in the modern period of thought? They were the famous *Cogito ergo sum,* "I think, therefore I am." These words are but a new turn upon the essential mystic Recognition. Descartes did not apparently enter fully, but in him a mystic phrase starts the current of modern thought. Newton, himself, clearly had a mystical side, much to the disgust of some scientists who imagine themselves to be tough. It is said that his original inspiration came from hints in the obscure writings of Jacob Boehme, a genuine Man of Recognition. And there is no greater sun in all our science than just this Sir Isaac Newton. What of Paracelsus, who occupies an important place in the history of chemistry? Clearly, He is a Man whose Fount is in the Beyond and One who possesses true Wisdom, even though He obscured It under the barbarisms of alchemical expression. What of Kepler? And what of Gustav Theodor Fechner, a man great in the science of physics and regarded by many as the founder of experimental psychology? This man has many of the marks of the real mystic, as revealed in certain of his less well-known writings, yet at the same time he was simply a tremendous force in science. But we must go on. We cannot pretend to complete the list. So let us turn to literature.

Consider men like Plato, Dante, the author of "Shakespeare," Balzac, Emerson. Every one of these Men carries the marks of Recognition in at least some degree. And what do They mean in literature? The best of all are in this list. Fortunately, in one of them we can trace the difference between the man before Recognition and the Man afterward. This one is Balzac. Before Realization, he produced voluminously a very inferior literature that has never lived at all, but afterward he rose to a literary height, comparable to that of the author of "Shakespeare." This same phenomenon can be seen in another man, this time in our own country, and while he does not occupy as high a place in literature as the others named, he is none the less gaining recognition as one of the great poets of all time, and he lived among us a life of nobility and enduring influence. I refer to Walt Whitman. Before his Recognition he, too, wrote inferior stuff that would not live, yet afterward he was able to infill with living richness a peculiarly obscure prosody.

I wish, finally, to call attention to an event almost of our present day. Consider the "Secret Doctrine" of H. P. Blavatsky, simply as a phenomenon, if not in a profounder sense. Let the reader examine this book, disregarding, if he can, the force of the thought contained therein, and regard simply the phenomenon of its erudition. The references alone might well require half a lifetime of research, yet the life of the writer, though fairly well known, reveals nothing like adequate scholarly labors. Competent testimony states that when she wrote her library resources were very meager. In addition, she was practically a sick woman throughout the productive part of her life. In her work, alone, we have a peculiarly compelling witness of some Power beyond the field of pure subject-object consciousness.

I might continue listing several cases. A volume could be written. But the reader, if he desires, can complete this for himself. The important point to note is that these Men all carry a somewhat which comes from Beyond. Many of Them have claimed that Beyondness as Their Source, but all carry the familiar earmarks in one form or another. Further, They all wield Powers in the moral, intellectual, or artistic fields of the very highest order. Education and breeding do not make Them. They can flame forth out of poor educational backgrounds as well as out of the best that education can offer. Their children, if They have any, do not show the same type of capacity, and thus it is clear that Their peculiar capacities are not due to special modifications of the genes. In some of Them, because of sufficiently complete biographical records, we can see the radical revolution between the man before and the Man after Recognition. Altogether, we have a strong case showing that Here is something from outside the range of understanding and control of the pure subject-object consciousness. Now, consider what a debt those within the subject-object field owe these Men. Just imagine this world as it would be without their influence, direct or indirect. Of religion, there would be little, if anything, more than animism left. Philosophy and science would lose their greatest classics. And how greatly impoverished would literature and art be! It is a very strong case, if fairly considered.

Let us now turn to other lines of evidence, admittedly of a distinctly inferior sort, but yet much more common. The cases considered have revealed the highest excellence in moral, intellectual, and artistic values. But there is a large number of other instances of weaker manifestation where the Sun of Recognition has not quite risen, and hence there has been but a Twilight of the Great Consciousness, or, if the Sun has risen, It has appeared but briefly or has been obscured as by a cloudy sky. Here we would have to include the lesser mystics, and at least much of genius.

In these cases again, we have that which neither education nor breeding explains. Here is a lesser Well of Mystery out of which choice values come to enrich the lives of men.

But below all this are other domains of progressively inferior character where some of the values are excellent and even exalted while others do reach to profound depths of ugliness in some sort of inferior world. But all of these are important to us as revealing one characteristic in common, i.e., a kind of consciousness that does not fit into the common framework of the subject-object manifold. Thus they all have a kind of mystic quality or consciousness-mode utterly alien to the dominant and common form of consciousness which we teach in our schools and which is the only form under the command of our pedagogical methods. All of these instances, from the lowest infernal ones up to those of the Christs or Buddhas, have in common the fact that a certain shell must be broken before a new domain of consciousness can be realized. No amount of development within the shell can attain this. Observation within the shell may be able to note certain phenomena that attend the "breaking through" and may be able to detect certain similarities that mark all such "breaking out," as well as some divergencies. Observers may very correctly find that such phenomena are contrary to the norm of usual behavior. But the observer, confined within the shell, is wholly incapable of evaluating the actuality beyond the shell. He may be able, in some degree, to evaluate the fruits from the Beyond as reflected back within the shell, but he does not and can not know their immediate content. He has no logical justification in concluding that that which is contrary to the norm is inferior. Some of it is inferior, to be sure, but also much of it is infinitely superior. But before one can be really competent in this differentiation he, himself, must have broken out of the shell. The one important fact that all this body of testimony does concur in, be it on the one hand noble, able, and beautiful, or, descending from that level progressively through inferior forms until we reach at the bottom something anything but admirable, is this: that there is another kind of consciousness or kinds of consciousness which do not fit within the forms governing the familiar subject-object consciousness.

Briefly, I would call attention to the very extensive but inferior field of evidence. Several volumes exist for the reference of those who are interested and qualified. There is a mass of testimony coming from the effects of various toxic substances, such as the common anaesthetics, alcohol, and the narcotic and hypnotic drugs. A few of these temporary unfoldings are of a high order, but most are distinctly inferior, and some very inferior. This sort of "breaking through" gives no voluntary command of the new level entered, and the capacity for cross-translation into the objective mind is very defective. But the reports show the presence of a consciousness of a nature quite different from that which is typical within the shell. Here we have, clearly, a kind of externally imposed violence that effects a sort of "breaking out." Most emphatically, this technique is not to be recommended, as it is very apt to prove a fatal barrier to the real Awakening, for the latter involves self-conscious Power. But since the drug-technique does exist in point of fact, and does produce a kind of result, it is of value as evidence.

Certain phenomena in connection with sickness supply further evidence. The wasting away caused by certain sicknesses and the process of dying, when it has been arrested before quite complete and the life-current is re-established, afford a number of instances of "breaking through" of variable value. Here there exists a considerable body of testimony revealing a consciousness or consciousness-mode quite alien to the form of common consciousness. There is also the large field of mediumship and the negative yoga-practices, but to these I shall only refer in passing, as there is an abundant literature covering them. In addition, within the more common and normal domain there are minor adumbrations of otherness that still are significant, if less striking. I refer to the effects often produced by strong emotions. In this class there is frequent partial "breaking through" to other values that do, in fact, point to a beyond.

If, now, we take the whole field of evidence, briefly summed above, there is built a presumption of tremendous strength to the effect that beyond the shell of the familiar subject-object consciousness there is another kind or are other kinds of consciousness. Further, the testimony is clear that in this other domain, or in some of these other domains, there are levels of Intelligence and Joy far transcending any that men have been able to find within the shell. The question of fact concerning this other domain or domains, regardless of what the values may be, is in any case one of scientific or epistemological interest of the very highest importance. For, so long as this other kind or kinds of knowledge are not understood, we can never justly evaluate the more familiar forms of knowledge. If there is a Domain where enduring Joy can be found and a kind of Knowledge which solves all problems that here distress the soul of man, then what is of greater importance than that men should find the Way to reach this Domain? Those who have witnessed to the actuality of such a Region have built an exceedingly strong presumption. Under these circumstances is it not the duty as well as the privilege of every man, whose courage is not too weak, to reduce that presumption to actual personal demonstration?

★ ★ ★

Much that I have written in this book is in the form of an intimate personal testimony. Other portions are in the form of reflective discussions, or more or less mystical compositions that are, in large measure at least, the fruit from a shift in consciousness level which I, individually, have experienced. My purpose in this was not merely the satisfying of a demand for self-expression—in fact I do not feel such a demand—but to report and reveal, as far as may be, a fact that I know to be of the very highest importance to myself, and a fact that is potentially calpable of having that same value for others. From previous training, I know something of the importance and technique of introspective observation. I have not neglected watching the personal transformation, while in process, with a view to keeping a record of as large an objective value as I could achieve. It has been my purpose not to neglect the recording of unpleasant or negative features if they should arise. In point of fact, I have found the unpleasant features to be of remarkably minor importance and only of temporary duration. Thus any ordinary athletic achievement in the fields of sport involves more bodily and emotional discomfort than I have experienced at any time since the 7th of last month, while on the other hand I have known the Joy of finding a World far greater and far more significant than all that which came out of the discoveries of Columbus. I simply wish that others may find the World, or have the Way made clearer to them because of what I have already accomplished.

There is one point that I wish to have understood very clearly. The initial Transformation did not just happen to me as something coming unexpectedly out of the blue. We have several records of such spontaneous Awakenings, and while there exists a rationale explaining such cases which shows that they are not quite so spontaneous as they seem, I shall not enter into that question at the present time. In point of fact, I have sought this Awakening for several years. I was finally convinced that, at least in all probability, there was such a thing or event, while I was in the midst of the discussions of a metaphysical seminary held at Harvard. I saw, at once, that if such Knowledge were an actuality it was of far greater importance than even the greatest intellectual achievement within the limits of the subject-object field. At that time I had a very imperfect idea of the Goal, but I knew that among the East Indians was to be found the greatest development of knowledge relative to It. I resolved to make the search and pay what price might be demanded. In the years since, I have been more than once discouraged and have permitted lateral desires to lead me into side-excursions. But I always returned to the search. I tested various different routes, finding values and defects in all, and then at last by combining the best that India has to offer in the field of metaphysics with the best of western science and philosophy, and then adding thereto some modifications of my own,* I found a road that has proved successful. While during the interim there have been partial Transformations and Recognitions, it has taken twenty-four years of search to attain a culminating point which I can recognize as definitely culminating. All of the steps within the subject-object field were conscious, and therefore I can formulate and evaluate them. Also, I am aware of the Transcendent Factor and know the Significance of the part It plays. If I had known in the beginning all that is here for the first time collected together between the covers of one book, many years of time would have been saved. Perhaps, also, for some others this book may have a similar value. But from the standpoint of evidence for a Beyondness, the point I wish to make is that in the present case an individual was finally convinced of the validity of a search from the discussions that formed a part of the classwork in one of the leading western universities. He tried to find the Way, at times following others, but in the end carving his own course, and did that without renouncing the western form of intellectuality. What one can do others also may do.

My final word on this particular subject is: I sought a Goal the existence of which I had become convinced was highly probable. I succeeded in finding this Goal, and now I KNOW, and can also say to all others: "IT IS ABSOLUTELY WORTH ANYTHING THAT IT MAY COST, AND IMMEASURABLY MORE."

---

*At the present time, some two and one-half years since writing the above, I have a further contribution to offer on the creative effort supplied by the individual himself. I have made many experiments with the meditative and yogic techniques given by the various authorities. In no case have I had any results that were worth the effort so long as I did not supply at least a self-devised modification of my own. Apparently the modification is suggested intuitively. Often I got results by a method diametrically opposite to that suggested by a given authority. At least, so far as my private experience is concerned, the successful method always had to be in some measure an original creation. I suspect the presence of a general principle here, but I am not at present able to deduce a conclusion of universal applicability.

54
A Poetic Interlude

September 11

Am I a man? Yet also am I a god,
For I am that which comprehends both gods and men.
I move among men in the form of a man,
Fallible, more or less good, like the rest.
Yet, also, I shine with the gods in Glory.
I compress Myself in the mineral,
Inert and long-enduring.
Ceaselessly I grow as a plant,
And am driven by desire as animal.
I am in all, yet ever Beyond all.
A Flame am I that nowhere remains;
I consume all.

★ ★ ★

As I write I am sitting on a pavement of cement.
A tree grows near, its roots, soft and brittle, beneath that pavement.
Ceaselessly, slowly, but inevitably, those roots expand.
The cement gives way, its resistance impotent.
So, too, I expand, inevitably, remorselessly, in this world.
Before Me no crystallization can stand.
In the end, all other powers fail;
My own, once more, return to Me.

★ ★ ★

What matters health, sickness or death;
Passing modes in the endless Stream of Life?
In health I go forth, perchance to forget;
In sickness I look within and remember.
Which is the greater blessing?
I know not.
Men seek health. I seek not at all.
I give health and accept the blessing of sickness.
Yet, beyond all these, AM *I*—Unbound.

★ ★ ★

Do I look for faults in men?
Then surely I will find them;
Dishonesty, lust, greed, hatred, and all the rest.
All these come with immense fecundity.
Do I look beyond to the good?
Then what a glorious paragon is man!
Generous, kind, and fair-dealing.
Which of these is the real?
Neither and both. Man reflects just what I seek.

55
The Real and the Unreal

We are in a position at this point to arrive at a clearer understanding of what is meant by the "Sangsara" of the Buddhists, the "Maya" of the Vedantists, and the "illusive nature of the phenomenal world" of the Hegelians. The State of the High Indifference is absolutely Real, and most emphatically not an airy abstraction. However, It may seem to be such an abstraction from the standpoint of relative consciousness. It is incorrect to imagine that when a man has Awakened to Real Consciousness then the objective universe vanishes in the photographic sense. In the Higher Consciousness the Inward and the outward blend, as do all other dualities, and are at once an eternal fact. So it is incorrect to regard the outward as unreal while, at the same time, predicating reality of the inward. No branch of any duality is real by itself. It is the separation of one or the other phase of inter-knit dualities that results in the vicious kind of abstraction, i.e., the kind that produces an illusion or Maya. It is because subject-object consciousness has characteristically produced such a disjunction of inseparables that it has been the great creative cause of unreality. When Shankara speaks of the universe, or the Buddhist of Sangsara, each means the subject-object manifold. And it is just because of the false abstraction in this manifold that life here below is essentially one of misery. Awakening is re-integration for the individual consciousness of the inseparable parts that have been, apparently, divided. Thus, this Awakening does genuinely destroy the universe, in the sense of Its being a power over the Awakened Man. The latter, after the Awakening, may focus attention upon and act within the relative universe at will, but the significance of his doing so is precisely that of entering a dream and consciously playing a part in it.

For the fully Realized Man, Sangsara or the illusive universe is without value. This is very difficult for the egoistic man to understand, and so the latter may be led to question the value of the Awakening. The Realized Man largely ignores those values which still seem important to the unawakened. The latter sees the apparent lack of ambition and desire in the former, and thus hands Him an utter mystery. Thus, for example, the man of the world makes a god of what he calls progress and laborious accomplishment; yet he sees these things, if not despised by the Illumined Men, at least looked upon with a certain detached aloofness. Quite naturally he resents this, though he may be forced to give respect when he finds that the Awakened Man, when acting within the relative manifold, wields an extraordinary and unconquerable skill. But, on the other hand, the Realized Man may choose not to act, in an apparent sense, and His life then is often judged as a wasted one both for Himself and for society. But the egoistic man is quite wrong here. In fact he is just as wrong in this attitude as would be the judgment of an animal, if it were capable of judgment, in viewing the scorn of the cultured man toward the essentially animal field of interest. The cultured man knows the superiority of his field of interests, when compared to anything possible to the strictly animal consciousness. Far more clearly, the Awakened Man Knows the superiority of the Infinite when contrasted to anything within the finite universe. This superiority is not measurable in finite terms, but is in fact infinitely superior. Life in the infinite is one with everything, and so the finite cannot possibly add anything to it. The last possible value of the finite, or subject-object domain, is realized once the Awakening has culminated within it. The Awakened One, who returns, does so not to learn more but to be of aid to those who are still sleeping. The best possible growth in this lower world is growth *toward* the Awakening in the Infinite. For Him who has Awakened in the Infinite, all Real Life is Life *in* the Infinite.

Too much emphasis cannot be placed upon the fact of the Reality and substantiality of the State of the High Indifference. Nothing here below is felt so immediately, so fully, and with such utter completeness. Nothing here is so completely *solid* or dependable in the essential sense. The Higher Reality merely *seems* abstract to the relative consciousness. Actually, what we call concrete here is abstract in the real and invidious sense.

The higher we rise in what we commonly call abstraction, the nearer we approach substantial actuality. It thus follows, that he who can arouse in himself the sense that the apparent abstractions of our language in fact mean real and substantial actualities, will be preparing himself for the Awakening.*

56
Integration

September 13

Most of yesterday was spent in the city. I found that I had better control of the problem of driving in traffic than had been the case for some weeks, and, in addition, I maintained my own center in the midst of the crowds more successfully than at any other time since the Transition. However, I found that this required quite a strong effort of will, and fatigue developed rather rapidly. Toward the end of the day, my control was not so strong, and at the same time I was thrown downward into the more barren levels of the personal consciousness in a larger degree than has been the case since the 7th of last month. Clearly, the whole problem is one of winning a new kind of control. Quite evidently, this can be accomplished, but a price is exacted. In this, experience confirms theory with respect to the principle that there can be no avoidance of the Law of Compensation on this outer plane of life. This leads to the following practical question: In what field, at a given time and under given circumstances, is one's functioning most useful, due consideration being given to the Law of Compensation? It is not merely a question of what one can do. In addition, consideration must be given to the probable value of an effort in comparison to its cost.

What is required in achieving the control necessary for meeting modern city-conditions is becoming clearer. Through the will, one must surround himself with a strong shield of integration. To accomplish this, the

---

*It should not be concluded that this is the only way of preparing for the Awakening. There is no one method that is exclusively valid. The process that proves effective for one psychological type may fail completely for a very different type. It is possible to outline an effective Route, but it is impossible to say that *only* by this means may anyone Attain.

aid of a certain kind of rhythm is required. I find it necessary to move, both mentally and physically, in a rather slow and stately rhythm, and refuse to accept impressions that I do not choose. Acting as a contrary force, the rush of traffic always threatens to break this rhythm, although yesterday it seemed as though circumstances were combining to favor me. Toward the end of the day the integration weakened to a degree, and then the interrupting cross-currents began to break through into my own consciousness. I find that when this happens, it begins to be dangerous and I have to struggle in order to secure simple physical safety. It appears that the action of subject-object consciousness is more certain, keener, and more powerful when supplemented by the Higher Consciousness, but when this correlation is interrupted, the personal control is less effective than it was in former days.

The meaning I am trying to convey by the word "integration" at this time may be illustrated by a familiar phenomenon in magnetism. When a bar of steel is made into a magnet, it is said that a certain force in the molecules or atoms is polarized in some measure, with the result that one end of the magnet is positive and the other negative. In a non-magnetized bar, this force exists but acts in all directions among the molecules so that there is little or no residual magnetic energy that acts beyond the bar itself. The result is that such a non-magnetized bar is a sort of neutral or closed field, although there is just as much force in it as in the magnetized bar. Now, subject-object consciousness may be thought of as a non-magnetized bar which forms a closed field within itself. In this way, the Beyond is shut off. But the man who is magnetized is in a position to pierce beyond the shell or closed field of relative consciousness, and so long as he maintains that magnetization, he stands correlated with the Beyond. Similarly, to the extent that that magnetism is lost, he tends to drop back into the field of mere subject-object consciousness. A magnetized steel bar can lose its magnetism very easily as it is brought into contact with non-magnetized pieces of iron, as in ordinary usage. The same phenomenon occurs when an individual with a magnetized consciousness moves in the field of ordinary consciousness. There is a dissipation of the integrated force, and the chaotic condition of the environing consciousness begins to invade the former. This leads to something analogous to demagnetization. But this demagnetized condition can be corrected subsequently by the action of the Current, just as a current of electricity may be employed in the re-magnetizing of a weak magnet. But all this takes effort, time, and the right conditions. It is true that so long as the Current is active, the magnetized man can dominate the demagnetizing influence of the environment, and in addition he will tend to magnetize the latter. However, it is not easy to maintain the Current under the conditions imposed by a modern city.

The magnetized condition is that which is meant by "Isolation." Physical solitude in the midst of wild nature, and particularly at high altitudes, affords an especially favorable condition, though this is not essential. This should make clear something of the rationale of the hermit-life of so many Sages, and also why the Illumined States are so sporadic and temporary in the cases of most of those who move in the midst of general society, particularly in the West. It also makes clear the rationale of the monastic or ashrama life. For in this, when it is genuine, we have a community formed of those who have attained some degree of Recognition, together with others who aspire to this State. Life in such a community is a great help to the latter and is not too severe a load for the former. Below the ashrama the next most favorable life is in communities where the population is not greatly concentrated and primitive nature dominates the environment. In contrast, the most unfavorable condition of all is afforded by the modern megalopolis, for in this we have the rushing and "jazzed" consciousness, heavily concentrated on the surface of things.

As a counterpoint to the foregoing fact is the other fact that it is precisely in the megalopolis that the human need of the God-Realized Man is greatest. The average city dweller faces the greatest soul-starvation and maiming of all. The city life supplies the greater bulk of suicides, insanity cases, and pathological radical movements, as well as a strong tendency toward sterility. All of these are symptoms of a very abnormal and unwholesome life. So the need in the city is the greatest of all, but likewise it is just in the city that the danger of suffocation of the Realized Consciousness is greatest. How can this problem be solved? It certainly calls for the highest kind of generalship.

57
The Gold Mine

September 14

These days I am facing the problem of embarrassment of riches. It seems I have a very peculiar gold mine. As the mine-car comes forth each morning, it brings a load of Gold Nuggets—Ideas, rich in the power of clarification and coordination. Always, I am unable to gather them all and store them in this vault of expression before the day closes. The remainder goes on the mine-dump of the hidden recesses of the mind where, while it is not exactly lost, it is hidden by other material and time is required to recover it. Meanwhile I have a vegetable garden—the merely practical and temporal concerns—and in this garden the weeds are growing. I am enough of a farmer to feel troubled about these weeds, but if I attend the weeding job, the Nuggets continue to roll over the dump. And it so happens that I am enough of a miner to appreciate the Value of the Nuggets. For the Gold commands all the lesser values, symbolized by the vegetables, while the latter do not command the Gold.

I choose the Gold before the rest.

58
The Power of Illumination

I have been dipping into Whitman during the last few days. With the perspective of the Consciousness I have called "Satisfaction" and the "High Indifference," he has become essentially clear. Most of the remaining obscurity in his writings has also been clarified by interpreting his language in the more obvious and simpler sense. In assuming in his work an involved meaning, as I have done heretofore, I found him baffling, but when I took his words as carrying the more simple and direct meaning, I found a very great increase of clarity. Whitman combines Illumination with a remarkable objective simplicity. It is the Illumination that makes Whitman great. There are some men who are so great on the level of relative consciousness alone that they are effective forces in the world for centuries and even millennia. Aristotle is an outstanding example of such greatness. I find nothing of this kind of greatness in

Whitman. If he had had a high order of capacity in the purely relative sense, it would hardly be conceivable that the great or Illumined Whitman could not have made his earlier writings—those written before Illumination—live. In fact, only his Illumined work has power, but it has unmistakably great power. This fact, however, simply increases the value of Whitman as an example of what Illumination means. On the other hand, men like Dante and Francis Bacon are not nearly so good examples for the study of Illumination, for both of these men, particularly the latter, were men of ability and training in the relative field. It is very probable that Bacon would have had a place in history even though he had not attained the Cosmic Consciousness. Hence, the contrast between the Illumined and the merely egoistic Bacon does not have the sharpness that is so marked in Whitman. It is hard to imagine that, without Illumination, Whitman would ever have been known beyond his own immediate circle.

How great, then, is the force of Illumination? An effective measure of It cannot be attained, but some men do show its force in relative "isolation." Whitman and Balzac are notable examples in recent times who afford us the marked contrast between the powers of the men before Illumination and what they became afterward. Western history gives us two other conspicuous examples. These are Jesus and Jacob Boehme, one a carpenter and the other a shoemaker. Each of these was a man of fine personal character, but neither of Them was great enough, in the purely egoistic sense, to have left any mark on history. It is unnecessary to remark upon the importance these Men achieved after winning the Higher Consciousness, especially in the case of the former. There are, undoubtedly, other men of this kind to be found, particularly in India, but some of these lived and died in retreats, or lived seen by men but under the vow of silence. Therefore, They have not constituted a recognizable force in history and do not live for the open record. Other men, of greater ability in terms of ordinary egoistic consciousness, who subsequently attained the Higher Consciousness, do not afford good examples, for the contrast between the two levels is not so marked. The difference between these two types may be illustrated in the following way: Nearly everyone can note the fact when a rather ordinary hill is raised to the magnitude of a high mountain as by the sudden action of geologic forces. On the other hand, if an already high mountain, with its top lost in the clouds, were suddenly raised to a still grander height, only a few would be able to appreciate this fact. Finally, only Those who dwell above the clouds can measure the relative altitude of the mighty peaks with just appreciation. So it is with the great Men of Illumination.

The Illumination is one fact. The form which Its partial expression takes within the subject-object field is something quite different. All Illumined Men form one Community; They are one Brotherhood grounded in mutual understanding and fundamental agreement. On the other hand, Their modes of expression in relative terms are as variable as are the differences in the development of personality. In principle, any mode of expression that exists in this world is a possible vehicle of Illumined Consciousness. In formal terms, not all these expressions are consistent with each other. They may even be far from correct in the scientific sense. But they all carry the Reality, in greater or less degree; Reality being understood as that which can be known only by Awakening to another dimension of Consciousness. Hence, any and all of these expressions from the Beyond are of the highest value to men. For a diamond is always a diamond, whether embedded in clay or washed clean, whether a rough stone or cut and polished. At one end of the scale, Illumined Men give us diamonds embedded in considerable clay, while at the other They supply us with diamonds well cleaned, cut to mathematically true angles that reflect most perfectly the contained Light, and polished to the last degree of refinement. The latter is, unquestionably, the more finished offering, but all are equal in this, that a diamond is a diamond. So, also, are all manifestations of Realized Consciousness equal, in that they are from a Source rooted in the Beyond or the Infinite.

For my own part, I much prefer the polishing of a Plato to the rough-hewing of a Whitman. But, unquestionably, Whitman is an "open Way" for some for whom Plato is a closed door. And all Ways that men need are acceptable to Me in the larger sense. But the Way of the rugged and simple man is no more *the* Divine Way than that which fits the needs of the highly cultured and aristocratic spirit. In fact, when it comes to the final showing, the real "snobs" in this world are not the highly cultured and aristocratic people, but a certain only partially finished group who feed their own pride by glorifying crudity, and insist that the crude way is the best way. The Illumined Man will do what is necessary to meet His people, and, if they require crudity, He will manifest through crudity, but this does not mean that He despises finished and polished workmanship nor those who prefer that Truth should be offered in a beautiful setting.

59
Expression and Transcendent Consciousness

Figures of speech or analogies seem to be absolutely essential to express the realities of Profundity. The direct meaning of language does not express the actuality of the Higher Consciousness. We might say that the Actuality envelops the expression but is not directly contained in it. Thus the reader should strive not so much to understand the formal meaning contained in these writings, but to make a certain turn in his own consciousness toward a Matrix that surrounds the expression. He should concentrate upon faint stirrings in his consciousness which he cannot really express, even to himself. They constitute a certain "plus" quantity added onto the formal meaning. The formal meaning serves as a sort of focal point that entrains the subtle "plus" value. It is very hard to reach the latter without the use of the focal point until a rather high level of spiritual development is attained. Hence it remains important to employ various means of expression. But if the expression is taken too much in the rigorous or defined sense, the real and deeper Meaning is lost. Therefore, the words of an Illumined Man should never be taken in the literal sense when He is giving a cross-translation from the Beyond. Now, the "plus" quality at first is almost indistinguishable from nothing or emptiness. It is like a breath that has just escaped, a momentary gleam caught from the corner of the eye that disappears when the full focus of sight is turned upon it. It must be reached for very gently, as one must act in seeking the confidence of a defenseless and fearful creature of the wilds. One should reach out almost as though not reaching at all.

A time will come when This that is so very subtle will be transformed into a Presence more palpable and stronger than the toughest granite. It will manifest a Power so great that It will dissolve not only the immediate field but even the whole universe. But the Great Power is rarely in the beginning a clearly dominant force, and It must be assimilated very carefully or It will disappear in the first stages. In the beginning, it may seem that one is walking a tight-rope over unmeasured spaces, and the necessary balance is extremely hard to hold. In the end, the rope becomes all Space, the Supreme Support of all universes but Itself in need of no support. Visible man, in that case, has been transformed and has become the all-containing Matrix. No longer, then, does he struggle to keep his balance on a rope, but he finds Himself everywhere and therefore Invulnerable.

60
The Symbol of the Fourth Dimension

There is a very beautiful and frequently employed analogy to be drawn from mathematics. It is that of the fourth dimension. Certain cross-correlations between subject-object consciousness and the Transcendent Consciousness are made considerably clearer by considering some of the properties of three-dimensioned and four-dimensioned space. While it is true that this symbol may be interpreted in a sense that gives a false impression, still this error may be avoided by divorcing the notion of "dimension" from metrical properties which, strictly considered, are significant only in applied mathematics. I have followed this course in the present discussion.

Subject-object consciousness may be likened unto three-dimensioned space. This relationship becomes clearer when it is realized that this kind of consciousness has three and not merely two aspects. For the sake of brevity I have called it subject-object consciousness, but actually it consists of the three following aspects:

1. The self, or subjective moment of consciousness that is aware of the content of consciousness.

2. The object of awareness that forms the external world, whether in the gross or subtle sense.

3. The awareness itself which occupies an intermediate position and has only a psychical existence.

Further, subject-object consciousness manifests under three types or modes, which I have designated and listed as follows:

1. Sensation. I have employed this term to include all that is directly connected with sense-perception. Thus, for the present purposes, I include not only raw sensation proper but as well "perception" and "recepts" or "generic images." All this is a mode of consciousness below the level of concepts proper, and therefore precedes the stage where language is possible. The dominant characteristic of this mode of consciousness, as commonly experienced, is that it is merely receptive and passive. Any state of consciousness involving a conscious reaction or thinking implies the presence of something more than sensation.

2. Affection. This term I am employing with the full meaning given to it in psychology and ethics, including the voluntary impulses to action that are sometimes called "conation." Thus, it includes all emotions, whether benevolent or malevolent, all passions, and all other impulses to

action. It is not restricted to the popular meaning of "love" alone, but includes, as well, hate, anger, desire, fear, the feeling for justice and beauty, etc. The affections are fundamental essentials of the moral sense and thus are of the very highest importance for religion. But the affections include more than the moral sense as they alone make possible conscious action and reaction in the whole field common to men and animals. Recognition has profound effects upon the affections, but Its effect upon sensation is of minor significance.

3. Cognition. This covers the domain of the conceptual life or understanding proper. Only where cognitive consciousness is awakened is thought and speech possible. It attains its highest degree of isolation from the other two modes in pure mathematical thinking. It is the prime mode in all philosophical and scientific thinking. It is the most important distinguishing mark separating man from the dumb animals. Affection and sensation extend downward over much wider ranges. The power of abstraction is one of the most important properties of cognition.

These three modes cover the field of subject-object consciousness and form the limits of ordinary human awareness. Rarely, if ever, would any concrete state of human consciousness consist of but one of these modes in its purity. But one or the other generally does predominate. Cognitive consciousness is usually maintained only with effort, particularly when there is a reaching toward high levels of thought. The other forms are so deeply habitual that they continue almost, if not quite, automatically, though their higher refinements require effort. Degenerative tendencies, manifested in insanity, show that the cognitive power and the higher affections are lost first, while capacity for sensation continues almost to the end.

It is easy to see that we may speak of human consciousness as three-dimensioned, because of the three aspects and the three modes. In contrast, we might call animal consciousness two-dimensional. The suggestion comes at once that in some way we may correlate the Higher Consciousness with the fourth and even higher dimensions. By so doing, a considerable clarification for the understanding is effected.

In the more common usage, the word "dimension" involves the notions of "extent" and "magnitude," but in the more rigorous thought of pure mathematics these notions are dropped. Here "dimension" has come to mean "degree of freedom." It is in this sense that the notion of "dimension" is of value for the present discussion. But as this usage is not generally familiar, it will be necessary to clarify just what is meant. For example, if a point is confined to all possible positions in a line, it is said to have one degree of freedom. It can occupy an infinite number of positions, but only in the restricted field or region defined by a line. Next, if a point is allowed to occupy positions on a plane or curved surface, it is said to have a two-fold degree of freedom. Thus, if we start with a straight line on a plane, at any point on that line we can draw another line at right angles to it. The number of possible positions on this second line is also infinite, and hence for every single position on the original line we have added an infinite number of new positions. The two-dimensioned world is, therefore, infinitely richer than the one-dimensioned world. It has within it a two-fold infinity of possible positions. By repeating this process we secure ordinary space or the world of threefold freedom, that is, one of infinitely greater possibility than existed in the two-dimensional world. This process can be carried on indefinitely, and this is done in pure mathematics, so that we have not only four dimensions but actually an unlimited number of dimensions, for there is no logical stopping point. But, for our present purposes, we will go no further than the addition of the fourth dimension, i.e., the space or world having a four-fold degree of freedom.

A very important point to be noted is that while all the relationships expressed by "degree of freedom" may be correlated with points in an extended space, the extension is not essential to the idea. The same relationships may be expressed by abstract numbers alone, without attaching to the numbers the meaning of measurement at all. Thus we are dealing with notions that are far more fundamental than the notions of either extended space or time.

As is true with every symbol, the formal relationships involved in the above notions become significant by attaching to them the appropriate interpretation. Let us consider, then, what we will mean by "degree of freedom" and by the phrase "an infinitely greater freedom."

"Degree of freedom" will mean here the elaboration of all possible states of a given consciousness-mode, such as sensation. Every possible sensation or combinations of sensations, including percepts and recepts, will form one dimension or degree of freedom in consciousness. As we can place no limits upon these elaborations in their own direction, we regard their total possibility as a one-fold infinity. Sensation, together with affection, would give a two-fold infinity, while sensation, affection, and cognition would give a three-fold infinity.

"An infinitely greater freedom" carries the meaning that the elaborations in the sense of a higher dimension cannot be expressed in terms of lower dimensions. Thus, every step from one group of dimensions to the next larger one involves a transcendence that is equivalent to entering an infinitely greater world.

However, cross-representation from the world of a higher degree of freedom to a lower one is possible in a sense, and this is analogous to what is called "projection" in mathematics. Thus a three-dimensional configuration, such as a bridge, a building, etc., can be projected upon a two-dimensional field, such as a sheet of drawing paper, in such a way that an engineer can construct the bridge or building from the drawing and may determine the forms of all his materials before a stroke of physical work is done. But there are certain important things that can be done with the actual constructed object, a bridge, for instance, that cannot be done with the simple plan of it. Thus an automobile can travel across a real bridge but cannot cross on a two-dimensional drawing. This means that the three-dimensional actuality has something that can never be captured within the limits of any two-dimensional representation, however completely the latter may be elaborated.

This leads to the point where we are enabled to apply our symbol. Here the fourth dimension represents the Higher Consciousness, by whatever name we may know It, such as Cosmic Consciousness, Specialism, Christ Consciousness, Transcendental Consciousness, Nirvana, etc. We may call this dimension "Profundity." Now, the actuality of Profundity can be realized only by Awakening in the direction of this Fourth Dimension. It may be "projected" downward into the three-dimensional field of sensation-affection-cognition, but this projection is not any more the actuality of Profundity than the descriptive plan of a bridge is the bridge itself. But as an engineer by the aid of his peculiar knowledge can employ such a plan to construct an actual bridge, so also through the more or less aroused Consciousness of Profundity a man can use a projected expression from out of the Fourth Dimension to derive values in terms of the Higher Consciousness. In this way, even a latent Consciousness of Profundity may be stirred to life.

The sum-total of all possible Higher Consciousness may well involve many dimensions, perhaps an unlimited number, but for mankind, in general, the next step is well represented by the Fourth Dimension.

A very important point to note is that the birth from a narrower dimensionality to a higher is not conditional upon the complete exhaustion of every possibility on the lower level. Man has unfolded on both the sensation and affectional dimensions more than any animal, but much of this has become possible to him just because of the superior advantages he possessed by reason of being cognitively awake. Thus, sensuous art requires, in addition to sensuous capacity, a considerable development of affection and cognition. In fact, great art requires a special development of the affections. Likewise, a high development of character, of the love-nature, or of the moral side of man, requires the cooperation of the cognitive dimension. Any one of these three dimensions may be the most highly developed in an individual man, but the distinguishing mark which separates a man from an animal is the presence of the cognitive capacity, or that power which, among other things, makes rational thought and language possible. A man does not differ from an animal because he *has* affections, for animals as well as men can and do know love, loyalty, passion, anger, etc. But through the combination with cognition, man has increased the possibilities of the affections enormously beyond the highest possibility of any animal. As a matter of fact, it is only a minority of men whose highest excellence is in the pure cognitive dimension, while the majority excel in the affectional or sensational dimensions. The important point is that the lesser wakening which separates a man from an animal and the greater Awakening which separates or distinguishes a God-Man from the ordinary man involves the arousing of an entirely new capacity. Degree of development in terms of the new capacity is a matter of evolution on a higher level, but that which distinguishes an animal, a man, and a God-Man is not a question of *degree*, but of *awakening* to a new dimension of consciousness.

Now, just as awakening to cognitive capacity enormously enriches development in terms of sensation and affection, so also the Awakening to Higher Consciousness tremendously augments the capacity in the already partially unfolded inferior dimensions. The result is that the greater portion of the best in religion, morals, art, philosophy, science, etc., has come from the hands or lips of those Men who have had this Higher Awakening in at least some degree. Here is an effect that the man limited to three dimensions of consciousness can in some measure evaluate and appreciate, even though the Key Power is as yet beyond his understanding. In fact, two of the earmarks of the Illumined Man are afforded by an increase, amounting sometimes almost to a revolution, in the intellectual and affectional functions or dimensions. Now, an animal may well recognize that somehow man can excel it in its own field, as is revealed by the fact that man is a far more dangerous killer than the most predatory animal, but the animal has no idea of the key that gives man that peculiar power. Likewise, ordinary subject-object conscious man, however much he may appreciate the superior excellence of the God-Conscious Man in the former's field, is utterly unconscious of, or blind to, the Key that unlocks the latter's Power. As has been repeated over and over again, man must Awake to understand this, and it is quite useless for him to try to circumscribe that Awakening by attempting to divine what It actually is. When something of It is suggested, as in the present case, by the use of an analogy or symbol, It is not being circumscribed in the sense involved in all effective definition.

I wish again to call attention to the fact that the notion of "dimension" as employed in this discussion is taken in the sense characteristic in pure mathematics. Dimension, conceived as "degree of freedom," involves the notion of "manifoldness," but not necessarily that of measurement or metrical property. Strictly considered, measurement belongs only to applied mathematics where extension is pertinent, since it is a property of physical matter. Thus the first three dimensions, as well as the fourth, do not logically introduce the notion of measurement or extension. The manifolds may be given a purely qualitative interpretation, and thus the difficulty involved in thinking of four dimensions of extension is avoided. But the notion of manifoldness is essential and primary. Without this there could be no evolution nor differentiation in any sense on any level. In fact, we could regard all space in the extended sense as merely an illusion, and yet retain the whole of pure mathematics, with all its richness of diversified development remaining unaffected. Verily, if the reader can break down the power which the notion of extension has over his own mind, he will have gone a long way in preparing himself for the Awakening.

61
The Nature of Ponderable Matter

September 15

A couple of weeks prior to the 7th of last August, the final correlation in the development of an idea broke through into my mind. This idea had such a clarifying effect, relative to the nature of the phenomenal world, that it was decisive in clearing up the remaining intellectual barriers to Recognition. As this correlation was of high importance in my own case, it may prove to be of similar value to others, and in addition may have systematic objective significance. Accordingly, I shall strive to give it a clear formulation.

What is the nature of the phenomenal world? The non-critical Naturalist says that it is the actual "thing" itself, existing quite independently of the perceiving subject. He goes further and says, not only is it self-dependent apart from the observer, but it is, as well, substantially as it appears to be to the observer. But all philosophy that has attained any degree of the critical sense, as well as modern science, agrees that the facts force a modification of this naive view. Genuine philosophers concur in holding that whatever the real world may be, it is at least modified by the senses so that what man directly experiences is something different. Also, for the twentieth century physicist, ponderable matter, that is, matter and form as given through the senses, is definitely known not to be the actual physical reality. The ultimates of matter are apparently wave-systems of essentially the same nature as electromagnetic or light waves; and, further, these systems cannot be correctly imaged in any sensible model. Only mathematical equations are capable of representing the reality, whatever that may be, in a manner that is consonant with the observed effects.

Closely connected with modern science and mathematics, a school of philosophy has developed in which the world is conceived as composed of externally real existences, but these existences are viewed as other than their sensible appearance. This school is known as Neo-Realism. This philosophy is highly technical and acutely logical, and thus fundamentally quite beyond the understanding of any reader who is not well versed in modern studies on the foundations of mathematics. But for our present purposes only one point is of decisive importance in determining our relationship to this school. This school is in agreement with Naturalism in regarding Consciousness as irrelevant to Actuality. Things are regarded as being what they are, quite independently of any observer or thinker.

If either the Naturalistic or the Neo-Realistic views were the true one, there would be no meaning attaching to such words as "Recognition," "Higher Consciousness," the "Awakening," the notion of the "Self sustaining the universe," "Cosmic Consciousness," etc., except in a merely psychological sense. Neo-Realism, as well as Naturalism, denies that there is such a thing as a Metaphysical Reality, at any rate in the ontological sense. Our own standpoint is necessarily quite at variance with either of the foregoing schools. While we recognize that Neo-

Realism offers much of unquestionable value as a partial view of the sum-total of all possibilities of consciousness, yet we must challenge it as a system claiming exclusive validity.

It is not our present purpose to attempt a systematic criticism of Neo-Realism, but only to make clear that a challenge of that philosophy is implied by practically everything that this book contains. We may, at a later time, undertake a general criticism of Neo-Realism as well as other philosophies that occupy a position that is not compatible with our own, but such critical work is necessarily rather technical, and so does not properly belong here. At this time we merely wish to clarify our own philosophic position in the reader's mind and acknowledge the existence of the critical problem.

Both in India and the West, systematic philosophies exist wherein the ultimate Reality is posited as being pure Consciousness. The apparently inert and lifeless matter comes to be viewed as merely a partially obscured Consciousness. Thus, if we regard a portion of an originally homogeneous Consciousness as partly blanked-out or neutralized by its own other, the result is some degree of relative unconsciousness. This relative unconsciousness is the objective world, or, in other words, the basis of the whole universe as experienced through the senses. An extensive restatement of philosophy and science can be given from this standpoint, but this also is not our present purpose. I desire simply to emphasize the most important ontological features of this view. Now one decisively important consequence of this standpoint is that the experienced universe, including all ponderable matter and form, is essentially an abstraction from, rather than an addition to, the original unmanifested Reality. Starting from an original and eternal non-relative Consciousness, which comprehends time and space as well as all else, all notions such as external manifestation and development must be in the nature of a predication concerning something abstracted or subtracted from the Whole. Among other things, it is clear that nothing can be predicated of the Whole which necessarily presupposes the dominance of time, as for example, process or development. The Whole, since It comprehends space and time, is not conditioned by these. In the end, we find that no relative concept—and all concepts are relative—can be predicated of the Whole, not even Being. In fact, It is THAT which is neither Being nor non-Being, and thus remains essentially unthinkable, though It may be Realized through the Awakening to Identification.

It may now be said that the universe is produced by a process which we may call a partial blinding, and that the reverse process, i.e., that of Awakening, destroys the universe to just the extent that the Awakening has proceeded. This should make perfectly clear the rationale of the statement of the Mystic who says: "I sustain this universe and can produce or destroy it at will." When Shankara speaks of destroying the universe, he does not have in mind a physical cataclysm but a Transition in Consciousness such that the apperceptive Subject realizes Itself as Lord over the universe, instead of being a victim of it. The individual soul that has attained this position may choose continued cognizance of the universe, but the essential power of the latter over the former is destroyed unequivocally.

If, now, we substitute for the term "relative unconsciousness" another term which is fundamentally equivalent, i.e., "ponderable matter and form," we may give the foregoing philosophy a transformation that fits more closely the terminology of modern science. This leads to the judgment that ponderable matter and form constitute a state of relative vacuity or nothingness in the essential sense. It is interesting to note that we are now not far from a position formulated by the young English physicist Dirac, though he reached this view by means of a quite different approach. There is nothing in this standpoint that militates against the relative correctness of any physical determination. The only thing that is changed is the metaphysical interpretation of what those determinations Mean. There is in this no challenge of the scientist, so long as he confines his conclusions to the limits logically defined by his methodology. He remains our best authority in the determination of objective fact as seen from the perspective he assumes. If he generalizes beyond these limits, we need no more than his own logic to bring a counter-challenge. This logic, followed strictly, can go no further than agnosticism relative to metaphysical actuality, and We are content that as physical scientist he should stop there. But We are not content that, as a man, he should linger in that position, for it is barren of enduring Values.

Let us give an illustration of how our standpoint would affect the interpretation of a fundamentally important principle of physics. Long ago our science reached the point where it realized that the vast bulk of the sensible effects associated with matter do not afford the essential determinants of matter. As now understood, "matter" is defined by "mass," and this in turn is manifested through the property called "inertia." Thus, where there is matter there is inertia, and where there is inertia there is matter. Newton gave the law of inertia in the following form: "Every body perseveres in its state of rest or of uniform motion in a straight line, except insofar as it is compelled to change that state by impressed forces." The mechanics of Einstein gives this law a different form but does not change its essential characteristic. Now, inertia implies absence of inward or self-produced motion, and hence it also implies essential deadness. In contrast, the fundamental distinguishing mark of Consciousness is the capacity for Self-produced motion. Thus it is that Universal Consciousness is often represented by the term "Ceaseless Motion." But, from this standpoint, the state of relative motion as well as that of rest in a material body, mechanically considered, is simply the absence of *real* motion. Where Consciousness is full, there is no inertia. Only absolute absence of Consciousness—a state of real nothingness—would be absolutely inert. Thus, we would say, the physicist is right in making inertia the prime mark of that which he is studying, but he is wrong if he proceeds to predicate substantial reality of his object of study. Actually he is studying a relative nothingness. This fact does not detract in the least from the practical values of his studies, but simply means that he is dealing with the obverse of metaphysical actuality. Further, once it is realized that he is unfolding the laws governing the obverse of the Real, his knowledge can be employed as a Way to the Recognition of that Reality. I can see how our present physical science is unfolding a peculiarly beautiful Path to Yoga. So I certainly have no quarrel with physical science as such. In fact, I feel quite otherwise.

Today physicists have found that at least much of force is not external to matter. In radio-activity there is an element of unpredictable spontaneity that certainly looks like what We mean by self-produced motion, or energy arising from within. The result is that matter is now seen as not wholly inert, all of which simply opens wider a Door for Us.

Let us, then, take the standpoint that ponderable matter, or the sensuously perceived world, is to be regarded as relative emptiness, so that absolute matter in this sense would be an absolute vacuum. We then see that the relative world, or this seen universe, is produced by a kind of process of negation, and hence from the standpoint of metaphysical philosophy it would have to be regarded as a Maya or Illusion. From this it is not to be concluded that the universe is without value. But it does imply that if a man misplaces his predication of "Reality," he would then be caught in an illusion in the sense that produces bondage. None the less, it would still remain true that if he avoids this error he can, through the universe, find the Real. Most of humanity has fallen into the error, and that is the cause of all suffering. But the very agency that caused the fall may be used as a stepping-stone to Recognition. To achieve this, a certain Copernican shift in individual consciousness is necessary. Thus, instead of regarding the sensuously apparent as being substantial, the standpoint should be reversed. Then we would view the seeming emptiness of space, where there is a relative absence of physical matter, as being actually far more substantial than any ponderable matter. We would thus say: *Increase of ponderability implies decrease of substantiality and vice versa.* Consequently, in some sense, the laws governing the ponderable become the obverse of the laws governing the substantial.

The foregoing discussion gives us a new angle for interpreting the meaning of the technique designed to arouse Recognition by the systematic denial of all that is ponderable or thinkable. The end of the process is the arrival at a *seeming* nothingness, i.e., pure Consciousness-without-an-object. This stage, plus the identification of one's Self with that *seeming* nothingness, produces at once the Recognition. But at that moment the Nothingness becomes complete Fullness and absolute Substantiality. Then the Realized Man may turn toward the world and assert universally: "I am all things." But now it is the obverse of the ponderable universe of which he is speaking. We may regard this obverse as something like a matrix. This Matrix is a continuum, while the ponderable manifold is discrete. So far as we can see, this resolves the difficulties in the reconciliation between the many and the One in the logical sense. Actually, for myself, this view was the finally effective cognitive aid that made possible the Transition in consciousness.

★ ★ ★

I believe that in the foregoing I have discovered a new elaboration in the technique for arousing Recognition. It does not demand the radical silencing of the thought processes. However, in my own case, I did employ silencing in a different sense, i.e., in silencing the affections, so that at the crucial moment there was a high order of calmness. There was cognitive activity, but it was so nearly purely cognitive that it was highly dispassionate. The cognitive action was exceptionally keenly discriminative, but it had to be maintained on the outer side only very briefly until something very deep and strong took hold inwardly, and thereafter the activity centered in the personal consciousness ceased to have any really effective obscuring power. It is as though the whole complex nature of the organized man were, from that moment, entrained behind a commanding Power that dominated from then onward. The result is that I do not seem to feel troubled by the residual habits in the personal man that have grown out of the past. There is something more or less automatic in the progressive transformation of them.

62
Real Equality

We are now in a position to attach a valid meaning to the idea of "equality." It is perfectly clear that in the relative or phenomenal sense, no two things, persons, or creatures are equal, one to the other. In fact, of all the milliards of concrete states of consciousness, no two are actual duplicates, and, therefore, no two are equal. The notions of equality and inequality involve measurement, in some sense, and thus equality implies that all measurable aspects of one thing are precisely the same as those of another or of others. We do find such equality in mathematics, but not in the sensible world. Further, the notion of "equality" is incompatible with the notions of "development" and "freedom." For, if there is such a thing as growth, and if self-determinism has any effect upon it, then not all entities would develop in precisely the same way or to the same degree, even though at the hypothetical initial stage there were absolute equality. But if we turn from the phenomenal world to the Matrix of all relative things, creatures, men, etc., it at once becomes apparent that the Matrix of a blade of grass is equal to the Matrix of a man or of a planet. For the Matrix, taken in the inmost sense, is the universal homogeneous Plenum. But even here, in strict logic, we should not predicate "equality" but rather negate "inequality," since in the Great Continuum, measurement is irrelevant.

One consequence follows at once, that true Democracy exists only for God-Realized Men. All others, being as yet bound to the relative or subject-object world, do actually stand on a scaled ladder, marking the different stages of achieved development. We can thus see how Carpenter was right in calling his poem "Towards Democracy." It is simply one way of saying "Towards Recognition." Consequently, this Democracy properly has nothing to do with what is possible here and now in the matter of government, men being what they are. So he who would bring about a true democracy in the world, instead of the spurious kind which alone is known to history, should work toward the spread of Recognition among men.

There are only two senses in which it may be said that men are born equal. In the first place, all men, and as well all things from an atom to a star, are equal in the sense that at the heart of everything is the one unchanging and indivisible Spirit. In the second place, all men are equal in the bare fact that to be a man a creature must have awakened into consciousness on the cognitive level. But in the degree of relative development of powers, in any sense, no two men are equal. Further, no two men unfold during life their initial possibilities in exactly equal degree. Thus in the relative sense, there can be no equality among men.

The fundamental fact of the empiric inequality of men does have a vital bearing upon the problem of what kind of organization of society can endure effectively. Institutions built upon a false premise cannot really endure nor can they function effectively. No formulation of a law made by man can change this fact. Nature is what it is, and propaganda to the contrary can merely produce an illusion. Visible man is what he is, and not what an idealist may imagine him to be or wish him to be. Ultimately sound government must orient itself to actualities, however much administrators may labor toward an Ideal.

63
The Predicament of Buddha

September 16

I turn to the *Gospel of Buddha* and find these words: "He—the worldling—will call resignation what to the Enlightened One is purest Joy. He will see annihilation where the Perfected One finds Immortality. He will regard as death what the Conqueror of Self knows to be Life Everlasting."

According to the record, this was said soon after Gautama had attained Enlightenment under the Bodhi tree. At first the Tathagata was tempted to keep silence, for it seemed useless to preach a Message of Liberation which certainly could not be understood by most men. In the end, Buddha decided to give the Message for the benefit of those who could understand. But the problem He faced is a very fundamental one, since it is very difficult for the man who is bound to subject-object consciousness to conceive of another kind of Life where egoism ceases. The average man can imagine a heaven or a hell built upon the subject-object pattern where life is more intense, whether in a pleasurable or painful sense, but the truly Emancipated Life is beyond his comprehension. The Christian world has interpreted the Kingdom of Heaven as simply a sublimated subject-object domain, and thus quite missed the real meaning of Jesus. Christ brought a Message of Emancipation, just as Buddha did, and Its meaning was exactly the same, though stated in a form to fit the consciousness of a different people. Few, indeed, of the Christian world have ever truly understood His meaning. A subject-object world experienced after physical death as a highly blissful state is not Liberation. Essentially it is not different from this present world right here. Consequently such a world could be represented in terms of conceptual language just as this is. But such is not the case with respect to Nirvana or the Kingdom of Heaven.

The impossibility of genuinely formulating and conveying to others what the Liberated State is is not simply the difficulty afforded in trying to give expression to an unfamiliar experience. The problem, in the latter case, may be great but it is not, in principle, beyond solution. It is simply a question of inventing the appropriate concepts and word-signs, and this can be done by men who are sufficiently skillful. But the kind of consciousness that falls outside the subject-object field is more than difficult to express in relative terms. It is absolutely impossible to do so. It is not simply a question of our not yet having developed sufficient skill. The impossibility inheres in the fact that the subject-object form, essential to language as such, can only distort the Transcendent. The "Kingdom of Heaven" and "Nirvana" are simply names pointing to a deathless Reality. But that Reality is ever something other than anything that can be conceived in relative terms. Hence it is the negation of everything we know in the subject-object sense. Thus, It is not-evil and not-good, not-large and not-small, not-colored and not-colorless, and so on through all pairs of opposites. More than this, It is not-good and not not-good, not-large and not not-large, not-colored and not not colored, and so on, also, through all pairs of contradictories. This means that It is not to be found anywhere in the "universe of discourse," as understood in logic. Naturally, this must appear as annihilation to the subject-object consciousness.

Yet, in point of fact, It is Infinite Life. It is pure Joy, the utterly satisfying Richness. It is the absolutely certain Knowledge. But It can be Known only through Identity. Once It is Known, even though it be for but a moment, then It is realized as the one and only adequate solution of human misery. More than that, It supplies the basis which, alone, affords an adequate solution of the final problems of philosophy and science. The combined testimony of Those who have attained Realization builds well the case for the Reality of this Transcendent World, and something deep in the heart of every man whispers: "Yes, it is so." If only men would listen to this still, small Voice !

But man must be born again before he can Know. And He who is born again is There, whether or not He remains correlated with embodiment in the relative world. In being born again, he has died to subject-object consciousness, in the essential sense, even though he continues to function in this field. He has died in a far more fundamental sense than is true of the worldly man who merely departs from the physical body. The latter type of transition does not lead out of the subject-object domain. But the Great Transition leads beyond the ordinary heaven and hell, just as much as it does beyond this world.

That which man overcomes finally in the Great Transition is the vehicle of egoism. This is an entirely different matter from that of merely losing the instruments of action and of relative knowledge in a particular one of consciousness.

64
The Adept World

A rarely discussed question that arises is: "When all the units of mankind are finally Awakened, will the values of the subject-object consciousness be abandoned in every sense?" Theoretically such could be the case, but it is not necessarily so. Between the subject-object world and Nirvana or the Kingdom of Heaven there exists a domain, creatively produced, in which there abides a rare Community of Liberated Souls. Here the Real Man is embedded in the Transcendent, and yet He acts in the subject-object sense. The Members of this Community in part act for the redemption of the still-sleeping mankind, but even supposing this labor of love completed—and some day it will be—yet They will continue to act in the pursuance of a larger and longer-enduring purpose. This is the Great Domain of genuine creativeness. Here abides the Hierarchy of real manifested life, which rises in grandeur from minor levels up to modes of informed Consciousness so vast as to transcend the comprehension of even the greatest Adept.

This is a sort of Life which is more within the range of imagination and appreciation of the subject-object man than the pure Liberated State. There exists an Initiation wherein man may make a choice between this Life and pure Liberation. This kind of Life retains the essential values of the subject-object consciousness, though it is rooted in the Transcendent, and consciously so. There are many Worlds beyond—many possibilities—most of which are quite outside the capacity of the imagination of the present humanity. But Liberation is the Key to these Worlds, and thus it is said that Liberation is not the end but the beginning of Real Life. Liberation is the Goal to be envisaged by the once-born, subject-object man, but when he attains that State, He is twice-born and then faces alternative possibilities, one of which is continued expression through a Life that is real in the objective sense, though something quite different from the life in the familiar subject-object domain.

We have here taken a step beyond the usual occidental interpretation of the Nirmanakayas. The latter are those Men who have won to Nirvana, or the Kingdom of Heaven, and refused to "enter in" fully. Hence They remain embodied, though in a sense too lofty for the grasp of the ordinary understanding. Their choice of that course of action has been portrayed as due to a Compassion for the humanity that remains behind. But it is further stated that this involves a real Renunciation. This is only part of the story. The refusal of Nirvana opens the Way to the ascending Hierarchy of the World Builders—an Hierarchy which reaches upward to the stars and systems of stars. But, in a sense, that is a Life both in and outside of Nirvana. It is grounded in the Divine Indifference, which is as truly a manifested as a not-manifested State.

65
Manifestation without Evil

Any action, in the subject-object sense, does imply duality or polarity, but it is not essential that any particular manifested world shall arouse all possible dualities. In fact, even in this world, as we progress in our knowledge, we discover new dualities and perhaps create dualities that do not appear in the old cultures. The implication is that there is unlimited possibility in such dualistic expression. Other worlds may have dualistic forms utterly unknown to us, and we in our turn have forms quite unknown to them. Thus, at present, worlds may be existent or may become existent wherein the duality of good and evil simply does not exist. It is said that such is the case. Mayhap man may leave evil behind him forever and yet remain an actor in the objective sense. This opens up some interesting possibilities and shows how there may be an objective life which at the same time remains one of continuous happiness.

66
The One Element

Once one has had a glimpse of the Consciousness which I have called the High Indifference, it readily becomes clear that there can be but one ultimate Element. Spirit is not divided from matter in any final sense. This is simply the truth concerning the subject and the object, given in other terms. In that State where I realize Myself as identical with all space and with all objects, there is no division between an "I" and a "not-I." This is equivalent to saying there is but one Element. But the same thing cannot be said concerning the seeming relationships within the shell of the subject-object consciousness. For here the subject has the appearing of being different from the object, but these two stand in some relationship to each other. Likewise, here spirit and matter appear as though divided in some relationship, rather than united. Thus there is a sense in which the Sankhya dualism is valid. There is no transcending the dualism within the shell. It now becomes clear why the notion of only one Element misses the understanding of him who has not yet broken out of the shell, and also why "Spirit" seems to require a definition that delimits It by saying, "Whatever Spirit is, It is other than matter." It is not correct to say that Spirit becomes matter, and vice versa, within the limits of the subject-object manifold.

67
The Current of Numberless Dimensions

Before me there streams a Great Current of unnumbered dimensions.
This is the High Indifference of All in all,
Producing, sustaining, and consuming all;
Utter and eternal Completeness, the End and the Beginning and the Mid-point.
Within this Current, eddies, swirls, and grand sweeps, blended together.
These, the worlds, the stars, and systems manifold, yet continuous.
Within their midst, a few vortices, hard-cased, seemingly separate.
Therein, consciousness bound in separateness and misery.
There also, this world, forlorn orphan, sick and weary;
Snare of Mara, who, triumphant for a season,
Makes the unreal seem the real, meshing in bondage.
But Time! and the shell will crack,
Flowing on in the eternal gyrations;
Sorrow becoming Joy, and Ignorance transformed into Wisdom.

68
Concerning Duty

September 17

To the merely egoistic man, duty appears as in some sense an external constraint. It is a mode of conduct, as defined by the civil law, by the religious authority, by the social body of which he is a member, or by his own rational judgment. Impulses arising from the different aspects of the human nature are often at variance with the pronouncements of such duty. The result is a battle in the man between something that he calls "lower" and something else which he feels is "higher." Duty comes as an imposed discipline and implies more or less hardship although, in general, the fruit of faithfully performed duty is a sense of "having done well." As a rule, in the end, this feeling more than offsets the hardship. But it is unquestionably true that the urge to freedom, naturally great in some men, leads to restiveness under the sway of duty. It is also true that, among the variously imposed duties, there is very often an incompatibility, so that if the individual acts in faithful accordance with a given duty, he at the same time violates the requirements of another. This may happen even within the field of duties which the individual himself freely recognizes as proper. So it is impossible to say of a life confined strictly within the path of duty that it is free from conflict.

In the case of an Awakened Man, "duty" undergoes a radical transformation. Duty ceases to be or, more properly, progressively ceases to have the character of something externally imposed, even in the sense in which we may say that a man's own theoretical judgment of right and wrong is external. On this higher level, duty becomes the spontaneous impulse that flows out of the Illumined Consciousness, so that here the conflict between duty and impulse vanishes. From the standpoint of Illumination, the desired thing to do is the right thing to do. As a consequence, in one sense, the Illumined Man, while He is acting or judging in the Current of Illumination, is beyond duty. But this is true only so long as we give to "duty" the connotation of "something externally imposed." However, in some usages, the meaning of "duty" has been extended to cover a wider connotation than this.

"Duty" has been employed as a translation of the Sanskrit term "Dharma." Now, "Dharma" carries a meaning for which there is no adequate English equivalent, though "duty" carries a portion of that meaning. However, the inadequacy of this translation is made clear in the following illustration. It is perfectly proper to say: "It is the dharma of fire to burn." But if we substitute "duty" for "dharma" and say, "It is the duty of fire to burn," the effect is quite false with respect to the primary meaning we attach to the word "duty." In a similar sense, it is perfectly true that it is the Dharma of the God-Conscious Man to act in accordance with the Divine Impulse that springs up in Him. Clearly this Dharma is not an external constraint as it is at-one with an interior and Divine impulse. Such a Man is happy when acting in accordance with Dharma, and not otherwise. If, now, we agree to give to "duty" just precisely the meaning attached to "Dharma" then, it remains true, the Illumined Man does not transcend duty. But in this case, "duty" would cease to have the connotation of an external constraint.

The problem in connection with the word "duty" is psychological and emotional rather than rational. Intellectually we can say, "Let 'duty' have the connotation of 'Dharma'," and then proceed to use it in the changed sense. I have done this myself for some time and find no hardship in the notion of "duty," the only difficulty being the definition of just what the duty is in a given complex situation where different canons of action come into conflict. When a clear definition emerged, I always felt happy, but much of the time I found it difficult to attain that clarity. However, I find that many individuals are unable to overcome a certain negative emotional complex centering around the word "duty." So I suggest that we take over into our language the term "Dharma," as we have already assimilated many Latin and Greek words, and use it to cover the meaning for which "duty" is admittedly inadequate. From an electron to a God there is no creature beyond Dharma, but there is a level where duty is transcended, when understood in the usual sense.

It is a mistake to think that the Dharma of even the God-Conscious Man is without problems. As God-Conscious, His impulse is His Dharma, and thus there is no emotional conflict. But the question "What does that Dharma mean in practical action?" is quite another matter. Absolute solutions of relative problems, outside of mathematics, do not exist. The Higher Consciousness is certain on Its own Level; It does effect an enormous clarification of insight on the subject-object level; and It always manifests as an intent to effect the highest good of all; but in all dealings with human beings, unknown variables are involved, even from the perspective of high Adepts. As a consequence, Illumination by no means implies infallible action in the subject-object field. So there always remains the practical problem, which we may state in the form of the question, "What course in action best manifests the inwardly recognized Dharma?" Naturally, for the solution of this problem, the Illumined Man who has, in addition to His Illumination, a broad rational understanding of the science of ethics is also best equipped for making lofty intent to manifest as wise action.

Another important point which should be remembered is the fact that rarely if ever is the personality of the God-Conscious Man enveloped in the full Light of the Higher Consciousness at all times. Generally the period of the envelopment is brief, sometimes of only momentary duration, and in many cases it happens but once in a lifetime. Much of the time, even in the cases of Men who have Known a high order of Illumination, the consciousness sinks more or less into the subject-object field, with a corresponding obscuration of the insight. The lesser impulses, which have their ground in the subject-object man, are not completely transformed in one moment, although the purification of them proceeds progressively. There remains, therefore, a practical need for discrimination among the complex of all impulses that may arise. He who has had even no more than one moment of Illumination does have a modulus for such discrimination, and that gives Him a decisive advantage over other men. But nevertheless He has not transcended the need for discrimination in practical action.

69
Philosophic Reconciliations

One of the striking changes I find in my own consciousness is a marked increase in the capacity to see reconciliations between ideas that ordinarily seem quite incompatible. From my present perspective, I see a great deal of truth in all of the philosophical views that have come before me, with the possible exception of naive Naturalism. At the same time, it does not seem that any philosophy has succeeded in saying the final word. When translated into words, I find that the Recognition takes on a form that is fundamentally idealistic, a view of the Whole which gives primacy to Consciousness. I know of no report from the level of Mystical Consciousness that does not concur in this, and thus, in general, Mysticism does challenge all materialistic schools in the ontological sense. Yet it cannot be denied that even the materialistic outlook does have some relative value.

But within the idealistic group, my own spontaneous expression accords far more closely with rational monism than with the dualistic or voluntaristic systems of idealism. At this point there is no longer an agreement among those who have attained the mystic insight, though the preponderant expression tends toward monism in some sense. We have here to recognize the fact that the form which Realization takes when expressed in the subject-object world is determined by the predilections of the individual man, as these already exist at the time of the Realization. Recognition adds something that is held in common in all instances; but, inasmuch as no individual personality is itself universal, every expression is at best but a facet reflecting the Truth as near as may be. It would seem but the part of wisdom for each individual to recognize this fact and then be true to himself in the personal as well as the Higher sense.

As one who, by temperament and natural inclination, stands close to rational Idealism, it was inevitable that in the past I should have come into conflict with the main thesis of the Pragmatists, inasmuch as the latter have generally sought to establish themselves, first of all, by a challenge of the validity of rational Idealism. William James gives as one of the primary postulates of Pragmatism the principle, "There is no difference of truth that does not make a difference of fact somewhere." This criterion is then repeatedly employed to challenge the view of rational Idealism. I submit my own Recognition as an instance which controverts this challenge. I mounted to the Moment of the Transition in the framework of rational Idealism, and the critical step hinged upon the isolation of the pure apperceptive moment of consciousness itself. Thus Truth, as conceived by rational Idealism of the monistic type, did effect a difference of fact for me. The difference of fact is a new relationship to the subject-object consciousness and a state of far greater peace and happiness than had been known previously. But the cause of this "difference in fact" was not an experience but the attainment of "Knowledge through Identity," which, as I have already pointed out, is neither experience nor formal knowledge but a third kind of knowledge.

From the foregoing a partial reconciliation seems to follow. The Pragmatists are right in asserting that formal knowledge is not enough to determine effective or final Truth, but they are wrong in asserting that such Truth, or the knowledge of it, must depend upon experience. On the other hand, the rational Idealists are right in maintaining that the effective Truth must be absolute and, therefore, cannot be derived from experience, which of necessity must be finite. But they are wrong in so far as they claim to be able to establish this Truth by formal demonstration alone. The effective establishment of this Truth requires "Knowledge through Identity," i.e., a direct Recognition on the level of Infinity, which is never attainable by any expansion of experience alone.

70
Recognition as an Act of Transcendence

I cannot too strongly emphasize the fact that Recognition is not a natural result of simple growth or expansion in the subject-object field. It is an act of Transcendence, whereby a Man Awakens to find that, instead of being finite, He is an Infinite Being, has always been so, and always will be so. For a time his consciousness had been obscured and it seemed as though he were a finite being, but in one moment a finite world is destroyed in an essential sense. In principle, he may Awaken regardless of whether he has had much or little experience in a finite world, or of whether he may be highly or imperfectly evolved in the subject-object sense. Practically, it is a rule that a certain superiority of individual development is the antecedent condition of success. But this is so simply because it takes strength to resist the hypnotic effect of the subject-object field. However, it is not an invariable rule. Unquestionably, the Awakened Man of superior individual development after the Transition can offer more to His companions who remain bound within the relative world than is possible in the case of a man of inferior capacity. But all this has to do with expression and not with the fundamental nature of Recognition as such.

The Awakening, when viewed from the relative perspective, is a "being-born," and a "being born" is a "dying" to the antecedent condition. It is useless to try to dodge this fact. It is simply the anciently uttered and repeatedly formulated Law: "The self of matter and the Self of Spirit cannot meet." I have already explained how the Twice-Born has died to the ordinary life, and yet continues to act through the form of embodied consciousness in an entirely different sense from that which had obtained prior to the Transition. Now the antecedent condition of Awakening to THAT, is a dying to this, in a mystical sense. This is the rational basis of true asceticism. The asceticism may be a conscious and deliberate discipline, or its value may come through accepting what life brings with resignation. But for either to be effective there must be a turning to the Higher Life or, in other words, Aspiration. Now, after the ascetic discipline has finished its work and the new Birth has been accomplished, the old rules cease to be relevant. The new Life is Free, and the course of action in the subject-object world is Self-chosen.

★ ★ ★

Note: It has been drawn to my attention that the idea of the antecedent death, preceding the Second Birth, is a notion easily misunderstood and repellent to many natures. Perhaps the idea could be made clearer by noting the fact that it is a dying to what is already a state of relative death, when considered from the metaphysical or eternal standpoint. It is thus a case of a double negative giving a positive. This mystic death is not death of the body, nor the destruction of any principle or function in the constitution of human consciousness, though it does initiate a progressive spiritualization of those principles. In one sense, it is death of *attachment* to matter, or to the world as object. In a deeper sense, it is death of personal egoism. It is entirely useless to cavil at this for we are dealing with a Law of the Higher Nature that has been made clear, at least since the time of Gautama Buddha. To disguise this Law as a concession to psychological prejudice does not change the fact of its actuality. If a man would become consciously immortal, he must die to mortality. The fruit is abiding Joy and Life Everlasting.

71
The Record Continued

I find that, as the days go by, there is a re-organization and consolidation of life about a new center. The thrill of new Awakening, that at first so dominates and sweeps the personal consciousness, gradually becomes a quiet steadiness on a level of new confidence. I cannot say that I feel any regret for the old life. I do not find any inhibition that would restrain me from dipping into any phase of old experience if I desired and found it convenient to do so. I do not feel the restless urge for outer adventure that formerly I felt so strongly. Not that I cease to feel joy in the wild places, but the service that they rendered does not seem to be nearly so important. On the whole, outer interests generally have become quiescent in the presence of an all-consuming interest in a new activity. Still I do not anticipate that I have turned my back on nature entirely. I shall gladly receive the caress of the wilds when convenience makes that possible.

Most of the ordinary activities in which men commonly find pleasure either never did have an attraction for me or some time ago ceased to have that attraction. Many of these activities, I have long found distinctly distasteful. But I do not find myself under anything like an external compulsion to refrain from these. It may even prove expedient to devise some entertainment in which the physical personality may participate, but this personality does not seem to insist. The fact is, that the personality does share in the Higher Consciousness and is not a sacrifice. The sense of sacrifice belongs only to the antecedent stages; afterwards there is a Joy in which the whole nature participates. To be sure, now, as ever, the larger purpose must take precedence over minor interests, but there seems to be a quality of such inner harmony that the sense of conflict in such a choice is almost wholly gone.

In addition to the companionship of those immediately surrounding me, I have, as always, the rich companionship of those who have incarnated themselves in books. Only this has become much richer as I feel more keenly the presence of the men who wrote. Further, there is a tangible inner Communion, and this is something of very rare value. If at present I share in an objective responsibility, it is none the less true that I freely chose it, and so I do as I have chosen to do. Finally, I know that even though I move for a time in the restricted field of the external world, yet the High Indifference is not far away—in fact It is present everywhere and at all times.

There is always the intriguery of new discovery, perhaps just around the corner. Even that which I already Know, in the sense of the profound Abstraction, comes again to me as time goes on in the form of concrete discovery. I find It as It takes form in my mind while I write It down. Again, I recognize It in the words of Men who have attained the Recognition, as They bring to me, in terms of formation, That which I already Know in a profound sense. Also, they unfold new aspects of Myself that are not native to this personal consciousness of mine. It is a very satisfactory life, my brothers, and immeasurably more than life-restricted-to-the-shell has anywhere to offer. If the form of outer living which I choose is not the form some other one would choose, let such a one refrain from thinking he would have to cast his life over my form. Remember that Walt Whitman lived a very different life from that of John Yepes, yet both These were Men of high Recognition and both knew profound happiness. In Its deeps the Life is utterly Free, and in a surprising degree that Freedom is reflected in the outer life.

72
The Problem of Government

September 18

In these days when there is such a widespread "liquidation" of old governmental forms and the substitution of new forms of extreme illiberality and brutality, one who is interested in the welfare of man can scarcely be indifferent to the problem of government. It is clear that thus far all our attempts in government on a large scale have fallen far short of a really satisfactory success. Otherwise there would not be so much of change and demand for changes.

For a government to be truly successful, it must maintain, in high degree in the social body, three principles, (1) Freedom, (2) Justice, and (3) Efficiency.* Now, none of the forms of government that we have tried so far have afforded enduring success in all three respects. The rule of kings and aristocracies has at times worked reasonably well, but in recent as well as ancient, history we have seen very clearly how badly this form can fail when there is a decay of character and competency in the ruling classes. Under certain conditions, democracy does function fairly satisfactorily. These conditions seem to be the following:

1. That the unit of government is not so large as to be beyond the effective comprehension of the average voter.

2. That the intelligence and sense for responsibility in governmental affairs of the average voter is considerably above that of the average human being.

3. That the governmental problems are fairly simple.

In the modern large nations, with our extremely complex civilization and particularly where there is a considerable heterogeneity of population, these conditions are far from being fulfilled. The signs of the breakdown of that form of democracy involving universal suffrage are painfully evident today. Democracy has become too dangerously inefficient, and thus this system is being replaced in an increasing degree by the dictatorial form of power wherein efficiency in certain directions is secured at the price of radical loss of freedom and justice.

---

*I do not name "Order" among these for it seems that Order is a means to an end, rather than an end in itself. Practically, we find Order to be vital for the highest possible realization of Freedom, Justice, and Efficiency, and consequently it is important in the pragmatic sense.

It has certainly become clear that an excellent constitution is no guarantee of good government. For the government largely becomes what the ruling class makes it, within certain limits determined by the temperament and character of the people governed. In a government such as that of the United States, this ruling class actually is not the people, as it is supposed to be in theory. In practice it is the class of the professional politicians, who, in their turn, have been checked, balanced, and sometimes controlled by another class whose basis of power is economic. Now the professional politician is typically the kind of man who can command the vote of the average elector. Generally, this is a sort of man who stands upon a distinctly inferior intellectual and moral level, though there are some brilliant exceptions. The result is that, though the American government is based upon an admirably designed form, it is today showing the signs of serious weakness that may become fatal. If the right kind of men, in sufficient numbers, could be selected for positions of authority and responsibility, this need not be the case. But with the intelligence and moral character of the average elector being what it is, and the common denominator of the whole being still a great deal lower, it is too much to hope that these positions will ever be filled, in sufficient numbers, with the men of requisite capacity and character. We do not have a lack of men with these qualifications, but for the larger part they are not popular with, or comprehensible to, the average voter. Hence, their services, when made available for governmental purposes, are much more commonly located in appointive than in elective positions. But final judgments in matters of policy rest with those who occupy elective offices.

It may well be that a dispassionate study of the history of the American government will show that the checking and control of the politicians by strong men who wield economic power has been more a factor serving the ends of stability and soundness in government than the reverse. Two factors tend to produce such a condition. In the first place, the only important field on the American scene where men of administrative talent could find opportunity for the exercise of their capacities has been in the business and financial worlds. On the whole, in America there are more men in the business field who manifest the caliber of statesmanship, in the true sense of the word, than there are in the political arena. In the second place, economic necessity, in the long run, requires of the men who achieve and hold economic power that they shall develop the kind of thinking which is characteristic of the engineer and scientist, in some measure at least. It is a kind of thought based more upon fact in the objective sense than upon psychological prejudice. In contrast, the typical power of the politicians is psychological and thus capitalizes prejudice, superstition, etc., as instruments of popular appeal. They often win votes by promising something contrary to the laws of nature, and in the very fact that they are willing to make such impossible promises, they reveal a dangerous defect of character. The result is that it may well prove to have been the restraint exercised by business and professional men of high character that has, on the whole, proved to be the most beneficent influence affecting practical American government.

It seems to be pretty definitely demonstrated that excellence of system is a far less important determinant in good government than the presence of wise men in the positions of power. The real problem of government is one not of mechanics but of wisdom. Thus the effective key to the solution of the generally chaotic condition of the world today is finding the men of sufficient wisdom and giving them power. This simply means that the crux of the problem of sound government lies in finding and placing sages at the center of power. The true Sage is a Man of Recognition and is, therefore, One who has transcended the temptations that the world has to offer.* At the same time, He brings to the problems of the world a more than worldly wisdom. There are Sages who, like Buddha, have an ancient understanding of government. Mankind can secure the leadership of such Men. But mankind must call for Them and recognize Their authority when They respond.

In the meantime, I see no real hope in the governmental field. Brief palliations there may be here and there, but no healing of the fundamental disease. It may be that conditions will have to continue to grow worse, that mass-man will try, as never before, to wield decision with respect to problems hopelessly beyond his comprehension, and that, when he has failed utterly, as he must fail, and is entangled in the impossible maze of his own construction, then in true humility he will call for help from Those who alone can give that help. In that day, and not before, the problem of government can be solved. For the inescapable

---

*It is not suggested that all Sages are necessarily wise in the special field of government. There are different kinds of wisdom, and rarely, if ever, does any one individual attain the fullness of wisdom, in all directions, in a single embodiment. The Sages fitted for the government are those who have unfolded the sense for the art of administration in an especial degree.

fact is that the problem of practical government is too complex for mere subject-object consciousness, however highly developed. The perspective of the Higher Consciousness is an absolute requisite.

73
Compassion

September 21

O Compassion! More than the other loves of men, less than the High Indifference;
Calmly standing by and waiting; years, centuries, millennia;
Taking to Thyself the suffering of all; transforming toward Joy;
With Light restraining Darkness; with good, evil;
Refusing release while others are bound; melting differences;
Accepting impurity, giving purity;
Bound by no law, yet acquiescing in bondage;
Available for all as the light of the sun, yet forced on no man against his will;
Needing nought for Thyself, though giving to all need;
The Base of all hope for this humanity so low;
Pure Radiance Divine.
Sweet art Thou, unutterably sweet; melting within me all hardness;
Stirring inclusion of the low as the high; the evil as the good; the weak as the strong; the unclean as the pure; the violent as the considerate; none left out;
Awaking new understanding and patience beyond Time;
Arousing forgetfulness of the petty in the grand sweep of the noble;
Equalizing regard, yet exalting true worth;
Reaching beyond all contradiction.
To Thee I sing, glorious Spirit; grandest God mankind can know.

74
The Symbolism of the Butterfly

September 25

The life-cycle from the egg, through the caterpillar and the chrysalis, to the butterfly, constitutes one of the best symbols afforded by nature of the progress of the human soul from birth into the world, thence through the development of subject-object consciousness, and then finally culminating in the translation to the Transcendental Consciousness by means of the Second Birth. Since our interest is centered upon the Second Birth, we are concerned primarily with the transition from the caterpillar to the butterfly, rather than with the birth of the caterpillar. The caterpillar represents life on the level of subject-object consciousness, which is life centered in egoism. The butterfly symbolizes Cosmic or Transcendent Consciousness, while the chrysalis is a good representation of the ordeal of the Transition, known in the Christian world as the Passion, culminating in the Crucifixion.

The life of the caterpillar is one confined to crawling on surfaces, and thus it may be said to represent a kind of two-dimensional consciousness. The primary concern of this life is nutrition, and this consciousness can comprehend nothing save in terms of crass utility. Hence, the typical caterpillar philosophy, if for the moment we may assume on the part of the caterpillar enough self-consciousness to develop a philosophy, must be such as would predicate reality and value of that alone which affects sensation, particularly in relation to nutrition. Thus ideas would be significant only insofar as they serve as a means which effect a fuller sensuous life and supply creature utilities.

In radical contrast, the life of the butterfly involves free movement in the air and therefore very well symbolizes a three-dimensional consciousness, as contrasted to the two-dimensional life of the caterpillar. The primary concern of the butterfly-life is mating and depositing eggs, with nutrition reduced to a distinctly subordinate position. Further, the typical nutrition of the butterfly is confined to fluids and thus contrasts radically with the gross nutrition of the caterpillar. The butterfly-life and philosophy may be said to center around creativeness and joy, and so beauty becomes an end-in-itself instead of crass utility. Thus reality and value for the butterfly have a significance not only utterly different from that conceived by the caterpillar but quite beyond the comprehension of the latter.

The chrysalis represents a stage where the caterpillar dies as caterpillar. To the caterpillar-consciousness, this must seem like an annihilation or "blowing out," as Nirvana does seem to the unillumined subject-object consciousness. But when viewed from the other side, as it were, the chrysalis is the open door to the free life of the butterfly.

The butterfly consciousness has certain very clear advantages. The butterfly, as compared to the caterpillar, moves in a world of an infinitely vaster comprehension. It lives in space with the power to return to surfaces. It is thus in a position fully to understand surface relationships, the whole domain of the caterpillar, but, in addition, knows an infinitely richer world that is utterly unknown to the caterpillar. Further, it knows surfaces in relation to depth, and thus can master problems connected with surfaces that quite transcend the capacities of the caterpillar.

This symbol is a peculiarly beautiful one. The restrictions of caterpillar-life very well represent the limitations of the subject-object consciousness. From the perspective of the restricted subject-object consciousness, the final problems of philosophy remain without satisfactory solution, and often involve unreconciled contradictions. These solutions are attained and the contradictions reconciled by Those who have Awakened to Transcendental Levels. This is due to the fact that the latter have the higher perspective, symbolized by the butterfly, and thus can comprehend the subject-object, or surface world, within the higher integration of space, representing here the Higher Consciousness. But just as the world of the butterfly is inconceivable to the caterpillar, so likewise the integration of the God-Conscious Man is meaningless to those who have no glimpse of Reality beyond mere subject-object consciousness. Thus, without some degree of Recognition, the philosophies of men like Plato and Hegel seem like something purely abstract and unsubstantial. These higher philosophies admittedly are largely not concerned with the production of mere sensual or experiential values, and certainly give a very subordinate place to nutrition and the creature comforts generally. But when these philosophies are seen from the level of Consciousness on which they are based, they are found to deal most emphatically with substantial actualities. They are written from the perspective of a real Waking Consciousness.

Philosophies of the type of neo-realism, pragmatism, and naturalism are conceived from the perspective of the surface consciousness, symbolized by the caterpillar. At least, this latter form of consciousness dominates. If, now, we restrict ourselves to the subject-object or caterpillar standpoint, the proponents of these philosophies do have the best of the argument. Essentially they understand only the inductive or "foot" logic of the caterpillar. Their final authoritative basis is either the data of sensation or data derived indirectly through sensation. Their final thesis is that what is objective alone is real. On their own ground, they are apparently unanswerable, but for every Man who has Awakened to "Knowledge through Identity" they are at once known to be in a false position. A Plato knows, beyond any possibility of doubt, that he is substantially right, but he may well be quite incapable of doing more for the caterpillar type of consciousness than suggest a Reality beyond the caterpillar level. The result is that argumentative conflict between these two great groups of philosophies is largely a waste of time, because there can be no agreement on basic recognitions. Each may prove his case satisfactorily from his respective standpoint, but the effect is simply one of a sort of shadow-boxing that accomplishes very little, so far as convincing the opponent is concerned. The Awakened Man *Knows* the inadequacy of the caterpillar recognition, but cannot prove this to the caterpillar type of man. On the other hand, the latter cannot grasp the Recognition of the Awakened Man unless he, himself, Awakens. The result is a stalemate, unless the caterpillar-man has adumbrations of a Beyond.

Of all men who are confined in consciousness to the subject-object manifold, those who see the primary problem of mankind as the one connected with economics are the ones most bound to the caterpillar level. For them, life centers in gross nutrition and the creature comforts, and this is precisely the dominant characteristic of the actual caterpillar. It is a pitifully restricted view. Mere increase of nutrition can only produce larger caterpillars. It can never solve the primary cause of human misery. For man to realize the enduring Joy, he must become so transformed that he enters upon the free life symbolized by the butterfly. It is doubtless true that some human caterpillars need to become fatter before they are ready to enter and pass through the chrysalis stage, but also many are ready now for that Transition and are wasting their time in making themselves into overgrown caterpillars. If the latter think they are serving humanity by continuing in their present course, they are but fooling themselves. When they have Awakened, and only then, can they competently serve that humanity, even with respect to the problems of social and economic organization.

The primary significance of the chrysalis is that entering into the free state of space-life is possible only through dying to the caterpillar level. Mere evolution, in the caterpillar sense, merely produces bigger and juicier caterpillars. There comes a time when man must turn his back upon the whole of the form of life symbolized by the subject-object consciousness, if he is not to be caught in the cul-de-sac of a wasted and barren existence. Of course, from the standpoint of the lower level, this does involve for a brief period an essential asceticism in some form or other. But the end is something infinitely richer than anything contained in the old life, and in addition it is anything but ascetic. Attachment to lesser values serves as a barrier to the realization of greater values. This is a familiar principle, even within the limits of ordinary life. It applies even more forcefully with respect to the attainment of the Supreme Values. Yet many human beings cling to values that are relatively no more than child-toys, and thus refuse to take the steps that open up a Life of Glory, Freedom, and Power. Is not this the supreme folly?

75
Concerning Asceticism

October 1

Throughout the history of religion, asceticism has played a highly important part, both as an enjoined discipline and as a spontaneously accepted practice. Several reasons underlie such practices, many of which have been listed and discussed by William James in his "Varieties of Religious Experience." However, I shall add certain considerations relative to this subject that have grown out of my personal experience and reflection.

I am convinced that for most natures and perhaps for all, a certain degree of ascetic practice is necessary if the individual is to attain his highest possibilities. But while this is particularly true with respect to preparing the Way for the Awakening, the same principle applies none the less in the unfolding or developing of power or skill in any field whatsoever. Man wins power in any direction by concentration of effort in the appropriate sense, but this involves inevitably a suppression of diffused activity. Combined with the main interest at any given time, most men feel within themselves counter interests and desires, and if the latter are indulged, the former are sacrificed. Here is a sufficient basis for essentially ascetic practice which may in extreme cases have all the value of the mortifications characteristic of some of the religious disciplines. A man may do this for the mastery of an art, of a science, for the building of a business, etc., just as well as for an objective of the type more commonly classified as religious. If the main interest is so all-consuming that there hardly remains any conflicting interest or desire, it may well be that but little discomfort is felt in the practice. On the other hand, important competing interests may cause the discipline to have the effect of real hardship. But, in any case, mastery in any field does require such discipline.

In the foregoing type of asceticism, there is no question of the essential sinfulness of the carnal nature. In fact, a rationale of asceticism may be developed entirely apart from the question of sin. Sin has been given a far too important place in religious thought and feeling. Such sin as there may be is largely incidental and the result of Ignorance and thus fundamentally a delusion rather than an actuality. The result of giving to sin the respect and attention which underlies the idea that it is of sufficient importance to be a worthy object of warfare is that sin is actually given life and power. *We never destroy anything by fighting it.* A force that we fight may be temporarily crushed, because at the time we may be wielding a stronger force. But it remains true that we have won at the price of a certain exhaustion, and meanwhile the opposing force rebuilds itself, partly out of the very force we have expended. Then it comes back upon us when we are weak and may conquer us. No man escapes the action of this law simply by dying physically before the rebound. Somewhere he will live again, and in the next life he may find himself as much identified with evil as in the preceding life he thought himself to be identified with good.

Undoubtedly a strong carnal nature does have to be restrained, and in the case of those who do not have a sufficient balance-wheel of wisdom, possibly extreme effort in restraint may be necessary for a time. But unquestionably, it is far better if this discipline is looked upon in the rational spirit of regarding it as simply a form of training. The problem is vastly simplified if the individual, instead of taking an attitude of fighting or suppressing, will undertake to transmute the carnal energy. Every form of energy, regardless of how seemingly evil it may be, has its higher mode or aspect into which it can be transformed. If the effort is focused upon this transforming, the energy is released and becomes a positive power, and this is relatively easy to do.

But after all is said and done, asceticism related to the carnal nature belongs only to the kindergarten stage of the training for the Higher Life of man. The higher and genuinely adult asceticisms are of an entirely different nature. Thus, when a man learns to become detached with respect to his pet opinions or ideas, and is willing to accept conclusions quite counter to his preferences when either evidence or logic points that way, then he is practicing asceticism in a higher and nobler sense. This kind of asceticism does cut far deeper into the real vitals of a man than any restraint connected with the mere carnal nature, and if he can succeed in the higher discipline, then anything remaining in the lesser nature requiring to be purified becomes a mere detail. In the superior discipline, the will has become so highly developed that the carnal nature is controlled relatively easily, provided the effort is put forth.

I would reduce the whole problem of asceticism to the following simple formula: *Let the individual concentrate his effort upon that which he desires most and restrain or transform incompatible desires.* What a man desires most may change as there is growth toward maturity. One implication of the formula, then, is to drop action in the direction of the old desire when the new and more potent desire takes its place. Of course, discrimination must be made between a persistent new desire and the mere temporary uprising of an inferior desire. The rule is to be applied as indicated only in the former case. This course followed consistently will achieve for the individual ultimately his highest good, and sooner or later that will mean the Awakened Consciousness. The advantage in this form of discipline lies largely in the fact that the center of emphasis is placed upon the positive value to be achieved, rather than upon the negative or interfering quality. It makes for a life of greater happiness, and this, in turn, arouses a greater strength, all of which means that success will come the more quickly, at least as a rule. Of course, such a policy of life practice may very well involve one or more radical changes of direction in the life-activity. Thus a man may start his adult life with a desire to attain a great business success, but after having only partly completed this work, he may find that a greater desire takes its place. In that case, he might have to forego great success in the business sense and, remaining content with but moderate achievement in that field, throw the central focus of his energy in another direction. But while this would entail a smaller degree of success in the narrower field, the whole life of the individual, considered in the wider sense, would be more successful. Such a one would escape the tragedy of so many retired business men who, after leaving their businesses, find themselves quite helpless in a meaningless and barren life. From the standpoint of the Awakened Consciousness, all life here below is of value only in the sense of training for the Higher Life and has nothing in it that is valuable as an end-in-itself. So, from the higher point of view, the judgment of what constitutes success in the subject-object field is formed on quite a different basis from that of the usual world-standard. Everything here below is instrumental and only instrumental. So a life encompassing many but partial successes in the subject-object field may actually be making more progress toward the Awakening than a life which is highly successful in one concentrated field. From the higher standpoint, this lower life may be viewed in much the way a music-master views his pupil. The music-master has in mind finished perfection as the ultimate, but in the work-shop of the studio the time is given almost wholly to fragments, such as the technical handling of a phrase, the building of tone-quality, etc. This life here is such a studio and only that. The concert stage is Cosmic Consciousness.

Once a man has Awakened to the Higher Consciousness, he may make a decision that requires the very highest ascetic resolution. He Knows the infinite superiority of the Higher Life in every sense, and, if he had only himself individually to consider, naturally he would choose that Higher Life exclusively. But consideration for the needs of others may lead him to forego this and accept a life in the world while, at the same time, it is not a life *of* the world. As a part of his work, he may move rather freely in the field of sensation, emotion, etc., and may even seem self-indulgent to the superficial observer, yet all the while he would be practicing asceticism in the severest sense in the very living in that way. For him there is not any longer a question of resisting carnal temptation, for Knowledge of the higher Joy has reduced all this to husks and ashes, relatively speaking. He simply endures what the carnal man imagines to be enjoyment.

The whole problem of asceticism appears to me, from my present perspective, as merely one of rational judgment and wisdom and is quite divorced from the emotional unpleasantness that is usually associated with it. It is simply good sense to choose the greater value in any conflict of values. Why should this be regarded as an occasion for serious emotional stress?

76
Poverty and Obedience

October 2

As I read through the records of monastic practices, I find myself increasingly impressed with the feeling that on the whole there is more inadequacy in this kind of life than there is superiority. Undoubtedly for certain specialized natures, a larger human usefulness is achieved under the conditions of monastic life than is the case within the turmoil of worldly existence. Thus, in general, the scholar can be more effective in his work if he has the advantages of monastic insulation. Monasteries were sanctuaries for learning during the Dark Ages. Today the university performs that service very largely, but in its turn it continues some of the more important values of the monastic life. However the value of the monastery in this higher sense requires that the associated members shall be of superior intellectual or spiritual endowment. Further, it requires that the members shall be individuals of sufficient character so that they do not require the prod of worldly life to stir them out of slothfulness. In a word, they must be men who have a value of a superior sort to contribute to mankind that could not be contributed, or could not be so well contributed, in the midst of worldly confusions. But taken as a whole, monasteries have served more as places of retreat for weaklings than as universities for the exercise of specialized capacities. It is this broader use of the monastery that I find inadequate.

The vows of poverty and obedience are very common throughout monasticism, and the rationale underlying these disciplines is easy to understand. The fundamental idea in much of monasticism is a training that will effect a complete surrender of the personal will, so that the individual man will find room for nought save the Divine Consciousness. This technique unquestionably has been successful with some natures, but none the less I am convinced that the literal interpretation of the rules of poverty and obedience is grounded in superficiality rather than in profundity. Of course, I am not bringing into question the necessity for obedience in connection with specific programs of training, or in the case of the performance of an organized work where the directors are alone in a position to decide with respect to courses of action. Here obedience is a practical necessity. I have in mind simply the more general monastic concept of "obedience" as it has been developed specifically within the Christian Church. In this sense, "obedience" is intended as a device to destroy the capacity for self-determinism.

It is unquestionably true that private possessions and personal self-will have their origin in egoism, which, in turn, is the basis of the sense of separateness. In its valid sense, the discipline of poverty is a means for overcoming the feeling of exclusiveness that so commonly characterizes the private possession of property. Similarly, the practice of obedience is designed to awaken perfect conformity with the Divine Will. But subjective change of attitude toward possessions and the exercise of personal will can have all the value of the literal practice of poverty and obedience. In fact, in this subtler form, the discipline can become much more thorough and afford a better protection against the pitfall of spiritual pride or self-righteousness than in the case of the more literal practices.

In the matter of property, strict analysis will show that there actually is no such thing as private property in the absolute sense. Thus no man owns any external private possession any further than Death permits. Therefore, regardless of social policy, all objective possessions are merely temporary trusts. Now, while it is true that property affords opportunity in terms of indulgence and functioning, yet in even a larger degree it involves responsibility. The more spiritual a man is, the larger looms the factor of responsibility, and thus the acceptance of this responsibility has the value of genuine austerity. In addition, this austerity reaches deeper into the soul of a man than any hardships of poverty. In the case of a man who is not a householder, the ultimate outcome of poverty is hunger, thirst, and exposure to the rigors of weather until death supervenes. This by itself entails only a brief physical suffering. None of this cuts very deeply into a man unless he is of small caliber. But in contrast, when a man feels that his position of power makes him responsible for the wellbeing of hundreds, of thousands, and perhaps of millions of human beings, he is living under a discipline of such austerity as to make merely personal suffering quite trivial. This is a much more heroic life than that afforded by mere literal poverty.

The same principle applies to the exercise of decision. The willingness to dodge responsibility in this respect is a mark of real weakness and not of strength. So far as man is concerned, the Divine Will acts through the human will. The Universal Will is transformed very largely through the human mind in acting upon the concrete field. Becoming effective in the objective sense is achieved pragmatically. Thus, the higher courage, which marks the really strong man, is revealed in a willingness to assume responsibility for the making of unwise decisions. If the correct course in any situation were always clear, there would be no need in this world for real courage. Accepting responsibility for decision, then, is a much higher and a much more severe austerity than unquestioning obedience.

In the practice that I find unfolding in my own mind, I would make use of the householder form of life as the main objective instrument of discipline, up to the time that the individual is ready for special training. Further, this special training would be of purely technical significance leading toward a definite objective. The essential moral training would be secured through a combination of the problems arising out of actual life, together with the cultivation of a certain attitude toward those problems. I am convinced that on the whole this is a better way to build the higher resignation, at least in the case of men possessed of the western temperament. I would ask students not to dodge temptation but to face it until it was mastered. I would expect the cultivation of conscientiousness combined with detachment. Likewise, I would insist upon the practice of self-determinism and would regard him who dares, even though it be unwisely, as the better man than one who obeys blindly.

Conscientiousness has the moral value of poverty. Likewise detachment has the value of obedience. Literal obedience is of importance in connection with technical training for reasons that are quite obvious, but for moral discipline, self-determinism is by far the most effective austerity. What We desire is men, and the stronger they are, the better. We do not seek mere mediums. Strength, even though combined with the vices of the strong, is preferable to weak goodness. In all men, it is the essential value that is important, not the details. For the latter can be handled easily if the central core is sound.

77

The Higher Consciousness and the Mind

It is often stated in mystical literature that the activity of the mind is in a peculiar sense a barrier to the Realization of the Higher Consciousness, while at the same time the action of the higher affections is viewed as not such a barrier or as an obstruction in only a minor sense. The primary reasons why mental activity is so regarded are twofold: First, the sheer activity, as such, produces an effect which we may liken unto a great noise that hides the subtle sound of the Voice of the Silence. In the second place, mind-action is a fruitful cause of egoism, and the latter is the basis of the sense of separateness. Both logic and my own experience concur with respect to the contention that action in the objective sense and egoism are barriers. But barriers may be overcome by being surmounted as well as by being removed. Thus a perfect silencing of all activity and a complete eradication of egoism are not absolute necessities upon which the Recognition is contingent. If this were not so, it would seem to follow necessarily that Recognition could never be achieved save in full trance, and thus values from the Recognition could never really descend into the personal consciousness. As was noted in the first section of this book, at the time of the Transition in August, the mind and the senses were active, I was self-conscious, and thus egoism was not completely blanked out. However, both the intellectual and the sensuous consciousness were substantially subdued, and another, a more Universal Consciousness, assumed a position of predominance. Further, prior to the substantially larger unfolding on the evening of the 8th of September, the mind was intensely active. But in this case, the higher level of energy was so great that whatever obstruction was interposed by the activity was easily swept aside. In fact, if the mind had not been as active as it was, there is reason to doubt whether the subject-object consciousness could have remained as witness, or whether there would have been force enough to draw me back into objective functioning.

It seems that the mystics must have employed overstatement in their definition of conditions. This may have been deliberate for psychological reasons, and, in some cases at least, it may have been due to an insufficiently acute power of introspection on the part of the mystic writers. We know that overstatement is one of the principal vices of the Orient, and it is in this region that we find the greater number of genuine mystics. Further, it certainly is true that—with mystics as a class—psychological factors have been given greater attention than logical or factual correctness.

But the foregoing is not the whole explanation of the confusion. In general, the mystical and occult use of the word "mind" does not carry the same connotation that western philosophy or the most authoritative usage gives that term. If for "mind" we substitute the word "manas," at once the mystic's statement becomes more correct. "Manas" is commonly translated as "mind," since there is no other single English word that approximates its meaning. But whatever the original or etymological meaning of "mind" may have been, its meaning, as defined today by the most competent and authoritative usage, comprehends much more than the Indian philosophers and mystics mean when they say "manas." Unless this distinction is born in mind, confusion is almost inevitable. For my own part, this confusion caused me some years of needless misunderstanding. What I read violated what I felt intuitively and subsequently demonstrated to be the case. It was not the competent mystical philosophers who were in error, but the translators and the western students of mysticism and occultism.

Another point to be noted is that—in the profounder and more complete Oriental philosophy—"manas" is divided into two aspects, a lower and a higher. Now, it is in the lower aspect that manas is called the "destroyer of the Real," and thus it is this aspect that must be conquered by him who would attain real Knowledge. This lower manas is united to desire and thus is merely the chief of the organs of sense. It is even called the "raja" of the senses. Thus conquering of the lower mind means "conquering the senses through the raja of the senses." This is obviously important, as the senses afford the basis of objective experience and accordingly make possible a desire that is directed toward the objective and thus away from the purely Subjective upon which the whole objective universe rests.

Now, while the meaning of lower manas is partly comprehended within the western usage of the word "mind," the latter is employed to mean much more. Let us refer to the definitions given in a good dictionary. Thus in the "Century Dictionary" we find the following definitions: "That which feels, wills and thinks; the conscious subject; the ego; the soul." This is very much nearer the real meaning of "Atman" or the "I AM" than to "manas," whether in the lower or higher sense, except that "egoism" is closely related to manas. Again, we have the following definition: "The intellect, or cognitive faculty or part of the soul, as distinguished from feeling and volition; intelligence." In part, this is close to the meaning of "Chit" and also, it gives much of the meaning of higher manas, but does not, as such, involve the association with desire which is an essential aspect of lower manas. Third: "The field of consciousness; contemplation; thought, opinion." This covers a wide field of meaning which, most certainly, should be differentiated. In Oriental philosophy, to cover this ground, we have terms, such as "Nirvana," "Sangsara," "Samshaya" and "Mata." Only with the last meaning, that of "opinion," do we begin to enter the lower manasic field proper, for desire and sensation are very apt to form a part in determining opinion. Philosophic usage also connotes by "mind" qualities such as "Reason," "Understanding," "Discernment" and "Discrimination" and much of "Intuition." It would seem that we must conclude that, however close "mind" may be to "manas" in its philological background, yet, given the meaning that it now has, it is a peculiarly bad translation of "manas," particularly when the latter is taken in the lower sense. Our words "sensation" and "desire" come much nearer to the meaning of lower manas, though they also fail to give a really satisfactory translation.

In the broad sense, "The Critique of Pure Reason" is devoted to an analysis of the faculties and functions of the human mind, covering, in the first part, the functions and the forms of the faculty of receptivity, which is fairly equivalent to the lower manas and the senses, while in the second part the spontaneity of the understanding is discussed. This second part covers the ground designated by "Atman," "Buddhi" and "Manas," the latter being taken in the higher sense. Kant's "Intellect" very largely overlaps Shankara's "Buddhi." These points are quite important, for Kant's usage is probably more influential than that of any other western thinker.

I have entered into this point at some length, partly for the reason that in my earlier studies the mis-translation of "lower manas" seemed to require of me a crushing of faculties of the soul that are vitally important for even the Realization Itself, for I was quite familiar with what the word "mind" meant in western usage. Others may be facing the same difficulty. Literally, to crush or suppress "mind," giving to that word the meaning it has in western thought, is to crush or suppress the soul. No true mystic means that, whatever he may seem to say as a result of not being familiar with the English term.

In these discussions I am trying to convey the fundamental meaning of the Recognition and to elucidate the factors favorable to it. As should now be clear to the reader who has understood all that has been written so far, by "Recognition," when taken in its full sense, I mean exactly what Buddha meant by "Enlightenment," Shankara by "Liberation" and Jesus by "The Kingdom of Heaven." Pursuing this aim and at the same time retaining as high a degree of accuracy as I can, I divided the modes of human awareness into three types: sensation, affection, and cognition. "Sensation" is made to cover the whole field of reception, such as sensation proper, perception, and reception. "Affection" covers qualities such as Love, Confidence, Desire, Faith, Joy, and in general all emotional qualities, both positive and negative. "Cognition" is made to include pure intellect or thought, discernment, reason, etc.

It should be clear that pure cognition as here understood is not sufficient to bring to birth egoism, but for it to do so it must be united with the quality of desire and perhaps other phases of affection and sensation. Actually, with the mass of men, cognition is bound to egoism, but a divorce of these two is possible. In the cognitive activity of pure mathematics, we do find such a divorce in high degree, for here the desire is almost wholly directed toward Truth and Beauty, with little or no attachment to any preconception of what Truth may ultimately prove to be. Cognitive activity of this type is most emphatically not a barrier to Recognition, and if my experience is any criterion, may well prove to be one of the most powerful subsidiary aids for those who can make use of it. In any case, I must conclude that if by "mind," cognitive activity is meant, then it is not true that the mind must be stilled in order to attain Recognition. But it is true that the cognitive action must be within a matrix of a high order of *dispassion.*

The higher affections, such as love, compassion and faith, are also most emphatically an aid. But upon this point I do not need to dwell, for here agreement among the mystics seems to be practically universal. Further, this phase of the subject has been much more clearly presented and better understood. This is the Road through Bliss, the Way most widely appreciated and most commonly followed by Those who have attained God-Realization.

By means of pure cognition, it is possible to enter through Intelligence (Chit). Or, again, one may Enter through various combinations of the higher affections and pure cognition. Such a course is naturally the most synthetic. But it is not necessary that the balance between the two should be perfect. The individual may be more developed on the one side or the other at the time of the Entering. But once he is grounded in the Higher Consciousness, there is a tendency for the nature to unfold toward balance, so that finally such a Man is symbolized by the "Great Bird" which has two wings equally developed. And these two are Compassion and Intelligence.

★ ★ ★

Note: Since writing the above I have made a considerable study of modern work on the psychology of types and this has brought to light further important considerations which I propose to discuss at some length in a later work. At this time I wish to make the following notation: The thinking of any non-thinking psychologic type tends to be negative or destructive when it is not guided by the function which is dominant with the given individual. With such individuals, the force of thought may easily seem to be destructive of the real, or Satanic. This makes clear much of the criticism of the mind on the part of mystics. What they have said in such cases is no doubt valid with respect to the kind of thinking with which they are familiar, but they have erred in universalizing what is no more than a peculiarity of certain psychological types. The thinking of the well-developed thinking type has quite a different character, as it is positive and constructive. He, in his turn, is negative or destructive in terms of the independent action of his repressed functions.

78
The Atlantean Sage

October 4

THOU ART DIVINE, yet also human, most comfortably human;
Knowing the breadth and the depth and the weakness of man,
Ever remembering the God within the mask;
Trusting with certainty that God,
Regarding not too seriously the mask;
Speaking most often the word of encouragement and comfort,
Yet not neglecting needed rebuke;
Fearing no enjoyment, here below,
Intrigued to forgetfulness by none;
Living in unbroken Joy, balanced by sage judgment;
Wise Teacher ever, yet One who never ceases to learn;
Ancient ruler of men, wise in the ways of men,
Knowing them better than they themselves;
Not scorning convenience, yet ready preference to forego,
Once need makes demand;
With touch tender as a woman's ministering to pain,
Stern, also, meeting enthroned perverseness;
Beyond discouragement, certain of triumph,
Freed from the tyranny of Time;
Ever expecting the best, accepting what is;
Unbounded in nameless majesty,
Beyond the entanglements of earthly man;
One who makes more easy the Path, seemingly so hard,
Discovering unsuspected alleviations of difficulty;

Master of the Inner Powers, melting Darkness with Light,
Transforming enemy-victories into defeat,
Thou Artist of strategy supreme, High Commander on the Staff Divine.
How greatly dost Thou awaken the love of those who come near Thee,
And confidence in a wise strength;
How greatly dost Thou remove the sting of dread austerity,
Bringing the Beyond within the compass of reasonable achievement.
Honored, I feel, that I should have known Thee,
And count most precious our days of communion.
Ever will I remember that day, on a northern mount,
Crested with pines, mantled with white sternness of winter;
Below us the deep carving streams;
In a little house, remnant of the days of the argonauts,
Now humble and decaying, but rich in memory of great adventure;
Ah! ever will I remember that day when first Thou camest!
I knew Thee, not knowing quite how I knew,
And recognized Authority to countermand the old pronouncements.
Saidst Thou: "In this new day in a newer land,
With customs and perspectives also new,
Old Realities needst must be, in new garments, clothed.
Balancing the strength and weakness of old, there is now another strength and another frailty.
It is but Wisdom's part to adapt effort to these.
Underlying is the unchanging Truth,
The Way to Recognition manifold.
Be not attached to the method, but to the End."
With much hesitation, I finally learned,
If not largely, still considerable store
Of this new, yet old, Wisdom.
Upon Thy promise, I dared and found Thee ever true.
A blessing art Thou to this mankind;
Unknown, save to the few.
May a monument be built to Thee,
Not of inert stone, so easily the victim of Time's ceaseless wearing,
But of the living, growing hearts of men.
In Thee abides a Presence Divine, yet also a man.

79
The Barriers to Recognition

In his Gifford Lectures, *The Varieties of Religious Experience*, William James sought to establish an outline of the basis for a philosophic science of religion. This entailed a search through all the greater religions for the common objective elements of all varieties. He found the two following common elements:

1. An uneasiness due to a sense of something being wrong about human beings as they naturally stand.

2. A solution that in some sense saves man from the wrongness by making the right kind of connection with higher powers.

Neither from the standpoint of my own individual experience, nor from that of my objective studies of religious thought, do I find any basis for questioning the correctness of the above conclusion. Without a sense of something not being right in the life as we find it manifested in this world, there would be no meaning in the programs of the religious movements as we actually find them. So we may say that the typical religious and religio-philosophical problems grow out of a condition which may be designated, in the broad sense, as pathological. Consequently, when this condition is cured in the case of any individual, the latter transcends the need of any religion, in the sense that "religion" is more commonly understood. Now, in point of fact, the God-Realized Men are superior to all religions in this sense. While it is true that such Men may become founders of religious movements, They are no longer the mere followers of already given religious disciplines. This very largely explains why so often They appear as atheistic to the followers of the various established religions. But the fact is that the God-Realized Men alone have found the solution and are cured of the usual pathological condition that envelops all other men.

What is wrong with man that, instead of God-Realization being the usual state of consciousness, it has been the Attainment of but a bare handful out of the mass? I see four factors which, while they do not cover the whole of the problem, certainly do comprehend it sufficiently, so that if all these factors are mastered, then the important barriers to Recognition will be removed. It may well be that these four factors are so interrelated that in the last analysis they would reduce to one. But, in any case, they would represent four approaches to the fundamental problem. I shall list the four without giving prior importance to any one of them at the present time. These four are:

1. Egoism.
2. Somnambulistic consciousness.
3. Sensual desire.
4. False predication. By this is meant predicating properties of the subject that are true only of the object, and the complementary error of predicating qualities of the object that are true only of the subject.

1. In "egoism," we have the "ahamkara" of the Vedantins. It is the negative aspect of individuality. It is the name for that state of consciousness expressed by the feeling, "I am I and none other." Consequently it is the cause of the sense of separateness, the strife of individuals, groups, and nations, of all destructive competition, and in general of all unbrotherliness. Without egoism, there could be no pride, conceit, jealousy nor either the inferiority or superiority complex. Egoism tends to crystallize and hold closed the microcosm of the individual. That it is a barrier to Cosmic Consciousness is quite obvious, for the latter is a State of Consciousness extending throughout the spatial matrix which contains all microcosms. The shell of the microcosm must be cracked or melted so that the individual consciousness may become one with Universal Consciousness. Now, inasmuch as the microcosmic needs can never be completely supplied by the resources of the microcosm alone, the individual so encased must, sooner or later, realize that something is wrong. Just so long as the individual seeks for the solution of this wrongness within the limits of egoism, he is doomed to failure. Thus he must overcome egoism and, by so doing, melt the shell of the microcosm and then—but not before then—he is united consciously with the infinite supply that is adequate for satisfying every need.

The mistake has often been made of regarding the mastering of egoism as equivalent to the destruction of individuality. In other words, Liberation is sought as pure Universal Consciousness without any element of self-consciousness. It is possible to do this, but such a course results in something less than the highest destiny of man. Individuality, the essential basis of self-consciousness or the power to know that one knows, can be retained in a form so freed from the dross of egoism that it is blended with Universal Consciousness. In this case, the microcosm is melted, as it were, so that it is no longer crystallized but remains as a fluidic vortex of force, continuous with the Universal Force, yet, in a sense, distinguishable as a vortex. This is the Path that leads to the highest Destiny of man.

Both a strong intellectuality and a powerful personal will or desire tend to build dominant egoism. Now, it is precisely men of these types who have the greatest powers of all those who are still confined within the limits of the subject-object manifold. They supply the greater number of the leaders of men and have great world-influence. Because of the influence and the power of these men, it is of special importance that as many of these as possible should attain to the Higher Consciousness. But owing to their greater development of egoism, they have unusual difficulty in rendering their microcosms fluidic. On the credit side of the ledger, they bring to the task of solving this problem a greater power than most others possess, and if they are successful, they will in general go further than others.

2. In Chapter 49, I have already discussed somnamblistic consciousness at some length and will not repeat here what I said there. Somnambulism is a barrier through weakness rather than one due to too much strength in the subject-object field. Often it is not difficult to awaken adumbrations of the Higher Consciousness in representatives of this class, but characteristically they lack the power to imprint these adumbrations within the personal consciousness in such a way as to organize them into a permanent value for the relative consciousness. In general, egoism is less developed in them, but likewise so is the quality of individuality, and consequently, if they do effect the Transition without first having strengthened their individuality, they are peculiarly apt to flow into Universal Consciousness without retaining self-consciousness. Thus they require first of all a strengthening of the capacity for self-determinism and self-directed thought. If they can accomplish this, at the same time retaining their greater natural capacity to receive adumbrations of the Higher Consciousness through the action of induction, then they have the definite advantage of being more responsive than most other types to the assistance of Those who have already Arrived. In any case, their course of training differs in important respects from that which is requisite for those falling in class No. 1.

3. Sensuality is the opposite of spirituality. Hence, desire directed primarily toward the objects of sensation tends to carry consciousness outward and away from inwardness where alone the universal Key is to be found. To follow sensation is to go toward ponderable objects, and this

means movement toward essential nothingness or illusion. The primary agent in this movement is the sensual mind, or, more correctly, the lower manas. As has already been shown in a previous discussion,* it is when it is taken in this sense that the Sages have traditionally viewed the mastery of mind as the central problem. As I explained in that section, the real meaning of "mind," when so employed, is better expressed in our usage of terms by the phrase, "desire directed toward sensation."

It is perfectly true that sensation can be used as a stepping-stone to Recognition. But this is done by viewing the objects of sensation as symbols rather than as actualities existing in themselves. It is possible, then, to use the direct object of sensation as an instrument to awaken consciousness of that Matrix which is the Fullness that comprehends or encloses the relative emptiness of ponderable objects.

I question greatly whether this technique is practical for any extensive application to occidental humanity in its present stage of consciousness. There is a tradition that a certain ancient race did employ this method as a systematic technique, but that race had a much higher development of sensual purity than is now the case. So it would seem that, on the whole, with men being what they are now, the technique with overly great sensual desire must be in the form of replacing the sensual with super-sensual objects. Gradually, then, the desire can be molded or directed toward genuinely spiritual objectives.

4. This may be called a barrier that grows out of the nature of subject-object consciousness as such. A man who is relatively free from egoism, as is true of many scientists and philosophers, may have a strong intellectual development and be little, if in any degree, involved in somnambulism, and in addition he may have a strong control of sensual desire, and yet with all this fall into the error of "false predication." With respect to this class more than any other, the problem of Recognition falls in the field of philosophy. In my judgment, this constitutes the really crucial problem relative to the Liberation of human consciousness from the state of bondage. Accordingly, I shall discuss this barrier to Recognition at some length.

The problem of false predication arises in the following way: The Self, or the purely subjective moment in consciousness, is the primary reality of the subject-object manifold. It is the Light, or the Intelligence, or the Consciousness on which the whole universe depends for its exis-

---

*See Chapter 78.

tence. It is unitary and above space, time, and causality and, therefore, not subject to conditions. The objective world, including the human body as well as other objects, is dependent and bound within space, time, and causality and, therefore, subject to conditions. It is also multiple in appearance.* Thus it is, in all respects, of a nature both opposite and complementary to the Subject.

Now, it is a widespread habit among human beings to reverse the above predications. So we have the custom, explicitly or implicitly manifested, of predicating self-existence of the objects of consciousness. As a result, things or objects come to be taken as primary, and then it may actually become a problem as to how a self-conscious Self ever became introduced into this world. Many a good scientist has addled his brains over this quite falsely stated problem. The fact is that a problem concerning nature has as its essential basis a conscious self that makes the apperceiving of the problem possible. In a purely blind and dead nature, there never could arise a scientific or any other kind of problem. Of primary importance, then, for the understanding of any problem concerning nature is a knowledge of the Self and of the knowledge-forms through which It acts in cognizing or sensing the world. The most primary fact of all is the Self that thinks and senses. Its presence is the one completely immediate reality that can neither be proved by logic nor found through experience, for it is the absolutely necessary basis for both these forms of consciousness. Thus it is only of the Self that we may properly predicate self-existence. It alone is that which is the original indubitable "given" on which all the rest depends. So the real problem is: How does the external universe come to have existence? It is a complete misconception to state the problem in the form: How did the Self come to be injected into the universe?

The Self, then, is the one Reality of which we can be absolutely certain, for It is presupposed as much in false as in real knowledge and underlies dreams as well as waking states. Now what can we predicate at once concerning this Self in addition to self-existence? A simple answer comes immediately: The Self is an unchanging power of awareness. This bare awareness is not affected, as such, by the modes or qualities of the

---

*I will not at this time develop the logic that supports this position, but that logic is well unfolded in existent philosophy and in addition has the overwhelming support of the testimony of the mystics. For the present I shall ask the reader to assume the essential correctness of the above statement of primary fact.

contents of that awareness. Thus, the states of objects, including the body of man, do not affect the Self. For instance, a man may have a sick body, but he makes an absolutely false predication when he says: "I am sick." The experiencing of the state of sickness in the body is a fact, but to predicate this sickness as attaching to the Self is to build the typical binding illusion which holds human consciousness in thralldom. Similarly, man's manifold instrument of body, mind, etc., is limited, but the Self is not limited. Thus to say "I am limited in such and such respects" is to produce but another of the illusions of nescience. It would have been perfectly correct to predicate these limitations as attaching to the individual and personal instruments. The application of this principle should now be clear.

The final consequence of both classes of false predication is the production of a state of Nescience or Avidya. The effect is a sort of superimposition upon the originally given universe of a secondary or false universe which enthralls the bulk of human consciousness. It is this secondary universe that is an Illusion or Maya in the invidious sense. Problems relative to nature and Being, taken from the standpoint of this secondary universe, involve a fundamentally false perspective, and therefore it is impossible to find effective solutions for them. On the contrary, they simply lead into ever greater and greater entanglements, in the effort to elaborate solutions. The fact is, that this superimposed universe has no more real existence than a dream. Now, the whole conscious field of a dream, together with its problems, is destroyed by the simple process of waking-up. This leads us to a very important point in metaphysical logic. Whenever we recognize any state of consciousness as being a dream, at that moment we have discovered that it is unreal, or, in other words, is devoid of self-existence. A man suffers while in the midst of the ordinary dream simply for the reason that at the time of dreaming he believes the state to be real. But this belief in the reality of the dream is caused by a superimposition that the dreamer himself has produced. The awakening is equivalent to a removal of this superimposition. At that moment, the state which was imagined as real, and therefore as having self-existence, is recognized to be no more than a dream. This destroys that particular world or *loka* of consciousness. Now we come to an especially important point. That world or *loka* is not simply destroyed for the future, but it is equally destroyed in the sense that *it never has been*. This does not mean that it is not a fact in the historic sense that at a certain time the individual in question was deluded while in the state of the dreamer. It simply means that the self-existence or actuality which was imagined as true of the dream never was in reality a fact. The same principle is true of the secondary universe in which the bulk of mankind lives somnambulistically. When a man Awakes to the Higher Consciousness, he destroys this universe, both in the sense of futurity and in the sense of realizing that it never has been. Right here we are dealing with one of the most important principles of the higher epistemology and logic, but also one that has been very widely misunderstood. It is not the field of subject-object consciousness, as such, that is an Illusion or Maya *in the invidious sense*, but the secondary universe. It is this that the Oriental Sage has in mind when He speaks of destroying the universe, but He has simply failed to make himself clear to the western mind.

There is a considerable group of western students who, through an imperfect understanding of the oriental doctrine of Maya, have developed a philosophy in which "Illusion" is predicated of the whole field of relative consciousness in a sense that is valid only of the secondary universe. The result is, that instead of destroying an illusion by their technique, they have simply succeeded in imposing a new kind of illusion and produced for themselves a state of autohypnosis, which results in a deeper state of dream-consciousness than is true of the average individual. In this deeper dream-state, only the evidence which seems to confirm preconceptions is recognized readily and the acceptance of contrary evidence becomes almost impossible. It is a state in which real discrimination is paralyzed. It is practically useless to try to help any individual who is in this state, until the force of auto-hypnosis exhausts itself.

Properly understood, the whole doctrine of *Maya* is entirely compatible with the idea that within the relative or subject-object consciousness there can be a correct view of the universe. But this view is correct only in so far as it is taken as true with respect to the subject-object base of reference. Critically self-conscious modern science is well aware that its knowledge is not valid beyond the limits imposed by the base of reference that has been assumed. From the standpoint of Recognition, there is no criticism to be made of a science built upon a background of such critical understanding. Confusion arises only when generalization goes beyond the theoretical limits of the base of reference. From the perspective of Transcendent or Cosmic Consciousness, the problem of nature and Being takes quite a different form. But this fact does not imply a challenge of the relative reality of a body of knowledge developed by sound method within the relative field.

Once one recognizes the fact that the relative world, or primary universe, is a valid part within the Whole and is relatively real, then the problem of cross-translation from the level of Cosmic Consciousness to that of subject-object consciousness is realized as being of high importance. The possibilities of cross-translation are admittedly limited. The immediate content of the Higher Consciousness cannot be cross-translated, but certain formal properties can be through the use of systematic symbols. In some respects, it is like the old problem of the evaluation of irrationals in terms of rational numbers. The ultimate content of the irrationals cannot be given in the form of the rationals, yet, in the radical signs, we have symbols representing the essential unity binding the two sets of numbers. Just so soon as the mathematicians abandoned the effort completely to reduce the irrationals to rational form, and accepted the radical sign as an irreducible symbol of profound meaning, then they did succeed in integrating in their consciousness two quite differently formed domains of reality. This integration meant that the two domains were found to be logically harmonious, although that which we might call the "affective" content was discrete. Cross-translation, in something of this sense, is possible with respect to Cosmic and subject-object consciousness. In fact, if the consciousness-equivalents of the entities and operations of pure mathematics were realized, we would find that, in that great science and art, cross-translation in a lofty sense already exists. The Root Source of pure mathematics is the Higher or Transcendent Consciousness, and this is the reason universal conclusions can be drawn with unequivocal validity in pure mathematics. The greater bulk of mathematicians fall short of being Sages or Men of Recognition because their knowledge is not balanced by genuine metaphysical insight. But they do have one-half of the Royal Science. Up to the present, at any rate, the Fountainhead of the other half is to be found mainly in the Orient. The union of these two represents the synthesis of the East and the West, in the highest sense, and is the prerequisite of the development of a culture which will transcend anything the world has known so far.

It is a mistake to regard the primary universe as being in some sense a great error. With respect to this point some of the exoteric Vedantins have not seen clearly, for they have said that the universe was a Divine Mistake. At the same time, from the transcendent level of the High Indifference, it is a mistake to give the universe a teleological interpretation. But from the subject-object standpoint, we can see purposive value in it, and so long as we confine our predication to the latter base of reference, this value is real. But a radical error is introduced when purposiveness is extrapolated as predicative of the High Indifference. In the highest sense, the universe is neither a mistake nor a purposive necessity. But it is an empiric fact, and it is the part of wisdom to accept it as such. The actual primary and empiric universe is not an ontological necessity. It is rather to be regarded as an existent and creative actuality, within the limits of ontological possibility. Ontologically, the universe might have been other than what it actually is, but empirically it is what we actually find it to be. To understand the fundamental meaning of the universe, one must rise in Consciousness to the level beyond Creative Ideation.

The state of subject-object consciousness, in the sense of the primary universe, is not to be regarded as pathological. However, the genuinely illusive secondary universe does involve a pathological or hypnotic type of consciousness. This is the universe that is produced by Ignorance and is destroyed when Ignorance is destroyed. When We speak of this world as being a sort of asylum or hospital, We have in mind earth-humanity en masse. We are not including all beings who are functioning within the subject-object manifold. The state of this humanity is abnormal, and thus is in a condition not typical of other humanities. This mankind, through a failure of discrimination, confused the subject and the object, producing thereby the false predication. To this was added the innate creativeness derived from the Divine Spark, resting at the center of every man. The combination of these two produced the secondary universe, which is not other than an illusion in the invidious sense. Actually, it is a hell that was so created; and, so far as most human beings are concerned, this life right here is the worst hell they will ever know. It would take considerable perverse skill to produce anything much worse. The only hope for individual and collective man lies in his utterly destroying his perversely produced secondary universe. Then, and only then, does he take up once more his course of development along the lines of genuine evolution.

In the philosophical sense, the crux of the problem of the effective destruction of the secondary or superimposed universe lies in the awakening of the power of real Discrimination. This is essentially the act of rigorously distinguishing between the Self and not-Self, or, in other words, the careful differentiation between the properties true of the object of consciousness and the qualities true only of the Subject. The practice of this discrimination has the value of a de-hypnotizing force, and once it is carried far enough, the man Awakes. This Awakening is equivalent to a discharge from a hospital. The methods that do actually effect de-hypnotizing for different individuals vary considerably, as has already been noted. But in the end, all methods, when they have been carried to the point of effective results, lead to true Discrimination, and thus it is Discrimination that remains the ultimately effective agent for Liberation. That is why Recognition is more than a *means* to Liberation; it actually *is* Liberation.

Religion, in the forms commonly known in this world, is but a treatment designed to meet the needs of sick souls. The really healthy soul has no need of religion, in this sense, for such a one is not only Divine, but in addition recognizes that fact. He is thus identical with the Object of religious worship. The "wrongness," almost universally felt by men in this world, is not something produced by an original Divine Plan, but is the production of a perverse creativeness on the part of man himself through the method already noted. Once the wrongness is corrected, there remains a continuation of evolution in the relative as well as in the Cosmic sense, in which the development is normal. This normal evolution does not have evil and misery as constituents of its make-up. On the contrary, it proceeds within the matrix of essential happiness and understanding. Thus Real Life begins only after man has Awakened.

80
The Nameless

October 7

Above below, to right, to left, all-encompassing,
Before and after and all between,
Within and without, at once everywhere,
Transforming and stable, ceaselessly;
Uncaused, while fathering all causes,
The Reason behind all reasoning,
Needing nought, yet ever supplying,
The One and Only, sustaining all variety,
The Source of all qualities, possessing no attributes,
Ever continuous, appearing discrete,
Inexpressible, the base of all expression,
Without number, making possible all number,
Containing the lover and the beloved as one,
Doing nought, remaining the Field of all action—

The actor and the action not different—
Indifferent in utter completion;
Diffused through all space, yet in the Point concentrated,
Beyond time, containing all time,
Without bounds, making bounds possible,
Knowing no change;
Inconceivable, yet through It all conceiving becoming;
Nameless ever and unmastered;
THAT am I, and so art Thou.

81
The Record Continued

October 15

At the close of the noon-day meal of last Sunday, there occurred the third significant event of this series. I had made a certain inward call, but had not anticipated the nature of the response. Presently there was evident an unusual field of energy of a quality I recognized from previous experience, but of an unprecedented degree of intensity. All who were present were aware of this field. I felt a tension which led to a spontaneous straightening of the spine, in a vertical position, and an exerting of the will in a very positive sense. Everyone reported feeling a quality of extraordinary Peace, but in addition I felt the Presence of a most unusual Power. I felt quite sure that I recognized what this Presence was, but it must remain nameless. The quality of the State was similar to that where I reported the thinking of thoughts of extreme abstractness and also to that which enveloped us on the evening of September 8th.

One quality of these fields of energy is analogous to that of a certain physical experience with which a number of individuals are familiar. When a moderately sensitive individual is placed in the electro-magnetic field of a powerful generator, he will feel a curious kind of tension, quite difficult to describe. He may even find it necessary to set his will very positively. He may not know why he has to do this, and the willed response seems largely spontaneous. Now the energetic Field of subjective Presence is similar, but is more subtle and may be much more potent. All of this simply supports the idea that Consciousness or Life is in some sense electrical. However this Energy may manifest in a number of different forms, of which terrestrial electricity is merely the most gross. This idea also helps to show how the phenomena of terrestrial electricity furnish analogues of certain of the actions or functions of the Higher Consciousness, such as that of induction.

The Presence of last Sunday continued with decreasing intensity throughout the rest of the day and since then has not seemed far away. One directly traceable consequence took the form of a rewriting of the experience of September 8th. The cross-translation of this inward State afforded peculiar difficulties, and my first effort was far from satisfactory. The rewriting last Tuesday was far more successful and is, I believe, the most difficult piece of formulation that I have so far attempted. However, I composed this quite readily, but all the while my thought was on an exceptionally high level. I was under a strong drive while writing and was unusually impatient of interruption before its completion.

During the last two days, I have become aware of a peculiar change of attitude on the part of my personality in a fundamental respect. This new attitude seems to be more in the nature of a gradual growth rather than a sudden development. Heretofore, and up to some point in the past two months, I have felt that there was such a thing as self-sacrifice. I have always felt that, wisely employed, it was a necessity, not only for the development of the higher moral life, but likewise even for the exercise of a merely decent moral code. My refusal to leave the world-field, when the opportunity to do so came, had the value of self-sacrifice, but the chosen course seemed to be the only honorable one to follow. In this there was a very real renouncing involved. But, in contrast to this, at the present moment, I do not feel that any course that I may choose to follow involves self-sacrifice. Studying this as objectively as I can, I must say that it is a very curious state. Admittedly, some courses of action remain relatively uncomfortable or difficult when compared to others. But, regardless of whether I am personally uncomfortable or comfortable, there does not seem to be any self-sacrifice involved. I find myself disposed not to predicate meritoriousness or its reverse to any course of action I now choose. I rather tend to judge whatever action may be chosen as more or less sound, or more or less wise, and so on. Folly seems to be the only possible mistake. Bear in mind that I am not presenting this outlook as a thesis relative to what should be, but simply as a report of a self-analysis of a state I now experience. Whether or not it is an enduring state, only the future will reveal.

The fact of this state of feeling with respect to self-sacrifice leads to a reflection concerning its significance. I can trace it directly as an effect of those hours of consciousness correlated with the High Indifference. There certainly is a persisting effect that is radically changing my attitude toward life. Now here is the logic as I see it. In the High Indifference, the "I AM" or the "Atman" is transformed, as nearly as I can express it, from a bare point of pure subjectivity to the whole of Space. The result is that I am not peculiarly involved in what happens to any one point in that Space, even though that point is this personal self-identity which I call myself, spelt with a small "m." A plus at one point in that Space is immediately balanced by a minus at another. However, since I am not confined to any one point but comprehend all points at once, I do not experience the effect of a "lessness" or of a "moreness," no matter what the course of action at any time may be. If self-sacrifice may be regarded as in some sense a "lessness" at a given point, it is, at the same time, a "moreness" at some other point or points. I, in reality, being the whole Space, comprehend at once both effects. Clearly, from the perspective of such a level, self-sacrifice is an impossibility. Literally, no circumstance can reduce Me, and equally no circumstance can exalt Me, and this remains true even though the personality were crushed out of existence on the one hand, or were given the highest honors on the other. I do not see how, logically, any other state of feeling would be compatible with genuine Indifference.

All of the foregoing simply further develops a quality I have found to be characteristic of the Recognitions I have had. They tend toward an integration of the whole nature, and thus the conflict between the affections and the logical demands of thought, a condition so common with most men in the usual state, is progressively eliminated. This is real purification and may well be more important for the eradication of misery than any other factor.

Is this State of fundamental Indifference in which I find myself a desirable one? I find it so. I would not choose anything else that I have known or heard of in preference to It. Yet, before my individual consciousness had been correlated with It, no reference to indifference that I had ever heard or read had succeeded in making it seem attractive. It seems that one's whole basis of valuation undergoes a fundamental change. From a distance, the State looks like negation, but when Realized it is Known to be more complete than any antecedent state. But it may well be that only by Realizing It does it become possible to prefer It to all others. I have no sense of being forced into This against my will. Perhaps, even now I could retreat from the effective memory of It, but that would be absolutely the last thing I would wish to do. I see no reason at all why anyone should fear it. There are States of real spiritual Bliss that do not involve this High Indifference, and it is possible for men to Realize that These are worth infinitely more than any of the offerings of the subject-object consciousness. I know of nothing that would cause men to abandon such States against their wills. If, when the Hour comes, some wish to continue on to the more comprehensive Consciousness, they are at liberty to go as far as they can. It is not a matter of outer constraint. Meanwhile, let me add my testimony: The State of the High Indifference is supremely worthwhile.

Concern is the earmark of a state that is incomplete. When completeness is realized, concern vanishes. The High Indifference is the hallmark of utter completeness. Action or inaction within the High Indifference is not the effect of concern. Concern may still be the basis of motivation within the personal consciousness, but at the same time in his deeper Consciousness the individual is quite aware of the irrelevancy of the concern. As the High Indifference is no more a state of inaction than It is of action, relative consciousness naturally puts the question, "What is the cause of action on that Level?" But the very form of this question makes an answer impossible, for a modulus of relative-world conduct is extrapolated into a State where it has no relevancy. Perhaps something of the truth may be suggested by saying that all Motion, in the highest sense, is spontaneous and is therefore not to be explained in terms of causal connection. Somehow, the Supreme and causal worlds are simultaneous facts. The Supreme IS, the causal world *apparently* is, and yet it is not. Let him who can resolve this apparent absurdity.

82
The Point-I and the Space-I

October 17

A new way of approaching the subject of Nirvana has come to my mind which may be helpful in clarifying certain difficulties relative to the nature of this State. The usual idea of Nirvana seems to be that It is a sort of blissful State produced by an extinguishing of personal life through the elimination of the will-to-live and the desire for enjoyment.

Since ordinarily men find themselves unable to conceive of consciousness unrelated to personality and the various cravings associated with sentient life, Nirvana appears to be something like an absolute non-existence or an annihilation in the full sense of the word. If, on the other hand, it is granted that Nirvana is some sort of State of Consciousness, it is often thought of as something undesirable. There is much misconception in all this. Anyone who has ever touched even the hem of Nirvanic Consciousness would not regard It as an undesirable State and most certainly would Know that It did not imply the cessation of Consciousness, although It is a kind of consciousness quite different from anything to be found within the relative field. Now the difficulty seems to me to grow out of a misunderstanding of what is meant when we say "I," and I believe that I can say something that will make this matter clearer.

Approached from the usual standpoint of relative consciousness, the "I" seems to be something like a point. This "point" in one man is different from the "I" in another man. One "I" can have interests that are incompatible with the interests of another "I," and the result is conflict. Further, the purpose of life seems to center around the attainment of enjoyment by the particular I-point which a given individual seems to be. It is true that in one sense the "I" is a point, and the first objective of the discriminative practice is the isolation of this point from all the material filling of relative consciousness, and then restricting self-identity to this point. For my own part, I finally applied this technique with success. But, almost immediately, at the moment of success, a very significant change in the meaning of the "I" began to develop. A sort of process of "spreading out" began that culminated in a kind of spatial self-identity. I found that the "I" had come to mean Space instead of a point. It was a Space that extended everywhere that my consciousness might happen to move. I found nowhere anything beyond Me, save that at the highest stage both "I" and Divinity blended in Being. But all of this process involved both an intensifying and broadening of Consciousness, and most emphatically not a narrowing or "pinching out" of it. For our present purposes, we may leave aside the State of Being, where both the subject and the object disappear. There remains, then, an "I" in two senses, which we may call the point-I and the Space-I. There is enough in this to clarify the fundamental problem of Nirvana, taken in the simpler sense, leaving out of account States called Paranirvana and Mahaparanirvana.

As a matter of formal properties alone, it should be clear at once that life-values take on very different forms when viewed respectively from the perspectives of the point-I and the Space-I. The point-I involves discreteness, separateness, difference, etc., and, as a consequence, there are possible attainments and failures to attain. This gives a certain meaning to desire-led action, resulting in all the features so common in ordinary life. In contrast, the Space-I is continuous, not-separate, not-different, etc. At least in a potential sense, the Space-I spreads over all possible consciousness-values. It thus stands above the need of experiencing (enjoyment). For the Space-I, consciousness-values are not attained by action, desire, etc., at least not in the common meaning of those terms. Consciousness may be focused anywhere within the given Space, and at once the corresponding consciousness-value is realized.* The important fact is that the Space-I does not have to strive in anything like a competitive sense to achieve any value. In a potential sense, the Space-I is all values at once; and by focusing, it makes any value whatsoever actual. Now, the Space-I includes all point-I's. Hence, in principle, any individual who has Realized his identity in the Space-I finds himself present in all point-I's. This also gives to him, in principle, the resources of all point-I experiences, and not merely those of one isolated point-I. It is easily seen that in such a Space-I there is no room for, nor meaning in, the separative affections of mere point-I consciousness. Further, the Space-I is a State of infinite completeness, as compared with the consciousness of any point-I or the compound effect of any number of point-I's. Of course, such a State is one of Bliss immeasurably transcending anything possible for any point-I. It is the Space-I Consciousness which is Nirvana.

Now, to have transcended the point-I state and achieved self-identity in Space, does not imply that no further evolution is possible. We are already familiar with the idea of one space being comprehended in other spaces of higher order. The Higher Evolution may be said to be a progressive Spatial integration, each advancing step being literally an infinite transcendence of the preceding stage. Thus, if point-I evolution may be said to be represented by finite numbers, the Space-I evolution would correspond to transfinite numbers. In this higher series of Transcendence, we very soon reach the limits of the most advanced pioneer of this humanity and, in fact, do not have to proceed very far before we

---

*Just what is meant by this "focusing" brings up an interesting philosophical problem, but I shall not enter into this at the present time.

have reached the utmost limit of man as man. Beyond the latter are fields that form the normal Level of Beings quite different from man as he is commonly conceived to be.

Formal mathematics has reached a long way ahead of the consciousness that is actually possible to man. Man will have long since ceased to be human, in the restricting meaning of that term, by the time he has Awakened in terms of Consciousness at the most advanced Levels represented by mathematical concepts and symbolic formulae. Mathematics thus constitutes a thread to the Beyond that has never been lost, even when mankind sank to the greatest deeps of materialistic consciousness. But there are very few who have realized just what that Royal Thread is.

83
Sangsara

October 28

Thou monster, spawned of Ignorance impregnated by human ideation;
Appearing glamorous, promising all,
Yet deceiving ever, rewarding fidelity with empty cups.
Like a beautiful lake thou appearest,
Offering rest and refreshment to the traveler weary;
But a mirage thou art, ever receding,
Leading on and on to desert barrenness.
Appearing again as multi-colored rainbow,
Promising the gold never to be found.
Intriguing with a seeming joy and victory,
Jeering at thy victims as they,
Compounding sorrow and defeat, die disillusioned.
Empty art thou, void of all value,
Ghost of that which might have been;
Beguiling all onward till, caught in thy web,
They struggle, helpless and forlorn;
Demanding full loyalty, rewarding with illusion's drug,
Dream-stuff, turning to ashes on the morrow of waking.
Binding in ceaseless travail thy victims,
Draining the substance of the soul,

Leaving man ever poorer and poorer and poorer.
Thee, I challenge to mortal combat,
To a war that knows no quarter,
Thou vampire, draining the life of this Great Orphan.
In that battle may there be no truce,
No end, until the Day of Victory Absolute.
Thou reduced shalt be, to a dream utterly forgotten.
Then man, once more Free,
Shall journey to his Destiny.

84
Nirvana

FELT DIMLY in the soul, by world-man unconceived;
Unknown Goal of all yearning;
The Fullness that fills the inner void,
Completing the half-forms of outer life;
The Eternal Beloved, veiled in the objects of human desire;
Undying, Timeless, Everlasting;
Old as Infinity, yet ever new as upspringing youth;
Pearl beyond price, Peace all-enveloping;
Divinity spreading through all.
"Blown-out" in the grand conflagration of Eternity,
Death destroyed as a dream no longer remembered.
Life below but a living death,
Nirvana the ever-living Reality.
Divine Elixir, the Breath of all creatures;
The Bliss of full Satisfaction;
Uncreated, though ceaseless Creativeness;
Ecstasy of ecstasies, thrilling through and through,
Freed from the price of ignoble pleasure;
The Rest of immeasurable refreshment,
Sustaining the labors embodied;
The one Meaning giving worth to all effort;
Balancing the emptiness of living death,
With values beyond conceiving.
The Goal of all searching, little understood,
By few yet attained, though free to all.

> Sought afar, but never found,
> For closer IT lies than all possession;
> Closer than home, country or race,
> Closer than friend, companion, or Guide,
> Closer than body, feeling, or thought,
> For closest of all IT lies,
> Thine own true SELF.

85
Conceiving and Perceiving

October 31

Which is the closer to Reality, the percept or the concept? In this we have a rather simple form of a very old question that has divided schools of philosophy from the time of Plato down to the present day. In an earlier time, before psychological analysis had developed as a recognizable field of research, the question took the form, "Which is more real, the universal or the particular?" But the underlying issue is fundamentally the same. Clearly, percepts give individuals or particulars, while every concept is either a generalization in some degree or a universal. At least in western philosophy no standpoint has emerged that has dissolved the issue this question has raised, although the form which the issue assumes is certainly not fixed. In Plato's time, we find the contention reflected in the contrast between Plato and Democritus on the one hand, and between Plato and Aristotle on the other. In the Middle Ages, it is reflected in the division between the Conceptualists and the Nominalists. The Conceptualists held that the universals were real and existed before things. In contrast, the Nominalists held that universals, or more properly generalizations, were merely abstractions from individual or particular existences which alone have reality. Later, at the beginning of the modern period, the division is represented by the Rationalists and the Empiricists. The former found primary reality in universal rational entities, such as those which form mathematics, while the Empiricists held that the data given through the senses was primary. Immanuel Kant found a road which in a measure united these two currents of thought, but, again, the division flows out of him in the form: "Which is the most primary or real, the *a priori* element in knowledge or the a *posteriori*?"

The subsequent current of thought, most influenced by Kant, certainly did give primacy to the *a priori* element. This current fruited in the Absolute Idealism of Hegel. In contrast to this school, today we have the Pragmatists who emphasize empiric utility in some sense as the mark of truth and reality. This latter form of division is sometimes contrasted as "Intellectualism vs. Vitalism." At this point, the question takes the form, "Which is the most primary, Consciousness or Life?" Finally Spengler gives the problem a new form by introducing the words "Physiognomic" and "Systematic." The Physiognomic is a mode of awareness or living process grounded in Life and Time, both of these being taken as original. The Systematic is a conceptual construction which conceives the Real in terms of Space. Spengler himself admittedly is grounded in the Physiognomic, but he concedes that other temperaments may be grounded in the Systematic. This latest presentation of the question takes two possible forms: (1) "Which is original and primary, the Physiognomic or the Systematic?" (2) "Which is most primary, Time or Space?"

The analysis of the basic problem which underlies all these various questions may be approached either from the genetic or the logical standpoints. Depending upon the line of approach, the conclusion seems to follow almost predictively. There does not seem to be any doubt but that in point of time cognitions of universals arise after experience. If the process in time is assumed as real and original, then it follows that percepts and particulars are really prior to concepts and universals. But it is entirely possible to regard space and number as more primary than time, and this is certainly the position of the modern physicist who has reduced nature to a four-dimensional manifold wherein the time-dimension has essentially the properties of space, and the final picture of physical reality becomes a group of differential equations, or in other words a system of relationships in terms of number. Further, in a more specifically philosophical sense, the genetic development may be viewed as simply an occasion for making a pre-existence manifest. Thus experience merely becomes the stimulus or catalytic agent that awakens sleeping Knowledge, but is not itself the source of that Knowledge.

The conflict of these two currents of thought has played a part of unquestionable value in philosophic development. Either stream by itself, almost certainly would have become crystallized long since. But the interaction between the two series of schools has led to greater refinements of understanding and profounder recognitions than could otherwise have been the case. Rarely, if ever, is a man converted from one school to the other, once he has become philosophically self-conscious. The arguments of one school fail essentially to convince the proponents of the currently opposite school. It would seem that the reason for this would lie in the fact that none of the arguments reach as deeply as the insight in which any philosopher is grounded. This insight is original, and the fundamentals of the system that spring from it follow necessarily. But the conflict between the implications of the different systems leads to mutual growth of self-consciousness in the two types of recognition.

This primary division in philosophy itself is reflected in a still broader field where philosophy is contrasted to mysticism. While there is such a thing as philosophical mysticism, or a mystical philosophy, the general rule is that mystics are typically not philosophical in their outlook. The latter class certainly does find the Real in something that is nearer the percept, or the physiognomic, than it is to the concept of the systematic. Poetry, symbolism, and what is called "living the life" afford their characteristic instruments of expression. In contrast, all philosophers, of whatever school, actually do work with concepts and more or less universal ideas. Now, in their higher manifestations, both Philosophers and Mystics are Awakened to the Higher Consciousness. Buddha and Shankara on the one hand, and the great Persian Mystics on the other, afford outstanding examples of these two groups. As a consequence, we see that this division runs deeper than ordinary subject-object consciousness, and in some sense extends into the Beyond. There must be something very fundamental in this.

The division is traceable further in the complemental and opposed Greek notions of Eros and Logos, with their more modern equivalents of Love and Wisdom. In Occultism, it is reflected in the complemental contrast of Buddhi and Manas or that of Ananda and Chit. As already noted in a previous discussion, each of these pairs represents modes of more ultimate realities, designated as Atman and Sat respectively. The ultimate Reality, when brought into expression, requires the mediation of one or the other of the respective modes, or a combination of the two. Whether or not any living man has achieved a perfect equilibrium between the two modes is a question which I find impossible to answer definitely at the present time. It would seem, however, that if the incarnation known as Gautama Buddha was not a case of perfect equilibrium in this sense, at any rate it comes nearer to it than any other case of which we have clear historic record. Shankara's predominant expression is clearly philosophical, while that of Jesus is notably mystical. But there is a subdominant mystical element in Shankara, and likewise a subordinate philosophical element in Jesus. All three, Buddha, Shankara, and Jesus, do seem to represent, when taken as a group, more balance than other historic incarnations. By uniting these Three and regarding them as one Reality in Three Persons, it would seem that we have the most synthetic spiritual manifestation lying within the limits of historic records that have any degree of exoteric definiteness.

My own contribution to this problem grows out of a Recognition of a third kind of Knowledge which I have called "Knowledge through Identity." This Knowledge, on Its own level, is neither conceptual nor perceptual and consequently can neither be defined in the strict sense of the word nor be experienced. Through Awakening, man can Recognize himself as identical with It. It is only when the Awakened Man seeks to achieve a correlation between that Knowledge and subject-object consciousness that any question arises as to whether It is nearer conception or perception. To me, It seems nearer conception, but in a subordinate degree I also express It in the physiognomic or mystical form. But considering this problem objectively or logically, I am quite unable to say that actually Knowledge through Identity is nearer conception than It is to perception. I do not see any practical escape from what might be called a coloring of the colorless, just so soon as the Inexpressible is reflected in expression. The most perfect vehicle of expression is, inevitably, a distortion in some measure. The alternatives are, therefore, either to refrain from all expression, or consistently to employ the instruments of expression which the individual has actually evolved, being careful, however, to warn all that the expression is only a reflection of THAT which on Its own level remains ever inexpressible. Expression helps as a Road to THAT, but where a given expression helps certain temperaments, quite a different form is needed for others.

86
A New Word

November 7

In the effort to give expression to Values which have their source in the Transcendent World, a serious difficulty is encountered, owing to the inadequate supply of words having the appropriate meaning. One result is, that very often the writer or speaker asserts ineffability in a wider sense than is necessarily the case. The Transcendent as such is inexpressible within the relative manifold, but there is an intermediate domain, between the Transcendent proper and the more restricted subject-object consciousness, where partial expression is possible. If this were not so, it would be entirely useless to write or say anything on these subjects. But when we come to the question of how far expression is possible, there is no definite answer. The problem seems to be much like that of the evaluation of an irrational number in terms of rational numbers. We know that a perfect evaluation is a theoretical or absolute impossibility, but at the same time the evaluation can approach perfection without limit. In actual practice, the mathematician proceeds in this evaluation just so far as is significant for his purposes, and stops there. With respect to the expression of the Higher Values, there is likewise no theoretical limit to the process of approximation. The absence of the conceptual tools or the limitations of the intellectual capacity of a given individual determine the limits for him, but do not define the limits of possibility for other individuals. This is all a question of relative skill and equipment. The higher approximations are, admittedly, very difficult to produce and they are, progressively, less and less easy to understand as they are extended into the unknown. Yet the process in approximation releases ever more and more power of an increasing inclusiveness. So work of this kind is important for mankind as a whole, even though those who *directly* benefit by it are necessarily quite limited in number.

For the expression of the Transcendent, the Sanskrit is unquestionably the best of the fairly well known vehicles, for in this language there are many words representing metaphysical significance, for which there are no equivalents to be found in western languages. But outside a limited group of specialized scholars, an extensive use of Sanskrit is impractical. A few Sanskrit words may be introduced with appropriate explanation, and that is all. One who confines himself to the more common portion of the English language is restricted to the Anglo-Saxon and derivatives of Latin and Greek. Without the aid of the latter derivatives, the writer would be all but incoherent, once he reaches beyond very simple levels of thought; and, even with all three resources, a certain straining of the meaning of words is often unavoidable. A great deal of the actual expression which one encounters in his various readings involves a very careless use of words, and the result is often one of needless confusion. I believe that this confusion should be avoided wherever possible. Part of this confusion grows out of a usage of words that is neither in accordance with their etymological meaning nor with current dictionary definition. Often this can be guarded against by a more careful selection of words and word-combinations and, where this is impossible, by taking pains to define the new usage of a given term. Sometimes new words may be coined in accordance with the established rules of word-building. It is not good practice to employ this device if adequate word-tools already exist, but where it actually clarifies meaning it would seem to be beyond criticism.

I have coined a new word that seems to supply an unfilled need. It is the noun, "introception," with the verb form, "introceive." This word is from the combining forms "intro," meaning "within," "into," and "in," and "capere," meaning "take." Hence it has the primary meaning "to take into or in." The principal meaning for which I find this word useful is: "The process or mode of consciousness which penetrates to profundity through the affective function." Thus, it is the kind of insight aroused through music, poetry, and the fine arts in general. Both the words "understanding" and "perception" have been, at times, stretched in their meaning to carry this significance. But such usage is not consonant with the current meaning of these terms. "Understanding," properly, is related to cognition, while "perception" is grounded in sensation. An idea or a concept may be understood; a sensory datum, either in a subtle or gross sense, may produce a perception; but the quality of consciousness, associated with the affections, is something of quite a different sort from either of these.

In principle, inward penetration is possible through any of the three modes of consciousness, or various combinations of them; but, practically, perception as a complex of sensation—not intuition—is rarely a Road in this cycle. Thus, in general, man Enters through understanding, or introception, or *intuitive* perception; or rather with one or the other of these as the predominant mode of his consciousness. With most individuals who reach the Outer Court of the Path, introception or intuitive perception is more developed than understanding, and thus he who would directly influence the greater number of people should speak mostly to the introceptive or intuitively perceptive consciousness. On the other hand, those who have attained a considerable development of power are likely to have exceptional understanding, at least in some fields. Thus, he who would effect an influence with the latter group must appeal, in large measure, to the understanding.

★ ★ ★

Note: Subsequently, I have broadened the meaning of introception so as to designate a third function of consciousness defined as: "The Power whereby the Light of Consciousness turns upon Itself toward Its Source."

87
The Conflict between Space and Time

November 13

We are indebted to Spengler for having given us one of the clearest and most significant statements of a very ancient and profound conflict; one which even underlies some of the old stories of the wars of the angels. It is a conflict traceable through many phases of human consciousness and beyond. It has its sources in the very beginnings of manifestation itself, and is transcended by man only when he has again found himself in the pre-cosmic consciousness. It appears under many disguises and assumes variable forms, but its most basic representation is a conflict between Space and Time.

As space and time are commonly conceived, the notion of a war between these two hardly seems intelligible. For we have formed a habit of regarding these as purely formal pre-existences, quite independent of matter and consciousness. This is not the standpoint of Idealistic philosophy nor of theoretical physics, since the epochal contributions of Albert Einstein. However, it is a view practically and commonly held, and it must be discredited before meaning can be attached to conflict between space and time.

As should be clear by this time, I do not regard space and time as external to consciousness, but rather as modes and forms determining the play of relative consciousness or, in other words, as setting the stage for the drama of evolution. Neither space nor time are limitations imposed upon the ultimate Reality. On the contrary, they have their origin within that Reality and are simply the most primary circumscribing forms that serve the purpose of delimiting consciousness or nature as this appears to human consciousness. The most basic forms, whether in terms of perception, conception or of law, involve the notions of space and time. These underlie logic, relationship, periodicity, causality, etc. Not all modes of relative consciousness in equal degree involve these primary forms. Some are nearly altogether, if not wholly, temporal in their nature, while others are predominantly, perhaps exclusively, spatial. Thus perceptual consciousness is on the whole in closer connection with time than with space, although the spatial quality is peculiarly strong in the case of the sense of sight. In contrast, concepts are very strongly spatial and, in their more developed forms, essentially reduce time to a kind of spatial extension. In general, the closest union of concepts with percepts occurs in connection with the sense of sight or the world of light.

We can see at once one of the manifestations of the space-time conflict in the war between perception and conception. It has already been shown* how this conflict has led to the most fundamental division between the various schools of philosophy. Which of these two is closer to Reality? This is a very old question which has not only divided philosophers, but likewise caused conflicts between classes and groups carrying powers of the one kind or the other. The old war between religion and civil power is one phase of the issue, and this persists strongly, even in our own day. If we are to understand these age-old struggles, with all their practical bearing upon the happiness and well-being of man, it is necessary to determine and understand the significance of their primary source. To attain this, we cannot stop short of acquiring some understanding of space and time in their primary relationship to consciousness.

Time is involved whenever we speak of "becoming," "periodicity," "life," "birth," "decay," "evolution," "progress," "loss," "gain," and so on through a multitude of terms implying process in some sense. On the other hand, space underlies notions, such as, "law," "all at once," "essential identity of cause and effect," "freedom from sin, guilt, or karma," "immortality," "logic," "calculation," "reversible time," etc. Tragic time or the time that is one with embodied life, birth, death, etc., is irreversible. It is tragic because of the irreversibility. That which has happened cannot be recalled; the unused opportunity of the moment is gone forever; death closes relationships, etc. If time were ultimately real, it would never be possible to transcend the tragic drama of life. In such a case, to be sure, creative becoming would have genuine reality, but as the becoming always involves a complemental destroying, the joy of the former would always be dogged by the pain of the latter without hope of any ultimate resolution of this pain. Spengler, on his part, recognizes this tragic quality of chronological time. He realizes that it entails essential pessimism, but glories in acceptance of that pessimism, holding that it is

---

*See Chapter 85.

the nobler part and the more heroic to accept this frankly. He definitely asserts the primacy of time and thus predicates its ultimate triumph in the conflict with space.

Contrasted to Spengler stand the religious, the scientific, and the larger part of the philosophical thinkers. Outstanding among these are Buddha, Shankara, and Jesus. Let us isolate the fundamental viewpoint of these Men. When Gautama was aroused from his youthful sleep as an indulged Prince, the inciting cause was the witnessing of sickness, poverty, and death. These He readily saw as inevitable consequences of Becoming. He also saw that they were far more effective in producing misery or pain than any of the complemental life-processes were in producing happiness. Hence the final balance of the time-process was suffering. He anticipated Spengler in realizing that the world-life or Sangsara was primarily tragic, and accordingly He held a pessimistic view concerning this particular field of consciousness. But unlike Spengler, He refused to acquiesce in the tragedy. He searched for and ultimately found a power superior to the tragic field of Sangsara. This Power was a State of Consciousness that transcended the whole domain under the sway of time. This State of Consciousness is known to us today by the symbolic designating name, Nirvana. Now, while it is true that in the highest sense Nirvanic Consciousness transcends space as well as time, it is nevertheless approachable by human consciousness as being of a space-like quality. Nirvanic Consciousness implies a comprehension of beginning and end at once, thus destroying the tragic quality of time. But "comprehension" is essentially spatial. Further, the differentiation of levels of Nirvana also involves a fundamentally spatial notion. It is possible for embodied man to attain some degree of Nirvanic Consciousness while still possessing embodied consciousness. That such can be the case and at the same time be known to be the case here in this world implies that there is some degree of overlapping consciousness. This overlapping is necessarily spatial in the fundamental sense as revealed in the fact that the little more than inchoate reports of Nirvana are space-formed but in the radical sense not time-formed. Buddha brought a message of Liberation and Immortality, and hence in the proper sense he is optimistic. But the significance of the immediate step He offered mankind lies in the fact that He opposed the tragic time-world with a more potent Space-World. Liberation and Immortality are space-notions, freed from time-bondage.

The significance of the work of Shankara is precisely the same, though His approach and methods are different. In effect, He set up the notion of the monism of continuity—a spatial notion—in opposition to the discreteness of the universe. He asserted the unbroken and unbreakable continuity between the Soul (Atman) of man and Divinity (Brahman). He denied unequivocally the reality of the discrete world or seen universe. Now, the primary instance of discrete manifoldness, carrying within it the tragic quality, lies in the three-fold division of time, i.e., past, present, and future. Herein lies the root of multiplicity and the cause of all misery.

However large may have been the development of an optimistic attitude toward the world-field in the later centuries of western Christianity, it still remains true that the original Message of Jesus was just as completely other-worldly as were those of Buddha and Shankara. Repeatedly Jesus said: "My Kingdom is not of this world." He never asserted that Immortality, or the Kingdom of Peace, or the Saved Life was realizable as a mere world-field existence. Temporal power, which is always peculiarly time-centered, remorselessly fought Jesus and His followers for several centuries. True, He said: "Render unto Caesar the things that are Caesar's." But he completed this clause by adding: "But render unto God the things that are God's." And, indeed, He challenged Caesar-power far more fundamentally than any mere invading host. Such a host might have conquered even Rome, but this would have meant merely a change in the group that functioned the Caesar-power. Political wars never overthrow Caesar as a principle. But Jesus challenged the power of Caesar at its very roots, and so the Roman political sense was quite correct from its viewpoint in attempting to exterminate all that Jesus represented.* Jesus was willing to let Caesar play with the bodies of men for a

---

*That dialectic materialism is but a permutation of Caesar-power is afforded empiric demonstration in the development in Russia. The religion of other-worldliness was crushed along with independent money power. In their place was substituted an unchecked political power. We are thus afforded an excellent example of the rawness of Caesar-power when it has a free field of action. Rarely have there been manifestations of the sheer brutality of naked force of sharper delineation than is afforded by this example. The other totalitarian governments manifest the same quality. The differences between Fascism and dialectic materialism are only superficial. Essentially they are only counterpointal manifestations of the same spirit. In a peculiar sense, they incarnate anti-Christ. Theirs is the time-bound spirit manifested with an exceptional degree of purity. Perforce they are at war with the Liberating Spirit of the Spatial Consciousness. But in the end, they will fail as they are identified with the lesser power.

brief period of time, but He claimed the Souls of men, realizing well that the Soul is the only part of man that really counts. Without control of human souls the power of Caesar is a vain and empty thing. Realization of this fact is the explanation why great or ambitious temporal rulers so commonly seek to abrogate Divine prerogatives. Caesar succeeds in controlling man only so long as he can accomplish the binding of the soul of man to the body, and then dominate the latter. Therefore, He who can free the soul takes the enduring kernel and leaves to Caesar but the husk.

Jesus did most emphatically challenge the time-world, but in His case it was very largely that world as represented by Caesar-power. He offered an other-worldliness, a prime characteristic of which is immortality. Now, nothing that is subject to time-wearing is immortal. The essence of time-wearing is the negation of persistence. Only that which is not subject to time endures. That which we find through self-analysis to have the quality of durability in man is not under the sway of time. This realizable fact of a persistent element in human consciousness, when properly understood, is definite proof of a trans-temporal Reality underlying man. Jesus simply sought, as His predecessors before Him had done, to Awaken in men a Recognition of this trans-temporal Reality. That Recognition means "being born again," which, when achieved, at once destroys bondage to the time-world, including the dominion of Caesar.

All Caesar-power, whether in the specifically political sense or in the military form, is essentially a manifestation of the time-power. Nietzsche, as one of the prime exponents of time-power, saw this point clearly, and both frankly and aggressively taught anti-Christ. He exalted the time-violence of the will and hated the potency of the Christly non-resistance. All rulers whose souls are identical with political power are consciously or unconsciously disciples of Nietzsche, and with respect to them, all men and women who incarnate something of the Christly principle stand in counter relationship.

★   ★   ★

The time-principle dominates in the case of consciousness manifesting in primitive forms. It is thus in the massive or numerical sense preponderant, for not only is the bulk of human life under its sway, but as well all of sub-human life. In the historic sense, Spengler is right when he says that spatial comprehension comes into dominance only as a culture flowers. It is born and sustained in this world only with difficulty. But, on the other hand, it wields the ultimately victorious force. The cosmic integration of Sir Isaac Newton is a good illustration of the power of the spatial principle. He gave an especially strong impetus to the conceptual grasp of the universe under law. By supplying a command over a planted time-mystery that had held humanity in its thralldom before his day, he effected a substantial degree of liberation for human consciousness. A considerable sector of time-mobilized nature now stands definitely conquered by man as a result of the spatial understanding introduced by Newton and other men like him. But as a biologic fighting animal, Newton would have proven peculiarly ineffective. The impact of the massive brute-force, which constitutes the ultimate instrument of Caesar-power, would be easily fatal to Newton and those of his type. Yet the science of which these men are masters has caused even the Caesars of this day to be nervous in the exercise of their own peculiar power. Adaptation of space-power to brute force threatens to become a boomerang, offering not victory, but mutual annihilation. It is utterly foreign to the native genius of Caesar as a type to be able to master the key to space-power so that he may employ it with safety. This key may be effectively mastered only by a peculiarly developed and rare type of man that from the standpoint of the standards of Caesar would be regarded as effeminate and weak. On a lower level, it is the same contrast that is afforded in the case of Jesus when He is contrasted with the political power of His day. A simple and saintly Man for a few years wandered up and down the roads of Palestine and spoke a few words also simple in form, though often obscure in meaning. Yet temporal and priestly power hated Him, as few men have been hated, and did all that it could, even over a period of centuries, to seek the destruction of the living stream that incarnated His words. Yet this Caesar-power, with all its impressive showing of material power, was forced to give way until ultimately it formally surrendered. Is not all this highly significant as revealing the hidden potency of Space-power?

It is true that the time-power, under the form of the Caesar-principle, does attain some degree of subsequent victory. In the instance of the history of Christianity, this was manifested through an apparent surrender of the former, followed by a subsequent adaptation of the new Force to its own purposes. In its purity, the Power, represented by Men like Jesus on the one hand, and by the philosophers and scientists on the other, is spiritual and is manifested through intellectual and moral vehicles. Subsequently, when through "boring from within" the Caesar-power gains control of the movements that originated in a spiritual impetus, the latter becomes largely crystallized and bound through being formalized in elaborate ritualism, genuflection, and convention. The emphasis of formal religion is then placed upon the story of the life of the Teacher, rather than upon the meaning of the Teaching. Finally, in greater or lesser degree, Caesar succeeds in capturing the force of space-power to serve his ends. The extreme manifestation of this we find in the wars of Christendom that Caesar succeeded in having fought in the name of the Prince of Peace!

But while all this reveals a certain tactical victory for time-power as incarnated in the Caesar-principle, the latter has actually incurred an important strategic weakening. The new power that Caesar has invoked actually contradicts him. This weakens Caesar's hand in the end. The result is that no political force in the West has ever been as fully successful as was Genghis Khan, who was an almost pure incarnation of the time-force in the political field. Today, Caesar is very much weaker than he seems. Sheer necessity forces him to restrain his will in the face of the knowledge of the technician. This simply means that the technician, together with the intelligences back of him, wields the ultimately higher power. Caesar may bluster and storm, but the quiet knowledge of law on the part of a few keen and some profound minds is a fatal curb upon his potency. To be sure, Caesar has a certain Samson-like power which he could will to use, but, like Samson, he would be crushed himself in the resulting debacle. So, all in all, if we compare the extent of Caesar-power before the Christian era with that which now exists after the leavening work of the thought of Jesus, supplemented later by that of the philosophers and scientists, we find Caesar in a much weaker position relatively. While he wields greater potencies than ever before, yet he is matched by powers of a still higher order. And temperamentally Caesar is disqualified to meet these higher powers. He can win in a temporary sense by destroying civilization and re-enslaving man, but he does not understand, and therefore cannot control, the powers which alone can lead to the genuinely higher culture wherein man attains more and more freedom.

★ ★ ★

In our day, the conflict between space and time is exemplified especially in the war between science and technology on the one hand, and politics on the other. Further, since money-power by psychological affinity lies close to technology, it must be aligned with science and technology in this conflict.* There is a deep reason for this conflict which should be understood as the issue is vital and of great current importance.

The space-power, whether represented in philosophic religion, technical philosophy, science, technology, or money-thought—in the modern sense—requires a careful use of a very vital instrument, i.e., concepts together with their enrobement in language. In order to attain understanding in any of these fields, particularly in those involving the use of the more subtle and intricate ideas, many years of careful discipline are required in the use of concepts and language. While a high order of imagination is required both for understanding and for creative activity in the higher phases of this domain, yet without the training in concepts and language this imagination is impotent. The requisite correctness and precision in the use of concepts is sometimes extreme. Even with an original endowment of natural talent or genius for these fields, the necessary skill is attained only by the most exacting kind of effort. Sometimes the precondition of the sufficiently precise concept is protracted labor on the part of very high talent. Naturally, such a vitally important and difficultly achieved instrument comes to have a value that is all but sacred. For it must be remembered, without these concepts no functioning in this domain can be effective. To give this point a more concrete form, I call attention to the fact that the machines of this age could not have been originated, then started into operation, and be kept in motion without the appropriate concepts and the men who had mastered them. There is but a handful of such men existing, but they make the machine-age possible. In contrast, a brute force which is far from intelligent can easily stop the machine. In this latter fact lies a danger to our civilization that is second only to that of war.

In contrast, the exercise of time-power does not require the mastery of carefully developed concepts. In the form of political power, the final instrument is brute force, and this in turn is controlled by psychological means. Now, the psychological use of language obeys radically different canons from that required in scientific language. Correctness and preci-

---

*Financial thinking combines both the political and the scientific spirit. In the older process of trading, a superior skill in deception was an important factor in success, in which case the difference between business and politics was less marked than it is coming to be at present. But as financial thinking has acquired greater maturity and has to operate in settings of ever greater and greater technical complexity, soundness and reliability have grown in importance as the conditions of success. Thus we are witnessing in business the evolution of financial engineering, and thus money-power is becoming less and less political in its spirit.

sion have no meaning here. The man who uses language as a psychological power may be utterly self-contradictory, his ideas may have the loosest sort of relationship with their supposed objects, and yet he may be highly successful. What he is actually doing is effecting a control of a certain kind of force through the exercise of an emotional key. Such a man may have a moral code and his private motive may be excellent, but his attitude toward concepts is amoral at best. On the other hand, the space-power type of man has a highly developed moral sense with respect to the use of concepts. Naturally, he is outraged through and through by this political and psychological use of concepts and language.

A profound consequence of this conflicting use of concepts and language is that there can be no sympathy between political power and technological power. In fact, the clash between the two domains may well be underlaid by a subtle hatred. Inevitably, the technician must view control by political power as an invasion by something inferior and certainly something inimical. As a result, political power, if once dominant, can crush and destroy the fruits of technology, but cannot lead toward, much less command, further and better achievement.* On the other hand, money-power can achieve and has achieved managerial control of technology, but the reason for this is that, in spite of surface frictions, there is a fundamental sympathy between these two due to a similarity of attitude toward, and use of, concepts and language. Neither does the other a deep and unforgivable violence. Finance, on the higher levels, requires the engineering type of mind, and all engineers, whatever the differences in their specialties, can understand each other in a fundamental sense. So it is possible for technology and money-power to co-operate, but both are outraged in their deeps by the loose, and in some respects, irresponsible modes of procedure of the political mind.

An illustration may make possible a clearer understanding of the irreconcilable nature of this conflict between technology and moneypower on the one hand, and a dominant political power on the other. Of very fundamental importance for both of the former is the rule that standards of measure should remain invariable. Invariables may be regarded as a phase of fundamental concepts by which alone is it possible to achieve calculated control of variables and unknowns. It is therefore a necessity for effective functioning in these fields that standards should not change,

---

* In this connection, it is a significant fact that in the totalitarian states where political power is dominant, the most imporant technological development has been in the adaptation of technical instruments for war.

or if they do, that they should do so in accordance with a perfectly determinant formula accessible to all. As a consequence, arbitrary political manipulation of standards has the effect of outrage for it cuts under the whole structure which is dependent upon careful calculation. The revealed attitude of political power in this matter simply illustrates how impossible it is to achieve real cooperation between dominant political power and technology. Further, this runs deeper than mere personal reaction. The political mind is quite incapable of understanding the necessities of technology.

★ ★ ★

That space is the greater power as compared with time is indicated by my own Recognitions. While the most inward State of all stands in a position of superiority with respect to space as well as time, there are intermediate stages, in some of which the space-quality is recognizable while the time-quality is not, but in others there is added to the space-quality a sort of modified time-quality. It is significant that the last expressible mode or quality of Consciousness, as the penetration proceeds inward, is something that can be indicated only by words such as "depth," "height," "inwardness," etc. These words with their corresponding concepts are manifestly of the spatial type. They have nothing to do with time. It is true that I have used above the term, "penetration" and this word clearly carries the connotation of "process," a time-quality. But process is not a part of the content or quality of the Consciousness Itself. There is no sense that the seeming penetration required an actual lapse of time. In the metaphysical sense, it is not correct to speak of the Recognition as an event, however much It may seem to be so from the standpoint of relative consciousness. I simply Awakened to an eternal Thereness—which in a mysterious sense is Hereness as well—that had absolutely nothing to do with Becoming. It is true that the self-consciousness in playing the part of witness did pass through a series of notations of states and analyses of them, and thus it still remained in some sort of time-field. But the witnessing self-consciousness must be carefully distinguished from the Primeval Consciousness witnessed. Now, the Primeval Consciousness is enrobed in a Space-Field, in some sense, at a level where no time-element is recognizable. This seems quite clearly to imply that, as compared with time, space wields the more ultimate power.

It should be clear by this time that I am constrained to assert a position at variance with that maintained by Spengler, who saw time as the father of space. Spengler recognized all cultured consciousness as essentially space-like and also realized that culture ever turned upon time and embodied life with a view to conquering them. Thus the Crown of all culture is well represented by Buddha.* The Message of Buddha is one of Liberation from all life-process with all its tragedy. But Spengler granted to such a Message only a temporary success. He thought he saw the time-life current ultimately undermining the Liberated State and melting It all in the stream of Becoming. Undoubtedly such must seem to be the case to a consciousness confined to the perspective of the historic stream, since all that persists for history is necessarily in time. However, Spengler has only been able to trace that which has not yet been conquered by space. That consciousness in which the desire for sentient existence has not yet been conquered is manifestly still in thralldom to time. But the Higher Consciousness, in which this desire has been destroyed has disappeared from historic observation. No one speaking from the perspective of a Spengler can possibly know anything of this. On the other hand, it is possible to Awaken to a Level of Consciousness wherein the Realized Man may Know that it is Buddha and not Spengler who represents the ultimately Triumphant Principle.

Viewed from the relative perspective, it seems quite clear that the gains of the Force for Liberation are numerically quite limited so far. But it should not be forgotten that these gains are absolute, for the Liberated Soul is outside the jurisdiction of time, whereas consciousness-bound-to-time-bodies is always subject to attack by the Force of Spatial Liberation. The Caesar-principle, being the child of time, is subject to Nemesis, while the space-power is not. Herein lies the basis for the profound optimism which makes it possible to say with certainty that ultimately all souls will be Emancipated from time-bondage.

★ ★ ★

I have developed the present thesis in terms of a conflict or war between two principles. Obviously, this is valid only from the relative perspective or as it appears in the time-stream. Metaphysically consid-

---

*The word "Buddha" has a three-fold meaning. The popular understanding is that it refers uniquely to the historic personage known as Guatama. But fundamentally it means "Enlightenment" in a transcendental or world-conquering sense. All who have established self-conscious identity with the synthetic non-dual consciousness are Buddhas.

ered, there is no victory to be achieved, for Primeval Consciousness never has in reality been bound. Time-bondage is only an effect existing for relative consciousness. *Arriving* at a State of Liberation has meaning for self-conscious consciousness, but not for Primeval Consciousness, which, like Space, is unaffected by the presence or absence of events.

SPACE remains the highest Divinity that is in any sense knowable, however dim that knowledge may be. Beyond lies the Eternally Unknowable, surrounded by impenetrable Darkness, Silence, and Voidness.

88
The Final Record

November 16

It is now one hundred one days since the great day of the Ineffable Transition and three months since I began the record that is now drawing to a close. It has been for the writer a most extraordinary period. He has known what it is to enter a State where he found himself complete; where the problems that weary the soul find their resolution; where there is a Joy unutterable; where there is found the satisfying and certain Knowledge; where there may be known the Companionship that gives the value of deep Communion; and where there is real Emancipation. He knows today, with the certainty of immediate Knowledge, that there is a hidden Kernel of utterly satisfying values within this husk of outer life. He has found the solution of the great metaphysical question, and so for him the Quest of life is finished.

There remains a work to do. There are almost unimaginably enormous fields of knowledge lying below and within the inconceivable Cognition, and for the unfolding of these possibilities, veritable ages are required. There is the work of leaving a record so that some aid may be given to those others who also seek to travel this way. This writing is a part of that task.

★ ★ ★

This would seem to be the time for making a general survey of the culminating effect of the past hundred days, so as to afford a basis for the evaluation of the event that I have called the Ineffable Transition. Its value to me in my inner life is clear and beyond doubt, a fact which, it seems, should be obvious to anyone who has read this book. Ever must I say: It is the Value beyond all other values. There is no counter-interest which relative life can offer that in the smallest degree would lead me to wish to turn my back upon the Transcendental World. There is nothing remaining here below that intrigues me, though some phases of outer life still remain more enjoyable than others. I desire that other individuals should Realize that which I have come to Know; and if I can be of assistance toward that end, I shall be glad to do what may be done. But the message I would carry would be that of another World, of another Life, and not one of mere amelioration of the world-field life. In this, my own conviction fully accords with the central theme of the Message of Jesus, i.e., that man must be Born again and enter into Real Life in another "Kingdom" or on another Level of Consciousness. For myself, I have now demonstrated, what others have already told, that it is not necessary to die here, in the physical sense, in order to be born again in that other World. But it does seem clear that, so long as man occupies bodies formed of the gross material of this plane, he can Realize the Transcendental World in only a penumbral sense. Gross matter opposes too much resistance to that Consciousness not to serve as something of a barrier. Yet, by a partial refinement of the materials entering into the composition of the compound human form, it is possible to achieve variable degrees of cross-correlation between the Transcendent and the outer relative life. Here we come to a question that requires for its solution a considerable exercise of discrimination. Let us consider this problem briefly.

The grosser the encasement of man, the deeper he can descend into the sphere of evil, dark, and confused consciousness without endangering his continued existence upon this plane of life. But also, the grosser the encasement, the greater the insulation from the Current of Higher Consciousness. As a counterfact, it is to be noted, that the more subtilized a human body may be, the greater is its potentiality in serving as a carrier of the Transcendent or Cosmic Consciousness. Other things being equal, the highest possible cross-correlation would be achieved by a man who had a body so subtle that it was just barely able to endure life on this plane. There is here, then, the action of two counter principles between which a working balance must be achieved in order that the Other-World Consciousness may have some degree of objective manifestation. The records of the cases of Cosmic Consciousness show the balance to have been achieved at quite various levels. In the western world, Plotinus seems to have had the greatest conscious command of inward penetration. But he lived in retirement and had so profound a distaste for the grossly physical that it is said he was ashamed that he possessed a physical body. He gave His values to the world through a philosophical vehicle and through a few personal disciples. At the other pole is a man like Walt Whitman who frankly loved the physical and lived much of the time in distinctly adverse environments. Whitman certainly was able to do what would have been quite impossible for Plotinus. But, on the other hand, the Light is manifested in far greater clarity in the case of the latter, and He had a power to penetrate the inward States as the result of his own conscious effort, something Whitman did not have.

Which of these two achievements constitutes the greatest offering to the world? I do not believe that there is any absolute answer to this question. It all depends upon the need of the hour, the stratum of humanity which is influenced, and the native capacities of the individual who has attained the Cosmic Consciousness. One type of man may achieve a wider breadth of direct human contact, another can manifest the Light in greater purity and completeness but can reach relatively only the few who are better prepared to receive. Both services are needed.

For my own part, at this moment I have not yet consolidated a working balance. The better attuned I am to Inwardness, the harder I find it to endure the harsh world-forces which I find striking in various subtle ways, difficult to describe. In contrast, if I harden myself so that I can endure those forces more easily, I find that the Inward clarity is distinctly clouded. My inclination is to retreat to the wilds and work from there. What working basis will prove to be both possible and desirable has not yet been determined. At present, though living in a semi-retreat but within the psycho-sphere of a great center of population, I find the impact of the world-force difficult to meet, and it has been a strain on the organism. Whether or not I can build outer ruggedness without destroying the requisite inward sensitiveness remains for the future to determine. For my own part, it would only be with the greatest reluctance that I would accept a clouding of inward capacity in order to extend the range of direct personal contact. To accept that course, I would have to be convinced that the social values achieved were worth the cost.

During the past three months, I have focused nearly all my efforts upon the problem of expression and, as might be expected, the principal objective effects of the Transition are focused upon the faculties exercised in such work. I find a distinct increase of capacity in terms of understanding and introception. Never have I produced so much material in so short a time, and much of this deals with concepts that are difficult to capture.

I find a new kind of concept being born into my mind. It is not yet sufficiently tangible to give it a clear delineation, and it is questionable how far present word-forms and even logic may serve for enrobing it. If our more familiar concepts may be thought of as granular and capable of fixed definition, this other kind of concept might be called fluidic or functional and not possessed of fixed definition. As nearly as I can describe it, I would say that this new concept is something like this: An idea enters or is born into the mind, but at once the counter idea achieves recognition. Then the original idea takes on a sort of flowing quality which seems to proceed toward the level that synthesizes both it and the counter idea. There is something in this that suggests the dialectic form of Hegel, but the movement is fluidic rather than in a series of discrete triadic steps. In some respects these concepts seem like vortices in consciousness, as there is a certain quality that suggests a turning inside out that proceeds continuously. So long as I do not try to express this thought, it carries a high order of clarity. It does not involve a defiance of logic, but it seems to require further logical laws, not yet recognized. When I attempt to give this thought expression, I have difficulties. It tends to disappear, and I often feel something like a nascent dizziness. It leaves me with the feeling that what I write or say is only partly true, try as I will to be as correct as possible. Thus these sentences both reveal and veil at the same time. It is not an easy Sea in which to think, when one tries to retain correlation with the outer consciousness. Whatever success I do attain in navigating in this compound of the Sea and relative consciousness, I owe very largely to the years of training in higher mathematics. Often I feel tempted to fall back upon the relatively inchoate expression of poetry where the conceptual demands are less exacting.

This effort has entailed quite a considerable demand upon the forces of the physical organism. Since the beginning of this writing, I have scarcely lived in the field of the action and reception senses. As a consequence, they have been despoiled in a degree of the values that otherwise would have accrued to them out of the Transition. This simply illustrates the importance of the effect of focusing. The Higher Consciousness, in a greater or lesser degree, is formless and thus is in the nature of a general Power which may be made effective in whatever direction It is focused. So far, I have concentrated principally in the field of thought and consciousness-correlation; and thus quite naturally it is in this region that the main effects are to be noted. I chose this course spontaneously and deliberately, for this is a region toward which my interest gravitates naturally. Others, differently constituted, would not have had the same experience.

★ ★ ★

As the final and crowning word of this record, I wish to state my appreciation, and give my tribute, to her who has journeyed by my side in this quest of the ancient yet ever new World; that World which is at once the Source and final Home of all creatures. The completed human being is both man and woman, but on this objective level of consciousness the true balance of these two is not found in one embodiment. So here in this world, the best that may be attained is not achieved by one alone. Man and woman, each in his separate nature, have peculiar powers, and that which is visibly true here also has its higher analogue in the Greater World. Whereas the strongest impulse of man is a passion for Freedom, woman in contrast conceives and cherishes Form. Corresponding to these two types of genius are the grand principles of Liberation and Compassion. It is not in accordance with the nature of the exclusively masculine principle ever to turn back from the Liberation of the great and free Space. But the feminine nature never forgets the needs of embodied form. It is the Woman in Men like Buddha and Christ that has made them Masters of Compassion, as the Man in Them made them conquerors of Mara. Emancipation for an individual soul is but a partial achievement, for the weal of units is not the Liberation of mankind. It is the others, whom man alone might easily forget, that woman never forgets.

In many ways, down through the years, Sherifa has never allowed me to forget the call whispered through the suffering of others. For my own part, I was content to unite with Space alone, but the justice of her claim for these others I could not deny. So, if at the final moment when Consciousness rested Free in the High Indifference and it was too late to form a genuinely new decision, for no desire is born There, if at the final moment, previously formed decision ruled my return to action in this bound-world below, it was the words and love of Sherifa, who never forgets those others, that were ultimately decisive. There is, within this book, a short poem to "Compassion" (Chapter 73), for which, while I supplied the words, Sherifa gave the Soul. Left to myself alone, it is highly probable that I would never have troubled to embody in words this that is written here but, rather, would have sailed on in an utterly satisfying Consciousness. So, if this book has values for other human souls, if, because of it, some other wanderers are led to seek for the Great Pearl, then thanks are due most to her who never forgot them. It is true that I brought to the task a certain skill and the advantage of some training, but withal I inclined to be far too aloof and indifferent to care to put forth the effort. But the Compassion instilled from her heart would not let it be so. Thus this book is sent forth as our common offering to those others who, soul-sick and weary in the meshes and mazes of Sangsara, yearn for the Light.

May Peace and final Victory come to all those who, having found the emptiness of life external, hunger for the Life that is Everlasting.

OM TAT SAT

89
The Supreme Adventure

AT LONG LAST the forest lay behind,
Before stretched a desert, bleak and empty,
Beyond, a mountain, dim in the dancing haze,
Reaching upward, defeating all measure.
I sat resting in the shade of the forest-rim,
The last cool stream at my feet.
Deeply I drank refreshment and pondered:
Long had the journey been and weary
In the maze and the dark of the forest,
Oft had I drifted down false lanes,
Oft had courage been shaken,
Yet I never quite failed to try again
And at last the dim trails were finished.
Behind lay desires, vain and incomplete,
Ambitions inadequate, yearnings now stilled;
Before, reaching all but endlessly,
A dreary waste, trailess and void of sign.
It seemed I beheld the Goal, dim in the distance,
But, again, It seemed not there.
Was uncertain possibility worth the effort?
Could anything be worth the cost

Paid, and yet remaining to be paid?
Oh! for the rest without ending,
If not the rest of Victory,
Then the surcease of defeat,
But in any case rest.
Thus I pondered while a new strength grew
And resolution again was born
Of the ashes of burned desires and yearnings.
Methought: "Better onward continue,
Else all this effort uncompleted
Useless would lie in the void of vain endeavor.
If thought of achievement thrills no longer,
Yet 'twere better to complete the half-finished.
Behind lie values exhausted and lost,
No longer potent to 'rouse the soul
That, in vision, a Beyond hath glimpsed.
Onward alone lieth hope
To fill the void."
At last I arose, resolution firm,
Gathered my staff and compass—
Sole possessions of the final hour—
And strode me forth beyond visible trail.
Ere long the forest behind me vanished,
Consumed in refracting desert haze;
Then all about the emptiness of burning waste.
On I journeyed in time-expanding void,
Unafraid, but weary with the seeming endlessness;
On I journeyed o'er rock and sand and thorn,
Alone in the stillness that is not Peace;
On I journeyed, thirsting ever more and more
For refreshing waters of the forest past recall;
Yet on I journeyed as thirst grew numb,
The mountain, haze consumed, as the forest.
And time, my tread less resolute became;
The void without become likewise a void within,
All endeavor unavailing.
I sank me down upon a rock,
Caring nought, accepting what might be.
Then spoke the VOICE,
In accents strong, cheering, comforting,

Calling from out the Beyond,
Telling of the Glory There,
Recalling the need of forest wanderers.
Within me a new courage grew, a new determination.
Once more I 'rose, onward moving,
Feeling more clear, though not yet seeing
The ancient Mount of untellable Majesty.
The desert journey, all but finished,
Now lay behind.
Already the slopes, mounting in steeper gradient,
Promise of final fulfillment offered.
Steeper grew the Way, but easier,
Strange paradox of a World, inverting former values.
Quickly I ascended, filled with strength
Born downward from Beyond.
The haze grew thin and vanished.
Then, before me, immeasurable Largeness,
Buttresses of the ancient Mountain;
Height rising on height, beyond all vision.
Filled anew with cheer and rich assurance,
Fast I climbed, until at last
Above me stretched the awful cliff,
Transcending the final reach of thought.
Here I lingered but briefest hour,
Extracting from thought its inmost core,
Seeking the Power above all powers.
Success crowned effort beyond all hope
And, as it were, in Time's briefest instant,
Outreaching time and space and cause, I rose
To unthinkable heights beyond unthinkable heights,
Finding at last the ancient Home,
Long forgotten, yet Known so well.
Gone was the forest-world, a new World mine;
Joy untellable, Knowledge all-consuming,
Eternity stretching everywhere;
Not anywhere aught but I
Sustaining all universes,
Their origin and consummation.
Darkness of ineffable LIGHT
Enveloping all.

II

Darkness, Silence, Voidness, utter,
At once, Fullness in every sense;
Deeps beyond seeing, beyond feeling, beyond thought;
At the inmost Core of all I AM,
Sustaining all, not different from all.
Untellable ages, a moment of time,
All time, but one moment there.
From the inmost Core, descending—downward, outward—
Distances immeasurable I came,
'Til finding the Thought unutterable,
Here, lingering, I dwelt for a season,
Thinking what I could not say,
Understanding transcending human conceiving,
Pure Meaning close-packed and o'erflowing,
Containing of libraries the substance all
And more, ne'er yet told.
Filled to the brim, I descended, down through the haze,
Which, ever inclosing the world below,
Holds dispart the Mountain Top
From the nether world of outer life.
Gone was the desert and forest-maze,
Scenes of age-old wanderings.
The Way to Heights ineffable a mystery no more,
A new mystery spread below.
Seething multitudes rushing to and fro
O'er far-reaching plane;
Bent over, searching the earth,
Grubbing here and there, ne'er still,
Driven as slaves, joyless and dull,
Seeking the Gold, finding dross.
One here, one there, standing in pause
Looking upward, eyes dim with pain,
Yearning, questioning, searching,
Not Knowing, yet hungering.
These, aliens all in a foreign land;
Their Home forgotten, yet dimly recalled

As the memory of distant dream.
I stood upon a lofty Field
At the edge of thought articulate,
Pondering the scene below,
Recalling the days I, too, was there
Seeking blindly for I knew not what;
Remembering effort—misdirected, barren of harvest.
All these my brothers are,
All these, not different from Me;
I, Free, yet not wholly Free,
While these, bound, remain, travailing.
Questioning, I pondered their sad estate,
Wondering how might release
For all be won.
Then gazing about me, on that lofty Field,
Beheld I a Glorious Company
Of Men, rare, Divinely Noble,
All striving ceaselessly in deep Compassion
With multitudes far below.
From These, methought I saw
Rays of Light, out-reaching and down,
Search-lights seeking quickened hearts and minds.
Then peering close, beheld I those who,
Pausing, raised their eyes in questing, hungering search,
Each enveloped in Search-Light Ray.
Along these Beams a Call forth-send
Arousing to fuller wakefulness
Ancient Memory.
Some, responding, gropingly to seek began,
Hunting the dim-felt but unseen Light,
Greatly tripping, meandering hither and yon,
Yet falteringly drawing nearer and nearer.
Then spoke the Voice, well loved,
From out an ancient Day, another Life,
Uttering words of counsel sage.
"Thou would'st of this harvest share,
Of souls drawn Home to Peace and Joy?
Then seek again the way

In yon fields below.
None knows the final secret of human soul,
So ever We try and try again,
In every way, old memory to 'rouse.
Go forth and try thy way."
So again I pondered the trials I knew,
The effort wasted, endeavor fruitless,
The final Success, the Key thereto.
Methought:
" 'Tis needless, the journey so hard should be.
A little turn here, another there,
And many a barrier and morass deep,
Easily surmounted will be.
I shall tell of the Way
Which at last I found,
That others in a dearer Light may See."
So I drew a chart, the best I knew,
And here it is for all
Who, wandering in forest and desert drear,
Wish that a clearer Way might revealed be.

90
Addendum to the High Indifference

January 19

The High Indifference, interpreted in Chapter 52, constitutes the culminating point of the whole cycle. It occurred almost exactly thirty-three days after the initial Transition. This event was quite unexpected and there was no premonitory excitement as in the first instance. I had had a warning to be on the watch for something involving a time-cycle of thirty-three, but I had no hint as to whether it was a matter of years, months, weeks, or days. I had already discounted the idea that it was only a question of days. In any case, up to the 8th of September, I had not noted the fact that nearly thirty-three days had rolled around. In fact, my attention was almost exclusively occupied with the stream of ideas to which I was giving formulation. Certainly I was not seeking anything more and had not the faintest idea what something more could possibly be. Thus this second Transformation was thoroughly spontaneous or autonomous so far as any conscious effort or seeking on my part was concerned.

The interpretation of this culminating Transition afforded extraordinary difficulties. The result of the first effort was far from satisfactory. At the close of the second period of thirty-three days, again I found myself in a state of exceptional lucidiy. At that time I undertook a fresh interpretation and was much more successful. This is the formulation that is given in the above discussion. It is an universal characteristic of all mystical states that they cannot be conveyed adequately in any conceptual formulation. The reason for this is clear once it is realized that the essence of the mystical state is a Consciousness that does not fall within the subject-object framework. In contrast, all language presupposes that framework. Thus, the idea, which of necessity is an object of consciousness, cannot contain or represent in the usual sense a consciousness-value where the subject and the object become co-extensive. But the more usual mystical state has an effective content which can be suggested sufficiently well so that anybody can sense that it is desirable. For states that are blissful, happy, or joyous are quite naturally humanly desirable. Because of this, and so far as I can see only because of this, it is possible for the typical egoistic man to desire and therefore seek mystical Realization. But when we deal with the notion of a state of Consciousness which, in addition to transcending the subject-object framework, is also marked by being neutral with respect to Bliss and its opposite, it appears that here we have something that lies quite outside the range of either human conception or desire. That, in addition, such a state should have the highest superiority and could even be preferred to a state of Bliss, certainly seems fantastic to say the least. Yet I can testify that such is the case. However I have found from experience that every effort I have put forth to make this fact convincing to other individuals has been unsuccessful. Indeed, I find that those individuals who come closest to the meaning which I am seeking to convey tend to be appalled. Others simply are not aware of the implications, save perhaps in a detached or academic sense.

At times I have debated the wisdom of releasing for publication the report of this more profound state of Consciousness. Two considerations have finally led to a positive decision. In the first place, lack of understanding automatically protects those who have not yet attained the affective maturity to face the Reality. In the second place, it is just this culminating Transition that supplies the keystone in the philosophic statement that is coming to birth in my mind as a result of the whole cycle. It is because of this cycle of Recognitions, and only because of them, that the resultant philosophy stands on a much more fundamental basis than mere speculative system-building. It is not a philosophy of mere arbitrary concepts, but a reflection in the form of a philosophic symbol of a realized Reality. Thus, to exclude the report of the actual unfoldment in Consciousness would be to leave the resultant philosophy suspended in the thin air of pure abstraction.

None of my previous readings in Theosophic or Vedantic sources had prepared me for anything like the state of Consciousness which I have called the "High Indifference." Up to that time, my familiarity with the Buddhist teachings had been mostly confined to translations of selections from the southern Canon. I knew that Buddhism taught the doctrine of Anatma and Nastikata, that is, the unreality of the Self and of God. But I had understood this in the sense of the unreality of a personal or individual self and of the unreality of any anthropomorphic God. I had not realized that there was a still more profound interpretation of these doctrines. It was only considerably subsequent to the cycle of Recognition that I came into possession of the translations from Tibetan Buddhism, edited by Walter Y. Evans-Wentz, and the *Buddhist Bible*, edited by Dwight Goddard. In the literature thus made available, for the first time I was enabled to verify the content of the Recognition called the "High Indifference." The two-fold egolessness of the more philosophic Buddhist Sutras conforms with my own mystical discovery. The most profound depth of consciousness transcends the Supreme Self as well as the egoistic self. Likewise, the reality of God is co-extensive with the reality of the Self. Thus, so long as there is a seeming of a Self there is a seeming of God that has equal reality. God is the Other of the Self that with most men abides only in the psychologic unconscious. But from the highest level of Recognition, it is seen that there is no independent reality to be attached to either the notion of a Supreme Self or a Supreme Being. In a derived sense both are real, but in the ultimate underived sense there is neither a God nor a Self but simply pure Primordial Consciousness.

Like many other students, I had formerly supposed that the notion of Nirvana pointed toward the most ultimate possibility of consciousness. The Realization of the High Indifference revealed the actuality of a more comprehensive Consciousness. At the time I was rather dumbfounded by this discovery, and made an almost frantic search for confirmation in the literature that I had available at the time. I saw quite clearly that Nirvanic Consciousness stood in polar relationship to objective consciousness, and therefore was not really synthetic. But I felt that there should be some reference to this super-Nirvanic state somewhere in mystical literature. Ultimately I did find the reference, but only when the translations from Tibetan Buddhism came into my possession. The word "Nirvana" is not always used in the same sense, and this is a source of considerable confusion. Sometimes it refers to Shunyata—the state which I have elsewhere called "Consciousness-without-an-object" and "Consciousness-without-a-subject." For the purpose of clarity, I have confined the use of the term "Nirvana" to pure subjective Consciousness.

Many philosophic thinkers have not only taken the subject-object framework as a fundamental form of all consciousness, but they have regarded desire as an ultimate determinant. Thus, for instance, the Pragmatic school of philosophy introduces desire or purpose as an essential part of their theory of knowledge. To know the High Indifference is to know that this theory possesses only partial validity. Pragmatism defines only a limited sector of consciousness. It is the very essence of Emancipation that it transcends just this sector. On the level of the High Indifference, there is no desire whatsoever, but simply unlimited potentiality. To find the Real, it is absolutely necessary to transcend desire. But it is impossible for the desire-bound consciousness to imagine the supernal value of that Consciousness which is free from desire. In the whole notion of desiring Desirelessness there is an inherent contradiction until somehow one has Realized that superior State and thus Knows directly Its superiority. The pragmatic epistemology has only pragmatic value within a relatively narrow field of consciousness and no more. As compared to Enlightenment, Pragmatism seems cheap.

In the Sutras contained in the "Buddhist Bible," frequent references are to be found referring to the "turning about in the deepest seat of consciousness." I find that this also has a two-fold meaning. In the first place, ordinary consciousness is bound to the object by a force which we may call "gravitation." The early struggle for Emancipation is against this force until ultimately a point is reached where it has become neutralized. This is a point of peculiar difficulty on the Path, for the old motivation has ceased to operate, and the opposite force does not yet dominate. It can easily become a place of despair. One can continue at this point only through the exercise of the will without any affective aid. But, if the individual persists, presently he finds himself within the field of another force, which we may call "levitation." From this point on through the next phase, the attraction of the Subject acts as spontaneously as formerly did the attraction of the object. The battle with obstacles is finished and the formerly most difficult accomplishment becomes the easiest. This is clearly a kind of "turning about" in consciousness. But it is not the "turning about at the deepest seat of consciousness." The latter requires the turning away from the subject. The record of this second "turning away" is given in the above discussion. My own conscious part in it was merely the renunciation of private enjoyment of Bliss. For the rest, it just happened.

I consider it a fortunate fact that prior to the cycle in 1936, I had not been a student of the profounder Buddhist teachings. For thus it gives to this cycle the value of independent verification. It shows, further, that Buddha discovered universal a Reality, and not merely something that is valid for Oriental consciousness alone. In this, we are dealing with the underlying Roots of all Consciousness.

91
Conclusion: Two Years Later

January 30

A little more than two years has elapsed since the completion of the foregoing writings. Although immediate publication had been my intention, yet through one factor or another, this has been delayed. This has proved to be, on the whole, a fortunate circumstance, as the delay has afforded me the opportunity to view the whole cycle from the perspective of temporal distance. As a result of this longer view, it is possible to report a more objective evaluation of the whole event than I could effect at the time when I was more occupied with the freshness of the new Presence. In addition, during the interval I have devoted considerable time to the search of both oriental and occidental literature which had a bearing upon the more metaphysical states of consciousness. As has been noted in the body of the text, there were certain features in the second Transformation for which previous studies had not prepared me. Fortunately, through recent translations and publications of selections from the Northern Buddhist Canon that have come into my possession during the interim, I have been enabled to give the content of that transformed Consciousness something on the order of an objective verification. Presumptively, a brief report of both the evaluation and the verification will be of value to the interested reader, and so I am including them as an addendum to this book.

It is entirely natural that a western student, nurtured in the tradition of physical science, should ask for a scientific treatment of any material which he is expected to consider seriously. Unfortunately, the immediate or intimate elements or states of consciousness do not lend themselves to any such treatment, for our science is oriented exclusively to objective material. Value and meaning are elements of consciousness which cannot be observed. They can be realized through introception, but this, for any individual, is an intensely private matter. It is impossible, by western scientific method, to observe the inner consciousness of any individual other than that of one's own self. The objective behaviour of the organization of an individual, who reports the realization of an unusual inner state of consciousness, may be observed in the scientific sense. But only the crassest kind of extravert would affirm that the inwardly realized value and meaning can be appropriately measured and appreciated through the study of observable behaviour. So the question of the status of any reported inner state of consciousness falls quite outside the range of the methodological technique of western science.

However, I cannot help but feel sympathy with the reluctance of the critical western student to accept statements relative to the mystical states of consciousness, on the basis of faith alone. For my part, I ask anyone not to believe blindly, but merely to be open-minded. There is no final verification save through immediate realization. All that I, or anyone else, can do is to build a presumption which may be sufficient to lead the student to seek private verification himself. This last statement is strictly true with respect to the student who approaches the subject in the critical intellectual spirit exclusively. If, on the other hand, the individual seeker is willing to dare on the basis of faith, in the spirit of the true pioneer, something more can be done for him. In the body of the text I have spoken of the power of "induction" or "contagion." Since writing that I have had rather extensive experience with this power, and have found it even more potent than I then realized. On innumerable occasions, when, either spontaneously or deliberately, I entered the Field of the Current, responsive individuals, who were present, were carried into the same Field in greater or lesser degree. I have secured several written reports of these induced states, and, in many instances, have been astonished by the mystical depths revealed in them. I have a number of reports which would compare more than favorably with the bulk of those given in Bucke's "Cosmic Consciousness" or in William James' "Varieties of Religious Experience." Here is a method of individual verification that approaches something of the requirements of a scientific check.

But strict scientific methodology requires that the observer shall, himself, stand apart from that which he observes. Admittedly, for many purposes, this aloofness is of superior value. But it may be applied only to strictly objective material, and never to the content of inner consciousness itself. In the latter case, the observer must become his own object. Further, he must permit himself in the aspect of observer to occupy an inferior status as compared to Himself as the observed. This is apt to prove quite a strain upon the pride of the scientific mind, for the typical scientist has a distinctly over-weening superiority-complex with respect to his observing function. It is difficult for the scientific mind to acquire real humility in this respect; yet, if it is acquired, it becomes possible to investigate even the transcendent Level of Consciousness.

Yet, even for the individual who maintains the attitude of the aloof observer, I have found at least one phenomenon that can be isolated from the subject's report of the inner content of consciousness. This is the phenomenon of the psycho-physical heat. In the early days, following the first Transformation on August 7th, I soon had my attention attracted to this phenomenon. Personally, I had the sense of Fire, but through identifying myself with this Fire rather than with the organism, I rarely had the experience of heat. Fire is not hot to itself. But those near me very soon began reporting an experience of heat which was often so extreme as to be far from comfortable. This was an effect for which I had not been prepared by my previous studies. Since then, I have found several references to it in Tibetan Buddhism, but in these cases it was a deliberately developed phenomenon for the purpose of the very practical protection from intense cold. Ascetics, living in caves well above the timber-line, would either have to find some unusual protection from the cold or perish. But, in my case, there was no thought of seeking heat, and so the phenomenon was quite spontaneous. However, the most significant fact is that it is an effect that has been experienced principally by those who have been in my vicinity rather than by myself. Further, it is not an hallucination or the effect of suggestion. Often the observer can detect a noticeable flush or the breaking forth of perspiration. In addition, the body of the subject is frequently warm to the touch. It is, however, a very curious kind of warmth. To the touching hand, the surface of the body may not seem notably warm but, rather, it is felt in the forearm, a little above the hand. I have felt a similar warmth when touching the terminal of a high-frequency electro-magnetic current. The terminal itself seemed cool, but the arm became warm.

Now, in this effect of the psycho-physical heat there is something that deserves scientific study. What is it? What is its cause? For my own part, I am convinced that in this we are in the presence of a manifestation of the Libido, in the sense Dr. C. G. Jung has employed the term in his later writings. But I have proved to my satisfaction that it is a force which is subject to considerable conscious control. In the Tibetan Yogic Manuals there is a decidedly elaborate technique outlined for the development of the psycho-physical heat. Part of this technique consists of posturing and certain breathing practices. There are also fairly elaborate rituals and visualizations listed. In my own case, I have found none of this necessary. Often the inciting cause has been apparently nothing more than a rather abstract philosophic discussion or analysis of the various components of consciousness when suddenly the heat-effect was produced and experienced by the vast majority of those present. For my own part, in such cases, I have generally not been thinking of the heat-effect at all, but merely of the content of the thought I was developing. In the case of the philosophic discussions in the seminars or philosophic clubs of the university, I never experienced anything like this, nor have I heard of anyone else testifying to it. No; the heat is a witness of the presence of something more than merely the intellectual content of consciousness. I repeat: This is something that can be observed and should be studied.

★ ★ ★

At the present time, about two and one-half years after that 7th of August, the Door of Consciousness that then was opened still remains open. There is, however, a difference. In the beginning, the Higher Consciousness occupied the position of the central focus of my individual awareness. At present, It is more like a peripheral Matrix back of and surrounding the central focus of awareness, which in its turn is occupied the preponderant portion of the time with relative contents. My private center of consciousness seems to occupy a sort of intermediate zone, between the relative and non-relative. I find myself able to turn either way, but I am never as completely occupied with either mode of consciousness as formerly. When speaking or writing concerning the Higher Consciousness, even when enveloped in the Field of the Current, my private consciousness is more occupied with the problem of the situation than with the immediate value of the Higher Consciousness Itself. The effective psychical state for this kind of functioning calls for a very fine balance and a distinctly positive will. Thus there cannot be a self-abandonment to the affective or noetic value of the Consciousness at such times. I have indubitable evidence that a considerable number of individuals have received distinctly superior values from this kind of functioning. There have been some instances bordering on ecstatic trance, though the rule has been the experiencing of ecstatic or noetic values without any trance effect. When functioning on the platform or in the classroom, I enter considerably less into the ecstatic effect than is clearly evident in the case of several students. The work-effort of the functioning occupies by far the most of my private consciousness.

I find that the Higher Consciousness is partly spontaneous and partly under the control of a will that I can direct. The transition from the relative to the non-relative functioning is quite subtle. The pre-condition is an affective calmness. Any notable disturbance of my emotional state nullifies my control. However, the technique for paralyzing the affective disturbance does not seem to be difficult to master. All that is required is a certain exercise of the will that quickly erases the emotional complex. Then in a setting of substantial calmness and detachment, all that is needed is a turn of consciousness-focus which seems something like the manipulation of a butterfly-valve controlling alternative passages. All that seems necessary is the intent to do this with appropriate application of the will. I find it quite impossible to describe the detail of the process, but then there is nothing surprising in this, as I find myself equally unable to describe the process of energizing the muscles of my arm when seeking to perform some physical function. It is much easier to move one's arm than to describe all the psychical processes involved in the act. I find that the position of the body or of any parts of the body is entirely a matter of indifference, except that the body should be sufficiently comfortable not to divert the attention. I pay no attention to the breathing process. In fact, such experiments as I have made with the tantric techniques have been barren of any worthwhile result. I also find the use of mantramic intonations quite unnecessary, though on occasion I have used a few mantrams with success. But in the latter case, only those mantrams that carried a meaning with which I already concurred intellectually have had any value. On the whole, when I make use of this technique, I secure the quickest results from aphorisms that I have composed myself.

Sometimes the shift of the "butterfly-valve" occurs without my personal consciousness intending it. Thinking, reading, or talking about the Higher Consciousness, more often than not, will accomplish this. Sometimes I am so occupied with the content of the idea that others, who are present, are aware of the shift before I am. I can continue the process of mentation after the shift, but the thought assumes a greater depth-quality and there is a definite slowing of the rate of idea-formation. There is a necessity of "stepping gently" in order to avoid the breaking of a very fine balance.

The shifting back from the non-relative to the relative level of functioning is also under my control, but this shift involves a much more gradual process in the subsidence than is the case in connection with the initiation of the State. There is something in this analogous to residual magnetism. An iron bar may be almost instantaneously magnetized by turning on an electric current through a surrounding coiled wire, but a degree of magnetism may remain for some time after the current has been turned off.

The Field of the Higher Consciousness does make some demand upon the resources of the psycho-physical organism. Something like work-effort is involved with a resultant subtle fatigue. Wisdom requires that the function shall be restricted to the resources of the psycho-physical organism. However, the total effect upon the latter after the passage of time is an improvement of the general healthtone.

I find it necessary to use my own methods, which I have myself discovered or, at least, modified, if they were first suggested to me from some other source. I am unable to say whether this is a general rule or merely a peculiarity of my own psychical temperament. At any rate, I find the matter of technique to be highly individualistic.

As to the location of my private consciousness, it seems to be in a very solitary place. In a sense, I seem to stand between two worlds, one a Realm of Ecstasy, the other, a world of pain. The latter is this world of ordinary consciousness. I see into this lower world far more clearly than ever before. I see uncleanness of which I scarcely dreamed formerly. Empiric human nature is a sadly defective thing. At the central core of every human being is a very precious Jewel, but all too often it is covered with a case of unclean mud. The Jewel is to be trusted and valued, but not the case of outer human nature. To see realistically is a painful thing, and I do not recommend such a view to one who places a high value upon his personal comfort. It would be devastating to one who had no vision of the Jewel, unless he happened to be a lover of the mud. The only thing to recommend the life between the worlds is the fact that it affords the possibility to do something about the mud. The Inner Fire can so transform the psychical mud that it too may become part and parcel with the Jewel. It is a very significant fact that the diamond is chemically the same as soot and that the ruby is a compound of the commonest metal and the commonest element, both of which are important components of common clay.

This solitary place is one of pain and Joy. It unites qualities that tend to pull apart. From this place it is possible to shed Joy while accepting the offering of pain. It is useless to pretend that the function is a comfortable one, though there are deep satisfactions. It is not comfortable watching men sowing the seeds of pain, when another and joyful life is near at hand, just waiting to be accepted. It is not comfortable to have to stand by waiting for pain to perform its purifying office. It is not comfortable to resist the desire to leave forever this dreary and empty world. And yet, what else can one do when he knows that he has the means of release which can change the state of the few or the many who will accept?

★ ★ ★

In the body of the text I have already noted the fact that in the Recognition which I have called the "High Indifference," a quality of Consciousness was realized for which previous studies had not prepared me. The only conceptual pattern which would correspond to this State was one which placed Nirvana in a relative status with respect to the objective universe or Sangsara. In contrast, my former studies had led me to the belief that Nirvana was the absolutely non-relative State. My intuitive perception on the level of the culminating Recognition was very clear, but intellectually I desired verification. In the search of my old sources I drew a blank. It was only when, at a later date, I came into possession of *The Tibetan Book of the Dead*, *Tibetan Yoga and Secret Doctrines*, edited by Walter Y. Evans-Wentz, and *The Buddhist Bible*, edited by Dwight Goddard, that I found the verification which I sought. It is quite evident that the Enlightenment of Buddhism is not identical with the Nirvanic State of Consciousness—which is simply the counterpole of objective consciousness—but a still more profound Consciousness that is neither objective nor subjective. At present, it appears to me that simple logic should have made it clear that the ultimate synthetic Consciousness could not stand in polar relationship to the objective world. It must be

THAT which equally includes or nullifies both poles, thus enveloping subjectivity as well as objectivity. However, I had failed to think my thoughts through in this respect, thus having to wait upon the Realization before making the discovery. How much time is lost because of intellectual laziness!

The ultimate synthetic Consciousness is beyond the reach of thinking, feeling, sensation, and intuition, but depends upon another Way of Consciousness which simply has no recognition in western psychology and philosophy. The Buddhist name for this Way of Consciousness is Dhyana, which is a good deal more than "meditation" as generally understood. It is a latent function of consciousness that so far has been only rarely active among men. Its study is quite beyond the reach of western psychologic methodology, since the latter is oriented to observation rather than to introception. But it is possible, by the appropriate means, to arouse Dhyana to action and in It alone lies the Door to Enlightenment. The functioning of Dhyana is a mystery. Instructions in the practice of Dhyana exist, but anything that can be described is only a collateral objective aid that may be of use to certain psychological temperaments while it fails with others. It is simply impossible to describe the essential laws which govern the functioning of Dhyana, while the collateral aids which work with one psychologic type may have to be radically modified when applied to a different type. The psychical structure of the East Indian and especially of the Chinese is radically different from our own. Hence, merely to transplant methodologies which have been successful in the Orient into the Occident is a case of using the "right method with the wrong man." It is only the combination of the "right method with the right man" that works. This means that for the West the whole problem of devising the effective collateral aids has to be resolved in new terms. We shall have to employ the powers which we have unfolded in superior degree, rather than depend upon those which, while strongly developed in the Orient, are weak with us. Today this is a pioneering problem.

But while the problem of method varies with the type and even with the individual, the Goal is eternally the same. One does not have to be a Mystic to see that this must be so. The very fact that we instinctively integrate all men by calling them "humanity" or "mankind," and all creatures by uniting them under the concept of "living forms," reveals an instinctive recognition of underlying unity. It is only because of an underlying unity that it is possible for men to communicate with each other and be understood at all. Thus there must be a common denominator, and all those who find this common denominator, no matter who or where they are, will find exactly the same thing. This Common Denominator is the Goal of Dhyana.

Necessarily, the Common Denominator is nameless, since genuine naming always implies defining. It can be symbolized, but such a symbol merely points to the indefinable Reality. This necessity should also be clear, for the definable is merely that which can be comprehended by thinking. It is, therefore, less than the thought-power. On the other hand, that which comprehends the thought-power, as well as all other functions of consciousness, is ever beyond delimitation by any function or group of functions.

Several symbols for the Nameless do exist. In the first place, I symbolized It by the "High Indifference." Subsequently, I have called It "Consciousness-without-an-object which is also Consciousness-without- a-subject." But no one can really think such a Consciousness, for then at once It would have become an object, a something comprehended by the subject-object consciousness. In Buddhism, It is known as "Shunyata" and this is variously translated as "Voidness" or as "Suchness." It is also frequently referred to as the "Dharmakaya." The Chinese have symbolized It by "Tao." Perhaps as good a symbol as any is SPACE, provided the Space is understood as being unaffected by either the presence or absence of a universe within it. Thus, the space of the Einstein-relativity would not serve as an adequate symbol, since this is affected by the presence or absence of concentrations of matter.

The identification of the Common Denominator under diverse symbols is largely intuitive, but it is aided by observing the way in which they are used and by the statements made concerning the corresponding Consciousness. Very readily, I found that both "Tao" and "Shunyata" have the same symbolic reference as "Consciousness-without-an-object and without-a-subject." But while I find myself in ultimate agreement with the central Core of Taoistic and Buddhistic Enlightenment, I often find the discursive approaches of the Oriental far from convincing. There is reason to believe that I have to credit the Chinese mind with much of this difficulty. For, so far as I know, all of the profounder Buddhist philosophic statements have first been translated from the Sanskrit into the Chinese or Tibetan, with the English translation taken from one or the other of the latter. Now the Chinese conceptual processes are radically different from our own. On the one hand, they involve a much greater sensuous richness than is true of our conceptualism; but, on the other hand, they are peculiarly lacking in the concepts necessary for abstract thinking. According to Lin Yutang, there never has been a development of the higher mathematics among the Chinese, and there could not be without a radical alteration of the Chinese conceptual base. In addition, the Chinese genius, unlike the Indian, has always been weak in the direction of metaphysical speculation. What, then, must happen when the formulation of the crowning insight of the most metaphysical of all races is translated into the Chinese language? It seems that there must be an inevitable transformation of *thinkable* meaning. Then, when on top of this there is a further translation from the concrete Chinese imagery into the abstract form of western language, further distortion seems unavoidable.

In the case of direct translation from the Sanskrit, the problem is not so great, though there still exists the difficulty growing out of cross-transference from a metaphysical to a non-metaphysical genius. However, the rationalism of Shankara is enough like our own thinking to be fundamentally intelligible. But from the standpoint of our current conceptual style, Shankara is far from satisfactory. His method of reasoning is too scholastic, and scholasticism has been outmoded with us for the last two or three centuries. Further, Shankara's problem was enormously symplified, as compared with its analogue in the West, since he could establish his case for the Brahmin community by reference to Vedic sources. We of the West do not accept the Vedic tradition, and thus Shankara's argument is undermined at its base, so far as Occidental effectiveness is concerned. Consequently, the whole approach to Dhyana, in a form that will be acceptable to the western psyche, must be carved out of new material.

The latter problem has come to occupy the principal place in my present consciousness. Much of the time during the past two years, I have been engaged with this problem. I have in course of preparation another work in which I believe I have achieved a partial contribution in this direction. I believe that at least some sectors of western consciousness are now ready. At the present time, contributions in the form of "Analytic Psychology" by Dr. C. G. Jung form a real advance in this direction, but no one man's statement can be comprehensive. However, "Analytic Psychology" is reaching close to the Door, at least in the hands of its chief representative.

I am convinced that the greatest achievement of western genius has been in the development of the abstract thought which has its crown in higher mathematics. The freeing of thought from dependence upon the sensible image is an accomplishment of the very greatest difficulty. Until thought has won this power, it cannot penetrate into the Realm of Imageless Consciousness. Now, once it is realized how much has been accomplished in this direction in the field of higher mathematics, it is easy to see what a powerful instrument in the practice of Dhyana we have forged. In my own experience, thought on the level of Imageless Consciousness was possible by employing the intellectual capacities unfolded during the years of mathematical discipline. The demand made upon the imagination was a close replica of that required in the study of the higher analysis and the non-Euclidian systems of geometry. I believe that the purified western intellect at its highest state of development can carry thought further into the Realm of Profundity than has been possible up to this time. Feeling no longer has the "edge" upon thought.

What I have said so far applies to but one wing of Enlightenment. Full Enlightenment requires the development of Eros as well as Logos. It is just in the dimension of Eros that the West is peculiarly weak. The strong emphasis of Love in the Christian discipline is psychological proof of this. It is only a people weak in love who have to give the Eros-principle strong emphasis. In this we have the compensating action of the psychologic unconscious. Our love is weak and, when developed, often only sentimental. Otherwise the development of our intellect would not have been so destructive, a characteristic well illustrated by the world-situation since 1914. As a result of our weakness in the dimension of Eros, practical Dhyana will have to stress the appropriate compensating discipline. For the one-sided Enlightenment through the understanding is weak in Compassion, and thus falls short of the highest possibility. However, it is possible from the perspective of the one-sided Enlightenment to arouse the complementary phase through the action of the will upon the latent seed of Love.

The culture of the Higher Love is difficult. For it is much harder for feeling to win detachment from the object than it is for thought. It is a lofty achievement to be able to radiate Compassion without thought of return and with full willingness to grant complete freedom to the object. Yet until Love has reached this height, it remains sentimental. And to the merely sentimental lover, Compassion may seem cold, though in reality It is the warmth of the real SUN.

Just because thought is the highest cultured occidental function, I believe that the intellect must lead in western Dhyana. But it must be trained not to abandon the weaker Eros. Here is where the West will face its greatest trial. For a race-horse and a donkey do not make a good team. In such a set-up there is bound to be much conflict, with the race-horse trying to get away and the donkey becoming stubborn. Yes, right here is where the West will have its troubles. I perceive that this conflict is just the place where the Analytic Psychologists will render us the greatest help, provided they are sufficiently spiritualized themselves.

★ ★ ★

To the devoted followers of traditional disciplines, it may appear presumptuous that I should question old techniques and substitute a new symbolic interpretation. But in answer to any who feel this way, I need only quote the words of acknowledged Sages. All clinging to traditional method and interpretation is but a subtle form of attachment and, therefore, a barrier to Enlightenment. Any method that works is pragmatically justified, and no method as such is a sacred object. Then with respect to interpretation, I need but recall the fact that there is no such thing as an exclusively true symbolic representation of an unthinkable Reality. All too easily a valid symbol may through the power of attachment acquire the force of an heretical dogma. Further, the validity of a symbol is a relative matter. Though the unthinkable Reality is eternal, yet every symbol is a time-existence and subject to the process of aging. The power of every symbol is relative to the peculiar psychical complex of an age and a people. Just that symbol is most effective which serves as the best corrective of the psychical complex of the given situation. Symbols are not designed for the benefit of Those who have Awakened, but for those others who are in need of a corrective of their present states of consciousness.

But while there are many valid symbols having quite different appearance in form, yet all these have certain features in common. The most important common feature can be given very easily in abstract terms. For this purpose I call attention to a simple logical principle. Everything that can be experienced or thought exists through contrast with its contradictory, otherwise no particular element of consciousness can be isolated from the totality of all consciousness. The whole universe of all possible experience or thought can be divided into any particular object, state, or function, and its contradictory. Let the letter "A" stand for any such object, state, or function, then the whole universe of possible experience or thought is either "A" or "Not-A." But the ultimate Reality of Enlightened Consciousness lies in neither of these compartments, and thus we say that IT is neither "A" nor "not-A." A whole life-time could be devoted to listing all possible values of "A" and applying the principle in each individual case, yet all the meaning that would be conveyed by such laborious effort would be contained in the preceding two sentences. Such is the power of abstract thought. As one reads the more philosophic Buddhist Sutras, he finds large numbers of pages devoted to the detailed application of the above principle with almost endless repetition. Undoubtedly the repetition builds a psychological effect that is potent, but the essence of all this can be given logically in a sentence or two.

Now, just what is THAT which is neither "A" nor "not-A," when "A" is given any thinkable or experienceable value? To the pure thinker IT seems like nothing at all. Thus IT is called "Voidness," for thus IT appears to the consciousness bound to relativity. But through the Door of Dhyana, IT is found to be substantial Fullness, quite beyond the comprehension of all possible experience or thought. Modern sub-atomic physics affords us an illustration which is as beautiful as any that I know. When two material entities of which the one is just the negation of the other, such as a positron and an electron, are brought into conjunction, the result is mutual destruction. In their place is a flash of radiation that spreads indefinitely throughout all space. If, now, our capacity for physical observation were limited to the field of the electron and the positron, we might conclude that the result of the conjunction was absolute annihilation. But we are now able to see that this is not so, but rather that the destruction of matter in one state has resulted in its continuation in a totally different state. So, also, is the effect of the mutual cancellation of all dichotomies of experience and thought. The flash of radiation that spreads indefinitely throughout all space is the symbol of the Enlightened Consciousness.

By keeping in mind what has been said in the last two paragraphs, the rationale of the various methods of practicing Dhyana, as well as the basis of the various symbols for Noble Wisdom, become clear. But while the rationale is simple, the practice is generally very difficult. To achieve the mutual cancellation practically is to effect the mystic Death, and this always requires faith and courage. It is also possible that success will result in individual unconsciousness. Hence, the actual practice of Dhyana is to be recommended only for those who are prepared. The essence of the preparation is the building of the capacity to maintain consciousness apart from all objects. This kind of Consciousness is present all the time surrounding the functioning of the relative consciousness. It can be isolated through Self-analysis while observing the phantasmagoria of the appearing and disappearing of the objects in the stream of time. It is

THAT which remains unaltered through all change. When awareness has learned to turn its focus upon this ever-present Matrix of Consciousness so that Consciousness becomes its own object, the power to remain individually conscious through the mutual cancellation has been achieved. Then the time has come for the Transition from the embodied to the Radiant State. There is nothing simpler than all this, and yet there is nothing more difficult.

THE PHILOSOPHY
OF CONSCIOUSNESS
WITHOUT AN OBJECT

Part I
The Ground of Knowledge

1
The Idea and Its Reference

The office of great philosophy is to be a Way of Realization, and not solely a monitor of *doing*. This the ancients knew well, but in these later, more sordid, days this truth is all but forgotten. The serious citizen of the present-day world may well blush when he thinks of what must be the judgment of the future historian who, when he writes of our age, notes how superb genius and skill served mainly the mundane needs and convenience of a "plantigrade, featherless, biped mammal of the genus homo" in its adaptations to environment, or else studied how very intricate and technical devices might be adapted to the destruction of that same mammal in the most unpleasant way conceivable. Indeed, when knowledge serves such ends, ignorance is preferable. But though it is ill enough when technical knowledge finds no more worthy objective, far worse and darker is it when the royal Queen of Knowledge is dragged down to the status of handmaiden of earthly science. Admittedly, by its very form and method, earthly science can find its ultimate justification only in doing, but it is the true office of philosophy to serve a more worthy and ultimate end. For the eternal function of the Divine Sophia is to supply the knowing that serves *being* first of all and *doing* only in so far as action is instrumental to that being.

The present sad estate of much philosophy is largely the result of a critical acumen that has run far ahead of the unfoldment of balancing insight. Far be it from me to question the valid functions of the critical spirit, for I would be among the last who would care to abide in a fool's castle of illusion; but criticism by itself leads only to the dead end of universal skepticism. To be sure, this skepticism may be variously disguised, as revealed in statements such as "all knowledge is only probable knowledge," or "knowledge is only warranted assertibility which is tested by how far it serves adaptation of an organism to its environment," or it may lead to the outright denial that there is any such thing as Reality or Truth. But in any case, certainty is lost with even the hope that certainty may ever be found. There are men of strange taste who seem to like the resultant gambler's world of complete uncertainty wherein nothing may be trusted and only illusions are left to feed the yearning for belief. But for all those of deeper religious need, the death of hope for certainty is the ultimate tragedy of absolute pessimism—not the relative pessimism of a Buddha, a Christ, or a Schopenhauer, who each saw the hopeless darkness of this dark world as well as a Door leading to the undying Light, but rather a pessimism so deep that there is no hope for Light anywhere. Somewhere there must be certainty if the end of life is to be more than eternal despair. And to find this certainty something other than criticism is required.

As the stream of experience passes by us, we find no beginning and no end. With our science we slash arbitrary cuts across that stream and find innumerable relations intertwining indeterminate parts that we can define and organize into systems with considerable skill. But as to the ultimate nature of the parts in relation, we know nothing at all. From whence the stream and whither? That is the question that centuries and millenia of knowledge grounded only in the empirically given has never been able to answer. Hopeless is the estate of man if the source of all he knows is experience and nothing more.

But is there, mayhap, a source of knowledge other than experience and its (supposedly) one-parented child, the concept? The great among the ancients have affirmed that there is, and so have others throughout our racial history. I, too, affirm that there is this third organ of knowledge and that it may be realized by him who strives in the right direction. And I, also, confirm those ancients who say that through this other organ, the resolution of the ultimate questions may be found and a knowledge realized that is not sterile, though its form may be most unexpected. But do the barricades of modern criticism leave room for the forgotten Door? I believe that they do, once the structure of criticism is carefully analyzed and that which is sound is separated from that which is unsound. For philosophic criticism is no authoritarian absolute competent to close the door to testimony from the fount of immediacy.

Kant's Critique[1] seems to have established this important proposition: The pure reason by itself can establish judgments of possibility only and can predicate existence of that possibility solely as a possibility. In order to predicate actuality of an existence, something more is required. In general, the predication of actual existence becomes possible by means of the empiric material given through the senses. The combination of the principles of pure reason and the material given through the senses makes possible the unity of experience whereby raw immediacy can be incorporated in a totality organized under law. This establishes a basis for

---

1. See Notes at end of chapter.

confidence in the theoretic determinations of science as such, with all that follows from that. But there are demands within human consciousness that remain unsatisfied by this integration. Kant was aware of this fact and tried to resolve the problem in his *Critique of Practical Reason*, but he failed to achieve any adequate ground for assurance. Thus we stand today in a position where for thought there is no certain but only probable knowledge.

In the present philosophic outline, I do not challenge the essential validity of the above conclusion, drawn from the *Critique of Pure Reason*. I accept the principle that *pure* thought can give only judgments of possible existence. But I go further than Kant in maintaining that in the total organization of consciousness there are phases that are neither conceptual nor empiric—the latter term being understood as consciousness-value dependent upon the senses. I draw attention to such a phase which, while not commonly active among men, has yet been reported by a few individuals throughout the span of known history, and maintain that I have myself realized at least some measure of the operation of this phase. This phase has been known in the West under a number of designations, such as "Cosmic Consciousness," "Mystical Insight," "Specialism," "Transhumanism," and so forth. In the Orient it has been given a more systematic treatment and designation. Thus, it is recognizable under the terms "Samadhi," "Dhyana," and "Prajna." The character of this phase of consciousness, as it has been represented in existent discussions and as revealed in my own contact with it, is of the nature of immediate awareness of an existential content or value. This immediacy is of a far superior order as compared to that given through the senses, for the latter is dependent upon the instrumentality of sensuous organs and functions. As compared to experience through the senses, this rarer phase of consciousness gives a transcendent value immediately and renders possible the predication of its existence in a judgment without violating the fundamental principles laid down by Kant.

An epistemological critique of this transcendental phase of consciousness is possible only by one in whom it is operative. This is true for the reason that the epistemologist, unlike the psychologist, can work only upon the material he actually has within his own consciousness. His is the inside view, while the psychologist, so long as he is only a psychologist, is restricted to the material that can be observed externally. Thus, the epistemologist is concerned with an analysis of the base of judgments of significance and value, while the method of the psychologist confines him to the field of judgments concerning empirically existent fact. As a consequence, the findings of the psychologist are irrelevant with respect to the more interior field of value and meaning. Failure to keep this fact in mind has produced a considerable confusion and heartache that were quite unnecessary.

The problem before us at this point is largely outside the reach of the psychologist, as it is concerned with value and meaning and not with observable existences, save only in very incidental degree. Very likely, the operation of the transcendental phase of consciousness which is predicated here, may have coordinate effects that can be observed by the psychologist, and perhaps even the physiologist. But whatever may be thus observed has no bearing upon the standing of the inner and directly realized value and meaning. Apparently, deviation from psychological and physiological norm may be, and indeed has been, noted. Often this deviation from norm has been interpreted as an adverse criticism of the directly realized meaningful content. This procedure is both unscientific and unphilosophical, for it involves the blind assumption that the virtue of being superior attaches to the norm as such. By applying this same method consistently within, say, the setting of the life and consciousness of the Australian bushmen, we would be forced to an adverse judgment relative to all the higher human culture in all forms. As many of our psychologists and physiologists do not actually maintain this consistent position, we are forced to the conclusion that they permit personal prejudice the determinant part in their valuations.

In current discussions it has been frequently noted that some concepts refer to sensuously given existences directly, while others do not. These existences have been called "referents." This leads to the formulation: Some concepts have referents while others do not. Generally the former concepts are given the superior validity and the latter only such validity as they may acquire by leading to concepts that do have referents. Indeed, there are some writers who deny that there is any such thing as a concept, and admit only words. In any case, the concepts, or words, without referents, are viewed as mere abstractions. Now, while it may be valid to regard concepts as important only in so far as they lead to referents, it is an arbitrary assumption to maintain that the referent must always be an empirically given fact. The referent may be a content given by the transcendent phase of consciousness immediately. In this case, the abstract concept may have as genuine reference-value as the more concrete ideas. It is only through the mystical awakening that this question can be answered positively. It is part of the thesis of the present work that abstract concepts, or at any rate some abstract concepts, do in fact mean a content that can be realized immediately. Thus the most abstract phase of thought can lead to meaning at least as directly as concrete ideas. But this meaning is not a sensuously given content.

A fundamental implication is that some conceptual systems may be regarded as *symbols* of transcendental meaning. Perhaps we may regard this symbolical form of reference as characteristic of all concepts with respect to all referents, whether empiric or transcendental. Some of the more mature branches of modern science seem to be arriving at such an interpretation of their own theoretical constructions. Thus, in current physics the constructions are often spoken of as models that mean a reality or referent that in its own nature is not thinkable. The model, then, is not a mere photographic reproduction but a thinkable and logical pattern that corresponds to the observed relationships in the referent. Such a pattern is a symbol, though perhaps not in the special sense in which Dr. C. G. Jung uses this term. At any rate, in this case it is a symbol of relationships. In the transcendental sense, the symbol would represent substantialities. We have here, then, the essential difference between the intellect as used in science and as employed in connection with metaphysics. In the one case, it supplies a symbol for relationships, in the other a symbol of substantial realities.

The primary value of the intellect is that it gives command. By means of science, nature is manipulated and controlled in an ever-widening degree. This fact is too well known to need elaboration. The same principle applies to transcendent realities. Through the power of thought this domain, too, becomes one that can be navigated. Immature mystics are not navigators, and therefore realize the transcendent as a sea in which their boats of consciousness either drift or are propelled by powers that they, individually, do not control. In such cases, if the boats are controlled, other unseen intelligence does the work. Many mystics give this controlling power the blanket name of "God." The real and genuine reference here is to a Power beyond the individual and self-conscious personal self that is realized as operative but not understood in its character. On the other hand, the mystic who has control may drop the term "God," with its usual connotations, from his vocabulary. However, he knows that the term does refer to something quite real though very imperfectly understood by the larger number of mystics. This control depends upon the development of understanding and thought having quite a different order of reference from that which applies to experience through the senses.

★ ★ ★

The empirically given manifold of fact that constitutes the raw material of physical science is not itself the same as science, nor does it become so simply by being collected, recorded, and classified. To raise this body of fact to the status of science, it must *all* be incorporated within an interpretative theory that satisfies certain conditions. Two of these conditions are fundamental and ineluctable. First, the interpretative theory must be a logical and self-consistent whole from which deductive inferences can be drawn. This is an absolute necessity of science as such. Second, the theory must in addition be so selected and formulated that the sequential train of inferences therefrom shall at some stage suggest an empirically possible experiment or observation that can confirm or fail to confirm the inference. This condition is not a necessity of science in the ontological sense, but is an essential part of *empiric* science. This condition peculiarly marks the radical departure of modern science as contrasted to the science of the scholastics and of Aristotle. It is a principle of the highest pragmatic importance and is the prime key to the western and modern type of control of nature. Now, any organization of a collection of observed facts that satisfies these two conditions is science in the current sense of the word.

But while the above two principles are the only two necessary conditions for defining a body of knowledge as scientific, in the current sense, yet in practice scientists demand more. There is a third condition that serves convenience and even prejudice rather than logic. This is the requirement that the interpretative theory shall be congruent with already established or accepted scientific points of view, unless it is well proven that this third condition cannot be satisfied without violating the first or second. The long resistance to the acceptance of the Einstein dynamics was due to the fact that the relativity theory violated the third condition, though conforming to the first two. Only with reluctance could the body of scientists be induced to abandon the classical mechanics of Newton. For many years the latter was lovingly patched with the baling wire of *ad hoc* hypotheses, and the body of scientists—very much like a conservative farmer attached to a tumbledown wagon, ancient team, and disintegrating harness, held together and kept going by every device of ingenuity, and hating the modern truck that has been offered him as a present—refused to have anything to do with the new theory, even though it satisfied the first condition with exceptional beauty. But ultimately, because the relativity theory met the test of the second condition and the Newtonian view had indubitably lost its logical coherence in the domain of electrodynamics, due to heavy patching, the former was, perforce, accepted. This bit out of the history of science simply illustrates the fact that the third condition is merely arbitrary in the logical sense. However, it must be acknowledged that this condition does have a degree of practical and psychological justification. It is part and parcel of the conservative spirit that someone has given a rather aphoristic formulation in the following terms: "So long as it is not *necessary* to change, it is necessary *not* to change." Change that is too rapid for adjustment and assimilation is not without its danger.

The danger of change is a danger to the all-too-human nature of the scientist and not a danger to science itself. The third condition exists for the protection of the scientist because he is a human being, and is quite irrelevant so far as science as such is concerned. I have talked to scientifically oriented minds and developed conceptions implying or explicitly affirming the reality of the transcendent, to which they took no logical exception, but they then drew the protecting robes of the third condition about themselves and withdrew to what they imagined was the safety of their enclosure. It is not wise to treat scared children too roughly, and in so far as the third condition is used as a protective temenos for the fallible human nature of the scientist, it should be respected. But this third condition is no real part of science as science and may not be properly invoked to discredit the *truth* of any interpretative construction.

Today in the vast domain of the biopsychological sciences—which include the whole of man in so far as he is an object for science—and in much of philosophy, the predominant orientation is to Darwin. Darwinism has a twofold meaning, the lesser aspect of which is innocent and creditable enough, but the larger aspect of which is a sinister force—perhaps the most sinister— that seriously threatens the ultimate good of the human soul.

In the narrower sense, Darwin gave us a major scientific contribution. Through the facts observed by Darwin the notion of organic evolution is drawn into the focus of consciousness with a well-nigh ineluctable force. So far the contribution of Darwin is positive and, I believe, permanent. But in the larger sense, Darwinism involves a good deal more than this. The evolutionary process is interpreted as a blind and mechanical force operating in the primordial roots of life and responsible for every development, including man, even the most cultured. The facts may, and I believe do, require some conception of evolution for their interpretation. But there are other conceptions of the nature of evolution, differing radically from Darwin's idea, that do interpret the facts, or may be adapted to such interpretation. Evolution may be conceived as the technique of an intelligent process, and it may be conceived comprehensively as the complement of an involutionary process. Evolution thus conceived is not part of Darwinism in the invidious sense.

The first two conditions of scientific method do not impose the blind and mechanical view of evolution as a scientifically necessary interpretation. The orientation on the part of scientists to this radically anti-transcendental view is merely in conformity with the artificial third condition. Yet it must be confessed that the mechanistic interpretation does have certain advantages. To those who hate mystery, it seems as though here we have a key for understanding life, in all its elaborations, that is directly and objectively understandable. Thus the senses and the intellect are all that is necessary for the conquest of life. There is much of illusion in this. For when the biologist falls back on the chemist to explain his vital phenomena, the chemist gives him cold comfort when he says that he does not find chemical phenomena adequate to meet the requirements of the biologist; and then when the biologist turns to the most basic physical science of all, i.e., physics, he finds that since 1896 physics has laid the foundation for mysticism with a vengeance, and the materialistic biologist is left without fundamental support for his interpretative view.

The idea that in the purely naturalistic sense there is a tendency in living organism to rise in the scale is by no means a scientifically established fact. To be sure, we do find a vast difference of level in the hierarchy of living creatures, reaching from the mineral or near the mineral to the Buddhas, but it is not a scientifically established fact that this difference of elevation is not due to periodic or continuous impingement of energy from transcendental roots. If the cause of rise in the scale is transcendental, then it is not *naturalistic*.[2] Apart from this consideration—which for the moment I shall treat as only speculative—there is strong positive evidence that in the purely naturalistic sense all function in nature tends toward degradation. The physicists tell us that in all their observation from the laboratory up to astrophysics they find no exception to the second law of thermodynamics. In simple terms, this law says that all energy tends to flow down hill, that is, from centers of high concentration to regions of low concentration, as from the stars to the depths of space.

And further, energy is available for work only while it is on this flow, and is lost in the final stage of dissemination. All this simply leads to the view that the purely naturalistic tendency is toward degradation.

Are we not justified in viewing life as some kind of energy? Would not such a view be a peculiarly consistent application of the third condition? Because it constitutes an extension of an already accepted scientific viewpoint. But if natural life is to be viewed as an energy, is there not then a strong presumption that this energy does not constitute an exception to the general law, which seems to be universally confirmed by the observation of the physicist? If the answer to these three questions is affirmative, it follows that we must view natural life, taken in isolation from any transcendental impingement of energy, as tending toward degradation. The consequences of such an altered viewpoint are far reaching. For instance, the ethnologist would no longer find justification for viewing the culture of so-called primitive man as the interpretatively significant root-source of higher culture, since this primitive culture would actually be degraded culture and thus not a root but the near end-term of a process of degradation. We would no longer be justified in viewing something like the voodoo as the primitive form of religious consciousness, or the seed from which ultimately flowered the higher religious consciousness, but we would see in this form of religious practice the degraded state of religion—that which religion becomes in the hands of a race moving toward extinction. As another instance we would find that the reductive interpretation in analytic psychology would lose all really significant value.[3]

Later in this volume I shall have occasion to develop more fully the line of argument sketched above in its relation to much current psychological interpretation of mystical states of consciousness. For it appears that most of the disparagement found in such interpretations develops from the prejudicial attitude growing out of a predilection for the invidious extension of Darwinism. For the present I am concerned only with the development of a general orienting preview in relation to the general reference of ideas.

The following chapter is introduced to establish a ground of knowledge upon which the body of subsequent interpretation is largely based. This mainly descriptive-narrative statement is to be understood as having the same methodological significance that attaches to the laboratory record in the development of scientific theoretical interpretation. But in this case, the immediately given material is not of the objective sort studied in scientific laboratories; it is that which is found by a predominantly conscious penetration of the subjective pole of consciousness. In this case that which corresponds to the raw material of scientific theory is the qualities or states found by piercing into the "I" rather than by observing the "not-I." A referential ground for interpretation of this sort is far from being a commonplace in the sense that all the objective material of scientific theory may be called commonplace, since the latter is, in principle, available to any so-called five-sense consciousness. Very few human beings have conscious familiarity with the zone in question, but there are a few who do, and they understand each other when they meet. This latter fact is of the very highest significance, for it reveals that the subjective realm is not something absolutely unique in an individual and having nothing in common with anyone else. Unquestionably, there are detailed features of the subjective zone that are unique, as one individual is contrasted with another individual and as one type of individual is set off by another type. But these variants grow less and less with the depth of penetration, while there is a progressive growth in congruency of insight that in the end tends to become absolute. At the very center stands Enlightenment, which is fundamentally the same for all men. I must leave this statement in dogmatic form since it can neither be proved nor disproved in objective terms.

The initial and most superficial stage of the subjective penetration is, admittedly, intensely personal, for no man can start at any point save that of himself, a concrete individual living at some particular point in time and space. An early danger of the Way is that of becoming entrapped in this purely personal subjectivity for an indefinite period of time. But he who is caught at this point has scarcely taken the first step on the ladder. The real penetration lies beyond the personal self. Reaching beyond the personal stage, the "I" rapidly grows in impersonality until it acquires the value of a Universal Principle. Thus the inner ground is a common ground just as truly as is the objective content of consciousness common to all men. As empiric scientists, in general, understand each other's way of thinking, so those who know some measure of the impersonal "I" understand each other's peculiar language, at least in its primary reference. To be sure, there are variants here, just as there are differences of scientific specialty, that restrict the completeness of mutual understanding. In general, a specialist in subatomic physics would not talk the specific language of a specialist in biology, yet with respect to the general determinants of empirical science as such there is mutuality of understanding. The analogue of this is definitely to be found among the mystics. And this fact is a real cause for confusion on the part of a non-mystical investigator of mystical states of consciousness. There are agreements and differentiations not hard for him who has Vision to understand, but that are hopelessly confusing to the uninitiated.

In the record given in the next chapter, part of the material is doubtless unique with respect to the individual. In this respect there are several divergences from other records that can be found in literature. But very soon the content acquires a progressively universal character. Proof of this can be found, likewise, by reference to the appropriate literature. It is this more universally identical content that constitutes the main ground of reference of the later interpretation. Indeed, there is here a common ground for all men, but generally it is lost in the Unconscious, yet waiting, ever ready to be revealed when the Light of Consciousness turns upon Itself toward Its Source.

Notes to Chapter 1

1. The *Critique of Pure Reason* by Immanuel Kant, the most important work in the whole of western philosophical literature.

2. "Naturalism" here is taken to mean the theory that sensuously observed Nature is all that there is of Reality.

3. In analytic psychology the standpoint that views the reference of complexes welling up from the unconscious as being due to causal factors that lie in the conscious field of the past is called "reductive." This stands in contrast to the "constructive" standpoint that views such complexes as symbolically meaning, or also meaning, an end to be developed in the future. See "Definitions," Chapter XI, in Jung's *Psychological Types*.

2
A Mystical Unfoldment

It was during the period when I was a student in the Graduate School of Philosophy at Harvard University that, finally, I became convinced of the probable existence of a transcendent mode of consciousness that could not be comprehended within the limits of our ordinary forms of knowledge. Several factors converged in the forming of this conviction. For one thing, a considerable portion of western philosophy from the Greeks to the present day seemed to imply some sort of insight into Reality that was not reducible to observation or derivable from immediate experience by logical deduction, however acute the course of reasoning might be. At the same time, the profound assurance of truth I had realized in my studies in pure mathematics did not seem to be explained satisfactorily by any of those philosophical interpretations that aim to show that mathematics is derived from the facts of the external world by mere abstraction. Throughout all discussion, the feeling persisted that at the root of mathematics there lay a mystery, reaching far deeper than anything attained through the senses. In addition, for a period of some three years, I had had a degree of contact with the Buddhist, Vedantist, and Theosophical phases of oriental thought, and in all these the evidence of some sort of transcendental consciousness was peculiarly decisive. On the other hand, as a factor that acted in a sort of negative sense, the various philosophies that repudiated the actuality of any transcendental or mystical reality seemed to have the effect of barrenness, which left them far from satisfactory. Meanwhile, acting beneath the surface of my consciousness, there was a more or less inarticulate faith that insisted that the truly valid interpretation of reality must be such as would satisfy through and through, and thus not be barren. Yet the dialectical and polemical processes of the various western schools of thought were inadequate for supplying the completely satisfactory solution that, while affording the appropriate recognition of the needs of experience and of reason, at the same time satisfied the hunger for assurance and depth. However, the evidence from history seemed to make it clear that at least some few among mankind had achieved this assurance, which was both reasonable and full. So it seemed to me to be highly probable that there must be a mode of consciousness or knowledge not yet comprehended by epistemology and psychology as developed in the West.

At that time I had no clear idea of what this knowledge might be, or of the methods by which one might hope to attain it. I had had some brief contact with the oriental manuals on transformation and realized that they seemed to point to a kind of consciousness that, while not generally realized by mankind, yet was potentially within the range of human attainment. At first I attempted to interpret the material contained within these manuals in the conceptual forms of western thought, but always in these efforts I finally met failure. I soon found enough to know that there was something concealed within the manuals, because I noted certain subtle affective changes they induced within me, and there was aroused also a sense of something near that yet defeated the efforts of my understanding to comprehend. So I began to feel sure of a hidden somewhat to which these manuals were related, if for no other reason than that their first effect was to leave me disturbed and restless. The desire for peace of mind sometimes counseled me to turn away from them, but then the realization that the subsequent position would be arbitrary and artificial, and therefore a repudiation of an honest search for reality, whatever that might be, always forced me to return to those disturbing manuals.

It soon became clear, if this search in a new direction was to be successful, I had to reach beyond anything contained within the academic circles of the West. The manuals demanded a life-practice or attitude that involved the whole man, and thus the requirements were incompatible with the attitude of a tentative *trying*, while part of the man stood back enclosed in a sort of reserve. Again and again I found the statement that, if a man would attain the transcendent realization, he must renounce all, and not merely part, of what he personally is. I did not find this an easy step to consummate. For years I resisted it, offering part of myself, yet holding back a certain reserve. During all this time, I realized only imperfect and unsatisfactory results, and often regretted the experiment. But it was not long before I found that I had gone too far to turn back. I had realized enough to render forever barren the old pastures, and yet not enough to know either peace or satisfaction. For some years, I rested in this position of indecision, without achieving much visible progress. Yet meanwhile, as time rolled on, progressive exhaustion of the world-desire developed, while concomitantly there grew a greater willingness to abandon all that had been reserved and so complete the experiment.

As the years passed, I began to form a better idea of the goal and of the reasons underlying the requirements of the manuals. All this helped to arouse a greater will to effort, and so I began to experiment more deliberately with the various transformation techniques that came before my attention. All, or nearly all, these were of oriental origin, and in most cases I found them disappointing in their effectiveness. But, finally, I realized that there are several techniques and that these are designed to meet the needs of quite various temperaments and psychical organizations. In time, it became clear that there are important temperamental and psychical differences as between orientals and occidentals, and that this fact implied modification of methods. So I began seeking for the invariable elements in the different techniques, with a view to finding just what was essential. Ultimately, I found one oriental Sage with whose thought and temperament I felt a high degree of sympathetic rapport. This Sage was the Vedantic philosopher known as Shankara. I found myself in striking agreement with the more fundamental phases of his thought and quite willing to apply the highly intellectual technique that he had charted. It was in this Sage's writings that I finally found the means that were effective in producing the transformation I sought.

In the meantime I had met various individuals and groups who offered and rendered assistance in the direction I was seeking to go, and from all of them I must acknowledge having received positive values which had a progressively clarifying effect upon the understanding. But none of them offered methods that proved decisively effective with me. Nearly all these placed their predominant stress upon feeling-transformation and failed to satisfy the intellectual demands that, with me, always remained strong. Of all such Teachers whom I met, either through their living presence or their written word, Shankara, alone, adequately satisfied the intellectual side of my nature. So, while I owe much to many whom I have known in one way or another, it yet remained for Shankara to offer the hint that proved to be decisive.

However, even Shankara did not supply all the specifications for the method that became finally effective. Also, I had to discover adaptations that would satisfy the needs of an academically trained occidental nature. None of these adaptations violated any of the fundamentals of Shankara's teaching. But what I added as a sort of creative discovery was peculiarly decisive in its effect. At the present time, I am convinced that some such original discovery is vitally important in effecting a self-induced transformation.

In the period just preceding the hour when success finally crowned a search that covered nearly a quarter of a century, certain features characteristic of the transcendent consciousness had become theoretically clear. I had attained an intellectual grasp of the vitally important fact that transcendent consciousness differs from our ordinary consciousness in the primary respect that it is a state of consciousness wherein the disjunction between the subject to consciousness and the object of consciousness is destroyed. It is a state wherein self-identity and the field of consciousness are blended in one indissoluble whole. This supplied the prime characteristic by which all our common consciousness could be differentiated from the transcendent. The former is all of the type that may be called subject-object or relative consciousness.

The second fact of primary importance, that I now understand, was that the common denominator, as it were, of both kinds of consciousness lay in the subject or self. This fact is identical, in a significant degree, with the fundamental discovery of Descartes, i.e., that when everything is submitted to critical examination, it still remains impossible to doubt one's own being, however little one may be able to understand the nature of that being. I also discovered the essential timelessness of the subject, or self, and that in its purity, unmixed with any objective element, it can never truly be an *object* of consciousness. I readily realized that if pure subjectivity, or the bare power to be aware, was a permanent or unchanging element and therefore must, as a consequence, stand outside of time and be unaffected by any history, then it must be, of necessity, immortal. I saw that this kind of immortality is wholly impersonal and does not, by itself, imply the unlimited persistence of the quality of individuality that distinguishes one man from another. But the finding of one immortal element affords a definite anchorage and security, grounded in certainty of an order far superior to that of any kind of faith. When I had reached this point in the unfoldment of my understanding, I really had achieved the positive value of decisive importance that, some years later, was to prove the effective entering wedge for opening the Way to the transcendent level of consciousness.

While, in addition to the principles or facts just discussed, there are a number of other statements relative to the transcendent that can be found in literature, yet, in my judgment, the recognition of these is all that is absolutely essential to prepare the understanding for the Transcendental Awakening. These principles or facts are clearly of noetic value, and they can be appreciated quite apart from any affective transformation that may be associated with the arousing of transcendental apperception. In fact, it may be entirely possible that a sufficiently concentrated meditation upon the inner significance of these principles might prove an efficient means for effecting the transformation without the aid of any other subsidiary factor. However, they were not the sole factors that were operative in my experience, though they occupied the position of first importance.

Concurrently with the attainment of the preliminary noetic adjustment, certain important transformations were developing in the affective and conative side of my nature. Early in my studies I found that the manuals emphasized the necessity of killing out desire. This proved to be a difficult step to understand and far from easy to accomplish. Desire and sentient life are inseparable, and so it seemed as though this demand implied the equivalent of self-extinction. It was only after some time that

I discovered that the real meaning consisted in a changing of the polarization of desire. Ordinarily, desire moves toward objects and objective achievements, in some sense. It is necessary that this desire should be given another polarization so that, instead of objects and achievements in the world-field being sought, an eternal and all-encompassing consciousness should be desired. This interpretation clarified the meaning of the demand and rendered it intellectually acceptable, but did not at once effect the required repolarization. To accomplish, this the wearing power of time proved to be necessary. As the years passed, the outward polarization of the desire did grow weaker, and some months just prior to the hour when the radical transition in consciousness was consummated, it actually had become transformed into a distaste for practically everything belonging to the world-field. It seemed that all in the world-field was drained dry of every significant value. Though there still remained vast quantities of objective secular information of which I was ignorant and that I could have acquired, and there were many experiences that I had never sampled, yet I realized that, as such, they were void of depth and had no more value than David Hume's game of backgammon. If there had not been a compensating polarization of desire in another direction, it seems highly probable that at this stage my state of consciousness would have had a very pessimistic and depressed coloring, but as there was at the same time a strong growth of the desire for transcendent consciousness, the result was that the psychical energy did have an outlet. However, there was a critical point at which the shifting polarization had attained something like a neutral balance.[1] At this point there was no decisive wish to go either way and the whole field of interest took on a colorless quality. As I look back upon the whole experience, I would say that this stage was the only one that involved real danger. I found it necessary to supplement the neutral state of desire by a forcibly willed resolution, and thus proceed in the chosen direction regardless of the absence of inclination.[2] However, once past the critical point, the inward polarization of desire developed rapidly, and presently spontaneous inclination rendered the forcibly willed resolution unnecessary.

In addition to the barrier of desire directed toward external objects, the manuals specify a very important and closely related barrier to attainment. This is egoism. The strong feeling for, and attachment to, egoistic differentiation is an insurmountable barrier to a kind of consciousness that, instead of being discrete and ego bound, is continuous, free, and impersonal. So a certain critical degree of dissolution or solution of the egoistic crystallization must be effected if the transformation of consciousness is to be successful. I did not find it difficult to appreciate the logic of this requirement, but again, as in the case of outwardly polarized desire, the difficult part was the actual dissolution of the egoistic feeling. The ordinary technique is the practice of practical altruism until personal self-consideration sinks well into the background. But this is not the only means that effects this result. A desire for the transcendent Self and a love of universals also tend toward the required melting of the egoistic feeling. In this part of the discipline, I found that my already established love of mathematics and philosophy was an aid of radical importance that, supplemented by more tangible practices, finally produced the requisite degree of melting.

In my experience, the preliminary noetic adjustment required much less time and effort than the requisite affective and conative reorientation. With the latter, the wearing-down process of time proved to be necessary. Unquestionably, if the feelings and will could have been made to respond more readily to the leadership of understanding, then the transformation of the consciousness would have been achieved in much less time. But, as human nature is constituted, it appears this phase of the labor does require much patience and the assistance of the maturing that time brings in its natural course.

Preceding the hour of the radical transition in consciousness, there had been two premonitory recognitions of substantial adjustment value. The first occurred about fourteen years before, and the second only about nine months prior to, the culminating stage. The first of these illustrates the important difference between the theoretical appreciation of a fact or principle and a kind of adjustment to, or realization of, that which I have called "Recognition." For some years I had been familiar with the Indian concept of Atman and understood that it meant a spiritual "Self" conceived as being the irreducible center of consciousness on which all knowledge or consciousness in the relative sense depended. I had found no empiric or logical difficulty with this concept and had accepted it as valid. I understood quite well, as an immediate implication, that since I am the Self, therefore, the judgment "I am Atman" is practically a tautology. I did not see how any idea could have greater philosophical clarity. But on one occasion, when a friend was outlining a method of systematic discrimination between the Self and the not-Self, finally culminating in the judgment "I am Atman," I recognized in this a profound truth carrying the very highest significance. With this there came a sense of new insight and of joy. It made a difference in me that the theoretical acceptance and appreciation of the judgment had failed to do.

In analyzing the difference between the recognition and the theoretical acceptance without recognition, it seems that in the latter instance there is a quality that might be called mediative distance, while in the case of recognition there is the closeness of immediacy. There is something nonlogical that is added, but, while nonlogical, it is not antilogical. Part of the effect was an increased clarity in the apperception of the logical implications that followed. Spontaneously and with intellectual ease I began thinking consequences that were practically identical with a number of fundamental statements in the *Bhagavad-Gita*. But now these thoughts were my thoughts in a close and intimate sense, whereas prior to that time they were simply ideas that I had touched through my reading, often not feeling very sympathetic with them. Within a considerable range of consciousness, I now felt assurance, whereas previously I had merely believed or accepted because of theoretical considerations. Ideas that formerly had had the effect of constraint upon me now had a definitely joyous and freedom-giving value. And it was only a momentary flash of insight that had made all this difference! The effect persisted and has never been lost at any time since, though the freshness of the insight gradually waned and became a "matter of course" in the background of my thinking and valuation. Much that had been previously obscure in a certain class of oriental thinking I now found myself understanding with a greatly increased clarity.[3]

In connection with the foregoing recognition, it seems clear to me that the prior theoretical acceptance has prepared the soil of the mind, as it were, for the subsequent realization. While there is something additional in the recognition as compared to the theoretical acceptance, that "something" is not in the nature of concepts nor of an added experience in any perceptive sense. It rather belongs to some other dimension of consciousness, not contained in either concepts or percepts, but which has a radical effect upon value. It may lead a train of thought to new discovery, but is not itself revealed in a subsequent analysis of that train of thought. The formal relationships of the final expression of the thought may be quite clear and understandable to the trained intellect of a man who is without insight and they may stand up quite well under criticism. Yet the insight renders possible much that is beyond the power of the trained intellect that lacks the insight. It can lead the way in radical cognitive discovery and contribute a form to the timebound world that will have its effects, large or small, in the stream of time. But he who is blind to this dimension of consciousness that I have called "Value" will see only a form, a mere configuration on the surface. Yet another who is awake to Value will, at the same time, recognize depth in the configuration. Also, one who is not awakened may, by dwelling upon the configuration through a method that has long been known as meditation, find the value-dimension aroused to recognition in his consciousness. And it is just this something additional, this somewhat that is over and above the concept, with all its traceable ramifications, that makes all the difference in the world!

The second premonitory recognition had a markedly different background, since it expressed itself in a judgment for which I had not been prepared by prior theoretical acceptance. I had been meditating upon the concept of "Nirvana" when, suddenly, it dawned upon me that I, in the inmost sense, am identical with Nirvana. My previous ideas upon this subject had involved a confusion that, while logical analysis should have dispelled it, none the less persisted. Despite statements to the contrary, with which I was familiar, I had been thinking of Nirvana as a kind of other world standing in disparate relation to this world of relative consciousness. Of course, I should have realized the hidden error in this view, as such an interpretation involved placing Nirvana in the relative manifold. But probably through intellectual laziness, I failed to carry my thought through on this point. The result was that the recognition effected for me a new cognitive discovery as well as a deepening and illumining effect in the dimension of value. I readily saw the reason why so little had been said, and indeed why so little could be said, concerning Nirvana beyond the assertion of its reality. The inner core of the "I," like Nirvana, is not an objective existence but is, rather, the "thread" upon which the objective material of consciousness is strung. Relative consciousness deals with the objective material but never finds the "thread" as an object. Yet it is that "thread" that renders all else possible. In fact, it is the most immediate and ever-present reality of all. Nirvana, like the "I," cannot be located anywhere, as in a distinct place, for it is at once everywhere and nowhere, both in space and time. Upon this "thread," space and time are strung just as truly as all perceptual experience and all thought consciousness and any other mode of relative consciousness there may be.

This second recognition had implications that actually were to become clear to me at the deepest stage of realization some ten months later. Presumptively, a sufficiently acute thought would have developed the consequences beforehand, but I failed to do this. At any rate, I now see that this second recognition contained the seed of insight that renders clear the Buddhist doctrine of anatman, which in turn constitutes an important part of the central core of that philosophy, as well as one of its most obscure doctrines.[4] But I shall return to this point at a later time when the ground for its discussion has been better prepared.

For the last two or three years prior to the culminating transition in consciousness, I was aware of a decrease in my intellectual capacity. The meaning of philosophic and mathematical literature that formerly had been within the range of my working consciousness became obscure. The effort to understand much that I had formerly understood reasonably well simply produced drowsiness. At the time this caused me considerable concern, and I wondered whether it might be a sign of premature intellectual aging. However, it proved to be a passing phase, for shortly prior to the culminating point the intellectual alertness returned, and after that point it became more acute than it ever had been. The recognition, among other effects, proved to have the value of an intellectual rejuvenation. I mention this development since it seems to have some significance. When observed retrospectively, it would seem that there had been a withdrawal of the personal energy from the intellectual field into some level that was not consciously traceable. As yet, I have not found any records of an analogous experience on the part of others when approaching the mystical crisis. I am noting this development for such value as it may ultimately prove to have.[5]

During the last few weeks just preceding the transformation, there grew within me a strong expectation and a kind of inner excitement. I felt within me an indefinable assurance that, at last, the culminating success of a long search was within reach. I felt that I was near the discovery of the means whereby I could surmount the apparently unscalable walls that seemed to lie all about. I had been studying and meditating upon the philosophic writings of Shankara more seriously than at any prior time and sensed that in them was to be found the vital key. At the same time, I had a strong desire for a period of solitude. Presently the opportunity came to satisfy this desire, and taking a volume of Shankara's translated works with me, I spent several days in a wild and lonely place.[6] The study and thought of this period proved to be decisively effective. As a result of this effort an idea of cardinal importance was evolved in my mind. In this case, as in that of the first premonitory recognition, the value of the idea did not inhere in its being something new to thought as such. It exists in literature, and I had come across it in my reading, but at the time in question it came with the force of a new discovery in a matrix of assurance and with an affective quality that I can hardly express in any other way than to say it was "Light." While the moment of this discovery was not that of the culminating recognition, yet I have reason to believe that it was the critical or turning point that rendered the final recognition accessible. It altered the base of thought and valuation in a profound way and in a direction confirmed by the subsequent realization. Because of the important part this idea played, a brief elucidation of it seems necessary.

It is a common, and apparently quite natural, habit with us to regard the material given through the senses as being something actual. Our science and philosophy may fail to give an adequate interpretation of this material, but still we generally feel sure that it is something. So the larger portion of the human search for Reality is in the field of the things given to our consciousness through the senses. But in my reflecting upon the idea that this universe of things is derived from and dependent upon a primordial plenum, it suddenly struck me that in the midst of the bare and original fullness there could be nothing to arouse discrete or concrete consciousness. It is a familiar fact of psychology that a long-continued or unchanging state or quality tends to become unconscious. Thus, in a state of health an individual is only slightly conscious of his body in its organic functioning. But let there be some form of injury or sickness, and at once the individual is conscious of his organism as he was not before. Likewise, when a long-continued period of bodily pain has ceased, there is then a concrete consciousness of well-being such as did not exist before the pain. In such a case, simply to be free of the pain has the value of an active joy, though the same bodily state did not have that value formerly. Through pain the joy-consciousness of health was aroused to recognition. Now, applying this principle in an ontological sense, it follows that the Consciousness of the original Fullness can only be aroused by first passing through the experience of "absence" or "emptiness," in some degree. Thus the active, concrete, and perceptual consciousness is to be viewed as an arousal of specific awareness through a partial blanking out of the full and perfectly balanced consciousness of the Primordial State. As a result, the world of things, apparently given through the senses, is actually a domain of relative emptiness. We become concretely aware only when contacting voids. There is nothing in this to invalidate the positive findings of natural science. Science studies the direct or indirect determinations of the senses and finds those relationships binding the various parts that render possible the formulation of laws. The question as to whether the terms or facts of science have a substantial base, and if so, what its nature is, is a metaphysical question quite beyond the range of the methodology of natural science. Scientific philosophy reveals a real critical acumen in dropping the notion of "substance" as being relevant to our kind of science. It says—I think correctly—that science is concerned with terms in various relations, and nothing else. When it goes further than that and says specifically or in effect that scientific knowledge is the only kind of real knowledge possible to man, or possible at all, it trips on the very error it charges against certain other philosophies, i.e., that of "definition by initial predication."

Now, if it is relative emptiness that arouses to activity concrete consciousness, then it follows that actual substantiality is inversely proportional to sensibility or ponderability. There is most substance where the senses find least, and vice versa. Thus the terms-in-relation of the sensible world are to be viewed as relative emptiness contained in an unseen and substantial matrix. From this there follows, at once, a very important consequence. The discrete manifoldness and apparent pluralism of sensibly given things are quite compatible with a continuous and unitary substantial matrix. The monistic tendency of interpretations based upon mystical insight at once becomes clear, and here is afforded a reconciliation of the one and the many.[7]

It is not my purpose, at the present time, to enter upon an adequate philosophical defense of this interpretation, but simply to present the idea that was of decisive psychological importance with me in removing a barrier to mystical realization. At least, the validity of this idea was, and still remains, clear to me as an individual.

The idea I had just recognized made possible an effective conceptual reorientation. The totality of being had become divided into two phases. The higher phase I called the "substantial" or "transcendental." This was supersensible and monistic, and served as the base in which the lower phase inhered. The latter phase thus became, by contrast, the sensible and phenomenal world, existing only through a complete dependence upon the supersensible and substantial. Within the latter existed endless multiplicity and divisibility.

There remained now merely the clearing up of the residual barriers to the complete identification of the self with the supersensible and substantial world, accompanied by the thorough divorcement of the self-identity with the phenomenal world. But a few days were required for the completion of this effort. Meanwhile, I had returned from physical solitude to the active concerns of social life, although I remained in a state of considerable mental detachment and continued brooding. Finally, on the seventh of August, 1936, after having completed the reading of Shankara's discussion of "Liberation," as given in the System of the Vedanta by Paul Deussen, I entered upon a course of meditative reflection upon the material just read.[8] While engaged in this course of reflection, it suddenly dawned upon me that a common error in meditation—and one which I had been making right along—lay in the seeking of a subtle object or experience. Now, an object or an experience, no matter how subtle, remains a phenomenal time-space existence and therefore is other than the supersensible substantiality. Thus the consciousness to be sought is the state of pure subjectivity without an object. This consideration rendered clear to me the emphasis, repeatedly stated by the manuals, upon the closing out of the modifications of the mind. But I had never found it possible completely to silence thought. So it occurred to me that success might be attained simply by a discriminative isolation of the subjective pole of consciousness, with the focus of consciousness placed upon this aspect, but otherwise leaving the mental processes free to continue in their spontaneous functioning—they, however, remaining in the periphery of the attentive consciousness. Further, I realized that pure subjective consciousness without an object must appear to the relative consciousness to have objects. Hence Recognition did not, of itself, imply a new experiential content in consciousness.[9] I saw that genuine Recognition is simply a realization of Nothing, but a Nothing that is absolutely substantial and identical with the SELF. This was the final turn of the Key that opened the Door. I found myself at once identical with the Voidness, Darkness, and Silence, but realized them as utter, though ineffable, Fullness, in the sense of Substantiality, Light, in the sense of Illumination, and Sound, in the sense of pure formless Meaning and Value. The deepening of consciousness that followed at once is simply inconceivable and quite beyond the possibility of adequate representation. To suggest the Value of this transcendental state of consciousness requires concepts of the most intensive possible connotation and the modes of expression that indicate the most superlative value art can devise.[10] Yet the result of the best effort seems a sorry sort of thing when compared with the immediate Actuality. All language, as such, is defeated when used as an instrument of portrayal of the transcendent.

There are implications and consequences following from such an insight that do fall within the range of formulation, and in this a man who has the appropriate skill can certainly do more than one who has little knowledge of the art of expression. But the immediate noetic and affective values of the insight, while they may be directly realized, cannot be conveyed by any formulation or representation whatsoever.

A definite line of demarcation must be drawn between the transcendental state of consciousness itself and the precipitated effects within the relative consciousness. The former is not an experience, but a Recognition or an Awakening on a timeless level of consciousness. The latter is an effect precipitated into the time-world and therefore has experiential and relative value. At the final moment, I was prepared not to have the personal, time-bound man share in any of the values that might inhere in the insight. But, very quickly, values began to descend into the outer consciousness and have continued to do so, more or less periodically, to the present day. These precipitated values have much that is of definite noetic content and decided affective value, well within the range of expression.

The listing and delineation of the elements that were precipitated into the relative consciousness from the first stage of insight is the next step.[11]

1. The first discernible effect in consciousness was something that I may call a *shift in the base of consciousness.* From the relative point of view, the final step may be likened to a leap into Nothing. At once, that Nothing was resolved into utter Fullness, which in turn gave the relative world a dreamlike quality of unreality. I felt and knew myself to have arrived, at last, at the Real. I was not dissipated in a sort of spatial emptiness, but on the contrary was spread out in a Fullness beyond measure. The roots of my consciousness, which prior to this moment had been (seemingly) more or less deeply implanted in the field of relative consciousness, now were forcibly removed and instantaneously transplanted into a supernal region. This sense of being thus transplanted has continued to the present day, and it seems to be a much more normal state of emplacement than ever the old rooting had been.

2. Closely related to the foregoing is a *transformation in the meaning of the "Self," or "I."* Previously, pure subjectivity had seemed to me to be like a zero or vanishing point, a somewhat that had position in consciousness but no body. So long as that which man calls his "self" had body, it stood within the range of analytic observation. Stripping off the sheaths of this body until none is left is the function of the discriminative technique in meditation. At the end there remains that which is never an object and yet is the foundation upon which all relative consciousness is

strung like beads upon a string. As a symbol to represent this ultimate and irreducible subject to all consciousness, the "I" element, I know nothing better than zero or an evanescent point. The critical stage in the transformation is the realization of the "I" as zero. But, at once, that "I" spreads out into an unlimited "thickness." It is as though the "I" became the whole of space. The Self is no longer a pole or focal point, but it sweeps outward, everywhere, in a sort of unpolarized consciousness, which is at once self-identity and the objective content of consciousness. It is an unequivocal transcendence of the subject-object relationship. Herein lies the rationale of the inevitable ineffability of mystical insight. All language is grounded in the subject-object relationship, and so, at best, can only misrepresent transcendent consciousness when an effort is made to express its immediately given value.

3. There is a sense of enormous *depth penetration* with two phases barely distinguishable during this first stage of insight. The first phase is highly noetic but superconceptual.[12] I had awareness of a kind of thought of such an enormous degree of abstraction and universality that is was barely discernible as being of noetic character. If we were to regard our most abstract concepts as being of the nature of tangible bodies, containing a hidden but substantial meaning, then this transcendent thought would be of the nature of the meaning without the conceptual embodiment. It is the compacted essence of thought, the "sentences" of which would require entire lifetimes for their elaboration in objective form and yet remain unexhausted at the conclusion of such effort. In my relative consciousness, I knew that I was thinking such massive thoughts, and I felt the infiltration of value from them. In a curious way I knew that *I KNEW* in cosmical proportions. However, no brain substance could be so refined as to be capable of attunement to the grand cosmical tread of those Thoughts.

But still beyond the thoughts of cosmic proportions and illimitable abstraction there were further deeps transcending the furthest reaches of noetic and affective value. Yet, in this, the self-identity remained unbroken in a dimly sensed series of deeps reaching on to ever greater profundities of what, in one sense, was an impenetrable Darkness, and yet I knew It was the very essence of Light itself.

4. I knew myself to be *beyond space, time, and causality.* As the substantial, spatial, and transcendent "I," I knew that I sustained the whole phenomenal universe, and that time, space, and law are simply the Self-imposed forms whereby I am enabled to apprehend in the relative

sense.[13] I, thus, am not dependent upon the space-time manifold, but, on the contrary, that manifold is dependent upon the Self with which I am identical.

5. Closely associated with the foregoing realization, there is a feeling of *complete freedom*. I had broken out of the bondage to the space-time manifold and the law-form governing in this manifold. This is largely an affective value, but one which, to me, is of the very highest importance. The quest for me was less a search for bliss than an effort to satisfy a deep yearning for Freedom.

6. There is the sense of *freedom from guilt*. That feeling, which is variously called sense of sin, guilt, or karmic bondage, dropped completely away from me. The bindings of a discrete individuality no longer existed. The accounts were closed and the books balanced in one grand gesture. This came at once as an immediate affective value, but I realized readily the underlying rationale. As the individual and personal self, I was bound within the space-time field and necessarily incurred the rebound of all actions there, but, as the transcendent Self, I comprehended that field in its entirety, instead of being comprehended by it. So it might be said that all action and its rebounding were contained within ME, but left the Self, with which I am identical, unaffected in its totality.[14]

7. I both felt and knew that. at last, I had found the *solution of the "wrongness,"* the sensing of which constitutes the underlying driving force of all religion and much philosophical effort. Beneath the surface of life, in the world-field, there is a feeling of loneliness that is not dissipated by objective achievement or human companionship, however great the range and penetration of sympathetic adjustment. Religious and other literature afford abundant testimony that this feeling of solitude is very widely, if not universally, experienced. I am disposed to regard it as the driving motif of the religious quest. In common with others, I felt this solitude and realized that the sense of incompleteness that it engenders forces the individual to accept one or the other of two alternatives. He may accept the solitude and despair of ever attaining a resolution of it, in which case he accepts fundamental pessimism as part and parcel of the very core of his life. But the feeling of incompleteness may drive him on to a hopeful quest for that which will effect its resolution. The more common mystical resolution is a sense of Union with God, wherein a companionship with a transcendent otherness is attained. My own recognition had more the value of a sort of fusion in identity, wherein the self and the otherness entered into an indistinguishable blend. Before the final moment of the transformation, I was

aware of an otherness, in some sense, that I sought, but after the culminating moment that otherness vanished in identity. Consequently, I have no real need of the term "God" in my vocabulary. I find it useful, at times, to employ this term in a literary sense, because it suggests certain values I wish to convey. But its significance is psychological rather than metaphysical.

Through the Recognition, I attained a state wherein I could be at rest and contented in the most profound sense. For me, individually, it was not necessary to seek further, to achieve further, nor to express further in order to know full enjoyment. However, there was a blot on the contentment that grew out of the realization of the pain of the many millions who live in this world, and also out of the knowledge that a private solution of a problem is only a part of the great problem of the philosopher, which is the attainment of a general solution that shall be of the widest possible universality and availability. But all this is not a defect in the adequacy of the transformed state of consciousness itself.

8. There is a decided increase in the realization of the affective qualities of *calmness and serenity*. In the immediate presence of the transcendent state, the disturbing factors produced by the circumstances and forces of the world-field lose their effective potency. They are simply dissolved away as something irrelevant, or as something that acts so far below one as to leave him in his real being untouched. When in the mystical state, there is no need for trying to be calm and serene, but rather these qualities envelop the individual without his putting forth any specific effort. Subsequently, when I have been out of the immediate presence of the state, it has been easier for me to remain calm and serene than formerly, though the more I am out of the state, the greater is the effort required to retain these affective qualities.

9. The *significance and value of information is radically changed*. Formerly, I acquired information very largely as part of the search for the Real. In the transcendent state I felt myself to be grounded in the Real, in a sense of the utmost intimacy, and since then I have continued to feel this grounding, though involving sometimes less and sometimes more the sense of immediate Presence. At the present time, knowledge, in the sense of information, has value chiefly as an instrument of expression or a means to render manifest that which is already known to me in the most significant sense. This making manifest is valuable, not alone for the reaching of other individuals, but likewise for the enriching of my own personal consciousness. The abstract and superconceptual knowing attains a formal and experiential clarification through giving it concrete

embodiment in thought. Nevertheless, in all this, knowledge-as-information serves only a secondary role, quite inferior to the vital importance it formerly had. It seems as though, in an unseen and dark sense, I already know all that is to be known. If I so choose, I can give a portion of this knowledge manifested form so that it is revealed to the consciousness of others, as well as to my own personal consciousness. But there is no inner necessity, at least not one of which I am conscious, that drives me on to express and make manifest. I feel quite free to choose such course as I please.

10. The most marked affective quality precipitated within the relative consciousness is that of *felicity*. Joy is realized as a very definite experience. It is of a quality more intense and satisfying than that afforded by any of the experiences or achievements that I have known within the world-field. It is not easy to describe this state of felicity. It is in no sense orgiastic or violent in its nature; on the contrary, it is quite subtle, though highly potent. All world-pleasures are coarse and repellent by contrast. All enjoyment—using this term in the Indian sense—whether of a pleasurable or painful type, I found to be more or less distasteful by contrast. In particular, it is just as completely different from the pleasures experienced through vice as it is possible to imagine. The latter are foiled by a sense of guilt, and this guilt persists long after the pleasure-quality of the vicious experience has passed. The higher felicity seems almost, if not quite, identical with virtue itself. I find myself disposed to agree with Spinoza and say that real felicity is not simply the reward of virtue, but *is* virtue. One feels that there is nothing more right or more righteous, for that matter, than to be so harmonized in one's consciousness as to feel the Joy at all times. It is a dynamic sort of Joy that seems to dissolve such pain as may be in the vicinity of the one who realizes it. This Joy enriches rather than impoverishes others.

I doubt that anyone could possibly appreciate the tremendous value of this felicity without directly experiencing it. I felt, and feel, that no cost could be too high as the price of its attainment, and I find that this testimony is repeated over and over again in mystical literature. It seems as though but a brief experience of this Joy would be worth any effort and any amount of suffering that could be packed into a lifetime that might prove necessary for its realization. I understand now why so much of mystical expression is in the form of rhapsody. It requires an active restraint to avoid the overuse of superlatives, especially as one realizes that all superlatives, as they are understood in the ordinary range of experience, are, in fact, understatements. The flowery expressions of the Persian and Indian mystics are not at all overstatements. But this mode of expression is subject to the weakness that it suggests to the non-mystical reader a loss of critical perspective upon the part of the mystical writer. It is even quite possible to be abandoned in the Joy, and so a real meaning does attach to the idea of "God intoxication." On the whole, it seems probable that the most extreme experience of this Joy is realized by those in whom the affective side of their nature is most developed. If the cognitive interest is of comparable or of superior development, it seems likely that we would find more of the restraint that was evident in men like Spinoza and Buddha.

The Joy seems to be a dynamic force. If one is justified in saying there is such a thing as experiencing force, in the ordinary sense of "experience," then it certainly is true that one experiences a force either associated with, or identical with, the Joy derived from the transcendental level. In my experience, the nearest analogy is that afforded by a feeling of force I have sometimes experienced in the vicinity of a powerful electric generator.[15] There is something about it that suggests a "flowing through," though it is impossible to determine any direction of flow, in terms of our ordinary spatial relationships. It induces a sense of physiological, as well as emotional and intellectual, well-being. The sheer joy in life of a healthy youth, who is untroubled by problems, faintly suggests a phase of this sense of well-being. It gives a glow to life and casts a sort of sheath over the environment that tends toward an effect of beauty which at times is very strong. I have demonstrated to my satisfaction that this joyous force, or whatever else it may be called, is capable of being induced, in some measure, in those who may be in the vicinity. I find there are some who will report feeling the joyous quality, even though the state I might be experiencing was not announced or otherwise noted. It is not inconceivable that in this "force" we are dealing with something that may be within the range of detection by some subtle instrument. Clearly there are detectable physiological effects. Nervous tensions are reduced and the desire for ordinary physical food decreases. In fact, one does have a curious sense of feeling nourished. On the other hand, there are some after effects that suggest that one's organism has been subjected to the action of an energetic field of too intense or high an order for the nervous organism to endure easily. For my part, during the past eight months, I have experienced frequent alterations between being in this "force-field" and being more or less completely out of it. The latter I have come to regard as a sort of deflated state. Particularly in the early days and after periods when the "force" and joy qualities had been especially intense, I found that in the subsequent deflated states there was a subtle sense of fatigue throughout the whole body. Return of the joyous state would at once induce the feeling of well-being. However, I soon realized that a due regard for the capacities of the physical organism rendered necessary a discriminating restraint when inducing the joyous "force-field." I found that this "force" was subject to the will in its personal manifestation and could be held within the limits of intensity to which the organism could adapt itself. In the process of time, it does seem that my organism is undergoing a progressive adjustment to the higher energy level.

There are times when this "force" seems to be of the nature of a flame with which I am identical.[16] In general, this flame is not accompanied with a sense of heat, but under certain conditions it is. Thus, if, while in the "force-field," I permit myself to feel disturbing affections, I begin to feel heat in the organism. The effect is of such a nature as to suggest that the affective disturbance has a value analogous to resistance in an electric circuit. It is well known that an electric conductor of sufficiently high resistance will produce heat, and so the analogy is readily suggested. Further, the "force-field" does seem, at times, to produce a feeling of heat in others who are in the vicinity. These are objective effects, apparently well within the range of objective determination. Yet, the inciting cause is a state of consciousness that I find to be subject, in considerable degree, to conscious control through the intervention of purely mental control with no manual aids. Does this not confirm the suggestion of William James that there is such a thing as a penetration of energy into the objective field of consciousness from other zones of consciousness that are ordinarily in disparate relationship?

Though the symbols of the electromagnetic field and of fire go far in indicating the quality of this subtle and joy-giving "force," they fall short of full adequacy. The "force," at the same time, seems to be of fluidic character. There is something in it like breath and like water. At this point it is necessary in some measure to turn away from the mental habits of the modern chemist and physiologist and try to feel a meaning closer to that given by the ancients. It is important that the "water" should not be thought of as simply H_2O, and the breath as merely a pulmonary rhythm involving the inhalation and exhalation of air. In the present sense, the essence of the water and air lies in their being life-giving and life-sustaining fluids. The chemical and physical properties of these fluids are mere external incidents. In a sense that still remains a mystery to science, these fluids are vitally necessary to life. The joy-giving "force" is

Life, but it is life in some general and universal sense of which life-as-living-organism is a temporary modification. Thus, to be consciously identical with this "force" is to be consciously identical with Life as a principle. It gives a feeling of being alive, beside which the ordinary feeling of life is no more than a mere shadow. And just as the shadow life is obviously mortal, the higher Life is as clearly deathless. It may be said that time is the child of Life in the transcendent sense, while life-as-living organism is the creature of time. Right in this distinction lies one resolution of the whole problem of immortality. So long as the problem is stated in terms of life-as-living-organism, immortality remains inconceivable. In fact, in this sense, all life is no more than a "birthing"-dying flux with no real continuity or duration at all. But the higher Life is identical with duration itself. Hence, he who has consciously realized himself as identical with the higher Life has at the same time become consciously identical with duration. Thus, death-as-termination becomes unthinkable, but, equally, birth is no beginning.

11. There is also associated with the deep feeling of Joy a quality of *Benevolence*. It seems as though the usual self-interest, which tends to be highly developed in the midst of the struggles of objective life, spontaneously undergoes a weakening in force. It is not so much a feeling of active altruism as a being grounded in a kind of consciousness in which the conflict between self-interest and altruism is dissolved. It is more a feeling of interest in good being achieved than simply that I, as an individual, should realize the good. Before the attainment of the Recognition, I felt a distinct desire for the attainment of good as something that I, individually, might realize, but once I became identified in consciousness with the transcendent state, the individually self-centered motivation began to weaken. It is as though there is a spreading out of interest so that attainment on the part of any self is my concern as truly as my own individual attainment had been. There is not the usual sense of self-sacrifice in this, but, rather, a growing impersonality of outlook. In such a state of consciousness, one could readily accept a course of action that would involve personal hardship, if only it would serve the purpose of bringing the realization more generally within the range of attainment. It is not a motivation in which the thought of heroism, nobility, or reward plays any part. It simply seems to be the appropriate and sensible course to follow if circumstances indicate that it is necessary. All this is a spontaneous affective state born out of the very nature of the consciousness itself, without thought of an ethical imperative. In the more deflated states of consciousness, I find the force of the feeling considerably weakened, and

then it becomes necessary to translate it into the form of a moral imperative to set up a resistance to the old egoistic habits. But on the higher level, the moral imperative is replaced by a spontaneous tendency that, when viewed from the relative standpoint, would be called benevolent.

The underlying rationale of this induced attitude seems clear to me. When the "I" is realized as a sort of universal or "spatial" Self, synthesizing all selves, the distinction between the "me" and the "thou" simply becomes irrelevant. Thus the good of one self is part and parcel with the good of all selves. Consequently, altruism and self-interest come to mean essentially the same thing.[17]

12. Associated with the transcendent Life-force, there is a very curious kind of *cognition*. It is not the more familiar analytic kind of intellection. To me, this development has proved to be of especial interest, for by temperament and training my mental action, heretofore, has been predominantly analytic. Now analysis achieves its results through a laborious and painful dissection of given raw material from experience and a reintegration by means of *invented* concepts applied hypothetically. This gives only external relations and definitely involves "distance" between the concept and the object it denotes. But there is another kind of intellection in which the concept is born spontaneously and has a curious identity with its object. The Life-force either brings to birth in the mind the concepts without conscious intellectual labor or moves in parallelism with such birth. Subsequently, when these concepts are viewed analytically and critically, I find them almost invariably peculiarly correct. In fact, they generally suggest correlations that are remarkably clarifying and have enabled me to check my insight with the recognition of others.

Undoubtedly, this cognitive process is a phase of what has been called by many "intuition." For my part, however, I do not find this term wholly satisfactory, because "intuition" has been given a number of meanings that are not applicable to this kind of cognition. Accordingly, I have invented a term that seems much more satisfactory. I call it *"Knowledge through Identity."* As it is immediate knowledge, it is intuitive in the broad sense, but as it is highly noetic, it is to be distinguished from other forms of immediate awareness that are largely, if not wholly, non-cognitive. There are intuitive types of awareness that are quite alogical, and, therefore such that they do not lead to logical development from out their own nature. In contrast, Knowledge through Identity is potentially capable of expansive development of the type characteristic of pure mathematics. Knowledge through Identity may give the fundamental propositions or "indefinables" from which systems can grow at once by pure deductive process. Knowledge through Identity is not to be regarded as an analytic extraction from experience, but rather as a Knowledge that is original and coextensive with a Recognizable, but nonexperiential, Reality. It is capable of rendering experience intelligible, but is not itself dependent upon experience.

A realization of Knowledge through Identity does not seem to be an invariable, or even usual, consequence of mystical unfoldment. My studies of the record have led me to the tentative conclusion that it occurs in the case of certain types of mystical unfoldment, of which Spinoza, Plotinus, and Shankara afford instances. In such cases, the cognitive interest and capacity is peculiarly notable. But the larger class of cases in which the mystical sense is well developed seems to be of quite a different type. The well-known Persian mystics, presumptively the larger number of of the Indian mystics, most of the Christian mystics, and naturalistic mystics such as Whitman seem quite clearly to fall into some other classification or classifications. With all of these, the affective consciousness is dominant and the cognitive interest and capacity may be—though not necessarily—but poorly developed. With them, expression is almost wholly in terms of art or way of life, rather than in terms of philosophical systems. Apparently, the noetic quality of their mystical consciousness is quite subordinate to the affective, and in some cases, even to the sensuous, values.

13. *Atypical features.* There are certain respects in which the precipitated effects from the transcendent consciousness, as experienced by me, differ from typical mystical experience. I have not known the so-called automatisms, a class of psychical manifestations that are so commonly reported. My psychical organization does not seem to be of the type requisite for this kind of experience. I have never heard words coming as though uttered on another level of being and having the seeming of objective sound. Even the thought has not seemed to come from a source extraneous to myself. I have thought more deeply and more trenchantly than has hitherto been possible for me as personal man, but the sense of intimate union with the thought has been greater than was ever true of the former personal thinking. Never has my thought been less mediumistic. Formerly, my personal thought has often been a reflection of a thought originated by someone else and not fully made my own before I used it. There is a certain kind of mediumship in this, although in this sense practically everybody is a medium part of the time and many

all the time. The thought that I have found born in the Recognition is non-mediumistic in the strictest sense, since it is MY thought but more than my *personal* thought.

There never has been at any time a writing through my hand in an automatic sense. What I have written has been my own conscious thought, with full consciousness of the problems of word selection and grammatical construction. The effective words and the correct constructions I find myself able to produce much more easily than formerly, but there is a conscious selective effort required at all times.[18]

When in the field of the "Life-force," the action of the understanding is both more profound and more trenchant than when in the "deflated" state, but the difference is one of degree and not of two radically separated and discontinuous states of consciousness of such a nature that the inferior consciousness is quite incapable of understanding what is written under the guidance of the higher. The inferior phase of consciousness, when operating by itself, does not understand as easily nor does it have as wide a grasp of the bearings of the thought. But, in some degree, the inferior phase readily becomes more or less infused with the superior by the simple application of effort to understand. The effect is analogous to the superposition of two rays of light, with both of which I am identical, the resultant being an intensified consciousness that is at the same time relative and transcendent, in some way that is not wholly clear to introspective analysis.

These states of Recognition have never been associated with the so-called photisms. They most certainly had Light-value, and I frequently have occasion to use the word "Light" to express an important quality of the higher consciousness, but this is "Light" as an illuminating force in consciousness and not a sensible light apparently seen as with the eyes. There have been a very few of these so-called photisms when in a kind of dreaming state when half asleep, but these have not occurred at times close to the periods of the deeper Recognitions.

Never have I had experience of the type commonly called psychical clairvoyance. It is possible that the strength of my intellectual interest operates as a barrier to this kind of experience. I admit having an interest in such experience and would consider it a valuable object of study if it came my way. But I would not tolerate such a capacity for experience if the price exacted was a growth of confusion in understanding. On the whole, psychical clairvoyance seems to be quite frequently associated with mystical unfoldment, perhaps more the rule than the exception.

There even seems to be some tendency to confuse this clairvoyance with genuine mystical value. However, the two are by no means identical, nor are they necessarily associated.

I have found that there is a very important difference between psychical experience and noetic Recognition. The transcendent Consciousness is highly noetic, but on its own level is quite impersonal. In order that a correlation may be established between the personal consciousness and the transcendental state, there must be an active and conscious intermediating agent. The evidence is that this intermediating agent may be, and apparently generally is, an irrational psyche of which the individual is more or less conscious. But the intermediation may be intellectual with little or no conscious correlation with the irrational psyche. It seems practically certain that the precipitated effects within the personal consciousness by the two routes should not be congruent in form.

14. If *ecstasy* is to be regarded as a state of consciousness always involving a condition of trance, then that state of consciousness that I have realized and called "transcendental Recognition" is not one of ecstasy. However, there is considerable reason for believing that Ecstasy, or Samadhi—the Indian equivalent—is not necessarily associated with trance. It becomes very largely a question of the basis of classification. If the externally discernible marks or symptoms of a state are to be regarded as determinate, then ecstasy, as ordinarily conceived, is a trance or trancelike condition. But if the inner consciousness-value is to be the ground of classification, then there is excellent evidence that Ecstasy or Samadhi may be realized without trance.[19] The latter basis of classification seems to me to be of far more significance, for the external symptoms of trance mark widely different inner states of consciousness, such as those of hysteria, mediumship, and hypnosis, as well as Ecstasy in the higher sense.

By subsequent comparison it appears that the noetic and consciousness values that I have realized have a very great deal in common with those reported by Plotinus as characteristic of the state of Ecstasy. I find a marked congruency between my present outlook and that given in the teachings of Buddha and in the writing of Shankara. But neither of these men regarded the state of trance as necessary for the realization of the states they called Dhyana or Samadhi, although Buddha seemed to have no objection in principle to the use of trance as a means of attaining the higher state of consciousness. It seems rather clear that the state of the personal organism is a matter of only secondary importance, while other factors are primarily determinant.

For my own part, never in my life have I lost objective consciousness, save in normal sleep. At the time of the Recognition on August 7, I was at all times aware of my physical environment and could move the body freely at will. Further, I did not attempt to stop the activity of the mind, but simply very largely ignored the stream of thought. There was, however, a "fading down" of the objective consciousness, analogous to that of a dimming of a lamp without complete extinguishment. The result was that I was in a sort of compound state wherein I was both here and "There," with the objective consciousness less acute than normal. It is very probable that the concentrated inward state would have been fuller and more acute had the objective stream of consciousness been stopped entirely as in a trance, but with regard to this I cannot speak from personal experience.[20]

The literature on the subject of mystical states very clearly reveals their transiency. Often the state is only momentary and, it is said, rarely exceeds two hours in duration. Of course, the only phase of such states that affords a basis for time-measurement is that part that overlaps the objective consciousness. The inmost content of the state does not lend itself to time-measurement at all. Its value, therefore, is not a function of time. But if we take the perspective of the personal consciousness, it is possible to isolate a period during which the recognition was more or less full, and this can be measured. In my own experience, I am unable to give definite data with respect to this feature. For the first ten days following the awakening, I was far too greatly occupied with the contemplation of the values unfolding in my consciousness to think of the question of time-measurement, and in addition, at that time I had not been familiar with psychological studies of the subject and so knew nothing about duration norms. As I look at the whole period retrospectively, I do not see how a very definite time-measurement could have been made. There was a sharply defined moment at which the state was initiated, but there was no moment at which I could say it definitely closed. A series of alternate phases and variable degrees of depth of consciousness are discernible, so that at times I have been more transcendentally conscious and at others less so. A different base of life and valuation has become normal, so that, in one sense, the recognition has remained as a persistent state. Yet there are notable differences of phases.

During the first ten days, I was repeatedly in and out, or more in and more out—I am not sure which is the more correct statement—of what I have called the "Life-force" field. I soon found that the stronger intensity of the field was a real strain upon the organism and so I consciously imposed a certain restraint upon the tendency of the states to deepen until I finally achieved a certain adjustment and adaptation with respect to the nervous organism. After the close of the first ten days, it was suggested to me that it would be well to keep a record of the effects of the transformation, and so at that time I began to write and continued to do so for about four months. While the effort at formulation was a little difficult at first, the writing soon acquired momentum, and presently I found ideas developing in my consciousness faster than I could give them expression. During this whole period, there were many times when the consciousness was dominantly on the noetic level, with more objective intervals interspersed. At first, the range of oscillation was more notable than toward the end. In the course of time, it seems, the personal consciousness has gradually adapted itself to a higher level, so that the periods of inward penetration do not afford the same contrast as formerly. The first period of a little more than one month constitutes a phase that stands out by itself, with a fairly sharp dividing line at its culmination between the eighth and ninth of September. During this time the prime focus of my consciousness was toward the transcendent, while in the subsequent phase, continuing to the present, I have rather taken this transcendent consciousness as a base and focused more toward the relative world. The consequence is that there is a sense in which I look back to those first thirty-odd days as a sort of high point in consciousness, a seed-sowing period, from which various fruitings have followed ever since. Frankly, these thirty-odd days constitute a period that I view as the best I have ever known. Referring to a symbol that Plato has made immortal, I would say that this was a time when I stepped outside the "cave" and realized directly the glory of the "sun-illumined" world, after which I turned back again to the life in the "cave," but with this permanent difference in outlook—that I could never again regard the "cave life" with the same seriousness that I had once given it. Thus, in this cycle, there is something to be differentiated from all the rest.

During that first month, the current of bodily life was definitely weaker than during the preceding and following phases. The desire for sentient existence was decidedly below normal. The spontaneous inclination was all in the direction of the transcendent consciousness. Physical life was clearly a burden, a sort of blinder superimposed upon consciousness. I even felt a distaste for physical food. I am convinced that if I had not supplemented the weakened desire for physical existence by a definite and conscious will-to-live, the body would have started into a decline. I became hypersensitive and found it very difficult to drive an automobile in traffic. I had to exert the will consciously, where formerly I had acted through automatic habit. But on the other hand, I found the will more effective than previously, so I was enabled adequately to replace spontaneous inclination with conscious control. Fortunately, my earlier studies had prepared me for this state of feeling and I knew that I was facing a temptation that others had faced before me. For there is such a thing as a world-duty that remains even after the desire for sentient existence has disappeared. But this did not keep me from thinking how delightful it would be to abandon all to the transcendent consciousness.

Concomitantly with the loss of desire for sentient life, there was a growth in the sense of power. I felt I had a certain power of conscious control over forces that ordinarily operate beneath the level of consciousness, and my subsequent experience has tended to confirm this. It is a sort of raw power without the detailed knowledge of how to apply it. In other words, the knowledge of effective practical use had to be developed through experiment. But I have found, very clearly, that I possess a power that formerly I did not know. I can choose and will consciously, where formerly the current of unconscious forces was determinant.

Before the close of the first month, the decision to continue as an active factor in the world-field had become definite, despite the distaste I felt for this domain. It felt like turning one's back upon a rich mine of jewels after gathering but a handful, and then marching back into the dreary domain of iron and brass. However, I found that it could be done, and then I accepted what I thought would be a future in which the best would always be a memory. I had found what I sought during many years and could see nothing but anticlimax thereafter, so far as the immediately realized consciousness values were concerned. So the further Recognition, which closed the first cycle, came as a complete surprise, for not only did I not seek it, I did not even know that such a state existed, or if it existed, that it was within the range of human consciousness. I had now already known a state of consciousness that certainly had the value of Liberation. A subsequent search through mystical literature revealed that it was substantially congruent with mystical experience as such and was distinctly more comprehensive than many of the mystical unfoldments. So far as I was familiar with it, the Brahmanical literature always represented the Liberated State as the end-term of all attainment. In this literature, I had found nothing requiring more depth of insight than I now had glimpsed, although there was a vast mass of psychic detail quite foreign to my experience. So I was quite unprepared to find that there were even deeper levels of transcendence. However, had I understood a few obscure references in Buddhist literature, I would have been warned.

In order to reach some understanding of the culminating phase of the Recognition, certain contrasting facts concerning the first phase must be given emphasis. As I have already affirmed, there is sufficient evidence of the fact of mystical recognition, together with reported affective value, to render it an object of possible desire. Long ago I had learned enough to realize that it was desirable and had set forth in search of it. There also exists a sufficient statement of the reasons why an individual who has attained this Recognition should turn his back upon it, as it were, to show that such a course was desirable in its social bearings. But there does not seem to be anything further that could be conceived as an object of desire. Now, the culminating effect of the present Realization with respect to desire is that the latter has fulfilled its office in the individual sense, and there is nothing more to wish for. I certainly felt in the transcendent state abundant completion and vastly more than I had anticipated. So, what more could there be?

I see now that there was a defect in this completion that kept it from being a full state of equilibrium. It consisted pre-eminently of the positive end-terms of the best in human consciousness. Thus it was a state of superlative Joy, Peace, Rest, Freedom, and Knowledge; and all this stands in contrast to the world-field as fullness contrasts to emptiness.[21] Hence there did exist a tension in the sense of attractiveness that was incompatible with the perfection of balance. There was a distinction between being bound to embodied consciousness and not being so bound that made a difference to me. I had to resist the inclination toward the latter state in order to continue existence in the former. In other words, there are in this earlier phase of Recognition certain tensions that call for a higher resolution. But it was the perspective of the culminating Recognition that rendered all of this clear. The first stage did not, of itself, disclose any further possibility of conceivable attainment, and so I was disposed to give it a greater terminal value than it really possessed.

So far I have outlined three progressively comprehensive Recognitions. Each was realized after a period of conscious effort in the appropriate direction. In each case I had some reason to believe that there was a goal to be sought. In the first two instances I was aware that there was something more remaining to be realized, because the sense of incompleteness was only partly liquidated. In the third instance this liquidation seemed to be complete, and then I simply turned my back upon the full individual enjoyment of it for such period of time as might be necessary to fulfill some more comprehensive purpose reaching beyond individual concerns. In contrast, the culminating Recognition came with the force of an unexpected bestowal without my having put forth any conscious personal effort toward the attainment of it. Thus, in this case, my personal relationship or attitude was passive in a deep sense.

During the day preceding the final Recognition, I had been busy writing and my mind was exceptionally clear and acute. In fact, the intellectual energy was of an unusual degree of intensity. The mood was decidedly one of intellectual assertion and dominance. This feature is interesting for the reason that it is precisely the state of mind that ordinarily would be regarded as least favorable for the "breaking through" to mystical modes of consciousness. The rule seems to be that the thought must be silenced or at least reduced in intensity and ignored in the meditation.[22] In the records of mystical awakening, it is almost always made evident that preceding the state of Illumination there is at least a brief period of quiescence of conscious activity. Sometimes this appears as though there were a momentary standing still of all nature. For my part, I had previously been aware of a kind of antecedent stillness before each of the critical moments, though it was not translated as stillness of nature. But in the case of the fourth Recognition, the foreground was one of intense mental tension and exceptional intellectual activity. It was not now a question of capturing something of extreme subtlety that might be dispersed by a breath of mental or affective activity. It was more a case of facing an overwhelming power that required all the active phase of the resources of consciousness to face it.

The Event Came after retiring. I became aware of a deepening effect in consciousness that presently acquired or manifested a dominant affective quality. It was a state of utter Satisfaction. But here there enters a strange and almost weird feature. Language, considered as standing in a representative relationship to something other than the terms of the language, ceased to have any validity at this level of consciousness. In a sense, the words and that which they mean are interblended in a kind of identity. Abstract ideas cease to be artificial derivatives from a particularized experience, but are transformed into a sort of universal substantiality. The relative theories of knowledge simply do not apply at this level. So "Satisfaction" and the *state* of satisfaction possess a substantial and largely inexpressible identity. Further, this "Satisfaction," along with its substantiality, possesses a universal character. It is the value of all possible satisfactions at once and yet like a "thick" substance interpenetrating everywhere. I know how weird this effort at formulation must sound, but unless I abandon the attempt to interpret, I must constrain language to serve a purpose quite outside normal usage.[23]

This state of "Satisfaction" is a kind of integration of all previous values. It is the culminating fulfillment of all desires and thus renders the desire-tension, as such, impossible. One can desire only when there is in some sense a lack, an incompleteness, that needs to be fulfilled, or a sensed goal that remains to be attained. When in every conceivable or felt sense all is attained, desire simply has to drop out.[24] The result is a profound balance in consciousness, a state of thorough repose with no drawing or inclining in any direction. Hence, in the sum total, such a state is passive. Now, while this state is, in one sense, an integration of previous values, it also proved preliminary to a still deeper state. Gradually, the "Satisfaction" faded into the background and by insensible gradation became transformed into a state of "Indifference."[25] For while satisfaction carries the fullness of active affective and conative value, indifference is really affective-conative silence. It is the superior terminus of the affective-conative mode of human consciousness. There is another kind of indifference where this mode of consciousness has bogged down into a kind of death. This is to be found in deeply depressed states of human consciousness. The "High Indifference," however, is the superior or opposite pole beyond which motivation and feeling in the familiar human sense cannot reach. But, most emphatically, it is not a state of reduced life or consciousness.[26] On the contrary, it is both life and consciousness of an order of superiority quite beyond imagination. The concepts of relative consciousness simply cannot bound it. In one sense, it is a terminal state, but at the same time, in another sense, it is initial. Everything can be predicated of it so long as the predication is not privative, for in the privative sense nothing can be predicated of it. It is at once rest and action, and the same may be said with respect to all other polar qualities. I know of only one concept that would suggest its noetic value as a whole, and this is the concept of "Equilibrium," yet even this is a concession to the needs of relative thinking. It is both the culmination and beginning of all possibilities.

In contrast with the preceding Recognition, this state is not characterized by an intensive or active feeling of felicity. It could be called blissful only in the sense that there is an absence of all pain in any respect whatsoever. But I felt myself to be on a level of consciousness where there is no need of an active joy. Felicity, together with all other qualities, is part of the blended whole and by the appropriate focusing of individual attention can be isolated from the rest and thus actively realized, if one so desired. But for me, there seemed to be no need of such isolation. The consciousness was so utterly whole that it was unnecessary to administer any affective quality to give it a greater richness. I was superior to all affective modes, as such, and thus could command and manifest any of them that I might choose. I could bless with beneficent qualities or impose the negative ones as a curse. Still, the state itself was too thoroughly void of the element of desire for me to feel any reason why I should bless or curse. For within that perfection, there is no need for any augmentation or diminution.

While within this state, I recalled the basis of my previous motivation and realized that if this state had been outlined to me then as an abstract idea, it could not by any possibility have seemed attractive. But while fused with the state, all other states that could formerly have been objects of desire seemed flaccid by comparison. The highest conceivable human aspiration envisages a goal inevitably marred by the defects of immature imagination. Unavoidably, to the relative consciousness, the complete balance of the perfect consciousness must seem like a void, and thus the negation of every conceivable possible value. But to be identified with this supernal State implies abandonment of the very base of relative consciousness, and thus is a transcendence of all relative valuation. To reach back to that relative base involves a contraction and blinding of consciousness, an acceptance of an immeasurable lessness. In the months following the Recognition, when I had once again resumed the drama in the relative field, I have looked back to that Transcendent State as to a consciousness of a most superior and desirable excellence. All other values have become thin and shallow by contrast. Nevertheless, I carry with me always the memory, and more than a memory, of the immediate knowledge of it, and this is something quite different from a mediately conveyed and abstract portrayal of it as a merely possible consciousness.

As an intimate part of that supernal consciousness, there is a sense of power and authority literally of cosmic proportions.[27] By contrast, the marchings of the Caesars and the conquests of science are but the games of children. For these achievements, which seem so portentous and commanding upon the pages of human history, all inhere in a field of consciousness that in its very roots is subject to that Higher Power and Authority. Before mere cataclysms of nature, if they are on sufficiently large a scale, the resources of our mightiest rulers and of our science stand impotent. Yet those very forces of nature rest dependent upon that transcendent and seeming Void in order that they may have any existence whatsoever. The mystery before birth and after death lies encompassed within it. All this, all this play of visible and invisible forces seem no more than a dream-drama during a moment's sleep in the illimitable vastness of Eternity. And so, from out of that Eternity speaks the Voice of the never-sleeping Consciousness, and before the commanding Authority and irresistible Power of that Voice, all dreams, though of cosmic proportions, dissolve.

Now, as I write, there returns once again an adumbrative Presence of that awful Majesty. This time, as I am focused upon the problem of objective formulation, I am less blended in the Identity, and sense IT as "Presence." This mind, which once carved its way through the mysteries of the functions of the complex variable and the Kantian transcendental deduction of the categories, fairly trembles at its daring to apprehend THAT which threatens momentarily to dissolve the very power of apprehension itself. Fain would the intellect retreat into the pregnant and all-encompassing Silence, where the "Word-without-form" alone is true. This personal being trembles upon the brink of the illimitable Abyss of irrelevance that dissolves inevitably the mightiest worlds and suns. But there remains a task to be done and there may be no disembarking yet.

At the time of the culminating Recognition, I found myself spreading everywhere and identical with a kind of "Space" that embraced not merely the visible forms and worlds, but all modes and qualities of consciousness as well. However, all these are not There as disparate and objective existences; they are blended, as it were, in a sort of primordial and culminating totality. It seemed that the various aspects and modes that are revealed to the analysis of relative consciousness could have been projected into differentiated manifestation, if I chose so to will it, but all such projection would have left unaffected the perfect balance of that totality, and whether or not the projecting effort was made was completely a matter of indifference. That totality was, and is, not other than myself, so that the study of things and qualities was resolved into simple self-examination. Yet it would be a mistake to regard the state as purely subjective. The preceding Recognition had been definitely a subjective penetration, and during the following month, I found myself inwardly polarized to an exceptional degree. In contrast, the final Recognition seemed like a movement in consciousness toward objectivity, but not in the sense of a movement toward the relative world-field. The final State is, at once, as much objective as subjective, and also as much a state of action as of rest. But since it is all coexistent on a timeless level, the objectivity is not discrete and differentiated, and consequently is quite unlike the relative world. The Godless secular universe vanishes, and in its place there remains none other than the living and all-enveloping Presence of Divinity itself. So, speaking in the subjective sense, I am all there is, yet at the same time, objectively considered, there is nought but Divinity spreading everywhere. Thus the level of the High Indifference may be regarded as the terminal Value reached by delving into that which, in the relative world, man calls his "I," and yet, equally, the final culmination of all that appears objective. But this objectivity, in the final sense, is simply pure Divinity. So the sublimated object and the sublimated self are one and the same Reality, and this may be represented by the judgment: "I am the Divinity."[28] The Self is not of inferior dignity to the Divine, nor that Divinity subordinate to the Self. And it is only through the realization of this equality that it is possible for the individual to retain his integration before that tremendous all-encompassing Presence. In any case, the dissolving force is stupendous, and there is no inclination to resist it.

Throughout the whole period of this supreme state of consciousness, I was self-consciously awake in the physical body and quite aware of my environment. The thought-activity was not depressed, but on the contrary, alert and acute. I was continuously conscious of my self-identity, in two distinct senses. In one sense, I was, and am, the primordial Self and co-terminous with an unlimited and abstract Space, while at the same time the subject-object and self-analyzing consciousness was a sort of point-presence within that Space. An illustration is afforded by thinking of the former as being of the nature of an original Light, in itself substantial, spreading throughout, but not derived from any center, while the latter is a point centered and reflected light, such as that of a searchlight. The searchlight of the self-analyzing consciousness can be directed anywhere within the primordial Light, and thus serves to render chosen zones self-conscious. Through the latter process, I was enabled to capture values within the framework of the relative consciousness and thus am enabled to remember not merely a dimly sensed fact of an inchoate transcendence but, as well, all that I am now writing and a vastly more significant conscious integration that defeats all efforts at formulation. The primordial consciousness is timeless, but the self-analyzing action was a process occurring in time. And so that part that I have been enabled to carry with me in the relative state is just so much as I could think into the mind during the interval of penetration. Naturally, I centered my attention on the features that to me as an individual appeared to be of the greater significance.

It seems to me that this that I have called the Primordial Consciousness must be identical with von Hartmann's "Unconscious." For what is the difference between "consciousness" and "unconsciousness" if there is no self-consciousness present? Sheer consciousness that is not aware of itself, by reason of that very fact, would not know that it was conscious. Thus, an individual who has never known ill health or pain remains largely unconscious of his organism. But with the coming of pain, he is at once aware of that organism in a sense that was not true before. Then, later, with the passing of the pain, particularly if it has been of protracted duration, he becomes conscious of well-being in his organism. Well-being has taken on a new conscious value. It is at once suggested that self-consciousness is aroused through resistance in some sense, an interference with the free flow of the stream of consciousness. When this occurs, a distinction between consciousness and unconsciousness is produced that had no meaning before. Now this line of reflection has suggested to me that the real distinction should not be made between consciousness and unconsciousness, but rather between self-consciousness and the absence of self-consciousness. When there is no self-consciousness in a given zone, there is then no more valid basis for predicating sheer unconsciousness than there is for saying that it is a zone of consciousness that is not self-conscious. On the basis of such a view, would not the problem of interpreting how the so-called "unconscious" enters into consciousness become greatly simplified?

The Primordial Consciousness cannot be described as conceptual, affective, or perceptual. It seems that all these functions are potentially There, but the Consciousness as a whole is a blend of all these and something more. It is a deep, substantial, and vital sort of consciousness, the matter, form, and awareness functions of consciousness all at once. It is not a consciousness or knowledge "about," and thus is not a field of relationships. The substantiality and the consciousness do not exist as two separable actualities, but rather it would be more nearly correct to say that the consciousness is substance and the substance is consciousness, and thus that these are two interpenetrating modes of the whole. It is certainly a richly "thick" consciousness and quite other than an absolutely "thin" series of terms in relation.[29]

While in the State, I was particularly impressed with the fact that the logical principle of contradiction simply had no relevancy. It would not be correct to say that this principle was violated, but rather, that it had no application. For to isolate any phase of the State was to be immediately aware of the opposite phase as the necessary complementary part of the first. Thus the attempt of self-conscious thought to isolate anything resulted in the immediate initiation of a sort of flow in the very essence of consciousness itself, so that the nascent isolation was transformed into its opposite as co-partner in a timeless reality. Every attempt I made to capture the State within the categories of relative knowledge was defeated by this flow effect. Yet there was no sense of being in a strange world. I have never known another state of consciousness that seemed so natural, normal, and proper. I seemed to know that this was the nature that Reality must possess, and somehow, I had always known it. It rather seemed strange that for so many years I had been self-conscious in another form and imagined myself a stranger to this. It seemed to be the real underlying fact of all consciousness of all creatures.

I remembered my former belief in the reality of suffering in the world. It had no more force than the memory of a dream. I saw that, in reality, there is no suffering anywhere, that there is no creature in need of an aiding hand. The essential consciousness and life of all beings are already in that State, and both never had been, and could not be, divorced from it. The world-field with all its striving and pain, seemingly lasting through billions of years, actually is, or seems to be, a dream occurring during a passing wink of sleep. I simply could not feel any need or duty that would call me back to action in the world-field. There was no question of departing from or deserting anybody or any duty, for I found myself so identical with all, that the last most infinitesimal element of distance was dissolved. I remembered that it had been said that there were offices of compassion to be performed in the world, but this idea had no reality in the State because none there was or ever could be who had need for ought, although those who were playing with the dream of life in form might delude themselves with imagining that a need existed. But I knew there was no reality in this dream.[30]

The imperative of the moral law no longer existed, for there was not, and is not, either good or evil. It seemed I could invoke power, even in potentially unlimited degree. I could choose action or rest. If I acted, then I could proceed in any direction I might select. Yet, whether I acted or did not act, or whether I acted in one way or another, it all had absolutely the same significance. It was neither right nor wrong to choose anything, or putting it otherwise, there was neither merit nor demerit in any choice. It was as though any choice whatsoever became immediately Divinely ordained and superior to the review of any lesser tribunal.

To me, individually, the State was supremely attractive, and as the period continued, I seemed to be rising into an irrevocable blending with it. I recalled that if in the self-conscious sense I never returned from this State there would be some in this world who would miss me and would seem, in their relative consciousness, to suffer. Yet it was only with effort that I could give this thought any effective force. For many years I had known from my studies that reports existed of realizable states of consciousness such that the relative state could be completely and finally abandoned. I had also been impressed with the teaching that it was a wiser course to resist that tendency and hold correlation with the relative form of consciousness. I had been convinced by the reasoning supporting the latter course and had for some time resolved to follow it, if ever the opportunity to choose came to me. This doubtless established a habit-form in the personal consciousness, and so far as I can see, that habit alone, or at least mainly, was the decisive factor. For while in the State there simply is no basis for forming any kind of decision, unless that ground is already well established in the individual consciousness out of the life that has gone before. As a result, there was a real conflict between the attraction the State had for me, as a center of individual consciousness, and the impress of the earlier-formed choice, but *I*, in my inmost nature, was not a party to this conflict, rather standing back indifferent to the outcome, knowing quite well that any outcome was Divinely right. The issue seemed to be a closely drawn one, for as time went on—from the relative standpoint—the organized man appeared to be vanishing, but not in the sense of the disappearance of a visually apparent object. It was more a vanishing as irrelevance may cause an issue or a consideration to disappear. It was as though Space were progressively consuming the whole personal and thinking entity in a wholeness-comprehension, beside which all particularities are as nought. Personally, I seemed powerless in the process, not because I lacked command of potential power, but simply because there was no reason—no desire—for rendering the potential kinetic. In the end, I fell asleep, to awaken the next morning in full command of my relative faculties; and clearly the issue had been decided. Was it a victory? From certain points of view, yes. Yet, as I recall the profounder State of Consciousness, which has continued ever since to seem close in the deeper recesses of my private consciousness, I cannot say that in the ultimate sense there was either victory or defeat. The choice was right, *for no choice could possibly be wrong.*

The full cycle of this final Recognition lasted for some hours, with the self-consciousness alert throughout the period. But the depth of the State developed progressively, and at the final stage entered a peculiarly significant phase that strained my self-conscious resources to the utmost. There finally arrived a stage wherein both that which I have called the Self and that which had the value of Divinity were dissolved in a Somewhat, still more transcendent. There now remained nought but pure Being that could be called neither the Self nor God. No longer was "I" spreading everywhere through the whole of an illimitable and conscious Space, nor was there a Divine Presence all about me, but everywhere only Consciousness with no subjective nor objective element. Here, both symbols and concepts fail. But now I know that within and surrounding all there is a Core or Matrix within which are rooted all selves and all Gods, and that from this lofty Peak, veiled in the mists of timeless obscurity and surrounded by thick, impenetrable Silence, all worlds and beings, all spaces and all times lie suspended in utter dependence. On that highest Peak I could Know no more, for the Deeps of the deepest Darkness, and the SILENCE enshrouded in manifold sheaths of Silence rolled over me, and self-consciousness was blown out. But o'er this I heard as the faintest shadow of a breath of consciousness a Voice, as it were, from out a still vaster BEYOND.

There remains to be considered the effects of these Recognitions upon me as an individual center of consciousness, thinking, feeling, and acting within the relative world. Of course, in this, my own statement is necessarily incomplete, since it is confined to an introspective analysis, and lacks the objective valuation that only a witness could supply. But it can render explicit that which no one else could know, since it reveals, as far as it goes, the immediate conscious values.

The Recognition of September 8 and 9 initiated a radical change of phase in the individual consciousness, as compared to the cycle of the preceding month. As already noted, the latter was very largely an indrawn state of consciousness, and the physical organism tended to become overly sensitive to the conditions of physical life. It was more difficult than it had been to meet the ordinary problems arising from the circumstances of the environment. The tumultuous forces of the modern city seemed far too violent to be endured. Even though living in the relative isolation of a suburban community, there still remained the irritations of a mechanical age and subtle impingements of a nature very hard to define. My natural inclination was to seek the wilds where the competitions of objective life-pressures would be at a minimum. It was a real problem of endurance. In contrast, after the final Recognition I noted a distinct growth of organic ruggedness. And, although I have never come to enjoy the harsh dissonances and regimented existence of modern town life, yet I find I have a definitely increased strength for the making of the various needed adjustments. There is an increased capacity to assert command with respect to the various environmental factors. I seem to have the capacity to will embodied existence, regardless of inclination.

On the intellectual side, I have noted a definite revitalization. I have found myself able to sustain creative and analytic thought activity at a higher level than formerly and for longer periods of time. Difficult concepts have become easier of comprehension. The seeming aging effect in the mind, that had been troubling me for sometime, passed, and in its place there came a very definite increase of intellectual vitality; and this has remained to the present hour as a persistent asset.

The affective changes are in the direction of a greater degree of impersonality. There is certainly less personal emotional dependence, and as far as I can detect, a practical unconsciousness of anything like personal slights, if there has been anything of that sort. I do care deeply for the growth of durable well-being, especially for those who come within my orbit, but also in the sense of a general social growth. Yet I find myself considerably indifferent to, when not disgusted with, the rather trivial foibles that make up so large a part of the day-to-day life of most human beings. I am not yet superior to the feeling of indignation, but this feeling is mainly aroused when noting the rapid growth of wilful and violent irrationalism, which has so rapidly engulfed most of the present world. However, I recognize this as a defect due to insufficient personal detachment. For, philosophically, I do realize that men have the right to learn the lessons that folly has to teach, and it is but natural that a certain class of leaders should make capital of this fact. Still, it remains hard to reconcile current morally decadent tendencies with the decades and centuries of relative enlightenment that have been so recent. I find that I had had too high an opinion of the intelligence of the average man, and that the individual who is capable of understanding the wisdom contained in the fable of the goose that laid the golden egg is really quite above the average level of intelligence. Frankly, I have not yet completely adjusted myself to the disillusionment that comes with a more objective and realistic appreciation of what the average human being is, when considered as a relative entity. This comes partly from an increased clarification of insight, and while I am much more certainly aware of the Jewel hidden within the mud of the personal man, yet I see more clearly also the fact of the mud and its unwholesome composition. It is not a pretty sight and not such as to increase one's regard for this world-field. All in all, the more objective my understanding of the actualities of this relative life, the more attractive the Transcendent World becomes.

Probably the most important permanent effect of the whole group of Recognitions is the grounding of knowledge, affection, and the sense of assurance on a base that is neither empirical nor intellectual. This base is supersensible, superaffective, and superconceptual, yet it is both conscious and substantial and of unlimited dynamic potentiality. I feel myself closer to universals than to the particulars given through experience, the latter occupying an essentially derivative position and being only of instrumental value, significant solely as implements for the arousing of self-consciousness. As a consequence, my ultimate philosophic outlook cannot be comprehended within the forms that assume time, the subject-object relationship, and experience as original and irreducible constants of consciousness or reality. At the same time, although I find the Self to be an element of consciousness of more fundamental importance than the foregoing three, yet in the end it, also, is reduced to a derivative position in a more ultimate Reality. So my outlook must deviate from those forms of Idealism that represent the Self as the final Reality. In certain fundamental respects, at least, the formulation must accord with the anatmic doctrine of Buddha, and therefore differ in important respects from any extant western system.[31]

Notes to Chapter 2

1. In the symbolical language so commonly employed for portraying the stages on the Way, this "critical point" is represented by the desert symbolism. The field of consciousness is watered by the stream of libido (the term of analytic psychology), and when this stream is turned off, the garden or jungle that filled that field withers, leaving a desert. Between the turning off of the libido-stream and its subsequent breakthrough on another course, there is a lapse of more or less time, or at least so I found it. The resultant state is one of aridity with no interest anywhere. Mystical literature is full of references to this stage.

2. At this stage, encouragement from a Sage whom I knew was an important, perhaps decisive, help. But while this Sage encouraged and stimulated flagging interest, he would not tell me what to do, leaving me to my own devices.

3. In the contrast between the theoretical acceptance and the Recognition, I did not find any addition or diminution of thinkable content. But in the case of the recognition, the effect upon the mind was something like an insemination—a vitalizing force. In addition to the unseen, inward deepening of value, there was an objective effect, in that the thought flowed more spontaneously, more acutely, and with much greater assurance. The thought developed of itself, in high degree, without the sense of conscious labor. At the same time, I *knew* the truth of the thought and did not merely *believe* in it. Yet, everything that I could think and say might very well have been worked out by the ordinary methods of conscious intellectual labor. But in the later case, the sense of assurance is lacking, as well as the sense of supernal value. With these recognitions there is, in addition to the transcendental values, a genuine rejuvenation and vitalization of the mind. This fact became extremely notable at the time of the later radical transformation.

4. The doctrine of the nonexistence of the atman. This is equivalent to the denial of the reality of the self, either in the sense of the personal ego or in that more comprehensive sense of denial of substantive self-existence of the subject, whether pragmatic or transcendental.

5. About two months prior to the "breakthrough," while occupied with a course of lectures in a middle western city, I experienced a three-week period of heavy drowsiness. Except when actually on the platform, I desired to sleep practically all the time. I simply had to give way to this inclination a good many hours of each day, but it did not seem that I could ever get enough sleep. The condition broke very suddenly, and then my mind became more alert than it had been for some years. I was aware of the great inner excitement and somehow seemed to know that I was near the day of final success. In later studies of

Dr. C. G. Jung's contribution to the psychology of the transformation process, at least something of the meaning of this stage seemed to be clarified. In the language of analytic psychology, the transformation is preceded by a strong introversion of the libido, followed by a sort of brooding incubation. Normal sleep itself is manifestly an introversion, and so it is quite understandable that protracted introversion of psychical energy should produce a state of continuous drowsiness. From the standpoint of analytic psychology, the introversion of the libido and the incubation are the prior conditions of animation of contents of the unconscious depths of the psyche. I do not think that either von Hartmann or Jung has seen into the nature of the Unconscious as fully as is possible, since their views are limited by the methodology of objective empirical research, aided by intuition, but, judging by the content of their contributions, lack the perspective of direct mystical realization. Nonetheless, I would judge the recorded studies of these two men as lying on the highest level of Western literature. I would rate Dr. Jung, by far, as the greatest Western psychologist, and von Hartmann as a philosopher deserving much higher valuation than he has yet received.

6. At the time of writing *Pathways Through to Space*, one of the purposes was the keeping of a record, not only of the inner processes as far as they lay within the field of consciousness, but as well to note external circumstances that might conceivably have some relevance. I had been acquainted with this as a standard practice of the psychological laboratory where subjects, or human reagents, were required to note bodily and psychical states of themselves, as well as more objective facts, as state of weather, external sounds, etc. This data might or might not have a bearing upon the outcome of a specific experiment, but the fact of its relevance or irrelevance could not be determined until the results of experiment were later analyzed by the experimenter. I followed this rule of procedure in my record, not necessarily implying that every noted circumstance was significant, but rather aiming to record all that I could think of that might subsequently prove to be significant, although it might seem to have no bearing at the time. One noted circumstance of this sort has proved to be surprisingly significant. At the time of the period of solitude, I was engaged part of the time in the exploration of a gold prospect in the region of the Mother Lode country of California. This entailed considerable periods underground, and while my thought was necessarily engaged a good deal of the time with the concrete details of what I was doing, yet my mind would repeatedly return to reflection upon the material in Shankara's work, which I was reading much of the time when not actually otherwise occupied. At that time I did not know that it was a standard practice in the Orient to place candidates for the transformation inside caves at certain periods, and often for very long periods. It does, indeed, appear that there is some relation between the transformation of "rebirth" and the entering into the earth.

Jung's researches have shown that in the symbolism of the Unconscious, the Unconscious itself is often represented by water and the earth, as well as by other symbols, so that a dream or hypnogogic vision, wherein an individual appears to enter water or the earth, carries the meaning of introversion of the libido into the Unconscious. In connection with the transformation this has the value of entering the womb of the Great Mother Unconscious, preliminary to the Rebirth. Now, there is some mysterious interconnection between the physical ritualistic reproduction of the processes of transformation in dreams and hypnogogic visions and those dreams and visions themselves. That such is the case is at least a tentative conclusion that is forced upon one as one studies the Indian and Tibetan Tantric literature, and the study of western ritualism simply tends to reinforce this conclusion. As I, myself, have never been oriented to ritualism and have never sought from it a personal value, the conclusion forced upon me that it does have important transformation value is quite objective, all the more so as I find in retrospect that I actually performed an exercise, unconscious of what I was doing, which is a conscious practice in the Orient.

That entering the earth, literally, would have a suggestive value to the non-intellectual part of the psyche is at once evident. But I cannot escape the conclusion that more than suggestion is involved. In some manner, actual life springs from the earth and the sea and so there is a sense, more than figurative, that the earth is, indeed, the Mother. Now, anyone who has real acquaintance with the transformation literature from the ancients to our day is bound to be impressed with the widely current rebirth symbolism. Jesus, himself, said, "Ye must be born again." But all life comes from the womb. Nicodemus partly understood Jesus' dictum, but, being a materialist, he could derive only a stupidly literal interpretation. The real gestation of the new Birth is in the womb of the Unconscious, and for this the literal entering of the earth facilitates the process. To find a rationale for this, one must turn to the recurring content of mystical thought. The mystic ever finds the world in complete correspondential relationship with inner psychical realities. Hence, objective relations are not irrelevant, though the degree to which they are determinant varies from individual to individual. With some, slight contact with these objective factors is enough; for others, protracted discipline is necessary.

7. It has come to my mind that the reader might be inclined to question whether this account may be called a narrative description, as I did call it in the last chapter, since so much of the writing is manifestly discursive. However, it really is narrative description, on the whole, since it is a record of a process of thought that took place and had vitally determinant effects in the past. Only in subsidiary degree is this autobiographical material related to the objective life of a physical personality. In much higher degree is it an autobiography of intellectual steps and processes. Thus the discursive material that appears here is primarily not interpretative after fact, but rather part of a process in which

interpretative factors were traceably determinant in my own consciousness as it became more and more oriented to the transformation. These interpretations were pragmatically effective agents. Whether or not they have a larger objective truth-value is not the question that is before us at present. Later, I shall return to this larger problem.

8. At the time I was seated out of doors, a fact that may prove to be of some significance. References to a value attained by being under the sky with nothing intervening are to be found in mystical literature. Edward Carpenter has said that he could not write in the vein of *Towards Democracy* except when he was out of doors under the sky. It is significant that the Sanskrit word Akasha means "sky" as well as "space," "primordial matter," and, in a certain sense, the "higher mind." The sky is the matrix of Light. Thus the sun, the moon, and the stars are embedded in the sky, and the whole sky, from the perspective of the earth, is luminous. Thus, coming from underground out to under the sky is symbolical of leaving the dark place of gestation and entering the Light-world of new birth. That which was hidden becomes revealed; that which was unconscious becomes conscious.

9. The final thought before the "breakthrough" was the very clear realization that *there was nothing to be attained*. For attainment implied acquisition and acquisition implied change of content in consciousness. But the Goal is not change of content but divorcement from content. Thus Recognition has nothing to do with anything that happens. I am already That which I seek, and therefore, there is nothing to be sought. By the very seeking I hide Myself from myself. Therefore, abandon the search and expect nothing. This was the end of the long search. I died, and in the same instant was born again. Spontaneity took over in place of the old self-determined effort. After that I knew directly the Consciousness possessing the characteristics reported by the mystics again and again. Instead of this process being irrational, it is the very apogee of logic. It is reasoned thought carried to the end with mathematical completeness.

10. The Indian and Persian mystics have developed a sensuous poetic imagery for suggesting supernal Value, which reaches far beyond that of the representatives of any western race. To the western mind these portrayals seem extravagant. Actually, however, they are inadequate, since sensuous imagination is crippled at its root by its medium. Mathematical imagination, by being freed from sensuous limitation, soars much higher, but nearly everybody fails to have an appreciation of what has happened. As the reader may be interested in a sample of the Indian imagery, I shall quote a few lines from the opening part of the *Mahanirvana Tantra* (translated by Arthur Avalon):

> The enchanting summit of the Lord of Mountains,
> resplendent with all its various jewels, clad with many a
> tree and many a creeper, melodious with the song of many a

> bird, scented with the fragrance of all the season's
> flowers, most beautiful, fanned by soft, cool, and perfumed
> breezes, shadowed by the still shade of stately trees;
> where cool groves resound with the sweet-voiced songs of
> troops of Aspara, and in the forest depths flocks of kokila
> maddened with passion sing; where (Spring) Lord of the
> Seasons with his followers ever abide (the Lord of
> Mountains, Kailasa)....

The "Lord of the Mountains" is the Door to the Transcendent.

11. The reader is warned that this is still part of the record, and not the more systematic interpretation after fact. The contents precipitated into the relative consciousness as a result of the first insight had a more or less determinant part in preparing the ground for the culminating Recognition that came later, and thus are part of the aetiology of the process.

12. By "superconceptual" I mean beyond the form of all possible concepts that can be clothed in words. However, the nature of this knowledge is nearer to that of our purest concepts than it is to perceptual consciousness.

13. Surely no one will be so clumsy as to suppose this "universe-sustaining 'I'" is any more the personal "I" than the reflection of the sun in water is the real sun itself.

14. The residual personality continues to exist by karma, and continues to pay prices and reap rewards. But all this lies below the new base of reference.

15. In my reading some years subsequent to writing this, I was particularly impressed by a reference to the "fire" in C. G. Jung's *Integration of the Personality*. Dr. Jung quotes an uncanonical saying attributed to the Christ, which runs as follows: "Whoever is near unto me, is near unto the fire." (p. 141) Here, also, identification with the "fire" is implied, as well as effects upon those who are near. Fire is that which burns up and so transforms (sublimates) everything except the ash. To understand these mystical uses of words one must isolate and idealize the essential functions of the corresponding literal or physical process.

16. At the time of the transformation, I called this joy-filled "force" the "Current." The latter term broke into my mind spontaneously and was not the result of an objective reflective search for a descriptive term. A "sense of flow" is an immediate fact of the state, to be distinguished from the objective interpretative judgment: "It is a flow." The step from the immediately given to the conceptual interpretation involves the problem of criticism, which I shall have to face later. But this much I may say here—there are interpretations that one feels at once are substantially true to the sense of the immediate value, while others falsify it. True, in this spirit, was the description I gave of the seeming of the

Flow. I said it was a Flow that did not proceed from the past to the future, but rather, turned upon itself so that there was continuous motion with no progress or decline. I later found that this conception evoked no intelligible meaning in minds that were mystically blind. Certainly, in the sense of objective reference, it is meaningless; nonetheless I must still affirm its substantial truth with respect to the sense of the immediate realization. At the time I was not familiar with analogous references in mystical literature, but I have found them since. Thus, in the *Secret of the Golden Flower* the "circulation of the Light" stands as the critical accomplishment of the "Great Work." In this, among other effects, immortality is accomplished. Now, analysis of the symbol helps a good deal. Thus the "circulation" suggests self-containedness, while the straight line of chronological time has direction and is therefore dogged by the pairs of opposites. The time-line does not progress any more than it degrades. It gives life and takes it away. Hence, the philosophic pessimist is the one who has seen deeply. Only through the "circulation of the Light" is the tragedy of world-life mastered.

17. The first time I experienced the consciousness of benevolence certain consequences were striking. At the time, I was sitting in a very humble shack, quite alone, located on one of the creeks of the Mother Lode country of east central California. Insects and other creatures were rather overfamiliar companions. Spiders, scorpions, daddy longlegs (in great numbers), centipedes, slugs, gnats, and rattlesnakes were creatures one could never safely forget. But when the state of benevolence was superimposed upon my own private consciousness, it included all these creatures as much as any other. My goodwill included them equally with more evolved beings, and there was nothing forced in the attitude. It was no conscious moral victory, but just a state of natural feeling. This state of immediate feeling is transient just as is true of other phases of mystical states of consciousness. But it leaves a permanent effect upon the moral judgment. One can no longer kill anything, no matter how repulsive or destructive it may seem, without a feeling of guilt. This definitely increases the difficulty of objective life. For when the individual sees the objective realities clearly, he finds that there is no embodied living in this world that does not imply killing, and, therefore, guilt. The farmer must destroy the enemies of his plants and stock, or have the latter destroyed, and without the farmer no man has food. And then, within our blood there is constant war, with tiny creatures being killed and devoured all the time. Hence, all life here depends upon the taking of life. It is a very ugly world that comes into view when the blinders are removed from the eyes. Saints (who continue to live) and vegetarians share the guilt with all the rest. The amount of guilt does vary, of course, but difference of degree is not a difference of principle. All men who live in this world inevitably share guilt, and thus there are none who may cast the first stone. There are none who may sit in judgment upon others, unless at the same time they judge themselves and accept sentence along with the others. Release from guilt lies only in the Beyond.

18. There is at times a spontaneous upwelling that leads to the most effective production, but at the same time there is conscious selection and judging upon the part of the mind that was trained in the schools. The resultant product is thus a joint product of deeper and more superficial levels, both part of myself. I might suggest this compound action by a figure. If we were to think of the mental accumulations of a lifetime as being filed away in a sort of hall of records in which there is only a dim illumination so that, ordinarily, much of the material is hard to locate, and therefore not easily used, the state of illumination is like a brilliant light suddenly appearing in that hall that renders everything filed, at once available. The light has the additional effect of leading well nigh unerringly to the most appropriate selection of the material that is pertinent to the problem at hand. The once known and forgotten tends to become known again, and all this without laborious trying.

19. Thus, according to the handed-down record, Gautama Buddha discouraged the practicing of the trance state, though He did not repudiate it as a possible means. Yet, Samadhi is a fundamental part of the Buddhist Way. The implication is that bodily condition is essentially irrelevant.

20. A study of the word "ecstasy" in an adequate dictionary clarifies a good deal that is confusing about the word as it is employed in literature, particularly that of a medical sort. As the term is of high importance in relation to mysticism, this study is very helpful. The dictionary gives four uses, which cover a wide range of meanings, and I shall quote these in full. Ecstasy is defined (see *Century Dictionary and Cyclopedia*) as :

a. "A state in which the mind is exalted or liberated, as it were, from the body; a state in which the functions of the senses are suspended by the contemplation of some extraordinary or supernatural object, or by absorption in some overpowering idea, most frequently of a religious nature; entrancing rapture or transport.

b. "Overpowering emotion or exaltation, in which the mind is absorbed and the actions are controlled by the exciting subject; a sudden access of intense feeling.

c. "In medicine, a morbid state of the nervous system, allied to catalepsy or trance, in which the patient assumes the attitude and expression of rapture. ('Ecstasis' is a synonym for this usage.)

d. "Insanity; madness."

Etymologically, the word carries the meaning of "any displacement or removal from the proper place, a standing aside."

From the external point of view, all four meanings are consistent with the etymological sense of the word. But in the intensive sense, the difference of meaning is as great as the difference between a snake and an eel, which are only analogous but not homologous. In the sense of the first meaning, the "displacement from the proper place" is true only on the assumption that personal egoism is the proper place. It is a prime thesis of mystical philosophy that this assumption is a fundamental error.

The primary meaning of the Sanskrit word "Samadhi" reveals a much more profound insight into the real meaning of mystical Ecstasy. "Samadhi" has the significance of "putting together, joining with; union; combination; performance; adjustment, settlement; justification of a statement; proof; attention, intentness on; deep meditation on the supreme soul, profound devotion." Thus the prime meaning is that of "bringing together of that which is improperly separated". This gives a value that is highly positive and superior, while the etymology of "ecstasy" is depreciatory. It is a difference of viewpoint that parallels that between the Ptolemaic and the Copernican systems, with the profounder Indian view corresponding to placing the center in the sun. The typically ancient Greek orientation was not spiritual but sensuous-materialistic, the philosophers of the type of Plato and Plotinus being the exceptions. The Greeks realized bodies rather than space. Hence, a consciousness which stood disassociated from bodies appeared as not in the proper place. The general Greek insight is not as profound as supposed. It is the great exceptions who have lived to our day, just because they have seen more truly, and while these have deserved the honor we have given them, they have not justified us in extending that honor to the Greek civilization as a whole. Our own spatially oriented mathematics is nearer to the feeling of the Indian than the typical Greek.

21. So long as there is contrast and not indifference to the contrasting elements, the state is not *nirdvandva*—freed from the pairs of opposites. The feeling of superlative value is, after all, a dualistic state. In a genuinely absolute state, there is not, and could not be, any preference whatsoever. A consciousness of Bliss, of All Knowledge, or of Compassion is thus colored with something relative, so long as it is felt or known that there is anything else with different value. Any possible report of the state of *nirdvandva* inevitably seems to the relative consciousness as nothing at all. This adequately explains why the unillumined psychologists view the highest of mystical states of consciousness as identical with unconsciousness. There is a serious error in this interpretation, but only he who has known the actuality immediately can know, and he cannot tell what he knows to one who does not also know. One can only categorically affirm: "It is not unconscious." However, it is as little like what is ordinarily understood to be consciousness as to be indistinguishable from unconsciousness as viewed from the relative perspective.

22. The manuals are generally, if not universally, insistent upon mental quiescence and emotional calmness. I am not here developing a critique of the manuals, but simply reporting what actually happened. But there may be a valid need of such a critique.

23. The reader must have patience with these unusual combinations of conceptions if he would acquire any understanding at all. There is no word-combination that is strictly true to the meaning intended, and so the common medium is strained to suggest a most uncommon content. In any case, there is mystery enough in the relation of idea to its referent, even in ordinary usage. Habit has caused most of us to neglect this mystery, but it has led to the production of many volumes out of the minds of philosophers.

24. When to wish for is to have immediately, it is impossible to isolate desire from possession. The awareness of desire necessarily vanishes. Ordinarily we desire and achieve the object only imperfectly after much effort. Thus we are highly conscious of desire. If there were absolutely no barrier to complete fulfillment, there could be no more consciousness of desiring.

25. This is clearly a case of dialectic flow paralleling the thesis, antithesis, and synthesis of Hegelian logic. Corresponding to the thesis is consciousness conditioned by desire, to the antithesis is the State of Satisfaction, and to the synthesis the State of High Indifference. Hegel is correct in viewing the process as autonomous. However, I think we can trace the vital logic a little more in detail. There could be no satisfaction without an antecedent felt lack, from which desire grows. But at the moment lack vanishes, satisfaction withers as does a tree of which the roots are cut. Then the dualism is dissolved, leaving a nondual state, which, affectively and conatively considered, is Indifference.

26. At this point I must take radical exception to the thesis of Dr. Jung given in the first chapter of *The Integration of the Personality*. There Jung says: "In the end, consciousness becomes vast but dim . . ." It is no more dim than acute. It is really *nirdvandva*, and no contrasting description is really valid.

27. Surely, no one would be so stupid as to imagine that this is a personal power. The great power of the sun is not wholly manifested in the image of the sun reflected in the drop of water. Inwardly, *I* am the Sun, but as a personal ego I am the *image* of the Sun lying in the drop.

28. It was sometime after writing this that I became acquainted with the one figure in western history who reveals something of the great Buddha's depth of penetration. I refer to Meister Eckhart, recognized by some as the greatest mystic of the middle ages, and in my judgment one of the greatest in western history. He is the only instance I have found in the West, so far, who reveals acquaintance with what I have called the High Indifference. In other words than mine, he has expressed the same meaning as that given above, thus: "For man is truly God, and God truly man." Also, in the same spirit some centuries later, the poet Angelus Silesius (Johann Scheffler) wrote in beautiful simplicity:

> *I am as great as God,*
> *And He is small like me;*
> *He cannot be above,*
> *Nor I below Him be.*

There are always to be found witnesses of the Eternal Truth. (Quotations taken from Jung's *Psychological Types*.)

29. See James's use of the terms "thick" and "thin" in the *Pluralistic Universe*.

30. We are throughout all this presentation confronted with the old philosophic problem of Illusion and Reality. It is involved in all the great monistic philosophies. It appears that William James, at one stage in his philosophic life, earnestly strived to resolve certain fundamental difficulties inherent in such philosophies, at least in their western form. His effort failed and he gave up monism entirely, advancing in its place a frankly pluralistic philosophy. While he did not dogmatically close the door to the possibility of a speculative resolution of the problem, he left the impression of grave doubt that such resolution existed. James saw quite clearly that there are different states of consciousness that are ineluctable facts. If these are represented by the twenty-six letters of the alphabet, then the unity of them all would not be simply one fact, but the twenty-seventh fact. Thus there is no resolution of many-ness into unity.

James's critical analysis is acute and is probably sound if we restrict ourselves to the limitations of Aristotelian logic. But this is not the whole of logic, as is evidenced by the development of the logic of relatives, not to mention the dialectic of Hegel. There is no good reason to suppose that current western knowledge of logic is the whole of logic. Now, there is a logical principle that, I believe, so far clarifies the problem as to render the speculative resolution much more probable. I shall introduce the principle by reference to a very common oriental figure.

People who live in a country where venomous serpents are a serious hazard are familiar with the delusion of seeing a snake that is not there. We who have been much in the wilds of the far West know this delusion quite well. One early learns to be everlastingly on guard, so that near the surface of his mind he is always watching for snakes. Often it happens that a stick, piece of rope, or other long slim object will be perceived, half unconsciously, and lead to a reaction of the organism before rational recognition of the object is possible. One seems to see a snake, feels the shock, pauses, and perhaps jumps, before a rational judgment is possible. A moment later, he sees his error. I have had this experience many times, and on analysis find that it reveals a great deal. The snake, at first seemingly seen, a moment later is a stick, rope, or such other material object as it may be. The question then is, What happened to the snake? Did a snake become a stick? a rope? The final practical judgment is that the snake did not become a stick, but never was there. Yet there is no doubt that, in a psychical sense, experience of snake was there. Well, then, what is the nature of its existence? We certainly do not attribute to it substantial reality. It assuredly cannot bite or otherwise be dangerous in an objective sense. The moment after the rational recognition and judgment, there simply is no snake. Further—and this subtle point is the very crux of the matter—*the snake ceases to have ever been*. I know that the process works this way since I have observed it again and again. It remains true that there had been a state of psychical delusion, yet there is a vitally important sense in which the snake ceases to be, both as a present and past fact. The delusion neither added anything to the reality nor took anything away. There is thus no problem as to how to integrate it within reality.

Now, the speculative resolution of the monist's problem is found by applying the above principle of interpretation to the whole of relative experience. The latter differs from the snake experience in that it is massively collective and is, generally, not at once corrected by a rational recognition and judgment. It is to be viewed as like unto a vast delusional insanity and is to be corrected as a dream-problem is corrected, simply by waking up. Human suffering is of like nature to the suffering of the delusionally insane, and there is no real cure in terms of the premise of the insane state.

But what is the difference between reality and delusion, since the delusion is a psychical fact? Simply this. The reality is substantial, while the delusion is empty. In Buddhist terms, the only actuality in the delusional modification of consciousness lies in its being of one sameness with the essence of mind, but there is no actuality of content. All experience is simply the revelry of mind and has no substance in itself.

The adequacy of the snake-rope analogy has been ably challenged by Sri Aurobindo Ghose in his *The Life Divine*, with the consequent introduction of doubt as to the objective validity of the figure. However, the analogy does seem to be subjectively valid since the relative consciousness tends to vanish, like the snake into the rope, while the self-consciousness is immersed in the Transcendent. It appears that Aurobindo has made necessary a reexamination of the classical metaphysical theories grounded upon realizations of the above sort. This subject will be considered later in the present work.

31. The notes for this chapter were added seven years after the chapter was written. The notes reflect the expanded perspective afforded by a quite considerable study of the transformation problem, both in western psychological sources and in Buddhist sources that had not been available for me prior to the cycle reported. Though the problem has not had a wide consideration, it has attracted the attention of some of the best minds the world has ever known. I know now that although the ground covered has only rarely been traversed as far, to judge by the mystical records, yet all the Way has been pioneered long ago. This simply reveals the fundamental universality of the problem.

Part II

The Aphorisms on Consciousness Without an Object

3
The Levels of Thought

In the semi-esoteric psychology of Buddhism, Vedantism, and Theosophy, there is to be found a division of Mind into two parts or facets.[1] While it is affirmed that the essence of mind is unitary, yet in the process of manifestation, mind becomes like a two-faced mirror, one face oriented to the objective, the other to the subjective. Since the mind functions in considerable measure like a mirror, it takes on the appearance of that which it reflects, and thus its own essential nature tends to become hidden. The objectively oriented facet reflects the world and is colored by the conative-affective nature of the personal man. The inwardly directed facet, like that which it reflects, is marked by the undistorting colorlessness of dispassion.[2] But since both facets are of one and the same essence, there is a native affinity between them. Because of this, the consciousness of man, by the appropriate means, is enabled to cross what would otherwise be an impassible gulf of unconsciousness. This is not to say that the empiric or personal man, if unpossessed of mind, would actually have no connection with his roots, but it would mean that the relation is unconscious in the strict sense. Through the doubly reflecting mind of one essence it becomes possible, in principle, for the personally integrated consciousness to know the roots. Thus there is a Way whereby man may know the transcendent.

For western psychology and much of western philosophy, the acquaintance with mind is restricted to the outwardly oriented facet of the oriental conception. This is true for the reason that the exclusively objective methods of occidental science, at the outset, exclude the possibility of direct acquaintance with the more hidden facet. There would be little or no harm in this if it were realized that only a facet, and not the whole, was the real object of study, but all too commonly it is inferred that the method employed can provide conclusions justifying privative judgments. Thus we have the widely held attitude that the total possibilities of human consciousness are exclusively of the type that are true enough of the objective facet of mind. This standpoint simply is unsound, and this unsoundness can be verified by the appropriate means. Here science, in the familiar western sense, does not mean "to know fully," but rather "to know restrictedly," and therefore does not justify privative judgments. SCIENCE, in the sense of knowing fully, cannot be restricted to objective material, but must, as well, be open to other possibilities of awareness. Western psychology is limited in its possibilities through a restriction imposed at its roots by methodological presuppositions. Accordingly, mind can never be known in its totality by this means.

As it appears through the western method of research, the mind tends to appear as quite lacking in self-determination. Thinking seems to be entrained behind wishing and unable long to continue on its own momentum. Thus the conception has grown that thinking is only instrumental to action, the latter being the direct outgrowth of the conative factor in consciousness. Clearly, such a view greatly restricts the supposedly valid zone of the judgments of thought. Among other consequences, it excludes the possibility of a genuine knowledge of the transcendent, which is just the center of focus in the present work.

It is a tribute to the relative competency of western psychologic methodology that the derived interpretation of mind functioning is in substantial agreement with the oriental psychology with respect to the lower facet. This latter is often designated kama manas, but since kama is the Sanskrit equivalent of "desire", we derive the meaning of "desire mind", and this is very easily identified with thinking led by wishfulness. Wishfulness in thinking is undoubtedly a *part* truth, but it is not the whole truth.

No one may validly affirm the truth of a read or spoken statement merely because he has read it or heard it. Western science is by no means more insistent upon this than was the great Buddha himself. Indeed, the latter was the more exacting of the two. The individual must verify for himself, or at least be able to do so, before he may justifiably accept, save as possibility. Thus we cannot affirm the actuality of the inner facet of mind until we know it directly, as no more is ignorance competent to deny its actuality. I affirm the actuality of the inner facet on the ground of direct acquaintance, and further affirm that it may be known directly, through the transformation process, by any one who fulfills the conditions.

There is another kind of thought, dispassionate and self-directing, that stands in contrast with the thought that is guided by wishing. It may be said that this thought thinks itself, or tends to do so, depending upon the degree of its purity. It is not concerned with the preconceptions of the relative consciousness nor with the pragmatic interest of man. It tends to be authoritarian in its form, and while possessed of its own logic, yet ignores or tends to ignore that part of logical process oriented to objective referents. Most readily it expresses itself in aphoristic form, with more or less dissociation of statement from statement. But this dissociation is a surface appearance only. An analogous form is to be noted in the groups of postulates that form the bases of formally developed systems of mathematics that by themselves do not give an explicit logical whole, but rather provide the components from which a logical whole may be developed. However, the genuine aphorism differs from most groups of mathematical postulates in that the latter are generally inventions of the unillumined mind, while the aphorism is a spontaneous production out of an illumined state. They could well serve as postulates from which systematic logical development could be constructed, in which case they might well be conceived as authentic axioms and not merely as *fundamental assumptions*. Something of the character of this thought I have been able to isolate, and thus have been enabled to see somewhat of the root whence springs the aphoristic thought.

There are certainly four kinds of thought that I find discernible, with various gradations and intermixtures. Of these, three employ or can employ verbal concepts with more or less adequacy. The fourth has no relation whatsoever with any possible word-concept, as far as its inner content is concerned. Thus the latter is not related to communication as between different centers of consciousness. The other three serve communication in some sense.

In its most lowly form, thought is inextricably entangled with bodily existence. Here thought serves organic need and relation. It is the commonest thought of everybody and is not wholly beyond the comprehension of animals. This is the thought in absolute bondage to desire, which has no value save as it serves organism. Obviously it has no eternal worth. Its language may be just as well the grunt or the gesture as the more highly developed word.

Above this is a thought well known to cultured man. It is the thought of the liberated or partly liberated concept, and is thus the thought for which the word is the peculiarly adapted vehicle. This is the thought out of which grow science, philosophy, mathematics, and much of art. It is extremely articulate. In some manifestations, it attains a high order of purity, but may be more or less contaminated with the inferior kind of thought. Most actual human thinking is such a contamination. Even those who have known this thought on its levels of greater purity cannot maintain themselves at the requisite pitch of discipline during a large proportion of waking consciousness. It is consciously directed thinking and is achieved at the price of fatiguing labor. The writing here, at this moment, is of this class.

At the deepest level of discernible thought there is a thinking that flows of itself. In its purity it employs none of the concepts that could be captured in definable words. It is fluidic rather than granular. It never isolates a definitive divided part, but everlastingly interblends with all. Every thought includes the whole of Eternity, and yet there are distinguishable thoughts. The unbroken Eternal flows before the mind, yet is endlessly colored anew with unlimited possibility. There is no labor in this thought. It simply is. It is unrelated to all desiring, all images, and all symbols.

Between the deepest level of thought and the conscious and laborious thought, there is a fourth kind that, in a sense, is the child of these two. In high degree, this thought flows of itself, yet blends with verbal concepts. Here the conceptual thought and the transcendent thought combine in mutual action. But the lowly thought of the organic being has no part in this. It is a thought that is sweet and true, but fully clear only to him who has Vision.

The best of poetry has much of this kind of thought. It is the poetry that stirs the souls rather than the senses of men. It is the poetry of content rather than of form. But most of all, from this level of thought are born the aphorisms, that strange kind of thought that is both poetry and something more. For it stirs the thinking as well as the feeling and thus integrates the best of the whole man. Mystery is an inextricable part of this thought.

It should not be hard to recognize in the transcendental thought and the organic thought the purest forms of the superior and inferior facets of mind. The conceptual and aphoristic thinking are derivatives from these.

It is a misconception that conceptual thought is exclusively a child of the organic kind of thinking—something that developed *solely* to serve the adaptation of a living organism to its environment as the difficulties became more complex. It has possibilities of detachment that could never have been born out of organic life. At its best, it is more than lightly colored with the dispassionate otherworldliness of the transcendental thought. Something of both the transcendental and the organic is in it, sometimes more of one, at other times more of the other.

It is in the realm of this kind of thought that the West has outdistanced the East. It is peculiarly a western power. Its potential office in the transformation process is not to be found in the oriental manuals. Here we face new possibilities.

The aphoristic thought is the child of the transcendental and the conceptual. This is the highest form of articulate thought. He who would understand cannot do so with his conceptual powers alone. He must also let the understanding grow up from within him.

Notes to Chapter 3

1. In this instance, I am using "mind" as a synonym of "manas." While this practice is quite common, it is far from being strictly correct. The western definition and usage of "mind" is a good deal wider than that of "manas," which has a specifically restricted meaning. For a fuller discussion of this see *Pathways Through to Space*, p. 166 in this printing.

2. The distinction between the two facets of the mind seems to be approximately, if not identically, that given by Sri Aurobindo in his *The Life Divine* in his usage of the conceptions of "surface mind" and "subliminal mind."

4
Aphorisms on Consciousness Without an Object

1. Consciousness-without-an-object is.

•

2. Before objects were,
Consciousness-without-an-object is.

•

3. Though objects seem to exist,
Consciousness-without-an-object is.

•

4. When objects vanish,
yet remaining through all unaffected,
Consciousness-without-an-object is.

•

5. Outside of Consciousness-without-an-object,
nothing is.

•

6. Within the bosom of
Consciousness-without-an-object lies
the power of awareness that projects objects.

•

7. When objects are projected,
the power of awareness as subject is presupposed,
yet Consciousness-without-an-object
remains unchanged.

•

8. When consciousness of objects is born, then,
likewise, consciousness of absence of objects arises.

•

9. Consciousness of objects is the Universe.

•

10. Consciousness of absence of objects
is Nirvana.

•

11. Within Consciousness-without-an-object
lie both the Universe and Nirvana,
yet to Consciousness-without-an-object
these two are the same.

•

12. Within Consciousness-without-an-object
lies the seed of Time.

•

13. When awareness cognizes Time,
then knowledge of Timelessness is born.

•

14. To be aware of Time is to be aware of
the Universe, and to be aware of the Universe
is to be aware of Time.

•

15. To realize Timelessness is to attain Nirvana.

•

16. *But for Consciousness-without-an-object,
there is no difference between
Time and Timelessness.*

•

17. *Within Consciousness-without-an-object
lies the seed of the world-containing Space.*

•

18. *When awareness cognizes the
world-containing Space, then knowledge of
the Spatial Void is born.*

•

19. *To be aware of the world-containing Space
is to be aware of the Universe of Objects.*

•

20. *To realize the Spatial Void
is to awaken to Nirvanic Consciousness.*

•

21. *But for Consciousness-without-an-object,
there is no difference between the world-containing
Space and the Spatial Void.*

•

22. *Within Consciousness-without-an-object
lies the Seed of Law.*

•

23. *When consciousness of objects is born,
the Law is invoked as a Force
tending ever toward Equilibrium.*

•

24. *All objects exist as tensions within
Consciousness-without-an-object that tend ever
to flow into their own complements or others.*

•

25. *The ultimate effect of the flow of all objects
into their complements is mutual cancellation
in complete Equilibrium.*

•

26. *Consciousness of the field of tensions
is the Universe.*

•

27. Consciousness of Equilibrium is Nirvana.

•

28. But for Consciousness-without-an-object,
there is neither tension nor Equilibrium.

•

29. The state of tensions is the state of
ever-becoming.

•

30. Ever-becoming is endless-dying.

•

31. So the state of consciousness of objects
is a state of ever-renewing promises
that pass into death at the moment of fulfillment.

•

32. Thus when consciousness is attached to objects
the agony of birth and death never ceases.

•

33. In the state of Equilibrium
where birth cancels death,
the deathless Bliss of Nirvana is realized.

•

34. But Consciousness-without-an object
is neither agony nor bliss.

•

35. Out of the Great Void,
which is Consciousness-without-an-object,
the Universe is creatively projected.

•

36. The Universe as experienced is the
created negation that ever resists.

•

37. The creative act is bliss,
the resistance, unending pain.

•

38. Endless resistance is the
Universe of experience; the agony of crucifixion.

•

39. Ceaseless creativeness is Nirvana,
the Bliss beyond human conceiving.

•

40. But for Consciousness-without-an-object,
there is neither creativeness nor resistance.

•

41. Ever-becoming and ever-ceasing-to-be
are endless action.

•

42. When ever-becoming cancels the
ever-ceasing-to-be, then Rest is realized.

•

43. Ceaseless Action is the Universe.

•

44. Unending Rest is Nirvana.

•

45. But Consciousness-without-an-object
is neither Action nor Rest.

•

46. When consciousness is attached to objects,
it is restricted through the forms imposed by
the world-containing Space, by Time, and by Law.

•

47. When consciousness is disengaged from
objects, Liberation from the forms of the
world-containing Space, of Time, and of Law
is attained.

•

48. Attachment to objects is
consciousness bound within the Universe.

•

49. Liberation from such attachment is
the State of unlimited Nirvanic Freedom.

•

50. But Consciousness-without-an-object
is neither bondage nor freedom.

•

*51. Consciousness-without-an-object
may be symbolized by a SPACE that is
unaffected by the presence or absence of objects,
for which there is neither Time nor Timelessness;
neither a world-containing Space nor a Spatial Void,
neither Tension nor Equilibrium;
neither Resistance nor Creativeness;
neither Agony nor Bliss; neither Action nor Rest;
and neither Restriction nor Freedom.*

•

*52. As the GREAT SPACE is not to be
identified with the Universe,
so neither is It to be identified with any Self.*

•

*53. The GREAT SPACE is not God,
but the comprehender of all Gods,
as well as of all lesser creatures.*

•

*54. The GREAT SPACE, or
Consciousness-without-an-object, is the
Sole Reality upon which all objects
and all selves depend and derive their existence.*

•

*55. The GREAT SPACE comprehends both the
Path of the Universe and the Path of Nirvana.*

•

*56. Beside the GREAT SPACE
there is none other.*

•

OM TAT SAT

•

5
General Discussion of Consciousness Without an Object

The aphorisms that constitute the material of the preceding chapter are to be regarded as a symbolic representation of the culminating stage of the Recognition reported in the second chapter of Part I. The direct value of that Recognition is inexpressible and inconceivable in the sense of concepts meaning just what they are defined to mean and no more. Of necessity, all concepts deal with content in some sense, as they are born in the tension of a subject aware of objects and refer to objects. Consciousness-without-an-object is not an object on the level where it is realized. But just as soon as words are employed to refer to it, we have in place of the actuality a sort of shadowy reflection. This reflection may be useful as a symbol pointing toward the Reality, but becomes a deception just as soon as it is regarded as a comprehensive concept. Conceivable conclusions may be derived from the original symbol, but the full realization of That which is symbolized requires the dissolving of the very power of representation itself.

There are two lines of approach to, and employment of, the aphorisms. They may be regarded as seeds to be taken into the meditative state, in which case they will tend to arouse the essentially inexpressible Meaning and Realization which they symbolize. This we may call their mystical value. On the other hand, they may be regarded as primary indefinables upon which a systematic philosophy of the universe and its negation, Nirvana, may be developed. In this case, they may be viewed as a base of reference from which all thought and experience may be evaluated. From the standpoint of strict logic, they would have to be regarded as arbitrary in the same sense as the fundamental assumptions of any system of mathematics are logically arbitrary. For any individual to determine whether they are more than arbitrary would require a direct Gnostic Realization of the Truth symbolized by them, but for the individual lacking such a Realization, they may be evaluated as any system of pure mathematics or work of art is commonly evaluated. In the latter case, they are justified if they enrich the consciousness of man, entirely apart from any determination of their ontological validity. I offer the aphorisms to the reader in this sense, if he is unable to find any more fundamental justification for them.

It is a fundamental principle of this philosophy that the aphorisms are not derived from experience. In its employment here, I have restricted the term "experience" to the meaning formulated in Baldwin's *Dictionary of Philosophy and Psychology*. This rules out definitely any state of consciousness that may have an absolute or timeless character as being properly regarded as experience. It is a primary consideration that experience should be defined as a time-conditioned state of consciousness in which events or processes transpire. Whether or not thought with its products may be regarded as a part of experience, and likewise whether "experience" is to be restricted to the "raw immediacy" of phenomena before it is analysed by reflective thought is unimportant for my present purposes. It is important, simply, that "experience" should be understood as time conditioned. This seems to be sufficiently consonant with the meaning of the term as it is employed in the various empiric philosophies. So, when it is predicated that the aphorisms are not derived from experience, it is meant that they are derivative from a consciousness that is not conditioned by time. Of course, their formulation was an event and a process in time, but it is only as symbols that they are time conditioned. Their meaning and authority inhere in that which is beyond experience.

I am well aware that several philosophies affirm or imply that all consciousness is of necessity time conditioned. But since this is undemonstrable, it has only the value of arbitrary assertion, which is countered by simple denial. This affirmation or implication is incompatible with the basis realized or assumed here—whichever way it may be taken. At this point, I simply deny the validity of the affirmation and assert that there is a Root Consciousness that is not time conditioned. It may be valid enough to assert that human consciousness qua human is always time conditioned, but that would amount merely to a partial definition of what is meant by human consciousness. In that case, the consciousness that is not time conditioned would be something that is transhuman or nonhuman. I am entirely willing to accept this view, but would add that it is in the power of man to transcend the limits of human consciousness and thus come to a more or less complete understanding of the factors that limit the range of human consciousness qua human. The term "human" would thus define a certain range in the scale of consciousness—something like an octave in the scale of electromagnetic waves. In that case, the present system implies that it is, in principle, possible for a conscious being to shift his field of consciousness up and down the scale. When such an entity is focused within the human octave, it might be agreed to call him human, but something other than human when focused in other octaves. Logically, this is simply a matter of definition of terms, and I am more than willing to regard the human as merely a stage in consciousness, provided it is not asserted dogmatically that it is impossible for consciousness and self-identity to flow from stage to stage. On the basis of such a definition, this philosophy would not be a contribution to Humanism but to Transhumanism.

The Critique of Pure Reason I regard as a philosophical work of very high importance. The most significant conclusion of that work seems to be that the pure reason, acting by itself, cannot solve the ontological problems. The reason can work upon a material that is given, but cannot, itself, supply the original material. If material is given through experience, then the reason can derive consequences that are also valid within the field of experience. However, the reason operates within the matrix of a transcendental base, and thus is something more than experience, though it be ever so impossible to recognize and isolate reason before the conscious being has had experience. The transcendental base is a preexistence determined after the fact of experience. Now, if we regard Kant's criticism as a sort of circumscription of a certain field of consciousness, his work may well be permanently valid in its main outlines. I am disposed to think that it is. But I question whether his analysis was broad enough to cover the whole field of human consciousness. It would seem to fit more especially that particular phase of human consciousness in which lies western scientific knowledge. In any case, it is not an analysis of subhuman consciousness, such as that of the animal, nor is it competent as a study of the forms of consciousness realized in the various mystical states.

For my own part, I do not contend that the pure reason, either acting in a strictly formal sense or upon a material given by experience, can demonstrate a transcendental reality. On the contrary, this reality must be realized immediately, if it is to have more than a hypothetical existence. But assuming that a given individual has awakened to a transcendental realization, it is possible for him to reflect the transcendent through concepts, when the latter are taken in a symbolic sense. Such concepts may then serve as original material upon which the reason can operate and derive consequences. Some or all of these consequences may well prove to have value within the range of relative consciousness, including experience. I do not suggest that such a system will necessarily prove competent to render experience, as such, unnecessary. It may only supply that which experience, by itself, cannot supply, i.e., an integrative framework capable of comprehending all possible experience however unpredictable its specific quale may be. Experience as raw immediacy does not define its own meaning. A given "raw immediacy" cast in the framework of traditional Christian theology arouses a meaning that is quite different from that afforded when the base of reference is such as is assumed by physical science. Neither of these frameworks are derived from nor proved by experience. Logically, they are simply presuppositions from which observation, analysis, and interpretation proceed. Historically, each has supplied human consciousness with positive values, and for that reason has persisted over considerable periods of time. But today we know that both are inadequate. Our science has given command over external nature that the older theology failed to achieve, but in turn it leaves a very important part of the demands of human consciousness unsatisfied—a fact that is exemplified by the growth of psychosis and parapsychosis.

A transcendental reality cannot be proved by logic nor can it be experienced in the time-bound sense, but it may be *realized* mystically. It is impossible to prove the actuality of God, freedom, immortality, or any other supposed metaphysical reality, in the scientific sense of proof. With respect to these matters, either to affirm or to deny is unscientific. The competency of any scientist qua scientist need not be affected by either an attitude of belief or of disbelief. But an attitude of belief or disbelief may make a lot of difference to him as a complete human being. There is an enormous divergence between a human consciousness that is rich and filled with assurance compared to one that is starved and uncertain, and this difference is important to relative life itself, even though not affecting technical scientific competency. Practically, men assume much that they do not know and that cannot be known within the limits of the methodology of physical science. In spite of themselves, men do act upon transcendental assumptions, even when the assumption is in the form of a denial of the possibility of a transcendental reality. And all this does make a difference for life as actually lived.

The man who has not realized the transcendental, in the mystical sense of realization, is not freed from the necessity of acting "as if" with respect to some transcendental base that forms his outlook on life. Barring mystic certainty, the relative merits of one "as if" when compared to others is to be judged by the values afforded for life as actually lived. No dogmatist, whether ecclesiastical or scientific, has any right to challenge the freedom of any man in the selection of his purely transcendental "as if." Such an "as if" can never contradict the raw immediacy of experience, since the former is related to value or meaning, which is another dimension of consciousness entirely. For instance, a scientific determination that the secretions of the ductless glands, in the case of a given individual, differ from the norm, proves nothing concerning the value of the consciousness enjoyed by the individual. The deviation from the norm may or may not be favorable for a long life, but in any case this is irrelevant when we measure the value of the consciousness in question. We are simply dealing with another dimension of consciousness altogether.

The aphorisms may be regarded as affording a particular "as if" basis for integrating in terms of value the totality of relative consciousness. In this case, it is unnecessary to raise the question as to whether they are true or false in the scientific sense. In fact, they are neither true nor false when these judgments are employed as they are in physical science. They stand simply as the basis for the integration of relative consciousness. They may be viewed as of only psychological significance, though for me there is no doubt concerning their positive metaphysical rooting. They are not a mere "as if" for me, though I am quite willing to assume the "as if" status for them as a minimal basis for the purpose of discourse. However, entirely apart from the question of metaphysical actuality, it remains true that there is an enormous practical difference between a self that is out of harmony with the not-self and a self that has attained harmonious integration with the not-self. The steps toward such harmonious integration in their less comprehensive phases are known as "conversion," and when more profoundly developed, as "mystical awakening." That these aphorisms have the power to produce such transformations, I have already demonstrated empirically in connection with others than myself. This fact, alone, is sufficient to vindicate their use as an "as if" basis, at least in principle.

In his *Dance of Life*, Havelock Ellis has developed the thesis that both science and philosophy are arts and therefore have the same justification as any other art, at the very least. This is to say that both are creative constructions, whatever else they may be. In this respect Havelock Ellis's position is consonant with my own. It simply means that a real philosophy is a Way of Life, however much it may also be a system of notions. I regard the aphorisms as affording a base that is valid in both senses. However, criticism may give them quite a different evaluation, depending upon the sense taken. In any case, I insist upon their value in determining a Way of Life. That is to say, that before and above all other ways, they determine a religious attitude. But for me, individually, no religious attitude is satisfactory that is not, at least, philosophically and mathematically adequate, and ultimately, justly comprehensive of all phases of consciousness. However, I ask the reader to view, and if possible, to accept this philosophy as he would a work of art, even though he can go no farther.

The basis of integration afforded by the aphorisms is that of the radical assertion of the primacy of Consciousness. In this respect, the present thesis stands in a position counter to that of the so-called scientific philosophies. In the case of the latter, matter, things, or relations are assumed as original, and then consciousness is approached as a problem. "How did consciousness spring up in the universal machine?" This becomes the most baffling of mysteries. I affirm that this mystery is purely artificial and grows out of assuming an inadequate base of reference. For "matter," "thing," and "relation" are creatively constructed notions and by no means originally given material. On the contrary, consciousness is original and is presupposed in the very power to recognize and formulate a problem. There is something sterile in speculation concerning that which is eternally outside consciousness. Just as light can never comprehend darkness, for the simple reason that darkness vanishes as light penetrates it, so too the unconscious vanishes as consciousness pierces it. Thus every element that is brought into any speculation is, of necessity, within the field of consciousness. The eternally unconscious is indistinguishable, at any rate, from absolute nothingness, if it is not identical with it. It simply *is not* for any practical or valid theoretical purpose. This much we know, even though we know nothing else: "Consciousness is." For it is presupposed even in the acknowledgement of ignorance and in the agnostical and skeptical attitudes. But while every man is a living demonstration to himself that "consciousness is," not every man has realized that "consciousness-without-an-object is." The radical element in my philosophic departure inheres in the "without-an-object." Herein lies precisely the difference between a state of consciousness that is only relative or saturated in raw immediacy and no more, and one that involves profound mystical realization. However, consciousness is the

General Discussion of Consciousness Without an Object

common denominator underlying the possibility of any philosophy, world view, religious attitude, art, or science. I, therefore, affirm the systematic primacy of consciousness as such.

As soon as consciousness is concerned with objects, and inter-relations, other complexities are introduced and accordingly, all sorts of divergencies. Deleting content, only Consciousness-without-an-object remains as the common denominator. If approached in a purely theoretical spirit, this might have merely the value of an abstraction. I have demonstrated its actuality as a direct realization, but found it the most difficult of all things to attain when starting from the basis of reflective consciousness. However, when realized, it is the simplest of all things. When I say that Consciousness-without-an-object is, I imply its independence and self-existence. Everything else may be only a symbol. Problems concerning the genesis of specific symbols may become very difficult and require all the resources of highly trained capacity. But Consciousness-without-an-object is an unshakable base, and thus is an assurance transcending both unverifiable faith and relative knowledge.

As I assert the dependency of all contents upon Consciousness-without-an-object, so likewise do I affirm the concomitant dependency of the Self and all selves, because the existence of a self implies the existence of objects, whether subtle or gross, and as well, the existence of objects implies the presence of a self that is aware of them. The object and the self are polar existences that are interdependent. The notion of a self that is conscious without being conscious of anything does not correspond to any possible actuality. The object may be very abstract, such as a bare field of consciousness viewed as an object, but analysis will always reveal a polar relationship. The subject is the inverse or complement of the object, or in other words, its "other." Thus, for example, the object is the totality of all possible experience, and this is manifestly multiform and heterogeneous. In contrast, the pure self, conceived as the polarized power to be *aware*, is unitary and homogeneous. Taken in abstraction, the object, as such, is not a universe, but simply a multitude without interconnection and therefore not even a collection. The *universe* is the resultant of the interaction of the self and its object—that is, a disconnected multiplicity integrated through the unity of the self.

The technique of the higher Yoga would seem to imply the isolation of bare subjectivity as Self-consciousness totally devoid of content. The real meaning of this technique is, however, a shifting of the focus of consciousness toward bare subjectivity and away from objectivity, with the goal being in the nature of a limit that may be approached with unrestricted closeness of approximation, but that is never actually attained as long as any self remains. Fully to attain the goal is to destroy the subject as well as the object, and then there remains pure Consciousness-without-an-object—a state which is equally pure Consciousness-without-a-subject. But so long as the movement is toward pure subjectivity, the goal is unattainable, just as the last term of an infinite converging series is never reached through a step-by-step process.

The aspirant to Yoga starts with consciousness operating in the universe of experience and thought, and in a state of a self entangled with objects. This is the familiar state of human consciousness. The entanglement with objects leads to the superposition upon the self of qualities properly belonging to the objects alone. This state is akin to that of hypnosis, and is real bondage—the great cause of suffering. The first steps in Yoga technique have the significance of progressive disentanglement of the self and of dehypnotizing the consciousness. The process is one of radical dissociation of the self from objects. At the completion of the first stage, the self stands opposed to and other than the universe of objects. Objects, now, are simply witnessed as something outside, and the identification is dissolved. This stage may be represented by the judgment, "I am other than that"—the "that" referring to all possible objects. The second stage is ushered in by a radical readjustment in which the self shifts to another plane or base, where relations vanish and the self is realized as identical with content of consciousness. Superficially, this may seem like a recurrence of the original participation or entanglement, but such is not the case as there has been a shift of base. The content of consciousness now is the inverse of that with which the aspirant originally started. The difference may be suggested by conceiving all objects in the original state as being vortices, or voids in a supersensuous and continuous plenum. The consciousness with which the Yoga process starts is exclusively aware of the vortices, or voids, the whole world of supposed things—while the culminating consciousness, thus far, functions in the supersensuous plenum. That plenum is realized as the Self identical with content of consciousness—the state consistently reported by the mystics. It is as though the "I," which in the original state was like a bare point within the universe and circumscribed by objects, had suddenly transformed itself into a space that comprehended all objects. But there still remains a self that is aware, that maintains its own identity, and may be said to have a content that is the inverse of experience; for such a self certainly realizes values such as bliss, peace, and freedom. The more familiar name for this State is Nirvana.

Most of the literature on the subject represents Nirvana as the final culmination, but this is an error. Nirvana is simply the inverse of the universe—thus not the ultimate transcendence of the pairs of opposites. There is a still more advanced stage in Yoga. To facilitate understanding of this stage, it may help if we review the significance of the first step, considered as an affective transformation. In affective terms, the first step is frequently called a renunciation of the universe, i.e., the breaking of all attachment to objects. The successful accomplishment of the first step brings a very great reward, that is, consciousness operative in a subjective or inverse sense. The realization here is extremely attractive, but attractiveness implies a self that remains identical and that is still influenced by valuation. Now, the final stage of Yoga involves the renunciation of Nirvana, and that means the renunciation of all attractiveness and reward. Such a renunciation implies the final annulment of all claims of a self that remains in any sense unique. Both consciousness as object and consciousness as subject are now annulled. There remains simply Consciousness-without-an-object, which, in turn, comprehends both the universe and Nirvana as potentialities. This stage is the culmination of Yoga.

Modern physics and astronomy have developed a speculative conception that is, in some respects, an inverse reflection of the view elaborated here. This interpretation is derived from certain facts that have come to light in recent decades, partly as the result of the development of instrumental aids to observation and partly as the result of progress in interpretative theory. It now appears, quite clearly, that the older conception of matter as being composed of unchanging and indestructible atoms does not faithfully interpret the facts derived through experience.[1] It has become necessary to conceive of the atom as composed of still finer units, such as electrons, protons, positrons, and so forth, and these in turn as being subject to transformation under the appropriate conditions. When the transformation takes place, it appears that ponderable matter assumes a state of radiant energy. This process, seemingly, is proceeding in the stars continuously and is the source of the energy derived from them upon the surface of the earth. Apparently, then, the stars are disintegrating in the sense that matter concentrated in bodies at widely separated points in space is being transformed into radiant energy which spreads throughout all space. All this suggests that the various systems of stars will ultimately disappear as masses of ponderable matter, and in their place will be a space uniformly filled with radiant energy. On the other hand, observation of numerous extragalactic nebulae suggests, very convincingly, that both stars and systems of stars are generated by an aggregation of more or less homogeneous and amorphous matter into concentrated and more or less organized form. These various facts from observation, combined with theory, suggest the following conclusions:

a. That if the history of the stellar universe were traced back far enough in time, we would find a stage wherein there were no stars, but only a more or less homogeneous matter and radiation spread uniformly throughout space.[2]

b. That if we could follow the life of the systems of stars far enough into the future, we would come to a time when most matter, if not all, would be reduced or transformed into radiation extending throughout space.

c. That the two notions of conservation of mass and of energy must be united into the conception of a persistent Energy which may appear in the forms either of ponderable mass or of field energy, the latter including that which is termed radiation.

The above conceptions leave us with but one constant or "invariant," i.e., Energy, which may appear at certain times as ponderable matter, and at others as transformed into the state of radiant energy.[3] If now we substitute for "Consciousness-without-an-object" the notion of "Energy"; for the "Universe"—in the sense of all objects—the notion of "ponderable matter"; and for "Nirvana," the notion of "state of radiation," we can restate our first aphorisms as follows:

1. *Energy is.*

2. *Before ponderable matter was, Energy is.*

3. *Though ponderable matter seems to exist,*
Energy is.

4. *When ponderable matter vanishes,*
yet remaining through all unaffected, Energy is.

5. *Outside of Energy, there is no matter.*

11. *Within Energy lie*
both ponderable matter and radiant energy,
yet for Energy these two are the same.[4]

This physical conception has a high order of theoretical beauty, and I regard it as one of the finer products of scientific art. It effects a very great conceptual simplification, and enables us to picture a wide range of transformation in nature as experienced within the organization of an essentially simple unifying concept. However, what we have is a construction of the creative intellect, in part operating upon a material given through observation, and in part conditioning the observation. We have no right to say that this theory, or any modification that may take place in the future, is nature as it is apart from the consciousness of all thinkers. Any question of the truth or reality-value of the theory must be judged in relationship to a conscious thinker. Further, we have no right to assert dogmatically that, even though for our science this theory should prove to be ultimately valid, then it must necessarily be valid for any competent thinker whatsoever. In fact, it is entirely possible, nay more, quite probable, that the scientists of an entirely different culture, although of comparable capacity and supplied with comparable resources for investigation, would none the less construct an entirely different theoretical structure for the organization of their corresponding experience. Yet, this would not discredit the relative validity of the foregoing theory for our present culture.

The value of a theory or of any conceptual formulation lies in the fact that it gives the intelligent consciousness a basis for orienting itself and for achieving either purposive control of, or intelligent understanding in, the sea of existences. In the strictly metaphysical sense, i.e., in the sense that is not related to any concrete thinker, no conceptual formulation is either true or false. It is simply irrelevant. Nor, on the other hand, can experience prove the truth or falsity of any fundamental theory, though it can check the various derivative theories.[5]

If we regard the fundamental theories—the original bases or starting points—as only assumptions, then the whole of science is grounded in uncertainty and affords no security. But if the fundamental theories are grounded in insight—a mystical function—then it is valid for science to proceed with a basic assurance that is essentially of the same type as that attained through mystical awakening. All of which simply means that science, completely divorced from the religious spirit, is no more than sterile formalism. In point of fact, much of our science is far from sterile, but then there is actually much real religion in it. This factor should be given a larger theoretical recognition and its significance should be more adequately appreciated.

It is not difficult to see that the fundamental theories of science are of the nature of consciousness, since their existence is, for us, in thought alone—and a conscious thought at that. But such theories contain terms pointing to referents that in some sense have an objective existence. At first, one may be disposed to think that these referents must lie outside consciousness. However, it can easily be shown that even here we have actually drawn upon no material from beyond consciousness, though it lies or rests in another compartment of consciousness as contrasted to that of the interpretative theory. We can illustrate this by reference to what is one of the most objective notions of all physical science. This is the notion of "mass."[6]

When we ask, "What is mass?" we find that it is, in effect, defined in two ways, as follows:

1. Mass is measured by inertia in the field of a force.
2. Mass is measured by weight in the gravitational field of a standard piece of matter, i.e., the earth.

"Inertia" is the name given to the resistance that a body opposes to an effort ("force") to speed up its motion or to retard its motion. "Weight" is the name for the effort ("force") required to hold a body against the so-called force of gravity. But what do we mean by resistance and effort? Here we step out of the conceptual system into the realm of data from experience. Resistance and effort are sensory experiences, particularly involving the kinesthetic sense. Thus, at least in so far as man is concerned, both of these "forces" are existences in consciousness. To predicate that they correspond to existences outside of and independent of consciousness in every sense is to create a speculative dogma that in the very nature of the case can never be verified. For verification operates only within the field of consciousness. This is simply another instance of the principle that consciousness can never know absolute unconsciousness, for where consciousness is, unconsciousness is not. Undoubtedly, speculative theory can proceed upon the assumption that there are existences outside consciousness in every sense, but this is the assumption of an "as if" that can never be verified, either mystically or in any other way. The assumption may have a relative value, but it lacks all authority, and properly, may not be invoked to oppose the rational right of anybody to refuse to accept it.

We know immediately that consciousness is; but we do not know that mass is, immediately. All that we do know concerning the latter is that systematic constructions involving the concept of mass can be produced that give to man a greater command over nature and establish a greater harmony between conscious man and the apparent environment in which he finds himself. Yet both of these are values within consciousness.[7]

From the basis of Consciousness-without-an-object, there is no necessity of predicating absolutely unconscious existences. There would remain a distinction to be drawn between different kinds and levels of consciousness, and in particular, the distinction between consciousness that is not conscious of itself and consciousness that is conscious of itself. This leaves plenty of room for the existence of something beyond "consciousness-which-is-conscious-of-itself," or "self-consciousness," and thus there can be a flow into and out of the field of reflective consciousness. This, I submit, is all that science needs to interpret the fractional character of the data from experience. In addition, the view I am offering eliminates the question: How is it possible for that which is wholly outside consciousness, in every sense, to enter consciousness? Primeval Consciousness is the all in all, and only self-consciousness grows.

While it is a theoretical impossibility for consciousness to comprehend that which is absolutely outside consciousness, in every sense, there is no theoretical barrier that stands in the way of self-consciousness spreading out in Primeval Consciousness without limit, for self-consciousness is composed of the very stuff of consciousness itself. An extending comprehension of Primeval Consciousness by self-consciousness is simply a case of light assimilating Light. The Light cannot know darkness, because where light goes the darkness vanishes, but light can, in principle, know the light as it is of its own nature.

Opposed to consciousness as the only existence, there stands the counter notion of voidness. In this sense the void is a somewhat that is not, or has no substance. Now, without voids there would be nothing within the Primeval Plenum of Consciousness to arouse self-consciousness into action. The voids may be regarded as zones of tension wherein consciousness negates itself and thus blanks itself out in greater or less degree. Such voids have the value of disturbance in the primeval equilibrium. We may regard this disturbance as acting like an irritant that tends to arouse consciousness to an awareness of itself. It is an instance of *absence* arousing the power to be aware of *presence*. Here, then, we have a basis afforded for interpreting evolutionary development. Instead of that development being a means whereby consciousness is finally evolved out of the mechanical processes of dead nature, we have a progressive unfoldment of self-consciousness within a matrix of Primeval Consciousness. The play and interplay of voids, instead of atoms of an external and dead matter, are the background of the universe of objects. The voids arouse attention within consciousness simply because of their pain-value. The focusing power aroused by attention in time becomes self-consciousness, or the power to be conscious of consciousness. The multiform combinations of the voids produce all the configurations of experience and thought, and these in turn have the value of symbols, which in the last analysis are of instrumental value only. The symbols indicate a preexistent and formless Meaning. When, for any individual center of consciousness,[8] the Meaning can be assimilated directly without the instrumentality of the symbols, then for that individual the evolution of consciousness within the field of consciousness of objects has been completed. But until that time, symbols are necessary.

Now we are in a position to see the metaphysical function of science. It is concerned with the progressive development of a system of symbols, the raw material of which is given through experience. Science—at any rate in the sense of physical science—is not concerned with a study of actual existences. Its raw material consists of voids or absences. These are formed into a system of relations that has value in expanding self-consciousness and in forming a symbol of hidden Meaning. So, from the standpoint of this philosophy, the work of the scientists is quite valid, regardless of the form of the working hypotheses employed. The only point where this view could come into conflict with the thought of any individual scientist would arise in the case where the latter superimposes an extrascientific interpretation upon the material with which he works and upon his conclusions. The technical functions of science do not require that its materials should be a substantial existence. They only require that that material should fit into an intelligible system of relations.

The most fundamental principle of this philosophy is that consciousness, as such, is original and primary, and thus not merely an attribute of something else. But as here understood, "consciousness" is not a synonym of "spirit," since, generally, the spiritual or idealistic philosophies have regarded "spirit" as primary and represented consciousness as an attribute of spirit. This leaves the possibility that spirit, in some phase of its total character, may be unconscious, so that consciousness is reduced to a partial and derivative aspect. Let this be clear, that here it is not predicated that any spiritual or other kind of being is primary. On the contrary, Consciousness *is*, before any being *became*. Thus, "God," whether considered as an existence or simply as an integrating concept, is, in any case, derivative. We may properly view certain levels of consciousness, which transcend the human form of consciousness, as Divine. All terms derived from the notion of Divinity certainly have a very high order of psychological significance, at the very least, and I do make use of them. But I do not regard them as corresponding to the most ultimate values.

It seems to be in accord with well-established philosophical usage to regard "spirit" as having the same connotation as either the "Self" or "God." Following this custom we may say, when consciousness of objects is born, spirit also is born as the complemental or subjective principle. Objects being taken as the equivalent of matter, then spirit and matter stand as interdependent notions. Neither of these is possible without the other, though spirit may be regarded as positive, while matter is negative.

To predicate that consciousness is original and self-existent does not imply that *Being* is dependent upon *being known*. For while cognition is a mode of consciousness, it is not identical with consciousness. Thus affective and conative states are essentially noncognitive, though they are part and parcel of consciousness. I predicate that pure consciousness is the self-existent antecedent of all these modes of ordinary states of consciousness, also of the less familiar mystical states, and likewise of the forms of consciousness characteristic of nonhuman beings. On the other hand, "to know" does *imply* being, but the implication is of an antecedent, not of a consequent. To become aware of knowing is to become aware of the reality—in this case relative reality—of Being. The awareness of this reality is something achieved, but the achievement has not made the reality. However, to *be known* is to *exist*, and this is a true sequential or derivative existence. Being is *antecedent*, existence *derivative*.

To be known is to be an object. Since by "universe" I mean the totality of all possible objects, it then follows that the universe is dependent upon being known for its *existence*. The universe exists for one who experiences or thinks, but for none other. Even the Naturalist, who predicates the existence of *things* apart from all consciousness, actually is dealing with a notion that exists only in his consciousness. He has not arrived at something that lies outside consciousness, and only fools himself when he imagines that he has done so. Knowing is a Light that drives away the darkness, and thus forever fails to comprehend darkness. It is useless to predicate existence in the darkness of total and unresolvable unconsciousness, in every sense, for it is an absolute impossibility to verify any such predication. Such a predication is not only unphilosophic, it is, as well, unscientific, for science requires of all hypotheses that they shall be capable of verification. In fact, science even goes further than the mystic and requires that the verification must be of a type that falls within the range of the modes of consciousness of the ordinary non-mystical man. Thus the scientist who blossoms as a naturalistic philosopher violates his own scientific canons in the most violent manner. It is at this point that the Idealist is rigorous in his methodology, and not the so-called scientific philosopher.

All *things* exist as objects, and only so. Especially is this true for him who experiences or thinks. To anesthetize the powers of experiencing and thinking is to destroy the universe, but this does not imply the annihilation of consciousness in the Gnostic sense. Consciousness remains in the Nirvanic State. If self-consciousness has been developed to that degree of strength such that it can persist in the face of the process of anesthetizing, then the resultant is an awakening to realization of the Nirvanic State, otherwise this State is like dreamless sleep. But dreamless sleep is to be regarded simply as a state of consciousness where self-consciousness—that is, consciousness that is conscious of itself—is unawakened. All men are in Nirvana in the hinterland of their consciousness. The Nirvani, in the technical sense, differs essentially from the ordinary man only in that he has carried self-consciousness over into the hinterland.

Here I am introducing nothing that cannot be verified, for, by taking the appropriate steps, men can actually take self-consciousness across into the hinterland. Admittedly, this is not easy to do. It involves a good deal more than the process of verification adequate for the checking of ordinary scientific hypotheses. But it has been done. I have done it, and I find there is an abundant literature furnishing the testimony of others who have claimed to have done so. This literature springs up at all periods, as far as we have historic records, and through it all there is a common thread of meaning underlying a wide range of more or less incompatible overbelief. Representative men of all cultures, races, and creeds have supplied this common testimony. They agree with respect to a certain consciousness-quale and that the basis of this consciousness was direct, individual realization, transcending both faith and authority. Thus, in the present thesis, there is no violation of the scientific demand that a judgment of actuality or reality must be capable of verification. But the verification does require going beyond the ordinary modes of consciousness, and thus does transcend the secondary requirement of western physical science. However, this secondary requirement restricts our science to a delimited field and is of only pragmatic value so long as it cannot be proved that the ordinary modes of human consciousness are the only modes there possibly can be. No such proof exists, nor can it be made, for the most that any man could possibly say is that, so far, he, individually, has found no other ways of consciousness; and that proves nothing concerning consciousness *per se*.

Modern psychology distinguishes between objects that it calls real and objects that it calls hallucinations. From the standpoint of Consciousness-without-an-object, there is no important difference between these two sets of objects. The so-called real objects are experienced by groups of men in common, while the hallucinations are generally private. This is merely a social criterion of reality and has no logical force. Essentially it is as meaningless as determining physical laws by popular vote. Doubtless, if a Newton, with all his insight and intellectual power unimpaired, were transplanted to the environment of a primitive society and judged by his milieu, he would be regarded as a fool whose consciousness was filled with hallucinations. The social judgment of reality would be against him. Our society has reached a level where it can verify the insight of Newton, in considerable degree, but the validity of that insight exists independently of the social power to verify it. All of which simply means that the fact that objects exist for a given individual *privately* is not sufficient either to credit them with reality or to discredit them by calling them unreal hallucinations. The problem of reality is not to be handled in any such simple offhand manner. In fact, such a method is sheer intellectual tyranny. It is entirely possible that society, and not the individual man, is the greater fool. I am inclined to think so.

Objects, whether of the common social type or the so-called hallucinations, exist for the powers of experiencing and thinking, and thus both are derivative. If by "Reality" we mean the nonderivative, then both types of objects are unreal. In the narrower or pragmatic sense, the one type of object may be more real than the other, when taken in relation to a given purpose. It may well be that in the narrow sense of the purpose of western physical science, the social object is more real, but from the religious standpoint, in certain instances at any rate, the reverse valuation is far more likely to be true. But here we have no more than valuation with respect to specific purpose.

Some mystical states, probably the greater number, involve the experiencing of subtle objects of the type that the psychologist calls hallucination. Practically, this has the effect of classifying the mystic with the psychotic, apparently with the intent of common depreciation. Such a course involves both intellectual laziness and a failure in discrimination. Since a "hallucination" merely means private experience as opposed to social experience, it constitutes no true judgment of value. There is often a world of difference between one and another so-called hallucination. The difference between the state of consciousness of a drunkard, enjoying delirium tremens, and that of a seer like Swedenborg, is as far apart as the poles. All too often the psychologist calls both merely states of hallucination, and acts as though he thought that by giving a name he had solved the whole problem. As a matter of fact, the real problem here is one of valuation, just as it is with the social objects. The vital question in either case is: How far and on what level do the objects arouse the realization of Meaning? The objects that do this in higher degree and on a higher level may properly be regarded as possessing the greater relative reality. Thus, in a given case, the so-called hallucination may far outreach any social object in the relative reality. In any case, the type of the object, whether social or private, is not by itself, any measure of its value or reality. Neither type has nonderivative Reality or Meaning.

That in some sense the *Object* exists cannot be denied, for it is unquestionably a datum for immediate experience. But to affirm further that the *Thing* exists is to add an overbelief that is not necessary for either experience or reason. As these terms are here employed, the "Object" is to be regarded as always a content of consciousness, and thus implies a relationship to or within consciousness. In contrast, the "Thing" is that which is *supposed* to exist, quite independently of any relationship to or within consciousness. Thus the Thing is to be regarded as a sort of thing-in-itself that stands apart from any dependent relationship to consciousness as a source of its existence. It is not the present purpose to attempt to prove that a self-existent thing is impossible but simply that the supposition of its existence is neither practically nor theoretically necessary, and also that its existence cannot be demonstrated.

That the existence of the Thing cannot be demonstrated is very easily shown. For demonstration never gives us anything but an existence, a relationship, a value, and so forth, for consciousness. Hence, that which is demonstrated to be is already a content for consciousness, and therefore, an object. Unquestionably, new and unpredictable contents can enter *empiric* consciousness. To assume that the sudden arising of the new contents implies an existence wholly independent of consciousness, in every sense, that merely happened to enter into relationship with consciousness, may be natural enough. But for logic this assumption is not necessary, and by hypothesis, it cannot be empirically verified. For, so far as experience and logic can determine to the contrary, it is as readily thinkable that when the new content of consciousness arose it actually, then, came into existence for the first time. No doubt, the notion of the birth of an existence quite *de novo* or *ex nihilo* is repugnant to the deep-seated conviction that all existences are traceable to causal antecedents. But, whatever validity may attach to this conviction, it yet remains something other than a derivation from either experience or logic. That it is not a derivation from experience has already been well established by the critical analysis of David Hume, and accordingly, further discussion of this point is not necessary here. That it is not a derivation from pure logic is also clear, as we now understand quite well that logic supplies only the formal implications of the given material upon which it operates. The innate material of logic, itself, consists only of the original logical constants, and since the notion that every existence must have a causal antecedent is not one of these, it follows that this notion is neither a prerequisite of logic nor a consequence to be derived from logical process alone.

There remains the question of the claim imposed by the conviction that there is no existence that does not have an adequate causal antecedent, i.e., that no existence can be *ex nihilo* or *de novo*. I assume the validity of the claim of this conviction as a component part of consciousness, which is not derived either from logic or experience. The question then arises: Does this conviction require that the antecedent of a newly arisen object in relative consciousness shall be a thing existing independently of consciousness in every sense? The answer is no, since another adequate source is thinkable, and in addition, has already become a working hypothesis of Analytic Psychology. We can conceive of the antecedent of the newly arisen object as lying in the psychologic unconscious. This interpretation is already commonly employed in Analytic Psychology in the exposition of the aetiology of the phantasy products of introversion. In the case of the phantasy function, objects do appear suddenly from a hidden matrix, either in ideal or sensible form. Analytic Psychology has found it unnecessary to assume a causal antecedent of such objects in terms of things existing independently of the psyche in every sense. To extend this aetiology to the objects of the objective senses involves no logical or empiric difficulty, and merely extends a principle of explanation with radical consistency.

It may be objected that, in introducing the notion of the psychological unconscious as the causal antecedent of the newly arisen object, we have merely substituted a logical equivalent of the Thing, existing independently of consciousness in every sense. But this is not so. For, as has been shown already at some length, the psychological unconscious does not imply unconsciousness in every sense. It is merely that which is unconscious to ordinary waking consciousness, which is quite different from saying that it is unconscious with respect to consciousness in every sense. For it is clear that consciousness that is not conscious of itself is indistinguishable from unconsciousness. Philosophically, then, it is possible to affirm the exclusive existence of all objects and their antecedents in consciousness and yet employ the notion of the unconscious in the *psychological* sense.

From the foregoing, it should be clear that the demonstration of the existence of the independent Thing is impossible. At the same time, in the latter part of the above argument, it has been shown that its existence is not a necessary assumption for logic, experience, or the conviction that every existence must have an adequate causal antecedent. For I have suggested a thinkable aetiology that supplies what is necessary, and yet dispenses with the notion of a thing existing independently of consciousness, in every sense. This completes the formal argument. Let us now examine the extralogical considerations that may bear upon this proposed aetiology.

The requirements of a physical science are fundamentally simple. Chief among these are the following. (*a*) The objective content of the science must be of such a nature that it can be perceived by the objective senses, either directly or indirectly, through the intervention of instruments, and these senses must be exclusively those that are active in the typical representative of our culture, or of the human race. (*b*) This material becomes a science when, and only when, it has become organized into a rationally thinkable system that possesses internal coherence and that, in addition, makes possible the prediction of future objective events in such a way as to render either observational or experimental checking possible. These are the two principal requirements of a pure physical science. Applied science requires, in addition, that the organization of the raw material of a science shall be such that, at least, some degree of practical control of the object is achieved. Any theory as to the real nature of the objects that form the content of a science, that does not interfere with the action of these fundamental requirements of science, leaves to science the full freedom that science qua science can claim. If the behavior of the Object were wholly arbitrary or irrational in every sense, no science, pure or applied, could ever be possible. A science is possible only to the extent that the perceived object can enter into some relationship with a rationally thinkable system. It is not necessary that such a system shall be the only conceivable one or that it shall be the ultimately true or complete system. The objective of physical science is partial. (*a*) It does not aim to comprehend the totality of all possible knowledge. This is evident from the fact that it arbitrarily excludes all material that cannot be perceived directly or indirectly through the objective senses of the typical representative of our culture or our humanity. Thus, such material of consciousness as there may be that is available only through other doors or by other modes of consciousness is extrascientific—in the western sense—however much such material may be an object for knowledge. (*b*) It does not include in its structure those modes or aspects of consciousness that are not to be classed as knowledge of objective content. Thus Self-knowledge or the feeling of Love are not part of the structure of any physical science.

In contrast to the specialized demands of a physical science, philosophy has for its field all possible aspects of consciousness. It is concerned with the religious, ethical, and aesthetic values, just as truly as with the general problems that are vital to the existence of science. Further, its concern with the general problems of physical science is not greater then with the similar problems of any other possible type of science. That the existence of sciences other than physical science is more than an academic possibility is revealed by the development of the psychologies with *a psyche*.[9] However, philosophy overlaps the motif of physical science in that it seeks a systematic objective.

All philosophies fail that do not take into account every conceivable possibility of consciousness and also grant to every possibility full freedom in its proper domain. The current schools of philosophy, known as Naturalism, Neo-realism, and Pragmatism, have granted to natural science full recognition. In so far as the ethical problem is conceived as a matter of social relationship, Pragmatism has made valuable contributions to ethical theory and interpretation. But all these philosophies fail—some of them completely—to give adequate recognition to the necessities of the religious and mystical states of consciousness. They are, therefore, valuable only as partial philosophies. Much of consciousness-value, they either ignore or treat with an unacceptable coercion. They are all psychologically one-sided. They represent, either exclusively or predominantly, the extroverted attitude in individual or social psychology. They either neglect entirely the values that are immediately apparent to the introverted attitude, or they treat such values with the condescension of extroverted pride that is quite unacceptable to any well-developed introvert. On the other hand, the systems of philosophy classified under Idealism, while they give with greater or less adequacy recognition of the introvert and the religious and mystical values, yet they have failed with respect to the extroverted standpoint. Since these four types of philosophic system cover the ground of western philosophic contribution, we must conclude that the West has not yet produced the adequate philosophic statement.

Why is it that the western mind so predominantly attributes the reality-value to the material that is the peculiar concern of physical science? It is not simply because that material is given as objectively sensible. Ordinary phantasy often produces objects that are sensibly apparent, yet commonly these objects are considered to be unreal. It is not due to the fact that the material of science lends itself to a logically systematic statement. There are mathematical systems grounded upon freely created fundamental assumptions that have the character of logically coherent, systematic wholes. However, these are not commonly considered to be possessed of reality-value. It does not inhere in a positive demonstration that science deals with a knowledge of existent things independent of all consciousness as such, as has already been shown. There seems to be but one fact of experience that affords the explanation of this attribution of reality-value to the material of physical science and that is that this material is relatively common and constant with respect to the vast majority of observers, and that so far as is commonly known, no individual can successfully act as though this material were not. Here there seems to be an objective somewhat with which the conscious being must come to terms if he is so to adapt his life as to live successfully.

Certainly, there is something or somewhat, in some sense, with which the individual must make terms. But this fact by no means implies that that something or somewhat is an independent self-existent reality. For we can give it an interpretation that, while independent self-existence is denied of it, yet retains for it its conditioning character with respect to the functioning of conscious beings. We may regard it as a collective phantasy projected from the collective unconscious and possessing a relatively frozen or fixed form, which, in turn, is but a measure of the stability of the collective unconscious. This would give to the projected phantasy the characteristic of being an objective determinant, and thus it is easy to understand why it should have acquired the seeming of primary reality-value.

Is there any respect in which the above interpretation of the objective somewhat would be incompatible with the facts of experience? There seems to be no objection that will stand after examination. The objective material of consciousness is given through the senses and only through the senses. But the senses supply merely the forms of one of the functions of consciousness, namely that of sensation. Here we are forever confined to material that is reducible to sensation, save in so far as material from other functions of consciousness are added to it. Much material that has an objective appearance is given in ordinary phantasy, even though it is the general judgment that such appearance is not an objective existence-in-itself. By the technique of hypnotism, similar appearances have been produced in the consciousness of the subject through suggestion. Here, again, there is no question of a corresponding objective thing that is an independent existence-in-itself. Give to such an hypnoidal appearance the character of being a collective component of all human consciousness, and then we may ask: In what way would it be distinguishable from the material acquired by ordinary extroverted observation? It would seem that every possibility of natural science that now exists would still remain. The significance of the scientific product, alone, would be changed. But this level of significance-evaluation lies outside the domain of scientific determination, as such, and thus there would be no interference with the freedom of natural science in the field or sector of consciousness available to it.

We should be forced to interpret the facts and laws of science as being purely psychical existence, though of an order of relative stability. The laws, as well as the facts, would have their real abiding place in the psychological collective unconscious.

I believe this philosophy allows to science all requisite freedom to develop in its own dimension. The interpretation of the significance of its facts, processes, and products, alone, is changed. I merely challenge the pretended right of the scientist to hypostatize the material of his science into a supposedly substantial and independent Thing. With the abandonment of this hypostasis, there falls all right to the claim of any peculiar reality-value attaching to the object of science or of sensation in general. There remains a relative or pragmatic reality-value that has validity within the restricted sector of consciousness involved, but only that. In a word, the accusation that a given content of consciousness has a phantasy-origin would no longer, by itself, be sufficient to establish inferior reality-value, as compared with the products of physical science, since this too rests upon essentially the same ground. Thus the argument that serves to undermine the reality of religious or mystical hypostasis would be a two-edged sword that likewise undermines the reality of scientific or sensuous hypostasis. Thus far, the content of mystical insight would have a right to claim reality-value that is not inferior to that which the scientist or extroverted consciousness may claim for his material. In a word, the extrovert must renounce his arrogant claim to peculiar possession of the sense for reality. He is oriented to a sector of relative reality, and only that. It is by no means evident that this sector ultimately releases the greater power. At any rate, this question becomes an open one.

A vital consequence of the present thesis is that, if there is any power that can consciously operate upon the psychological collective unconscious, then that power would be superior to any of the products of phantasy, whether religious or scientific. For it would be a power acting upon the root-source of all contents of consciousness of whatever nature. Theoretically, such a power would have the capacity of causing all the material of objective perception, as well as of religious phantasy, to vanish or to be transformed through processes that could not be objectively traced. Such a power, it must be understood, does not imply the capacity to destroy consciousness as such, but simply to destroy, or rather, transform, all content. It should also be clear that such a power would lie closer to ultimate Reality than any of the content of consciousness over which it has mastery.

The practical question is: Does such a power exist? So far, at least, I do not find it possible to give an objectively satisfactory answer to this question. To my own satisfaction, I have verified its existence, but I do not find it possible to do more than build a more or less satisfactory presumption for its existence, with respect to empiric centers of consciousness other than my own. It seems that there is a Transcendent Somewhat that must be sampled, at least, to be known. While I do affirm the reality of this Transcendent Somewhat and the existence of a conscious Power that can operate upon the collective unconscious of psychology, I do not claim the capacity to coerce recognition of either.

The term "Universe" is here employed with the connotation of the Buddhist term "Sangsara" Thus I do not confine the meaning of "Universe" to the totality of all objects of ordinary waking consciousness. It includes, as well, the so-called hallucinations, dream states, and any other possible states of consciousness during physical life or after death in which there is consciousness of objects. Opposed to this is the Nirvanic state of consciousness in which there are no objects, for the simple reason that in that State there is no subject-object relationship. Thus, Nirvanic Consciousness is not identical with the totality of all mystical states of consciousness, but on the contrary is the culminating point of the mystical Path into the *subjective pole* of consciousness. Only a few, even among the mystics, have gone this far, to judge from the available records. It follows that there are mystical states that do not transcend Sangsara, and in general, such are the more understandable to objective consciousness.

But the further the mystic goes in his penetration to subjective deeps, the less he can say in terms that are intelligible to ordinary consciousness, when trying to report the value of his realization. The higher the point of attainment, the less effective does concrete sensuous imagery become as a symbol of its value. Abstract concepts remain as effective symbols longer, but in any case all that can be said is of value only as a symbol. This is necessarily so, since the representation must be in terms of objects, whether sensory or conceptual, whereas the actuality is not an object. A so-called hallucination or phantasy may, in a given case, supply a truer symbol than one formed out of the material of social experience, though this is not necessarily so. In any case, the vital point is that from the standpoint of Nirvanic Consciousness everything supplied by the Universe or Sangsara is of symbolic or instrumental significance only. At this point I am in accord with the epistemology of the Pragmatists, but I go further than any Pragmatist with whom I am familiar, for I regard all experience, as well as intellection, as being, in the last analysis, of only instrumental value, and even regard experience as no more than a catalytic agent, valuable as an arouser of self-consciousness.

It is only recently that western scholarship has begun to come to an intelligent understanding of the state of consciousness called "Nirvana." Recent translations of authentic northern Buddhist canonical literature should go far in the clarification of the older misconceptions. The etymology of the term "Nirvana" is unfortunate. To be "blown-out" naturally does seem like total annihilation. But this is a great misconception. A truer understanding is reached by regarding the Nirvanic State as that realized when the powers of experiencing and thinking are anesthetized *without destroying self-consciousness.* It is a way of consciousness that is blown-out, not consciousness per se. To understand the idea in a form that is at all valid, it is necessary to think of all form or objects and all structures of thought and in consciousness, in general, as being in the nature of limitations imposed upon the play of consciousness. Remove the limitations, while holding to self-consciousness, and the Nirvanic State is instantaneously realized. Since this is a freeing of consciousness from limitations, it has been traditionally called "Liberation." Thus "Freedom" is the prime keynote of the State. But from this Freedom, when realized, affective and noetic values are precipitated. The latter, in some degree, can irradiate both thought and experience, and thus be an illuminating and blessing force within the universe. Consequently, Nirvana is a State of consciousness that can and does produce a difference of fact within the universe of experience. This is sufficient to give it pragmatic value. But this pragmatic value is merely a derivative and transformed value and thus of only partial significance.

A critical study of the use of the terms "Nirvana" and "Moksha," in Buddhist and Hindu literature, reveals that the meaning intended is not always the same. At times one receives the impression that Nirvana is Absolute Consciousness, while at others one runs across a differentiation between different degrees or levels of Nirvanic Consciousness, and even the explicit statement that the Nirvanic State is not an absolute state. Clearly, some of the writers are stricter in their usage of the term than others. If we view the term as sometimes used to designate a genus, and at other times a species under that genus, the apparent incompatibility of usage is largely, if not wholly, clarified. The primary mark of the genus would be that it is a state of consciousness transcending the subject-object relationship, and therefore inevitably ineffable for relative consciousness. Differentiation of this genus into various species implies that within the consciousness transcending the subject-object relationship, there are differences of level or phase, though these differences must remain unintelligible for the subject-object type of consciousness, as such.

At the time of the deeper level of Recognition that occurred to me spontaneously on the eighth of September, I was completely surprised. Up to that time I had found nothing in my readings that had suggested to me the existence of such a state. I named it, tentatively, from its affective quale, which had the quality of thoroughgoing indifference. It seemed to transcend Nirvana in the usual sense, since the latter is always represented as having the affective quale of supermundane Bliss. I had previously known such a State, but while on the level of the High Indifference, I realized Bliss as lying below me, as something that I could participate in or refrain from at will. Subsequent to the period of being immersed in the Higher State, while functioning on the level of subject-object-consciousness, I was somewhat troubled lest I had made some error in my interpretation.[10] To check myself I made a search of the available literature, but I found no clear verification until I chanced upon the translation of Tibetan Buddhism, which Evans-Wentz has edited and published in English. Here I finally found the references in which the Primordial Consciousness, symbolized by the "Clear Light" and in other ways, is represented as the container of the Nirvanic as well as the Sangsaric State. This supplied a conceptual form that confirmed my own interpretation of the culminating stage of Recognition. It made clear, also, that "Nirvana," as sometimes employed, is made to include the "Clear Light," a state that is neither subjective nor objective, while in other connections it refers only to the purely subjective State. Finally, I developed the symbol of "Consciousness-without-an-object" as a representation with a meaning or reference analogous to, if not identical with, the "Clear Light," and thus was enabled to add a noetic designation to the affective one I had already found.

Consciousness-without-an-object is the keystone that completes the arch. It is the final step necessary to produce a self-contained system of consciousness. Nirvana stands as a phase of consciousness standing in contrapuntal relationship to the sum total of all Sangsaric states—the consciousness behind the Self that is focused upon objects. It is thus the "other" of all consciousness of the subject-object type. But the predication or realization of any state and its other, in discrete stages, is not a complete cycle, for the two imply a mutual container. This mutual container is found in Consciousness-without-an-object, and this latter affords a base from which Nirvana, as well as Sangsara, falls into comprehensive perspective. Consciousness-without-an-object is neutral with respect to every polarity and thus in principle gives command over all polarities. It affords the basis for a philosophic integration that is neither introversive nor extroversive. This implies a philosophy that, as a whole, is neither idealistic, in the subjective sense, nor realistic, but which may incorporate both idealistic and realistic aspects. It should be equally acceptable to religious and scientific consciousness.

The actual working consciousness of man is not purely Sangsaric. Man's bondage to subject-object consciousness inheres in the fact that, characteristically, his analysis of consciousness has succeeded in capturing only the Sangsaric element. For most men, the Nirvanic element moves in the darkness of the not-self-conscious, such as dreamless sleep. In our western philosophic analysis of relative consciousness, we have always come ultimately to a blank wall, though even at that limit consciousness is found to be a stream. Whence this stream and whither? For ordinary subject-object consciousness, the final answer is the Unknown and the Unknowable. But this is correct only for the type of consciousness in question. Consciousness in the sense of Gnosis can and has gone farther, driving the Unknown far back into the Transcendental Plenum. And who is there who can place a final theoretical limit on this recession of the Unknown?

The Nirvanic State is not far away, but near at hand, in fact closer than the universe of objects. There is no difference between the purely subjective element of the subject-object consciousness and Nirvana. And what is nearer to man than his most immediate Self, that which he calls "I," and which is always present, however much the content of consciousness may change? Man has the power to see, yet he constantly projects himself into the objects seen, and complementarily, introjects the object into himself, thereby superimposing upon himself the limitations of those objects. Every human problem grows out of this, and the never-ending stream of unresolved or half-resolved problems cannot be eliminated until this vicious habit is broken. Every other relief is meliorative or palliative and no more. Mayhap melioration does more harm than good. I am often inclined to think so, for individual man might often try harder to escape from a trap that had become completely unendurable, and thus succeed in the resolution of the life problem more frequently than he does. Merely making the trap more endurable by melioration may well have the effect of delaying the crisis, and so result in an increase of the sum total of suffering. Let man so change the polarization of his self-analyzing consciousness that he may see his seeing, as it were, and at once, he breaks the participation in objects. Of course, this seeing of seeing is expressed in the language of subject-object consciousness, because we have no other language. In the actual seeing of seeing, the self and the object become identical.

When an individual has at last learned the trick of dissociating his "I" or subject from the whole universe of objects, he has, seemingly, retreated into a bare point of consciousness. But the moment he succeeds in doing this, the point is metamorphosed into a kind of space in which the Self and the content of consciousness are blended in one inseparable whole. I have called this the Spatial Void. Now it must be understood that this is not a state wherein the individual merely finds himself in space, but he is, as a Self, identical with the whole of Space. It is not consciousness as functioning through bodies and aware of objects, but a subjective state dissociated from all bodies and not concerned with objects. Yet it would be incorrect to regard it as a purely homogeneous consciousness in the sense of a fixed state, totally devoid of variety. For consciousness and motion, in some sense, are inseparable.

To arrive at a symbolic concept that may fairly suggest motion in the Nirvanic sense, it is necessary to analyze motion in the universe of objects and then develop its inverse. The consciousness of objects is atomic. By this I mean that it is in the form of a series of discrete states or apprehensions, in the sense in which Kant spoke of the manifold given through experience. This is well illustrated by the cinematograph, where we actually have a series of still photographs thrown upon the screen in rapid succession. The spectator is not actually witnessing motion, but merely a series of still images. Only a fraction of the original drama was actually photographed. Yet the effect upon the spectator is very similar to that produced by original scenes enacted by living actors. Now, actually the camera reproduces essentially the process of visual seeing. A certain amount of time is required before an image can be seen, and thus the sensible motion of external objects is really no more than a series of images with gaps between. All of which means that we do not see continuity. The same is true of the other sense-impressions, as there is always a time-factor involved in any sensible recognition. Again, when we analyze motion, we always give it a granular structure, even though our ultimate fixed elements are infinitesimals. Thus, both experience and thought deal with manifolds, and never with true continua. In this connection, the analysis of Weierstrass is profoundly significant. By very careful thinking, Weierstrass reached the conclusion that there is no such thing as motion, but only a series of different states or positions occupied by objects. As a judgment or interpretation concerning the universe of objects in its purity as abstracted from the whole, I do not see how this statement can be seriously questioned. It simply means that the ceaseless becoming and endless dying, which mark the universe of objects, are series of instantaneous states rather than true continua. This would be the rigorous interpretation of being as it appears to objective consciousness in isolation from other dimensions of consciousness, and thus radically non-mystical. It reveals beautifully the absence of depth or substance in the universe when taken in abstraction as only objective. The series of states are no more than dead pictures, having no life or substance, but are merely empty terms in relation.

The inverse of the phantasmagoric series, which constitutes the universe of experience and thought in its purity as abstracted, is the true continuum. The one is a granular manifold, the other a flowing unity. Now it is true that man has arrived at the notion of continuity, although, as Weierstrass has shown, he never really thinks it. Continuity is the inverse of the manifold and is, of necessity, recognized at the moment man became conscious of manifoldness, but this recognition involves more than the action of consciousness in the objective sense. Continuity belongs to the hinterland of consciousness. This simply illustrates the eternal fact, i.e., that the actual consciousness of man continually operates in a Nirvanic as well as in a Sangsaric sense. However, analysis has grappled fairly well with the Sangsaric phase, but has remained generally not-self-conscious with respect to the Nirvanic.

This all leads us to the point that the unity of the Nirvanic Consciousness is better symbolized by the notion of the true continuum than by the finite number 1 (one). For the number one is a fixed entity representing a single empty term, which in turn always implies the manifold of all numbers. In other words, the unity of numeral one is an abstraction and not a concrete actuality. It is the unity of the continuum, in the true sense, that symbolizes the unity of the Nirvanic State. The Nirvanic Consciousness is not granular but flowing. It is without parts, in the sense of finite proper parts, but is a ceaselessly flowing and self-contained stream. It is not a stream from past to the future, that implies division by the point called the "present," but a flowing that comprehends the totality that appears in the universe of objects as the temporal series.

That which appears in man as the persistent Self—the Witness of the universe-drama—is the dividing and uniting point of two worlds of consciousness. Before our consciousness lies the universe of objects, but behind is the hinterland of the Self, and this is Nirvana. But the hinterland of the Self is also the hinterland of all objects. In this hinterland, we do not have merely empty terms in relation, perceived by the Self; we have a continuum in which the inverse of the self is identical with the inverse of all objects. Here consciousness, substance, and energy, or life, are interchangeable terms. Here, also, the sterile and empty terms-in-relation are replaced by a pregnant Meaning. Without this Meaning, man simply cannot live. The more closely man identifies himself with objects, or mere empty terms-in-relation, the more starved he becomes, and in the end, if this condition is continued too far, real death must follow. By real death, I mean the loss of self-consciousness.

Actually, man has rarely succeeded in completely isolating himself from the inflow of consciousness from the hinterland. For the greater part, he has simply received this inflow and has not succeeded in being self-conscious with respect to it. Unknowingly, he has received some nourishment, otherwise life in the universe of objects would have failed e'er now. Yet, except for a few among the human whole, the stream of nourishment has been so poor that man suffers the travail of slow starvation. Great is the need that the stream be increased. Now, this increase is accomplished by opening the gates to the hinterland through at least some degree of Recognition. This means becoming self-conscious, in at least some measure, of the stream of Nirvanic Consciousness and realizing oneself as identical with it. We need more philosophy conceived as a Way of Life and less emphasis upon systems of bare terms-in-relation.

It has been stated that the key to Nirvanic Consciousness consists of an anesthetizing of the power of experiencing and of thinking, combined with a continuing of self-consciousness. This is the essential process that reveals the significance of the step. Practically, the process of transformation may or may not involve the complete anesthetizing. If the anesthesia is complete, then the consciousness of the universe of objects is wholly annulled, either temporarily or permanently. This is the mystic destruction of the universe and the Awakening to the Nirvanic State. Objectively viewed, the individual who does this appears to enter a complete state of ecstatic trance, in which there is a suspension of vital and conscious process in the Sangsaric sense. This is all that the physical scientist qua physical scientist can observe. And if the observer holds to the theory that the Sangsaric type of consciousness is the only possible consciousness, then he would say the trance involved the total extinction of consciousness in every sense. Some psychologists take this position, but since they are unable to trace what they cannot see, they are quite unqualified to pass judgment upon the state in question. For in this matter, the bare observer is entirely helpless. The realizer may report the continuity of his self-consciousness, but the observer, as such, has no check whatsoever. If, in turn, he should become a realizer in his own right, then he would Know, but that knowing would not be the result of his observing external states or conditions. He would no longer be a bare observer.

Now, it is possible, by a modified technique, to become a realizer and remain, in some degree, an observer at the same time. In this case, there is substituted for the literal anesthetizing a process of dissociation of the two kinds of consciousness. The thinking and experiencing powers are set on one side, as it were, while the larger portion of the self-conscious principle, but not all, is withdrawn into the hinterland. In this case, there is no black-out trance-state but a sort of slowing down of the Sangsaric consciousness and the objective life-stream. It is a critical kind of balance to maintain, as there is a constant tendency for the consciousness principle to "flop over" completely to the one side or the other. But if, through steadiness of the will, the balance is maintained and the self-analyzing power functions with clear discrimination, then it is possible to be conscious on two levels without confusion. In this case, dissociation accomplishes the essential effect of the anesthesia.

The latter technique has a decided advantage in that it effects a conscious bridging of two levels of consciousness. This facilitates the construction of interpretative symbols, and as well, opens a door whereby a stream of Nirvanic Consciousness may be made to penetrate the universe of objects and be more or less consciously directed.

From the standpoint of Consciousness-without-an-object, there is no problem concerning immortality. The directly known truth is: "Immortality is, but no embodied or object-bound stage of consciousness is immortal." This simply means that the Sea of Consciousness is without beginning or end, being completely unconditioned by time, but the various stages wherein that Sea supports objects are temporary. Thus man as man is not immortal. Here it must be understood that "man", as well as any other name of an object, is only a designation for a stage along the Way. Immortality attaches to consciousness as a principle, not to the stages. Man may achieve immortality by superimposing his evolved power of self-consciousness upon the Primordial Consciousness itself, but in this case he simply ceases to be a man. The self-conscious Nirvani is no longer a man, though in his case the differentiated consciousness-principle once passed through the human stage. Actually, the Nirvani is a Divine, rather than a human, being. The consciousness-principle is the Pilgrim that passes through many stages, absorbing from those stages many values in terms of progressively awakened self-consciousness. When man succeeds in assimilating the Pilgrim by transference of his self-consciousness, then his self-identity is one with immortal consciousness, but the self-identity ceases to be merely human. Put in other terms, all somatic stages are temporary; the consciousness stream is without beginning or end.

But while immortality ceases to be a problem, an entirely different problem arises. This may be stated in the form: How is it possible, within a beginning-less and endless Primordial Consciousness, for transitory states to arise? I am not here attempting any solution of this problem but simply indicating the shift of problem form. This new problem, unlike the old one concerning immortality, has no tragic implications. Reflective consciousness, aided by insight and observation, may undertake its resolution at leisure, with all the time in the world to complete the search. For with the problem thus stated, there is no deep religious or psychological need at stake. The resolution of the problem would have theoretical and working value, but there is no time-pressure to drive reflective consciousness to a quick solution.

There is but one consideration that I shall suggest here. It is unthinkable that the formless and attribute-less Primordial Consciousness, all of a sudden, at a certain point, started to project Itself into the subject-object series of states. Rather, no beginning or end to the series of states is thinkable, one state being always the consequent of a preceding state and the cause of the one that follows. Consciousness-without-an-object is not a First Cause; it is the substratum underlying all possible states and causes.

For one who has made himself familiar with the stream of western philosophy from the time of the Greeks to the present day, it should be evident that there are certain differences of base and valuation that have divided philosophers throughout the whole of that period. The development of scientific knowledge, of mathematics, and of epistemological criticism has not succeeded in bridging these differences so that a philosophic agreement could be effected. All these developments have only had the effect of changing the form in which the differences appear, so that they have become more subtle and intellectually sophisticated; but the essential differences still remain, however much transformed in their statement. There still are incompatible philosophic schools, represented by men of comparable degrees of intellectual ability, training, and knowledge. All of which reveals, clearly, that the factors that make for philosophic differences run deeper than the material with which science can deal and resolve factually and interpretatively once for all.

Some psychologists have taken cognizance of these philosophical tendencies and have shown that they are connected with differences of psychological type. The immediately taken base and the accepted values are not the same for all men. And this immediate element belongs more to religion, in the broad and fundamental sense, than it does to science. It is something that precedes, rather than follows, science. In fact, that attitude that makes the scientific point of view itself possible is of the nature of these more fundamental and extra-scientific adjustments. Justice demands that we accept these differences of adjustment as relatively valid and renounce the hope and desire for universal philosophic conformity. The conflict of philosophic schools is both desirable and necessary.

Two important types of differences in valuation and immediate insight will account for the principle differences of philosophic systems. One is a difference in the valuation of the two principal groups of objects, i.e., objects of sense and objects of thought. The other is a difference in the valuation of objectivity, as such, as contrasted to the subjective pole of consciousness. These differences I shall discuss briefly, so as to relate my own system to them more clearly.

Evidently the overwhelming majority of men in thought and practice most of the time predicate substantial reality of the objects of sensation, particularly in terms of the social waking consciousness of our ordinary life. Most, though not all, physical scientists take this position, as well as the majority of the men of action. Among the current philosophical tendencies, Naturalism definitely, and sometimes quite naively, takes this standpoint. This is also true in considerable degree, but not entirely, of the representatives of Pragmatism. The position of Neo-realism is more involved, in that, while it is highly objective, its objects are not conceived as objects of sensation or of thought, but as independent existences that, in their real nature, are neither psychical nor physical, though capable of passing through both psychical and physical systems without being altered in their essential nature. However, Neorealism is frankly and intensely objective in its valuation, and therefore stands in closer relationship to both Pragmatism and Naturalism than it does to Idealism.

There is a smaller class of men who find the objects of thought more real than the objects of sensation. These are represented in the philosophical systems of rational Scholasticism, Rationalism proper, and in those philosophical systems currently called intellectualistic. There may be more or less blending between these philosophic currents and Naturalism, Neorealism, and Idealism, though they are definitely nonpragmatic, since the latter school seems pretty thoroughly united on the principle of anti-intellectualism, in the philosophic sense.

The two foregoing groups largely agree in that they attach primary importance to objects, in some sense, and may be divided by regarding one group as sensationalistic and the other as rationalistic or intellectualistic.

In contrast to both these groups, there stand those who attach the greater reality to the subjective pole of consciousness. In the philosophies, these are represented by Idealism and Vedantism. However, this class seems to be more widely represented by individuals whose dominant expression is not consciously philosophical. More often their expression appears in the form of a mysticism that is more poetic than philosophical. Yet, within the mystical group, there is a further differentiation to be made between those who emphasize union with God and those who emphasize union with the Self in a transcendental sense. However, the whole mystical movement is in a subjective direction, so, when the emphasis is placed upon more or less Divine objects, these objects are subtle rather than gross.

In the present system, all objects are regarded as derivative, and therefore possessing, at best, only a derivative or symbolic reality. Yet some objects may have a higher order of relative reality than others. I have already pointed out that the valuation here is relative to purpose and not absolute. Thus, the ordinary gross objects of sense, common to waking consciousness, are given no superior status as such. Essentially, dream objects and mystical objects are given the same validity. Relative to a particular purpose, the one or the other class of objects may be judged as possessing the superior order of reality. Concerning the two classes of objects, i.e., objects of sensation whether subtle or gross, and objects of thought, the same principle applies. Objects of thought, or some classes of the objects of thought, may, in some purposive situations, possess an inferior reality as compared to that attaching to the objects of sensation. On the other hand, the reverse is equally true in other purposive situations. To sum up: All objects of whatever type, whether objects for sensation or for thought, whether subtle or gross, whether abstract or concrete, in the last analysis possess only a derivative reality, and thus may be regarded finally as a *seeming* only.

There remains to be considered the view this system presents concerning the subjective pole of consciousness. In this, I am referring to that which is variously known as the "ego," whether in the personal or higher sense, the "I," the "self," or the "Atman," whether in the individual or supreme sense. In this subjective pole, there are discernible differentia, just as there are between different classes of objects. Now, in the present system, the subjective pole, both in its inferior and superior aspects, is viewed as the reflex or inverse of the object, as such, though in the higher sense it is viewed as essentially the higher pole. This means that the "I," in whatever sense, whether empiric or transcendental, is as much derivative as the objective world. Thus the present system is not to be identified with either Vedantism or current Idealism, though it is arrived at by a process of passing through these schools of interpretation and thus stands genetically, although not necessarily formally, closer to them.

The final position is: The One, nonderivative Reality, is THAT which I have symbolized by "Consciousness-without-an-object." This is Root Consciousness, per se, to be distinguished from consciousness as content or as state, on the one hand, and from consciousness as an attribute of a Self or Atman, in any sense whatsoever. It is Consciousness of which nothing can be predicated in the privative sense save abstract Being. Upon It all else depends, while It remains self-existent.

The question of the means by which any individual may arrive at a direct Realization of Consciousness-without-an-object is one that is very involved and the solution has many variants, corresponding to the psychical status of the various individuals. All evidence confirms the view that it is reached by a progressive series of steps, such that a lower attachment or identification is renounced for one that is superior, the process being repeated again and again until, from the vantage ground of a high transcendental position, the final step can be taken. Beyond this general statement, the question of technique cannot be entered into here.

Apart from the actual Realization of Consciousness-without-an-object, it is possible to take the symbol itself as an object of thought and use it for the purpose of philosophical and general mystical integration. This is the procedure of assuming the symbol as a fundamental premise and then observing the consequences that follow. There is some reason to believe that such a method of procedure is possible within the setting of western culture, as might not be the case for oriental culture or for any culture that has preceded ours of which any record exists. This possibility

I see as growing out of our peculiar mathematical development. In mathematics, we excel all other cultures, and as I see it, all other genuine superiority we may have has resulted from this mathematical excellence. In other respects, as far as the greater and durable values are concerned, there are other cultures in the Orient, whether of the present or the past, that just as clearly excel ours. Now, it is by its power, and not its weakness, that an individual or a class attains the best. Thus, I would select the mathematical road as the one of pre-eminent power so far as western culture is concerned.

Now the validity of mathematics is established upon a basis that is quite impersonal and universal. Its authority is not dependent upon the name of any writer of any mathematical treatise. In its purity, it deals only with the transcendental or ideal objects of the very highest order of thinkable abstraction or universality. In high degree, the consciousness of the mathematician qua mathematician is not concerned with either a self or objects. To be sure, this is not absolutely so, but this position is attained in mathematical consciousness in higher degree than anywhere else, except in states of Samadhi of a high order. Herein is revealed the power of pure mathematics as an instrument of consciousness-transformation on a very lofty level.

Again, pure mathematics is the only real invariant that we have in the ever-changing phantasmagoria of experience. When an individual undertakes to chart an unknown sea, he must have fixed bases of reference by which to navigate his course, if he would not run the risk of being hopelessly lost. To be sure, there is a profound sense in which the pure Self is a similar invariant, but the peculiar psychology of the West is too objective in its orientation to permit this Self to be generally and effectively accessible. It is otherwise in India. This profound psychological difference renders it impractical to hope to graft oriental method upon the western man, save in some exceptional cases. That would be using the right method with the wrong man, and such a procedure leads to wrong results. Hence, the western psychology being what it is, the available invariant seems to be pure mathematics.

I am not speaking with a naive ignorance of current philosophic and logical analysis of pure mathematics. But I shall not enter into this extremely technical question at this time. I am well aware that the invariant element does not lie in the fundamental assumptions, or so-called axioms, from which a mathematical system starts. These assumptions may be chosen as a largely free creative act, but just as soon as the process of deduction of theorems begins, free creativeness ceases. The law that governs the flow of consequences is tougher than tempered steel and harder than the hardest rock. Save in the Self, here, as nowhere else, is there something to which human consciousness can tie and give its trust, though all else became fluid and confusing. And this invulnerable core carries straight through to Consciousness-without-an-object. Only at the very last does the logical invariant vanish in the eternally Ineffable, but then the Wanderer has arrived at the place of Final Security and Completeness, beyond the relativity of all science, art, religion, and philosophy.

And supposing the Wanderer has at last arrived, is there nothing more than a ceaseless consciousness without content? No, before him there stand all possibilities, both those of the universe of objects, in every sense, and also of Nirvana, likewise in every sense. But the arrived Wanderer is now Enlightened and is secure against all dangers and all possible entanglements in all kingdoms or states of consciousness from the heavens to the Hells. He may produce creatively or not, but in any case He is superior to either action or refraining from action. In a word, He moves upon the plane of a higher order of evolution. This is the meaning of Consciousness-without-an-object.

Notes to Chapter 5

1. It would be more correct to say that the older conception can no longer interpret the facts as *simply* as the newer conception. It is always possible to make the older conception work by adding intricate interpretations through *ad hoc* hypotheses, but this is done at the price of clumsiness and complication. It is not change in the factual picture that compels change in theory, but the greater logical beauty and efficacy of the new theory.

2. According to latest theory, the radiation density at the early, highly condensed stage of the expanding universe was much higher than the matter density. What matter there was present was, however, spread out uniformly. At a later stage of expansion the radiation density had dropped to equality with that of matter, and at this point "gravitational instability" set in and the galaxies began forming.

3. Actually, the more generally valid space-time "invariant" concept is that of the directed quantity "Energy-Momentum," of which "Energy" is merely that part lying along the direction of increasing time. For the sake of simplicity of illustration, we use only the more familiar term "Energy."

4. This analogue is not employed to suggest that the aphorisms gain their authority from the physical conception. Physical conceptions change and so constructions based upon them are vulnerable. The real point made is that the aphorisms, as concepts, are not nearly as strange as they may seem at first. The above is a conceptual pattern that already exists and is used, though in a somewhat different sector of human knowledge. Of necessity, any conceptual symbol must be composed in terms of the conceptualism of its milieu, however unthinkable its roots may be in conceptual terms.

5. In this connection, by fundamental theory I mean one that is a primary assumption of a given type of intellect—its starting point for creative constructions. These fundamental theories are based in faith and really form part of the essential religious belief of a given culture. In order to think, we must always start with something that we cannot prove either by logic or by reference to experience. This something defines the form of experience as it becomes the material of thought, but it is not a derivative from experience. Thus, for example, our science rests upon a faith in the uniformity of nature. Discredit this faith and the science falls as a whole. Indeed, this faith may be perfectly justified, but it precedes science—it does not follow from science. In psychological terms, the fundamental theory wells out of the unconscious.

6. This is perhaps the most concrete special case of the energy-momentum concept described in a previous note.

7. An implication of the foregoing discussion is that physical science does not give us noumenal, metaphysical, or substantive knowledge. Rather it gives an only positivistic kind of knowledge, but a positivism that is logical as well as aesthetic.

8. The following questions have been raised: "What is the interpretation of an 'individual center of consciousness'?" "Is it a void too?" First, with respect to the individual center of consciousness, it may be said that we mean here the empiric cognizing entities that we commonly view as individuals, without raising at this point the question as to the ultimate status of individuality. But the second question raises problems having profound ramifications which are given serious consideration in a future volume. The whole issue between the Atma Vidya of the Vedantins and the Anatmic doctrine of the Buddhists is raised in this question. Briefly, it may be stated that the position taken here occupies an intermediate position. Thus it would be said that in the relative sense the individual center of consciousness is not a void or unreal as compared with the object, but in the absolute sense it may be viewed as a void in the sense of being ultimately derivative. It occupies a position analogous to that of the concept of the parameter as used in mathematics.

9. The older psychology without a psyche is merely a crude physical science.

10. The assurance of the transcendental states is by no means a certainty that the conceptual interpretation is the most correct possible. Interpretation is a relative function subject to criticism.

6
Commentaries on the Aphorisms

PRELIMINARY

In their depths, feeling and thought spring from the same root. This root, in its own nature as unmanifested, has a character that appears to the relative consciousness as both devoid of feeling and without conceptual form. But when realized, it has the value of fulfilled feeling and completed thought. Consciousness no longer feels a reaching out for an unattained completeness. With this, both thought and feeling lose their differentiated and, therefore, identifiable particularity. But when the root is projected into the actualizing consciousness, it loses some measure of its purity, since to actualize is to particularize, even though on the most abstract level of expression. The aphorisms on Consciousness-without-an-object constitute such a projection on a level of exceptional abstraction and universality, whereby the unthinkable becomes, in some measure, the thinkable. But since, in this act, the universal comprehender appears in the field of the comprehended, we stand, in the latter case, not in the presence of Truth herself, but we come into possession of a symbol of the Truth.

To step from the symbol to that which is symbolized, though this does afford a peculiarly exacting demand upon acuity of thought, yet requires much more. Here, feeling, in the best sense, must fuse with the thought. Thus the thinker must learn also to feel his thought, so that, in the highest degree, he thinks devotedly. It is not enough to think clearly, if the thinker stands aloof, not giving himself with his thought. The thinker arrives by surrendering himself to Truth, claiming for himself no rights save those that Truth herself bestows upon him. In the final state of perfection, he possesses no longer opinions of his own nor any private preference. Then Truth possesses him, not he, Truth.

He who would become one with the Eternal must first learn to be humble. He must offer, upon the sacrificial altar, the pride of the knower. He must become one who lays no possessive claim to knowledge or wisdom. This is the state of the mystic ignorance—of the emptied heart. He who has thus become as nothing in his own right then is prepared to become possessed by Wisdom herself. The completeness of self-emptying is the precondition to the realization of unutterable Fullness. Thus mere "knowledge about" becomes transformed into Knowledge as Reality.

To know THAT which the aphorisms symbolize is to be possessed by THAT and, then, to be one with THAT. Thenceforth, all thinking, all feeling, all particularization, and all selfhood lie below. To be sure, all these remain, but no longer as claimants to a Throne they could not possibly fill. They remain thenceforth as the actors in the Divine Drama, but no more.

Before the candidate, the ordeal of the mystic death appears as a terror-inspiring apparition. But he who, with stout heart challenging the seeming of ultimate dissolution, enters into the awful and terrible presence, finds only utter Glory. Terror has become beatitude. Only liabilities have been lost as he finds himself, not lost in the Eternal, but become that Eternal Itself. All the dangers of the Way are only ghosts, possessing no power save such as the candidate has himself projected upon them. However, since there is much darkness and fear in the heart of man, there are apparitions of terrible visage. But they have no power of their own and must vanish, helpless before the will of the undaunted candidate.

He who receives the aphorisms as guideposts along the Way will find in them powers to dissipate all apparitions, whether of terror or seduction. The threatening appearance of darkness will be dissipated before him as he journeys along his Path. In the end, the Door to Glory will loom clear before his gaze, and he will know no conflict with terror in any part of the Way. Yet he who does not find himself able to go so far, may yet find in the symbols content for his thought that will illumine that thought. Thought in the light is much better than thought groping in darkness. To think from the base of Light, though it be that that Light is not yet understood, is far better than thought grounded in the darkness of no vision. For upon some base all thought must be grounded if it is to be more than that absolute nescience that leads in darkness from nowhere to nowhere. To have more than such hopeless darkness, he, who is not yet Knowledge, must base himself upon faith, whether it be faith in the Eternal, or some lesser light. Lacking Knowledge, man must have faith if he would not perish.

1. *Consciousness-without-an-object is.*

The fundamental principle underlying all the aphorisms is that Consciousness is the original and self-existent Reality. This Consciousness is both Substance and Life. It would be possible to view the Primordial Principle in terms of Life or of Substance, as well as in terms of Consciousness, but I approach the subject from the standpoint of Consciousness for the reason that this is the phase of Reality of which we are most immediately certain. Consciousness, Life, and Substance are not to be regarded as three distinct realities, but as merely three facets of the non-dual Reality, as the latter appears to the analytic consciousness.

The Primordial Consciousness is not to be regarded as the consciousness of some transcendent being who is aware of some content. Herein lies, perhaps, the main difficulty with respect to understanding the idea contained in the symbol of Consciousness-without-an-object. We are in the habit of regarding consciousness as something derivative—a quality possessed by something else or a kind of relationship. It is necessary to abandon this view if the aphorisms are to be understood. Let this Consciousness be considered as original, and then both the subject and object become derivative. That which is primary and original, then, is a Great Void of Consciousness, to all consciousness of the type that depends upon the subject-object relationship. It is as though that Consciousness were nothing, while actually It is the all in all.

This Absolute Consciousness is, from the relative standpoint, indistinguishable from unconsciousness. Most generally, philosophy is written from the perspective that views the ultimate as unconscious, whether of psychical (e.g., von Hartmann's view) or non-psychical (e.g., the view of materialists) nature, and thus has taken the relative consciousness as the ground of approach, but the aphorisms are written as from the ultimate Transcendental Base, and then, from that viewpoint the problems of relative consciousness are approached. We are following a deductive process of descent from the most universal to the concrete or particular, rather than the inductive method that is so characteristic of physical science and much philosophy, including that of von Hartmann.

An inevitable question is: How can this Primordial Consciousness be known? To this it is answered, "Through a Recognition transcending the Nirvanic State." Complete verification of the validity of the aphorisms requires this. However, a partial or pragmatic verification may be achieved through willing to accept them *as though* they were true symbols of the Reality, and then drawing the consequences that follow from them, finally noting how they affect the problems of life and thought as practically experienced. If the investigator finds that they tend to simplify the problems and to bring the self into more harmonious adjustment with the not-self, then they prove to be an orientation that enriches life, and are thus pragmatically justified.

Naturally, it is implied that Recognition is a human possibility. Otherwise, the aphorisms would have to rest upon one or the other of two bases: (*a*) intellectual speculation grounded exclusively in relative consciousness; or (*b*) external superhuman revelation beyond the possibility of human verification. Both these standpoints are denied here, especially the latter. The notion of external superhuman revelation, when subjected to analysis, does not possess any really intelligible meaning, and belief in this tends toward both intellectual and moral suicide. From this belief follows the attitude made famous in the words of Tertullian: "I believe because it is against reason." Such a viewpoint is utterly foreign to the spirit in which the aphorisms are written.

It is affirmed that the aphorisms mean a content given through immediate Knowledge, and that for the Realization of this content the functioning of a generally latent organ is the proximate means. Hence they are not to be viewed as metaphysical speculations of which the concepts would have no real content, as Kant pointed out in his *Critique of Pure Reason* in relation to metaphysical subject-matter. Thus it is maintained that the aphorisms are not mere developments of the pure reason, and accordingly, avoid the challenge of the Kantian criticism. Therefore, philosophic criticism of the present philosophy, in so far as it is strictly philosophical, must assume the actuality of the inner organ.

The critical problem takes the form: Does the inner organ or Samadhindriya—as it is known in Sanskrit—exist? This is a psychological, or rather, metapsychological question. I have explored with care the possibilities of logical proof that such an organ must exist, but have been forced to conclude that no such demonstration is possible. Yet logical disproof is equally impossible. The only possible proof depends upon immediate experience of the activity of the organ. On the other hand, empiric disproof is impossible, since empiric disproof of any supposed psychical function or organ presupposes demonstrably complete knowledge of every psychical possibility. I am not aware that any psychologist lays claim to such omniscience.

Now, if any individual should have immediate acquaintance with the functioning of a psychical organ, which with most men either lies wholly inactive or functions in such a way as to be unrecognizable to the relative consciousness of the individual, he would know as a matter of genuine private knowledge that the function or organ is an actuality. But if he sought to prove this actuality to those in whom the function was wholly latent, he would face serious difficulties. Anything that he succeeded in introducing into the consciousness of the latter would, of necessity, be in terms of the functions that were already active in them. In general, this means in terms of the so-called five-sense rational consciousness. Anything more that was strictly peculiar to the new organ would stand in incommensurable relationship, and therefore, be ineffable; it could not be communicated at all. But that which could be communicated would be, as said, in terms of the usual five-sense rational content. And this could always be explained away by the appropriate ingenuity, so that it would appear to the unawakened consciousness that the hypothesis of a new organ was unnecessary. The inventive ingenuity of the human intellect is, undoubtedly, quite capable of inventing the appropriate hypotheses. But if, for instance, the born-blind could invent hypotheses that would explain everything that the seeing ones could convey to their consciousness, in terms that could dispense with the hypothesis that anybody had sight, this might be quite convincing to other blind men, but it would leave those who had sight quite unimpressed. The result would be a stalemate.

That the conception of a latent mystical sense, active in some instances but inactive with most men, can be interpreted in such a way as to supply a *sufficient* explanation of how a transcendental knowledge can be, I have not yet found questioned by anyone. It is the question of *necessity* that is raised. Now, if we assume the actuality of the mystical sense in an active state in a given case, then, although the content that could be conveyed into the zone of the ordinary five-sense rational consciousness would not necessarily require the predication of the mystical sense for its interpretation, yet there would remain the incommensurable or ineffable portion of the original content or state, which still would require explanation. So far as I have found, the hypotheses of the five-sense rational consciousness imply that the ineffable content or value is pure illusion. To the mystic, this is proof of the *insufficiency* of all such hypotheses, since he claims a greater reality-quale for the content or value realized through the mystical sense than for that possessed by all the other senses. Now, how is the five-sense rational consciousness going to challenge this? By basic assumption, the mystic has the five-sense rational consciousness plus all the consciousness-value realized through the mystic sense, and therefore, is in a position to establish a comparative valuation; and this the exclusively five-sense rational consciousness cannot do. At this point, the less gentlemanly of the psychologists descend to the street urchin's device of labeling the other fellow with bad names, though usually highly technical language is employed. I submit that this is beneath the dignity of true scholars and gentlemen.

It is a principle of logic that a rigorous argument shall satisfy the categories of both necessity and sufficiency. But this perfection is attained only in pure mathematics. No inductive, hence no scientific, hypothesis satisfies both these conditions. There is no scientific hypothesis that is necessary in the logical sense, since other hypotheses could be invented. But a scientific hypothesis must pass the test of sufficiency, i.e., it must be such as to incorporate all relevant facts into a systematic whole. Now, if we are to leave out mutual name-calling as a valid line of argument as between the possessors of the mystic sense and those of the exclusive five-sense type, then it is the five-sense type of interpretative theory that fails to satisfy the canons of scientific hypotheses. For these hypotheses do not satisfy the condition of sufficiency.

As to the ineffable content or quality of mystical states of consciousness, it may be pointed out that there is nothing at all strange about this. "Ineffable" means unspeakable or incommunicable. But incommunicability is not at all strange, for such a limitation attaches even to sense-experience. The peculiar quale of one sense cannot be communicated in terms that are understandable with respect to another sense. And indeed, there is something fundamentally ineffable in the relationship between percepts and concepts. Concepts convey perceptual values from one individual to another only to the extent that the two individuals have a commonality of perceptual experience. Since the referents are in common, the concepts convey meaning, but otherwise they do not. Now, the mystic knows an ineffable content or quality in the case of communication to a non-mystic, but in general, the concept, the sign, or symbol will convey this content, more or less adequately, to a fellow mystic. It is just a case of the concepts, signs, or symbols having a different kind of reference and of two or more individuals having common acquaintance with the relevant referents.

In the highest sense of Transcendental Consciousness, we have to abandon the whole idea of organ of consciousness, since the notion of organ implies delimitation. But so long as there are stages in mystical consciousness, the idea of an inner organ is valid.

2. Before objects were, Consciousness-without-an-object is.

This aphorism emphasizes the priority of Consciousness to content. But this is not a priority in time in the sense that a causal antecedent precedes a consequent. Primordial Consciousness is no more a cause of objects, *in the temporal sense*, than is space a cause of the stellar systems. But without space there could be no stellar systems, and likewise, there could be no objects without the support of Consciousness. Hence Consciousness-without-an-object is, not in the sense of a present that is a mere point in the flow of the future into the past, but in the sense of an Eternal Now. This "isness" is a denial of time. Consciousness-without-an-object is not a cause that determines any particularization, but it is the Causeless-Cause whereby all particularization is possible.

Here "Objects" must be understood in that most general sense of any modification of consciousness whatsoever. It is not only objects as seen or thought, but, as well, any feeling-toned state of consciousness. For, a feeling-toned state, being recognizable as such, is, therefore, a content or object.

We cannot conceive of a first object, since before that object there must be its causal antecedent. The stream of objects is a stream reaching from nowhere in the past to nowhere in the future. There is no substance in this time-stream, and hence an eon of eons is precisely the same as the smallest division of time, just as a finite section in a line is as rich in points as the infinite totality of the line. The drama of time is played in the Sea of Consciousness, and yet it is as though nothing at all had happened.

3. Though objects seem to exist, Consciousness-without-an-object is.

This aphorism relates to that state wherein objects, in any sense, appear to consciousness *now*, whereas the preceding aphorism refers to that which seems to be before the present appearance. All existence that objects may have is for the "now" only, though we may distinguish phases of the "now," such as existence in memory, existence as given in the present presentation, and existence in the imagination as future. There is a recognizable qualitative difference between these three phases of the "now," but no phase can be actually isolated from the "now" of consciousness and still have existence, in any sense, predicated of it. For predication is a present act within consciousness itself.

In the first part of this aphorism, the crucial word is "seem." No object requires more than seeming in order to exist for consciousness. Existence conceived in any other sense, than as for consciousness, is entirely meaningless. For that existence is found to be dependent upon *being conceived*, which, of necessity, is a conscious act or state. In the strictest logical sense, therefore, all objects rest upon the same base, i.e., that of *seeming*. To be sure, purposive interest will lead to the abstraction of certain objects as being important, while others will remain in greater or less degree irrelevant. Relative to purpose, then, degrees of reality or unreality may be predicated of the manifold of all objects. But this predication is valid only in relation to the given purpose, and confusion arises when this is forgotten. Thus, for some purposes, the dream-object may be more real than the objects of our so-called waking consciousness. For the purposes of our scientific culture, a certain class of objects belonging to the waking state is significant. We have formed the habit of calling these real, and of thinking of them as being real in some nonrelative sense. In this we forget that the reality that they possess is relative only to our specific scientific purpose. Our psychologists tend to distinguish between this class of objects and all, or nearly all, other objects by calling the latter phantasy. This is a terminology that is prejudicial to the latter class and is not logically justified, unless the condition is explictly implied that they are phantastic and unreal with respect to a certain scientific interest. Considered as such, apart from any purposive motive, we cannot distinguish any relative difference in degree or reality as attaching to any class of objects when contrasted to other objects. All objects are equal in that their existence is a *seeming* to consciousness and no more. But whether there is one kind of purpose or another, or a complete absence of all purpose, consciousness, per se, is an indisputable reality. This Consciousness is a Reality that unites, on the one hand, the youngest child, the idiot, or the insane, with the wisest and most developed intelligence, on the other. The differences that mark the gulf between these extremes are differences in content only, and not of Consciousness taken apart from content.

There is no doubt but that a valid significance attaches to difference in valuation of the various contents of consciousness. But these valuations are always relative to purpose and level, and not significant out of relation to all purpose or perspective. Thus valuation, itself, is but one of the derivative contents of consciousness, subject to development and decay. Beneath valuation, as the substratum that makes it, as well as all else, possible, is pure Consciousness apart from content.

> 4. *When objects vanish,*
> *yet remaining through all unaffected,*
> *Consciousness-without-an-object is.*

Objects have vanished when they are no longer present to consciousness as currently present, or present in memory, or finally, present in imagination. The fact of vanishing is not affected by the arising of other objects. Thus, vanishing operates as a principle, whether it is complete or only partial.

Consciousness-without-an-object is the binding principle underlying the progression and evanescence of states or objects of consciousness. This binding principle neither develops nor disintegrates. It is thus the invariant element associated with all variation. At certain stages in the analysis of consciousness, it appears as though the invariant element were the pure Subject or the Self, but at this stage the analysis has not isolated the subtle distinction between pure Subjectivity and Consciousness, as such. It thus appears as though the pure Self were a sort of permanent atomic nucleus, which is persistent through all states. But, when analysis is carried further, this notion is seen to fail. Ultimately, it is found that the Self is derivative as well as the objective pole of consciousness. Thus, there remains as the sole nonderivative principle the Pure Consciousness Itself.[1]

Just as we must regard the presence of objects as a seeming, and no more, so is the vanishing only a seeming. The nonderivative Reality is unaffected in either case.

> 5. *Outside of Consciousness-without-an-object,*
> *nothing is.*

Within the widely current realistic and naturalistic thought, both naive and critical, there is a deeply embedded habit of viewing objects as existing quite independently of consciousness. From this perspective, objects are viewed as self-existent things. But this is a hypothetical construction, in the invidious sense, for the simple reason that it is incapable of verification, either through experience or as a necessity of thought.

For verification necessarily implies the presence of consciousness, and so the, so-called, independent thing is reduced to the status of an object in dependent relationship to consciousness, at the moment of verification. There is no necessity, such as a logical necessity, that requires the predication of the existence of things quite independent of consciousness, in every sense, in order to account for the arising of objects. For objects arise and vanish with respect to a *state* of consciousness, and merely cease to be traceable beyond the borders of that state, for that state alone. Their continued existence for another state beyond those borders is not only in principle possible, but is verifiable through the use of the appropriate means. Though logic and the principle of causal connection may require that the arising of objects shall not be completely *de novo*, it is not necessary to predicate existence of things, totally independent of consciousness, in order to satisfy this requirement.

Objects, for the state of waking consciousness, vanish upon going to sleep, and an entirely different state or system of objects is realized. But though the system of objects that may be realized in the dream state is quite different, the analysis of dreams has often shown a connection between some of these objects and the contents of the waking state. Some dreams reveal a continuity of objects from past waking states, while others are prophetic with respect to objects experienced in future waking states. Here we have an instance of a widely experienced movement of consciousness from state to state with objects traceable in quite different systems of objects. These two examples of specific states, admittedly, are insufficient to trace the whole genetic and disintegrative history of objects. But they do afford empiric demonstration of the possibility of consciousness to shift from state to state, and thus render conceivable, in principle, the broader application of this possibility. Thus, again, there is no logical or epistemological need to predicate the existence of things apart from consciousness.

The aphorism goes further than barely to affirm that the predication of the existence of things, outside consciousness in every sense, is unnecessary. It asserts, categorically that "Outside of Consciousness-without-an-object, nothing is." This may be viewed as simply implying a primary definition of "something." Thus "something" is that which is an object in consciousness in some sense. Actually, no meaning attaches to the notion of "something" in any other sense. Such a notion is useless, as well as unnecessary. To say "outside of consciousness in every sense, there exists thus and so" is just to produce a meaningless collection of words, like the classical combination, "the barren woman's son."

6. Within the bosom of Consciousness-without-an-object lies the power of awareness that projects objects.

Pure Primordial Consciousness must be conceived as enveloping the subjective power of awareness, in relation to which objects exist. The subjective power of awareness and the content of consciousness stand in a relation of interdependence. In the most abstract case, wherein there is a consciousness of absence of objects, this absence has the value of content, since it stands in polar relationship to the subjective power of awareness. Thus there is no subject for which there is no content, in every sense, or stated conversely, where there is no content, there is no subjective pole of awareness.

Consciousness-without-an-object is not simply the power of awareness, for It comprehends the content along with the power of awareness itself. The power of awareness we may conceive as the first modification of the unmodified. It has its roots in, and derives its being from, the unmodified. It is this power that may be regarded as the First Cause—a Power that is Ever-Concealed, but renders possible the revealed and reflected.

Ordinarily we think of the power of awareness as playing a purely passive or receptive role in the receiving of impressions. It is true that on the empiric level it does function, in some measure, in the receptive sense. But in the ordinary creative activity of men, even, we can see that this is not its exclusive function. Thus, a work of art is first creatively imagined, then projected into objective form, and finally, received back as an impression. In turn, the received impression may arouse further creative activity and lead to a repetition of the same process. However, in this series, the function of the received impression is that of a catalytic agent, which simply arouses the creatively projective power. It is the impression from the object that is passive and not the power of awareness. Clarity with respect to this point is of the very highest importance, as it is right here that the invidious participation in objects begins. When an individual views the power of awareness as standing in passive relationship to impressions from objects, he places himself in a position of subordination to objects, and this constitutes the essence of bondage. The universe of objects then becomes a great prison-house, instead of the playground of free creative activity. As a prison-house, the universe of objects takes on the seeming of evil—the great adversary of man—but as the playground of free creative activity, it is an invaluable agent for the progressive arousal of self-consciousness.

The projective power of awareness is *a priori*, i.e., it precedes experience. It is true that experience, in turn, reacts upon this power, but it acts as a stimulating, rather than as an essential, agent. The whole externally causal series consists only of such stimulating agents. While the stimulating agent may be viewed as a sort of trigger cause of subsequent creative projection, it is not the material cause. The purely creative phase of the projective power is a first cause from which effects follow, but that is not itself an effect of previous causes. At this point, energy flows into the universe of objects. It is a misconception that an equation may be set up between any two states of the universe of objects, as between any two such states there may be an actual increase or decrease of content. The creative projection effects an increase of content.

> 7. *When objects are projected,*
> *the power of awareness as subject is presupposed,*
> *yet Consciousness-without-an-object*
> *remains unchanged.*

The projected objects become the experienced objects, and the latter appear to be a restricting environment. The restriction is a constant irritation, and thus is the basis of the ubiquitous suffering that runs through the worlds of objective experience. The ultimate effect of this irritation is to arouse the latent power of consciousness to be conscious of itself, an effect that could not be developed where there is no seeming of restriction placed upon the free play of consciousness. Out of consciousness of the consciousness of objects, there is finally aroused the inverse realization of the subjective principle. We thus find the substratum on which all objects rest. By superimposing an objective character upon this substratum, we evolve the notion of an ego having an atomic existence analogous to that of objects, save that we give to it a fixed character in contradistinction to the ever-changing character of all genuine objects. The ego is thus produced as a compound of the atomic nature of objects and the relatively deathless persistence of pure subjectivity. But this atomic ego is a false construction, and not the genuine subjectivity. It is, in fact, but another object in the universe of objects; however, it is the peculiarly invidious object whereby consciousness is especially bound.

The true Recognition of the pure Subject is something quite different, in that the Self must be so recognized as never to become a new subtle object. It is that which underlies all notions, but is never itself a notion.

The aphorism reasserts the immutability of Consciousness-without-an-object. The point is that no degree of development of consciousness in terms of content, or in terms of the recognition of the subjective principle, has any effect upon the pure principle of Consciousness per se.

> 8. *When consciousness of objects is born, then, likewise, consciousness of absence of objects arises.*

To be able to cognize any thing or object implies the isolation of it from that which it is not. While the degree to which this is accomplished does vary, yet the isolation must have proceeded to some discernible degree before an object can exist, either for thought or perception. Where an object is completely defined, the isolation is perfected. In that case, the universe of discourse is divided into two classes, i.e., the class of those instances that fall within the limits of the definition and the class of those that fall outside. But always, in order to form any definition, there must be a cognizance of the excluded class as well as of the included class. This is a process that proceeds continuously on the part of all individuals whose consciousness is concerned with objects in any sense, even in the case of those with whom the process lies very largely in the background, where it is more or less "unconscious" or "subconscious."

To have reached the point in the evolution of consciousness such that the cognition of the class of all possible objects, in any sense whatsoever, is born, is also to have attained at least a shadowy awareness of *absence* of objects, in every sense, as a state or condition that stands in contrast. This awareness of the absence of objects, in its purity, is not a cognition of an object, but another form of consciousness that is not concerned with objects. However, a reflection of this state of consciousness may be produced so that a special cognition arises, of such a nature that its content is definable as the inverse of all objects. This produces a sort of ideal world that is neither the universe of objects, proper, nor Nirvana, but one that partakes, in some measure, of the nature of both. This sort of ideal creation is very well illustrated in mathematics in connection with the development of the notions of negative, imaginary, infinitesimal, and transfinite numbers. All these may be regarded as of the nature of inverse cognitions. But they are not, therefore, cognitions devoid of meaning; however, their meaning is of a more transcendental and ineffable nature than that which is connected with the original positive real numbers, particularly the integers, which have been significantly called the natural numbers. These inverse numerical cognitions have been not only valuable but, in some respects, even necessary for the development of certain phases of western culture. They are unquestionably significant.

Now, when the awareness of the absence of objects has become embodied in a sort of inverse concept, the latter has a different kind of meaning as compared with that of the direct cognitions from which they rose genetically. This meaning stands in purely symbolic relationship to the inverse cognitions and lies outside the definitions, in a sense and degree, which is not true of the meaning of the direct cognitions, where the meaning in some degree or some sense lies within the definition. There is a sense in which we may say that we comprehend the direct cognitions with their meanings in a non-mystical manner, but in the case of the inverse cognitions, the meaning is realized only through mystical insight. If, however, the inverse cognitions are interpreted as comprehensions in the non-mystical sense, then we have merely created a subtle sub-universe of objects, with the consequence that the consciousness-principle has not destroyed its bondage to objects, as such, but merely sublimated the field of objects. None the less, such sublimation may very well mean progress toward true Liberation. It may serve very much like a scaffolding, from the upper platform of which the step to true Liberation may be much facilitated.

The kind of consciousness symbolized by the system of inverse objects is of a totally different quality from anything entering into ordinary relative consciousness. It is an ineffable State of the type realized in the higher mystical states of consciousness or in Samadhi.

9. *Consciousness of objects is the Universe.*

In one sense, this aphorism may be viewed as a definition of what is meant by the term "Universe." It is that domain of consciousness wherein a self is aware of objects, the latter standing as opposed to, or in contradistinction to, the self that is aware of them. In this sense, the Universe is much more than that which is connoted by the term "physical universe," since it includes as its field, in addition to waking physical consciousness, the fields of all dream objects, of all objects of the type that psychologists call "hallucinations" or hypnogogic visions, and of any other objects that may be experienced during objective life or after death that there may be. In this sense, the psychical states in which the phantasies, so called, are experienced are classed as part of the Universe.

Since the whole field of western science is restricted to the study of the objects of consciousness, it can never extend into that realm of consciousness that is other than the universe. This science takes as its most primary base of operation the subject-object relationship in the structure of consciousness. This fact, at once, defines the limits of its field of possible action. Such delimitation does not exclude the possibility that science, in the western sense, may develop without limit in the particular dimension defined by the subject-object relationship, but this science, as such, is forever excluded from the dimensions of consciousness not conditioned by the subject-object relationship. Nor is science capable of critical evaluation of its own base, as this base is the original "given" with which it starts and is implied in its own criticism. Competent criticism of this base is possible only from that perspective that is freed from exclusive dependence upon the subject-object relationship.

10. Consciousness of absence of objects is Nirvana.

Here it is necessary to employ a Sanskrit term to suggest a meaning for which no western term seems to exist. By "Nirvana" is meant a somewhat which has been peculiarly baffling to western scholars, as is revealed in the preponderant portion of the discussion of this notion. The reason for this is not hard to find. It lies in the typically intense and exclusive polarization of the western mind toward the *object* of consciousness. Even western mystics have rarely attained a degree of subjective penetration sufficient to reach the genuine Nirvanic State. Western subjectivity scarcely means more than a domain of subtle objects, even with most of the mystics, and this is a domain still within the range of meaning of "Universe," as defined in the last aphorism.

Etymologically, "Nirvana" means "blown-out," and this, in turn, carries the popular connotation of annihilation. It is true that it does mean annihilation in a sense, but it is the annihilation of a *phase* or *way* of consciousness, not of the principle of consciousness, as such. A careful study of the Buddhist canon reveals quite clearly that Gautama Buddha never meant by "Nirvana" the destruction of the principle of consciousness, but only of consciousness operating in a certain way.

As employed in the present aphorism, "Nirvana" means that state of consciousness wherein the self does not stand in the relation to objects such that the self is to be contrasted to, and aware of, objects. Only one part of the meaning of "Nirvana" is suggested in this aphorism, i.e., that "Nirvana" designates the consciousness wherein there is absence of objects. Yet the subject to consciousness is not here considered to be annulled in the deeper sense. Something of this quality of consciousness, but generally not in its purity, is to be found even in western mysticism. It is revealed in the expressions of the mystics, wherein they report realization of identity between themselves and content of consciousness. This content is so often mixed with an objective meaning that the mystical states in question must be judged as not pure, but rather, a blend of a degree of the Nirvanic State with the typical consciousness of the universe of objects. Yet always, with the mystic, there is an ineffable substratum that he never succeeds in more than suggesting in his expression. Often his effort to do justice to this substratum leads to a formulation that simply does not make sense, when judged by the canons of subject-object language. The result is that only a mystic really understands another mystic.

The ineffability of the genuinely mystical consciousness is not due to an imperfect knowledge of language on the part of the mystic. While many mystics have had a very defective knowledge of language, and are consequently especially obscure, yet others have not been so limited in their equipment. However, in either case, the ineffable and obscure element remains. The fact is, this ineffability can never be conveyed through language, any more than an irrational number can be completely equated to a rational number. All our language, as such, is based upon the subject-object relationship. Thus, consciousness that transcends that relationship cannot be truly represented through language built upon that base. Therefore, the expressions of the mystics must be regarded as symbols, rather than as concepts that mean what they are defined to mean and no more.

The pure Nirvanic State of Consciousness is a Void, a Darkness, and a Silence, from the standpoint of relative or subject-object consciousness. But taken on its own level, it is an extremely rich state of consciousness that is anything but empty. It cannot be conceived, but must be realized directly to be known.

11. Within Consciousness-without-an-object
lie both the Universe and Nirvana,
yet to Consciousness-without-an-object,
these two are the same.

Superficially considered, nothing may seem more incomprehensible than a state of consciousness from which two dissimilar states, such as the Universe and Nirvana, have the same value. But actually, the difficulty is not so great when once analysis has led to the realization that consciousness, as such, is unaffected by superimposed states or forms. Neither the Nirvani nor the man in the Universe is outside of Consciousness, as an abstract and universal principle. If a conception from mathematics may be borrowed, it may be said that the Universe and Nirvana have the same modulus but are different in sense. The notions of "modulus" and "sense," as employed in mathematics, have the following meaning: In the series of positive and negative numbers we have an unlimited number of pairs of numbers having the same absolute magnitude, but of opposite signs.[2] In this case, it is said that the members of such pairs have the same modulus, but are opposite in sense. Applying this analogy, the modulus that is common to both the Nirvanic State and to consciousness in the Universe is the common quality of being *Consciousness*. The difference in "sense" refers to the opposed qualities of being objectively polarized, in the case of consciousness in the Universe, and subjectively polarized, in the Nirvanic State. Now, when the "modulus" of a number alone is important, then the positive and negative "sense" of the number is irrelevant, and therefore, may be regarded as having the same significance. By applying this analogy, the meaning of the aphorism should become clearer.

There is a profound Level of Realization wherein the two states of the Universe of Objects and Nirvana, instead of seeming like forever separated domains, become interblended coexistences. In other words, at that Level of Recognition, consciousness of objects and consciousness of absence of objects are known to be mutually complementary states, the one dependent upon the other, just as the notion of negative numbers is dependent upon the notion of positive numbers, and vice versa. And just as the student of mathematics very soon reaches the point where the notion of number, as such, comprehends the positive and negative "sense" of number, so that he no longer thinks of two distinct domains of number, so, also, is it at that higher Level of Recognition. Nirvana and the Universe of objects are simply phases of a more ultimate Reality.

Consciousness-without-an-object is not simply consciousness of absence of objects. It is THAT which is neutral with respect to the presence or absence of objects. As such, IT stands in a position of Indifference to this presence or absence. In contrast, the consciousness of absence has a positive affective quale, just as truly as is the case with the consciousness of presence of objects, and this is not a state of indifference. The actuality of positive affective quale both during presence and absence may be noted by studying the effect produced after the performance of a fine musical composition. If a period of silence is allowed to follow the performance, and the listener notes the effects upon his consciousness, he will find that there is a development of musical value in that silence. Actually, this value has a greater richness for feeling than the music had as audible sound. Further, that silence is not like any other silence, but on the contrary has an affective quale that is specifically related to the particular composition that has been rendered. We may call this the nirvanic aspect of the given musical selection. Now Nirvana, as a whole, stands in analogous relationship to the totality of the Universe of Objects. The Universe of objects is an affective privation, which becomes a corresponding affective richness in the Nirvanic Aspect. Also, the form-bound knowledge of the Universe of Objects becomes the free-flowing Gnosis, having inconceivably rich noetic content. But Consciousness-without-an-object stands in neutral relationship to both these aspects.

In the strict sense, from the standpoint of Consciousness-without-an-object, objects are neither present nor absent. Presence or absence has meaning only from a lower level. The older notion of space, as being that which is affected neither by the presence nor absence of bodies, suggests the idea.

12. *Within Consciousness-without-an-object lies the seed of Time.*

Although consciousness-as-experience is time bound, Consciousness, as such, is superior to time. That this is so is revealed in the fact that intellectual consciousness has been able to isolate and cognize time, and then, in turn, analyze it into its component parts as past, present, and future. This is further evidenced in analytic mechanics wherein time appears as a contained conception. It is impossible to analyze that which is superior to the level on which, in a given case at a given time, the consciousness-principle is operating. The roots of any mode or form of consciousness are dark with respect to that particular mode or form. If, at any time, consciousness becomes aware of those roots and succeeds in analyzing them, it is of necessity implied that the principle of consciousness has risen to a perspective superior to the mode of consciousness in question. Thus, while consciousness-as-experience is time bound, yet, as thought, it has risen to a level where it can apprehend the time-binding roots. In this instance, we do not have to call upon the deeper mystic states of consciousness to reach to the necessary superiority of level. It is to be found in philosophy and theoretical mechanics. This is enough to show that Consciousness, as such, is not time bound, but only consciousness-as-experience.

Time is thus to be regarded as a form under which certain modes of consciousness operate, but not as an external existence, outside of consciousness in every sense. This idea is sufficiently familiar since the time of Kant not to require extensive elaboration. In the terms of Kant, time is a transcendental form imposed upon phenomena. But, it follows, consciousness, in so far as it is not concerned with phenomena, is not so bound.

The "seed of Time" may be thought of as the possibility of time. Time is an eternal possibility within Consciousness-without-an-object. Time is not to be thought of as something suddenly brought to birth, for the notion of "suddenly" presupposes time. On the time-bound level, time is without conceivable beginning or end. It is in the deeps of consciousness that time is transcended. It is quite possible so to penetrate these deeps that it is found that no difference of significance attaches to the notions of an "instant of time" or "incalculable ages of time." Yet, all the while on its own level, time continues to be a binding form. We have here one of the greatest of mysteries.

Through time it is possible to reconcile judgments that would otherwise be contradictory. This principle is so familiar as not to require elucidation. But he who reaches in Recognition to Consciousness-without-an-object finds that the logical law of contradiction no longer applies.[3] Judgments that otherwise would stand in contradictory relationships are brought into reconciliation without the mediation of time. This is an even greater mystery than the mystery of time.

*13. When awareness cognizes Time,
then knowledge of Timelessness is born.*

This aphorism exemplifies another application of the principle that governs the action of consciousness that was discussed in the commentary on aphorism number 8. We are able to recognize time as a distinct form only when we are able to isolate it from what it is not. This is done not only in philosophy, but, as well, in many of the theoretical constructions of science. In these cases, however, we have an isolation for thought. The immensely important philosophical question then arises as to how far, or in what way, a necessity or possibility for thought or for reason is likewise an actuality. This question is so fundamental that it seems advisable to discuss it at some length.

The issue involved here is essentially identical with that present in the ontological argument for the existence of a Supreme Being. This argument is based upon the assumption that the existence of an idea implies the existence of a reality corresponding to it. Hence the idea of a Supreme Being implies that such a Being is. The analysis to which Kant submitted this argument is a classic in philosophical criticism, and it is generally felt that Kant has, once for all, undermined the force of this argument. Yet, despite all this, it continues to have psychological force and has reappeared more than once since Kant's time.

The aphorisms and the philosophy surrounding them do not make use of the notion of a Supreme Being, though they leave open the possibility of evolved Beings that may very well be regarded as God-like when contrasted to man.[4] But this philosophy establishes its base upon the reality of a Transcendental Principle. Hence, the essential problem involved in the analysis of the ontological argument arises here. So, to bring this question out into clear form the following quotation is taken from Kant:

> Our conception of an object may thus contain whatever and how much it will; nevertheless we must ourselves stand away from the conception, in order to bestow existence upon it. This happens with sense-objects through the connection with anyone of our perceptions in accordance with empirical laws; but for objects of pure thought, there is no sort of means for perceiving their existence because it is wholly *a priori* that they can be known; our consciousness of all existence, however, belongs altogether to a unity of experience, and an existence outside this field cannot absolutely be explained away as impossible. But it is a supposition we have no means of justifying.

Let us, for the present purpose, assume the general validity of this argument. Then, in simple terms, the conclusion reached is that for an object of the reason or thought to have, or correspond to, an existence, in any other sense, that existence must be determined through some other mode of consciousness. In the case of experience, the senses perform this necessary function, in that sense-impression is necessary to determine experiential existence. At the close of the quotation, Kant admits that the possibility of a non-experiential existence cannot be denied, but goes on to say that we have no means of justifying this supposition. Now, so far as the field of consciousness that is the proper field of physical science is concerned, Kant's conclusion seems to be valid enough. But the domain of consciousness comprehended by science is only a part of the sum total of all possible consciousness. Once this is granted, then, in principle, it must be admitted that the supposition of a non-experiential or transcendent existence or reality can possibly be justified. Epistemological logic does not rule out this possibility; it simply establishes the point that by means of pure conceptions and logic alone, transcendental existences or realities cannot be proved.

In the present philosophy, all effort to establish such a proof is abandoned. Logic and analysis of consciousness are employed simply to build a reasonable presumption, without laying any claim to coercive demonstration. It is, however, asserted that direct extra-logical and extra-empirical verification is possible. All this implies that there is a way of consciousness that is not, on the one hand, to be regarded as presentation through the senses, or in the form of conceptions, on the other. Nor, further, is it to be regarded as no more than affective and conative attitude. It is, rather, a way of consciousness that sleeps in most men, but has become awakened and active in the case of a small minority, which is to be found represented by individuals scattered thinly throughout the whole span of history. This way of consciousness has been known by different designations, but in the West it is most commonly called "mystical insight."

In introducing this notion of another way of consciousness, called "mystical insight," certain obvious difficulties arise, owing to its not being a commonly active mode of consciousness. The individual in whom this insight is sleeping is necessarily quite incapable of evaluating it directly. To be sure, he may study the phenomena connected with the mystical function, as exemplified in historic personalities, as has been done by some psychologists. But this is a very different matter from the direct epistemological evaluation of the noetic content of the mystical insight.[5] A work like that of Kant's *Critique of Pure Reason* can be accomplished only by a man who finds in the operation of his own consciousness the very contents that he is analyzing. The study of the forms and processes of consciousness is, of necessity, only in subordinate degree a matter for observation. In the present case, it depends preeminently upon the introceptive penetration. As a result, the psychologist, who is not himself also a mystic, is not competent in this field, for he of necessity judges from the base of a consciousness operating through the senses and the forms of the intellectual understanding alone, so far as cognitive content is concerned. Recognizing this difficulty, I have abandoned in the present work the effort to force agreement by means of logic and reference to a widely common ground of experience.

However, the *possibility* of a noetic insight must be indicated. The chapter on "A Mystical Unfoldment" was introduced earlier in this work to meet that need. Admittedly the reader is in a difficult position when it comes to the question of evaluation of the honesty and competency of the writer in the forming of his interpretations in this chapter. But there simply is no way of presenting the material and processes of mystical insight in terms that are generally objective. The record of historic instances of mystical insight that have led to the formulation of a noetic meaning adds to the presumption of the validity of the insight, but does not help the reader directly unless, he too, has known at least some modicum of the mystical sense. Consequently, all that can be asked of the general reader is that he entertain the idea of the possibility of mystical insight, and then judge the philosophic consequences from that base.

It is predicated here that one important consequence, which does follow, is that an existence or reality outside the field of experience through the senses can be justified directly without falling into the error of the ontological argument. It would follow that Kant's *Critique of Pure Reason* is, in principle, valid only with respect to the relationship between the understanding and the material given empirically through the senses. But mystical insight gives another order of material or viewpoint that, also, in combination with the understanding, has noetic value. Undoubtedly there are problems concerning possibly valid and false interpretations here, analogous to those that arise in the relationship between understanding and experience through the senses, that Kant treated so trenchantly. But only the mystic who is also a critical philosopher could possibly be qualified to handle these. In this domain Kant hardly seems to qualify, for his is the scientific, rather than mystical, mind.

Once it is granted that there are two domains from which the material filling of conceptual consciousness may be derived, instead of the one through the senses alone, then the field of cognition has a threefold, instead of a twofold, division. There would then be the domain of pure understanding or conceptual thought in a sort of neutral position, with material through the senses standing on one side, and material or viewpoint from mystical insight on the other. This, in turn, would lead to something like a division in understanding, which may be called the higher and lower phases of intellection. Another consequence is that some men may have the lower phase of intellection, that operates in connection with the material given through the senses, developed in high degree, and yet remain quite blind to the higher phase. More than extensive scholarship or superior scientific ability is required to awaken recognition of the higher phase. On the other hand, there is a considerable dearth of superior intellectual training among those who are, in some measure, awakened to the higher phase of intellection, though history affords us some brilliant exceptions. Thus, there are not many who realize that here, too, is a problem for critical philosophy.

In any case, the aphorisms must be taken as material derived from mystical insight. As a consequence, their verification in the full sense is possible only from the perspective of a similar insight. Logic and experience can provide only a partial presumption for them, at best, and that is all that is attempted in these commentaries.

14. To be aware of Time is to be aware of the Universe, and to be aware of the Universe is to be aware of Time.

This aphorism emphasizes the interdependence of consciousness under the form of time and of consciousness of objects. Formerly, in the days when our scientific thought was governed by the Newtonian mechanics, we were in the habit of regarding time, space, and matter as three independent existences. Explicitly, Newton held the view that these three were not interdependent. However, as knowledge of the subtler phases of physical nature has grown, it has become evident that this view is no longer tenable. The new relativity, which has been largely developed through the insight and coordinating thought of Albert Einstein, definitely asserts the interdependence of these three notions of time, space, and matter. Now, while this integrating conception was developed to unify actually existent knowledge of physical fact, it is, at the same time, the formulation of a profound metaphysical principle. The notion of time is meaningless apart from the notion of change. Further, there is no change save in connection with objects. Thus, at once, it should become clear that awareness of objects implies change, and consequently, time, while on the other hand time becomes existent only in connection with objects.

It should be clearly understood that the ground on which this aphorism is based is not the above theory of mathematical physics, but is genuinely transcendental. However, the physical theory is a beautiful illustration of the essential idea.

15. To realize Timelessness is to attain Nirvana.

In this work the terms "realize" and "realization" are used in a special sense, which is to be clearly distinguished from "perception" and "conception." Whereas the latter two terms refer to a relationship between a self and objects, whether in the form of sense objects or ideas, the terms "realize" and "realization" are employed to designate a mode of consciousness wherein there is identity between the self and content, in other words, a state of consciousness not concerned with objects in objective relation. Thus "realization" means a mystical state. The Nirvanic State is not something conceived or perceived, though it is possible to conceive or perceive a symbol that means the Nirvanic State. If the latter possibility did not exist, it would be impossible to say anything at all in reference to Nirvana.

The realization of Timelessness should not be confused with the concept of timelessness that frequently occurs in philosophy, nor with the notion of simultaneity that is employed in classical theoretical mechanics. In the case of the mere concept of timelessness, the thinking and experiencing self is actually, in terms of awareness, moving within the time-world of objects. Thus his creating of the concept is a time-process. In this case, the self is not fused into identity with that which it has conceived. But when genuine realization has been attained, the self is found identical with Timelessness. The difference here is of crucial importance, though one that is difficult to convey adequately with ideas. Not only is it not merely "knowledge about," but it is an even more intimate state than "knowledge through acquaintance," such as that which comes through immediate experience. It is, rather, a state of "knowledge through Identity." This consciousness has a peculiar quality that is quite ineffable, but it may be suggested in the following way: If we may regard all concepts and percepts as being a sort of "thin" consciousness of surfaces only, then the state of realization would be like a "thick"—substantial—consciousness extending into the "depth" dimension. All presentation and representation deal with surfaces only, and all expression in its direct meaning is solely of this nature, whatever its symbolic reference may be. But the realization gives "depth-value" immediately. It may, therefore, be called substantial in a sense that may never be predicated of mere presentations or representations. This "depth-value" actually feeds that which some modern psychologists have called the "psyche." On the other hand, mere experience and intellection do not supply this nutritive value. They may arouse self-consciousness and afford something that has the value of control, but they do not themselves give sustenance.

To attain the Nirvanic State is to reach the source of sustenance for the psyche. This is the genuine goal of the religious effort, however inadequately that goal may be envisaged in the majority of religious conceptions and programs. Religion is concerned with the sustenance of the psyche; it is a search for a durable "Manna."

To realize Timelessness is to transcend the tragic drama of Time. Time is tragic because it destroys the beloved object, and because it is constantly annulling the unused possibilities. In the Timeless State there is none of this tragedy; hence it is a State of Bliss without alloy. But Bliss without alloy is simply another name for Nirvana.

16. But for Consciousness-without-an-object,
there is no difference between
Time and Timelessness.

This is another instance wherein the meaning is more easily seen by consideration of the fact that Consciousness as a principle is unaffected by the nature of content or state. But this is not the whole meaning of the aphorism, for Consciousness-without-an-object is not merely an analytic abstraction from the totality of common consciousness. It is also a symbol of That which may be directly realized. On the level of That, there is no differentiation of Significance. In other words, it is neutral with respect to Meaning as well as to affective value. It is a level above all relative valuation, both in the affective and noetic sense. Stated in another way, all differentiation has the same significance, and this significance is simply irrelevancy.

Consciousness-without-an-object represents all possibilities, but is specifically identified with no particular possibility. If IT were especially close to any one tendency, then IT would cease to be perfectly neutral. Thus all judgment or valuation lies on some lesser level, wherein the principle of relativity operates. But this lesser level depends upon the superior for its possibility and existence.

17. Within Consciousness-without-an-object
lies the seed of the world-containing Space.

"Space" is a generic concept, as there are many kinds of space. Thus the perspective-space of the eye has characteristics quite different from those of the space with which the engineer works. The latter is generally the familiar Euclidian space. But, whereas we formerly thought that the Euclidian space was the sole real space, today we know there are many kinds of space. Most of these exist only for mathematics, but within our own day we have seen one of these purely mathematical spaces become adapted to the uses of mathematical physics. So, now the notion of a multiplicity of types of spaces is definitely extended beyond the domain of pure mathematics.

In the present aphorism, the reference is to the space in which all objects seem to exist. In the broadest sense, this is not a single space, but several sorts of spaces, all having in common the property of containing objects. Two of these spaces that are generally familiar are: (*a*) the ordinary space of waking consciousness, in which all physical bodies from the stars to the electrons rest; and (*b*) the spaces of the dreamworld, wherein distance takes on quite a different meaning. It is characteristic of these spaces, at least as far as we are commonly familiar with them, that distance and quantity are significant notions. Such notions, however, are not essential to space as such, as is revealed in the mathematical interpretation of space as "degrees of freedom."[6]

Space is to be regarded as the framework or field of each particular level of differentiated consciousness. The world-containing space is that framework in which objects appear. The normal framework of the space of waking consciousness vanishes for the dream-state, and a space having discernibly different properties replaces it The latter is a space filled with objects quite distinguishable from the objects filling the space of waking consciousness, even though they may be related. Different laws of relationship and operation apply.

The superiority of consciousness to a specific space is revealed in the fact that the external space of waking consciousness can be annulled by the simple act of going to sleep. The dream space is annulled by the reverse process of waking to the external space. This fact, which is part of the common experience of all men, is of profound significance, for it reveals the overlordship of the principle of consciousness with respect to these two kinds of space. It is a constant reminder that, in reality, man as a conscious being is not bound to the space that defines the form of his experiencing or thinking while in a particular state. The delusion of bondage is truly a sort of auto-hypnosis, produced through man's predicating of himself as a subjective consciousness-principle those spatial dependencies that apply only to objects, including his own body. In reality, the consciousness-principle supports and contains the universe, instead of the reverse being true, as commonly supposed.

The world-containing space is derived from, and is dependent upon, Consciousness-without-an-object. The latter comprehends the former, both as potentiality and as actuality.

> 18. *When awareness cognizes the
> world-containing Space, then knowledge of
> the Spatial Void is born.*

As the underlying principle of the complementary or inverse awareness has already been discussed in the commentaries on aphorisms 8 and 13, it will not be further considered here. Our attention will be devoted to the meaning of the Spatial Void.

The Spatial Void stands in polar relationship to the world-containing Space. The latter is preeminently a space with content involving the notions of quantity and distance. The Spatial Void is without content and involves no notion of quantity and distance. The more qualitative spaces of mathematics suggest the idea. It is predominantly Space as Freedom, and not space as restraining and constricting form. Any differentiation that would apply here would be analogous to that which attaches to the notion of transfinite numbers, and not like the sharply bound differentia of finite manifolds.

The direct realization of Consciousness as the Spatial Void has an inconceivably lofty value. It is a state in which the lonely self has found its own other in the fullest possible sense. Symbolically expressed, it is as though the lonely self, regarded as a bare point, had suddenly been metamorphosed into an unlimited space, wherein content-value and the subject—the "I"—were completely fused and co-extensive. More commonly, this is expressed as union with God. The latter statement is sound enough so long as it is understood as a symbol and does not assume an arbitrary preinterpretation. The Reality realized is Presence, in the sense of envelopment in the Eternal Other. This is the final resolution of all the problems of the tragic life in the world. It is the Terminal Value, with respect to which all consciousness concerned with objects is of instrumental significance only.

> 19. *To be aware of the world-containing Space
> is to be aware of the Universe of Objects.*

This aphorism asserts the interdependence of our ordinary space and the objects contained within it. This involves a departure from the older Newtonian view wherein space was regarded as independent of the presence or absence of objects. While it is possible to conceive of such a space, it would be a space taken in a different sense from that of the world-containing space. The view developed in the new relativity is consonant with the present aphorism, for in this latter theory matter and space are viewed as interdependent. This space is not simply an empty abstraction, but actually has what might be called a substantial quality. Thus, the very form or "properties" of the space is affected by the degree in which matter is concentrated in different portions of it. It becomes warped in the vicinity of large stellar bodies, so that the shortest distance between two points is no longer a straight line, in the old sense, but a curved line, analogous to an arc of a great circle on the surface of a sphere. Modern astrophysics has even developed the idea of an expanding space, implying therewith the possibility of a contracting space. This notion, at the very least, renders intelligible and plausible in physical terms the ancient notion of a pulsating universe on the analogy of a great breath.

Once we have the notion of a space expanding with the matter, which is coextensive with it, and the consequent possibility of its contraction in another phase of the life-history of matter, then there at once emerges the further implication of the dependence of matter-space upon a somewhat still more ultimate. For pulsation implies a matrix in which it inheres. In these aphorisms, that matrix is symbolized by Consciousness-without-an-object. The objective phase of the pulsation, that which is marked especially by the expanding of the universe, is the state of consciousness polarized toward objects. The contracting phase develops while consciousness is being progressively withdrawn from objects. This may be viewed first as the macrocosmic picture—a process in the grand cosmos. The same principle applies to the microcosmic or individual consciousness.

These two senses are not generally distinguished in these commentaries, as the latter are concerned with general principles that may be applied in either sense. Thus, what is said may be interpreted either in reference to an individualized human consciousness, or to consciousness in the more comprehensive sense.

20. *To realize the Spatial Void is to awaken to Nirvanic Consciousness.*

This aphorism effects a further expansion of the meaning of Nirvana. The latter may be viewed as a spatial consciousness, but not in the sense of a world-containing space. Nirvanic Consciousness is not to be regarded as simply the total consciousness of the manifested universe. If such a total consciousness could be envisaged, it would be very appropriate to call it Cosmic Consciousness, and it would stand as a whole, in contradistinction to Nirvanic Consciousness. These two, Nirvanic Consciousness and Cosmic Consciousness, would contrast in the relation of polarization, analogous to the familiar polarity of subject and object. In spatial symbols, the polarity is between the world-containing Space and the Spatial Void.

Now, a more complete interpretation of the pulsation noted in the last commentary becomes possible. The expansion of the world-containing Space corresponds to contraction of consciousness in the sense of the Spatial Void, or a reduction of consciousness concerned with the Self, while there is an expansion of consciousness in the field of objects. In psychological terms, it is the predominantly extroverted phase. While in such a cosmically expansive phase, the balance of human consciousness, as of all other consciousness, is bound to be predominantly extroverted, yet particular individuals may be relatively only more or less extroverted. In this setting, the so-called introverted individuals are only relatively introverted, and cannot be predominantly introverted so long as they possess physical bodies. To become predominantly introverted is to cease to exist objectively, and thus, to have consciousness centered in the Spatial Void or Nirvana.

For most individuals, the centering of consciousness in the Spatial Void is a state like dreamless sleep, in other words, a psychical state that analytic psychology has called the "Unconscious". In this philosophy, this state is not viewed as unconscious in the unconditional sense, but is conceived as a state of consciousness that is not conscious of itself, and therefore, indistinguishable from unconsciousness from the subject-object standpoint. It is possible, however, to transfer the principle of self-consciousness into the Spatial Void, in which case it is no longer a state like dreamless sleep. But this is not an easy step to effect, as it requires a high development of the principle of self-consciousness, combined with its isolation from the object. If, in the case of a given individual, this power is sufficiently developed, beyond the average of the race, it is possible for such a one to become focused in the Spatial Void, in advance of the race as a whole. When this is actually accomplished, the individual is faced with two possibilities. Either he may then become locked in the Spatial Void, in a sense analogous to that of the binding of most men to the universe of objects, or he may acquire the power to move his consciousness freely between the world-containing Space and the Spatial Void. In the latter case, the individual's base is neither the universe of objects nor Nirvana, but lies in THAT which comprehends both these. The latter is here symbolized by Consciousness-without-an-object, which is neither introverted nor extroverted, but occupies a neutral position between these two accentuations.

> 21. *But for Consciousness-without-an-object,*
> *there is no difference between the world-containing*
> *Space and the Spatial Void.*

In one sense there is no difference because Space or Consciousness, in either sense, is irrelevant. From the standpoint of a profound metaphysical perspective, both are irrelevant, as the just forgotten dream is irrelevant to the consciousness of the man who has awakened from sleep. Yet, while dreaming, the dream was real enough to the dreamer. We can thus distinguish a sense in which we would say the dream is not, i.e., from the perspective of the awakened consciousness for which it has been forgotten, yet, at the same time, in another sense, for the dreamer while dreaming, the dream is a real existence. Shifting now to the highest transcendental sense, we can say that both the world-containing Space and the Spatial Void both are and are not. In the sense that from the level of Consciousness-without-an-object both the universe of objects and Nirvana are not, there is no difference between them.

It is possible for an individual to achieve a state wherein consciousness is so divided that in one aspect of that divided consciousness he realizes the irrelevance or essential nonexistence of both Nirvana and the universe of objects, while at the same time in another aspect of that consciousness he is aware of the relative and interdependent reality of these two grand phases of consciousness. The synthetic judgment from this level of dual consciousness would be: "The universe of objects and Nirvana both are and are not." There is something here that can be realized immediately, but which defeats every effort of the intellective consciousness to capture and represent in really intelligible terms, but there can be no doubt of the superior authority of the State of Realization itself, for the individual who has acquaintance with it. To be sure, intellectual dialectic may confuse and veil the memory of the immense authority of the Realization, but this veiling process has no more significance than the power of the ordinary dream to veil the judgment of the waking state. Whereas the dream is generally something inferior to the waking intellectual judgment, the Realization has a transcendent superiority with respect to the latter. But can the intellectual consciousness of the man who has had no glimpse of the Realization be convinced of this? It is certainly quite difficult for the dreamer, while dreaming, to realize the purely relative existence of his dream. Has the waking intellectual judgment a superior capacity with respect to the acknowledgment of its own Transcendental Roots?

22. Within Consciousness-without-an-object lies the Seed of Law.

Consciousness-without-an-object is not Itself law bound or law determined. It is rather the Root-source of all law, as of all else. Thus, when by means of Recognition an individual self is brought into direct realization of Consciousness-without-an-object, it is found that that most fundamental of all laws, the law of contradiction, no longer applies. Here no affirmation is a denial of the possibility of its contradictory. Also, Consciousness-without-an-object is that excluded middle that is neither A nor not-A. Hence, the actuality that Consciousness-without-an-object symbolizes is unthinkable, and so in order to think toward IT, a thinkable symbol must be employed.

All law, conceived as law of nature, or of consciousness in its various forms and states, or of relationships, is dependent upon law of thought. For such states of consciousness as there may be in which there is no thought, in any sense, there is no awareness of law, and, hence, no existence of law within the content of such states. But for a thinking consciousness that contains or is associated with those states, the operation of law is realized. Thus we may regard a law-bound domain as a thought-bound domain, though such thought is not necessarily restricted to the familiar form commonly known to men. This implies, among other consequences, that there is no universe, save for a thinker.

23. When consciousness of objects is born, the Law is invoked as a Force tending ever toward Equilibrium.

The school of English Empiricism performed a fundamental service for philosophy, in a negative way, by trying to interpret the mind as an empty tablet on which uncolored impressions from objects were imprinted. The culmination of this line of thought was finally achieved by Kant when he demonstrated that the only way to avoid absolute agnosticism was through the recognition of a positive contribution by the mind itself, that is, a contribution not derived from experience, however much experience might be necessary for arousing this factor into action. Kant showed that, *pari passu* with the development of awareness of objects through the senses, there was aroused knowledge of a form within which the objects were organized as a whole of experience. This "organization as a whole of experience" is simply the principle of Law in the general sense.

The most fundamental meaning of Law is Equilibrium. For equilibrium is that which distinguishes a cosmos from a chaos. The very essence of the notions of "law" and "equilibrium" is contained in the notion of "invariant." The counter-notion is that of an "absolutely formless flux." If we abstract from experience all the notion of law, then all that is left is such a formless flux, devoid of all meaning. This would be a state of absolute nescience. Therefore, the existence of any knowledge, or of any dependability in consciousness, implies the presence of law. But the moment that we apprehend an object as object, we have invoked both knowledge and dependability. This is shown in the fact that the apprehension of an object implies the subject, which stands in relation to the object. Thus, Law appears as subject-object relationship. Now, at once, the factor of Equilibrium is apparent, for opposed to the object stands the complementary principle of the subject.

Laws are not discovered in nature, considered as something apart from all consciousness. Rather it is the truth that organized nature is a product of thinking consciousness. In a profound sense, the Law is known before it is empirically discovered. This is revealed in the fact, noted by psychology, that law-formations are developed out of "phantasy" processes. In notable instances, as in the case of Riemann, a form principle was evolved as a purely phantastic geometrical construction, which several decades later supplied the form for Einstein's general theory of relativity, to which current physical experience conforms better than it does to any preceding theory. The form that a given law takes when constructed in relation to a certain segment of empiric determination may be, and generally seems to be, inadequate. However, this should not be understood as implying the merely approximate or pragmatic character of Law per se. It should rather be understood as an imperfect objective apprehension of the Law, "known" prior to experience. The real Knowledge of Law lies somewhere in what the analytic psychologist calls the "Unconscious." Man is born with this hidden knowledge, which rises more or less imperfectly to the surface as an intuition. Even when scientific laws are interpreted as the product of a relative purpose, the notion of Law in the deeper sense is presupposed. For the affirmation of a productive relationship between purpose and the scientific law implies a deeper Law, whereon faith in that productive relationship rests. Even the Pragmatist rests upon a base of a non-pragmatic Assurance, however little the latter may be in the foreground of consciousness.

> 24. *All objects exist as tensions within Consciousness-without-an-object that tend ever to flow into their own complements or others.*

The principle involved here is illustrated by the law in psychology known as "enantiodromia." This is the law that any psychical state tends to be transformed into its opposite. The operation of this law is most evident in the case of those individuals who are extremely one-sided, since they manifest correspondingly exaggerated reversal of phase. But the principle always operates, even in the most balanced natures, though in these cases the two phases are conjoined and function together.

The operation of the principle can be observed quite widely. Thus, growth is balanced by decay, birth by death, light by darkness, evolution by the reverse process of involution, and so on. A particularly impressive illustration is afforded by the interaction of electrons and positrons when coming into conjunction. Here we have a flow of phase into counterphase, resulting in mutual cancellation and the production of a different state of matter. The dialectic logic of Hegel is a systematic application of this principle.

No object of consciousness is stable—remaining ever the same—but is, on the contrary, a state of tension that tends to transform into its complement. Consciousness-without-an-object is the universal solvent within which the centers of tension, or objects, have their field of play. All tendency in that play is counterbalanced by its countertendency, the culminating effect being an expression equated to zero. It is the zero that symbolizes the durable Reality, or Consciousness-without-an-object. Within the field of Consciousness-without-an-object, in principle, any creative tension may be produced, but unavoidably, the countertension is invoked. This is the reason why all creativeness involves a resistance that renders every construction something more than merely what one chooses that it should be. From this there results the positive consequence that any construction, however phantastic, when taken in conjunction with its counterphase, is true, while every construction whatsoever, when taken in isolation from its counterphase, is false. Thus, if the initial construction is even the most phantastic conceivable, and as far as possible from that which is generally regarded as reality, nevertheless, if the counterphase is given full recognition, the resultant is durable Truth. While, on the other hand, if the original construction is in terms of the generally conceded objective material, and grounded in the most careful observation, but is not taken in conjunction with the counterphase, the resultant effect is a false conception and, if believed in, produces a state of real delusion. In this way, it is possible for the so-called practical and scientific man to occupy an essentially false position, while some highly introvert poet, who lives quite aloof from the so-called world of real experience and who allows the initial impulse of his imagination the greatest possible freedom, but who, at the same time, carefully regards and incorporates the counterphase of his phantasy, will render manifest profound and lasting Truth. Now, all this leads to a very important consequence, namely, that starting from any state of consciousness whatsoever, it is possible to arrive at the final and durable Reality and Truth, provided that the resources of the counterphase are incorporated in the self-conscious consciousness. Thus, no particular merit attaches to that peculiarly valued phase of consciousness—the extroverted phase of the so-called practical and scientific man—as a starting point for the attainment of the Real. This base may serve as an effective starting point, but equally well, may any other. In fact, it is quite possible that some present inmate of a psychiatric institution may outdistance all the philistines in the world who pride themselves on their sanity.

> 25. *The ultimate effect of the flow of all objects into their complements is mutual cancellation in complete Equilibrium.*

The illustration of the positron and the electron applies here. The state of each of these units, by itself, may be regarded as one of tension, hence one is called a positive and the other a negative charge of electricity. For such isolated charges there can be no rest, as each is driven ceaselessly toward its own complement. So long as the goal of mutual fusion is not effected, they operate as the dynamic forces that underlie the existence of ponderable matter. But because these units are in a state of tension, no ponderable matter can remain stable. It is subject to the disruption that results when the positive and negative charges are fused. The labor of these charges to gain the goal of fusion may be regarded as one aspect of the dynamic force that manifests as evolution. To such extent as the fusion is effected, visible evolution terminates and ponderable matter vanishes. The resultant of the fusion is a flash of radiation. The latter may be regarded as the Nirvanic State of matter, for the radiant state is one of freedom and equilibrium.

The radiant state of matter is just another name for light. Now, while there is a wide range of wavelength and wave rate in the known scale of light-octaves, there is one constant element that has become highly significant in modern physical theory, and that is the velocity of light. Regardless of wavelength, all light travels at uniform velocity. Here we have a fact intimately related to the principle of equilibrium—a most important invariant. When ponderable matter finally vanishes, it enters a state subject to this invariant. Wavelength is so equilibrated to wave rate that the resultant is always the same.

Now, as revealed in the modern theory of relativity, the constant velocity of light becomes determinant of the form of the physical universe. It forces the view of a finite world-containing space. While it is true that from the standpoint of consciousness-bound-to-objects, the high velocity gives the impression of enormous activity, with respect to which the object-world seems relatively stable, yet, if we shift our base and place our consciousness, as it were, in the sea of radiant energy, the universe of ponderable matter has the value of violent turmoil.[7] For consciousness thus centered, the high-potential of the radiant state has the value of peace and equilibrium. Further, radiant energy, through its property of uniformity of velocity, has the effect of bounding the universe of objects.

In psychological terms, by means of the law of enantiodromia, one psychical state draws forth its opposite. Ordinarily, through the tension of these two phases, the restless movement of embodied consciousness is maintained. This leads to the development of life as experience. The self is driven by problems that are essentially insoluble, but by ever striving to reach the rainbow's end of a satisfactory solution, the self is forced by those problems to the development of potential psychical powers. And when the phase and counterphase of psychical states are blended in the Self, instead of continuing in a condition like that of a dog chasing his own tail, the state of tensions is dissolved in Equilibrium. In this case, the phase and counterphase cease to exist, just as the electron and positron vanish when united, and in their p]ace is a state of consciousness of quite a different order. Throughout mystical literature, one finds an oft recurring reference to this state as one of "Light." Does this not rather beautifully complete the analogy with the corresponding radiant state of matter?

26. Consciousness of the field of tensions is the Universe.

This consequence follows at once when it is realized that an object exists as a tension. Although, in the ultimate sense, every tension is balanced by its opposite phase, so the equilibrium is never actually destroyed, yet consciousness, taken in a partial aspect, may comprehend only one phase, or may be only imperfectly conscious of the counter-phase. For this partial aspect of consciousness, equilibrium does not exist. The consciousness of the universe of objects, taken in more or less complete abstraction from the totality of all consciousness, is preeminently consciousness in the field of tensions. One result is that any view of a segment of the universe of objects gives an impression of development, as in some direction. The usual scientific name for this apparently directed development is "evolution," and a familiar social interpretation is called "progress." Each of these terms reveals a recognition of a tension in the field of consciousness or life that forces any present given state to change into another. The fact that this change can be described as evolution or progress implies, in addition, that some directedness that is recognizable is involved in the change.

The more common view of evolution and progress is of a form that may be called linear. By this is meant a movement that could be represented approximately by a straight-line vector, the direction being given usually not only toward the future but also inclined upward. This linear form of the interpretation seems to be sustained when the segment observed is short enough and appropriately selected. Larger segments, such as those afforded through the study of geologic records, reveal a periodicity more or less clearly, and thus make it clear that the linear interpretation must be modified. It is, in fact, a profounder view to regard the form of change as like a pulsating breath or heartbeat, one phase being the diastole, the other the systole. As a result, it is impossible to predicate "progress" of the process taken as a whole. For while an individual of the extroverted type might predicate progress as characteristic of the diastolic phase, he would be inclined to regard the systolic phase as a regression, and on the other hand, the introverted type would most likely give a reverse valuation. For, to predicate "progress," some base of valuation is, of necessity, assumed, and there is no one base common to all individual valuation. Consequently, it is possible only with respect to restricted segments of experience and from the base of particular valuation to predicate either evolution and progress or devolution and retrogression.

However, regardless of how the tendency of change may be evaluated in any given case, the common fact of experience is that objects and objective states of consciousness are subject to a tension that continually forces transformation, be the rate rapid or slow. In other words, there is no rest or balance in the universe of objects taken in abstraction. For individuals who are in the more active phase of their interests, there may be nothing profoundly distasteful in this fact, but when they begin to feel the need of stability and rest, the total significance of the universe of objects becomes tragic. These differences, probably more than anything else, afford the explanation of why some men are optimists in their attitude toward the universe of objects, while others are pessimists. This difference is also that which marks the general characteristic attitudes of youth and maturity. It should be noted that pessimism and optimism are attitudes toward a phase of consciousness, and not to be interpreted as general attitudes toward all phases.

27. *Consciousness of Equilibrium is Nirvana.*

The idea of "Nirvana," as employed in the present exposition, is not a notion of exclusively religious significance. Unquestionably, in the historic sense, this notion has been given a predominantly religious and religio-philosophical value, but when the two following considerations are taken into account, the reason for this should become clear. In the first place, the notion is introduced to the West from the East, and the oriental focus of interest is predominantly religious. In addition, the Nirvanic State is more readily accessible to the introverted type of individual polarization in consciousness, and the typical focus of interest of the introvert is more religious than scientific. As a consequence, the full value of the notion of "Nirvana" has not so far been developed. It is significant for the scientific focus of interest, as well as the religious, and is, in fact, implied in the development of science, though in this connection it is more deeply buried in the so-called "unconscious" than is the case where the focus of interest is in the direction naturally taken by the more introverted religious type. The scientific importance of the notion is nowhere more clearly revealed than in the value the idea of "equilibrium" has for scientific thinking. The profound tendency to find equilibrium in an hypothesis, theory, or law, that is so strongly manifested in the great coordinative scientific thinkers, reveals this fact. The objective material with which science is concerned never gives the hypotheses, theories, and laws. These are actually created out of phantasy, using the latter term in the sense employed by analytic psychology. To be sure, the selection of the form of the phantastic creation is guided by a due consideration of data from experience, but it is a creative act, added to pure experience, that provides the form. Now, as one studies the various hypotheses, theories, and laws of all departments of science, a very important tendency in the selection is noted. This tendency gains its clearest and most perfect expression in mathematics and mathematical physics, but is nonetheless recognizable in the other sciences. It is the tendency to express the unification of the original collection of scientific data in the form of equations. So far has this gone in modern physics—the most fundamental of natural sciences—that the culminating statements are more and more in the form of differential equations, with sensuously conceived models occupying a progressively inferior place of importance. Now, what is the psychical significance of the equation, as such? It is simply this, that in the equation we have manifested the sense or feeling for equilibrium. So long as a segment of experience is not reduced to an equation, the state of consciousness is one of tension and restlessness, and not of equilibrium. The investigator is driven on because his current position affords no resting place, and therefore, no peace. But when an adequate equation has been found, then there is a sense of conquest, rest, and peace. There is no need in man more profound than just this. If no success in this direction were ever attained, life would become unendurable, sooner or later. The sense of hunger for the equilibrating equation is simply one phase of the hunger for Nirvana—that inner Core that sustains the whole universe of experience.

The less there is of realization of equilibrium, the more painful life becomes, and likewise, the more realization of equilibrium achieved, the greater the joy and peace. Without consciousness of equilibrium, life is only a painful battle and a storm of conflicts that leads nowhere. This is Suffering, spelled with a capital S. On the other hand, the more complete the realization of equilibrium, the less the suffering, until, in the culminating state of pure Nirvanic Consciousness, there is total absence of suffering. The great difficulty is that, whereas suffering tends to stir self-consciousness into wider and wider fullness, the State of Equilibrium tends to lull it to sleep. The latter is usually the state known as dreamless sleep, when taken in its purity. But when self-consciousness has been sufficiently developed so that it can resist the lulling effect of Equilibrium, then the purely Nirvanic State can be entered without loss of self-consciousness. This is the Great Victory, the reward for the travail of living-form down the ages.

Some writers conceive Nirvana as being like the state of the newly born infant, wherein there is little or no self-consciousness. Thus it is seen as a retreat to a purely nascent consciousness, which is much inferior to genuine adult consciousness. In this view there is a part truth and a great error. Without full self-consciousness, this state may be likened to a sort of original nascent consciousness, such as must precede the development of organized consciousness. It is entirely possible for an individual who is not sufficiently developed in the capacities of organized consciousness to sink back into such a nascent stage. Therefore, Nirvana is not the immediate Goal for immature men and women. In fact, the immature entering of the state is a sort of failure. But the situation becomes wholly different when the debt to life, in the essential sense, has been completed. When any human being has reached the stage wherein experience has been substantially exhausted as a source of vital value, when this pasture has become a desert with only a few scattered bunches of grass in isolated corners, and when, in addition, the capacity for self-consciousness has been highly developed, then the only remaining significant Path lies in or through the Nirvanic Domain of Consciousness. Nirvana, in this case, is transformed from a nascent state of consciousness to the Supreme human Goal, wherein at long last the insoluble problems of life receive a final resolution and the greatest possible richness of consciousness replaces the old poverty.

This work is not written for immature men and women. It is believed that the inherent difficulty of the subject, when viewed from the standpoint of the intellect, will automatically serve as a means of selection, so that only those will read and understand who are prepared to do so. For the others—the immature ones—there are other needs that may often, for a time, seem to lead in quite different directions. Such are not the special concern of the present work. Largely, instinct and the lash of both circumstance and ambition will perform that function that the immature still require.

But those who have attained substantial maturity, whether in the scientific or religious direction, reach, sooner or later, a cul-de-sac wherein further development in the old directions has only a sort of meaningless "treadmill" value—a place wherein all action means little more than "mark time, march." When this time comes, the only hope for the avoidance of a life in utter poverty of consciousness-values lies in a shift in the focus of consciousness. In the end, this shift will lead to durable and adequate results only by attainment of the Nirvanic State with full self-consciousness.

> 28. *But for Consciousness-without-an-object*
> *there is neither tension nor Equilibrium.*

This is true for the simple reason that Consciousness-without-an-object can never be comprehended by any partial or fractional phase of consciousness. Any phase implies its other, and Consciousness-without-an-object is their mutual comprehender, or rather, the conceptual symbol of that forever inconceivable Reality that underlies and envelops all partial aspects. Where there is no awareness of tension, no meaning attaches to equilibrium. Here we may think of the "equals sign" in mathematics as symbolizing equilibrium, while zero symbolizes Consciousness-without-an-object. As an actually realized consciousness, the distinction here is extremely subtle, and yet of vital significance. It is very easy for the mystic to combine these two states into one and simply call them both "Nirvana." In most, but not all, literature on the subject this seems to have been done, and the result on the whole seems to have been confusing, at least to the western mind. For this treatment gives to the Reality an overly introverted interpretation, and this is quite naturally repugnant to the extremely extroverted West. On the other hand, when Consciousness-without-an-object is distinguished from the purely subjective Nirvanic phase, a kind of mathematical clarity results. The subjective and objective are then seen to inhere in a neutral and more primary principle, and thus they acquire a more thinkable perspective. In the final analysis, this means that the peculiar genius of neither the East nor the West is nearer the ultimate Reality. Both are seen to stand as partial phases of a more comprehensive whole. Each has a half-truth, which is unavoidably blended with error when taken in the partial form alone. And each must add its neglected half to its recognized half to find the ultimately durable.

> 29. *The state of tensions is the state of*
> *ever-becoming.*

A state of tension is a state of instability, since it implies a tendency to become other than what it now is. Every state of relative balance that is under tension can never be permanently durable, since the ever-present tendency to break away from the balance will become actual at the first opportunity. All the balance we find in the universe is of this sort, as is easily seen by considering that the atom exists as a state of tension between the nucleus and the surrounding electrons.

Since a tension is a tendency to become other, it follows readily that a state of tension implies becoming. Nothing in the worlds of experience or thought remains permanently stable, but is ever subject to becoming something else. Some elements remain relatively stable, while others change rapidly. But every objective "invariant" is, in the last analysis, only stable in the sense that a parameter is fixed for a certain phase of mathematical analysis, while for the completed analysis, it also changes. All objective life or experience is thus a process of becoming other, and taken by itself in abstraction, it is a becoming other that leads nowhere.

30. Ever-becoming is endless-dying.

That which becomes ceases to be that which it was—The flash of radiation that was born upon the coalescence of the electron and the positron implies the death of the units of ponderable matter. The acorn ceases to be as it becomes the oak. As the man comes forth, the child, that was, is no more. As a new social organization occupies the field of the present, the old society is entombed in the pages of the historic past. No form or state in the empiric field is permanent, but ever develops into something else. The passing may be as imperceptible as the changes of massive geologic transformation, or as the birth and decay of stars, yet it may be as inconceivably rapid as that of the most instable species of radium. But, in any case, all things change. This is an ineluctable law of all empiric existence.

At every moment, a new child is born out of a dying past. But if the death implies a birth, it is equally true that the new birth implies death. And what is good and valued in the old dies along with the not-good and that which is not valued. So long as we are restricted to objective consciousness, this dying is a tragic finality.

31. So the state of consciousness of objects is a state of ever-renewing promises that pass into death at the moment of fulfillment.

Because of the law of becoming, that which we wish for and work for will ultimately come forth. But also because of this same law, that which is thus brought forth will not endure. Since becoming and dying never cease, the fulfillment of the newborn is also the moment at which it begins to decay. The beloved leaves us at the moment she is found, never to be regained as just that beloved object.

With much effort we climb to the top of a high mountain, and at the very moment we have attained the heights and cry, "Eureka, I have attained the goal," at that very moment only depths reaching down into darkness loom before our vision. Only descent is possible after attaining the crowning heights. Attainment ever initiates decline.

The vitalizing current of embodied life rises up within us whispering, "Look out there and see the vision of my new promises." And we look out and behold the vision of just what we wish, the value that we have cared for so dearly. Then we move toward it. At first the travel may not be so hard, but in time we face difficulties that we must needs surmount. But the vision holds and seems well worth the effort. Yet, beyond one difficulty there lies another, and still another, mounting in ever larger and larger proportions until, finally, we can overcome only by straining our last resources. But at that moment the vision has become actual as our accomplishment. And then we say, "Aye, this is good," and we rest in contemplation of the hard-earned accomplishment. Then as we hold the object of fulfillment in our hands, feasting our heart upon it, we feel it melting in those hands, like a beautous sculpture of ice in a warm place. It melts and melts and our heart grieves, and we pray to the powers that be that this desired object of beauty shall not leave us. But all this is in vain. Despite everything it melts and melts away, until, in the end, the fulfilling object of promise is no more. And then we are cast down for a season, until once more the current of embodied life rises and bids us look forth again and see still another vision. Then, again, we proceed as before, to achieve as before, and to lose as before. So it is throughout the whole of outer life, and mayhap, a long series of outer lives.

In the end, the wandering soul after many ages learns to abandon all hope. But this hour of deep despair brings the soul close to the Eternal. Vision of another Way begins to clear.

> *32. Thus when consciousness is attached to objects the agony of birth and death never ceases.*

That birth and death are ceaseless follows from aphorisms 29, 30, and 31. But birth and death are also agony. That this is a fact, in the familiar biological sense, is very well known indeed. Creatures are generally born through suffering and die in suffering. And beyond this physical or sensuous suffering there is a more subtle suffering that envelops all becoming, whether physical or ideal. The loss of the valued object is suffering, and the dying to a world of valued objects is likewise suffering. And in travail new ideals are born. On one side of its total meaning, the whole drama of becoming is one grand symphony of agony.

The attainment of a desired object is the birth of an object for the self that seeks. But the process through which this object is born rests in a field of desire-tension. When there is desire, there is want or craving, and this is a state of suffering. Then when the desired object is born to the individual as possession, forthwith it begins to die as the no-longer-wished-for. Attainment becomes boredom. This, again, is suffering.

Attachment to objects is, in all ways, a state of suffering, lightened only briefly by satisfaction at the moment of success. But the satisfaction is born to bloom for but a fleeting moment, then to decay in the long dying of boredom. Suffering reigns supreme over the world-focused consciousness.

33. *In the state of Equilibrium where birth cancels death, the deathless Bliss of Nirvana is realized.*

Birth and death are strung on a continuum of Life that is not born, nor ever dies. Life does not come into being with birth, nor does it cease with death. It is the living object that is born and dies. In the end, death just equals birth, and that which underlies remains unaffected. Here Equilibrium reigns eternally and unaffected. When self-consciousness abides in the underlying Life, birth and death are realized as just cancelling each other, and so have no reality. Thus, there is no suffering, but only the eternal Bliss of undying Life. This is Nirvana.

34. *But Consciousness-without-an-object is neither agony nor bliss.*

Agony or bliss are experienced or realized states, but the experiencing and realizing inhere in pure Consciousness. The latter is unaffected by that which it contains. Like Space, It is a universal support that remains ever the same no matter what the nature of the supported may be. When self-consciousness fuses with the pure Consciousness, no longer is modification or coloring of consciousness known. Hence, there is neither agony nor bliss, but only eternal possibility.

35. *Out of the Great Void,*
which is Consciousness-without-an-object,
the Universe is creatively projected.

THAT, which is here symbolized by "Consciousness-without-an-object," has long been called the "Great Void." It is the "Shunyata"—Voidness—of the Buddhists, and the "Nothing" of Jacob Behmen. It is that which, when defined exactly rather than represented symbolically, is designated only by the negation of every possible predicate. But that of which only negations are strictly true can seem solely as nothing at all to relative consciousness. Hence IT has been, repeatedly, called the "Void" or the "Nothing." IT is not a possible content of any conception whatsoever. For thought, and also for sense, IT truly is Nothing. But to say, therefore, that it is nothing in every sense whatsoever is to imply that all being is necessarily a being for sense or thought. No man has the knowledge that would enable him to say, justifiably, that thought and sense comprehend all possibilities of Being; while, on the other hand, there are those who know that there is Being beyond the possibility of sense and thought. Kant implied such Being in his "thing-in-itself," and von Hartmann located it in the collective "Unconscious," while Schopenhauer called it "Will." The mystic has proclaimed it in the most ancient of literature, and reaffirmed it from time to time down to the present.

"Creative projection," as here understood, is wholly other than the theological conception of "creationism." There is here no creative act of a Deity that stands, essentially and substantially, separate from the created, nor does the creative projection produce souls *de novo*. Essentially, "creative projection" is identical with "emanation," but with the additional implication that the emanation depends upon an initial act of will, which was not necessary. That is, the act of will is not necessary in the sense that it might not have been, but necessary in the sense that without the act of will there would have been no universe. An absolutely necessary emanation would not be a creative projection.

The standpoint here is in substantial agreement with that of von Hartmann, in that the Universe as its *possibility* is predetermined by the ideas that lie in privation of form eternally in THAT, but as to its *actuality* is the effect of a free act of Will. Since the Will is free, it could have failed to will actualization. But It has so willed, and thereby invoked necessity as the law that determined the form of the Universe. Science discovers, or rather, uncovers, the necessity in the Universe, but never finds the Thatness without which there never would be any actuality whatsoever.

This creative power does not transcend man when man drives his self-consciousness to his ultimate roots. But as long as man is in a state of consciousness seemingly isolated from the Roots, he seems to be merely an effect of causes that transcend him. Hence it is only for man as isolated—as the Great Orphan—that the Divinity appears transcendent, i.e., lying at a distance. However, when man has carried self-consciousness into the ultimate Roots, he becomes, in his own right, a potential center of creative projection, and consciously so. At this inmost state of consciousness, he may choose to will actualization, or may refrain from so choosing. If he chooses to will actualization, he creatively projects, in conformation with the idea that he thinks. Thus, finally, it is seen, man is his own creator.

As conscious creator, man is God-man; as the created, he is creature, in the sense long used by the mystics. In the mystic Way, the denial of creature-man is but preliminary to the realization of the God-man. Theistic preconception has led many Christian mystics to misinterpret the real meaning of the deepest phase of their realization, but they have reported the schematic pattern correctly. Actually, in the state of ultimate realization, it is not Otherness—i.e., God—who replaces the man, but the true self-identity of man replaces the false image that led man to conceive himself as creature only. It is true that mystical insight is a revelation of Man, rather than a revelation of God, provided the total meaning of "man" is sufficiently deepened. But "Man," understood in this adequate sense, is as much inaccessible to objective psychology as ever was the God of the Theists.

36. *The Universe as experienced is the created negation that ever resists.*

The creative act is entirely free or spontaneous, but the created effect is subject to the law of necessity. The creative act may be quite consciously chosen, yet the necessity invoked may be only imperfectly understood. In this case, I find that *I* have willed more than I knew, and thus face compulsive necessity in the environment that *I* have creatively produced. As a result, further willing is conditioned by this necessity. Hence, the created projection resists me. I must conform to its conditions, though *I* was its source.

37. The creative act is bliss,
the resistance, unending pain.

In creativeness, the stream of Life flows freely, and the free-flowing is Joy. The Bliss of the mystic is consciousness fused with the free-flowing Life. Before embodied life was, the free-flowing Life is. Though embodied life seems to exist, yet the free-flowing Life continues, quite unaffected. And when embodied life is no more, still the free-flowing Life remains as always. The ordinary consciousness belongs to the somatic life, but the mystic consciousness is part and parcel of the germinal Life. Creativeness is of the very essence of germinal Life, while the somatic life is bound by the restraint of form. The one is all-bliss, the other all-enveloping pain. Since the consciousness of the concrete man is mainly, but not exclusively, somatic, there are brief moments of joy in the usual life, but pain predominates, overwhelmingly. This, any man can see, if he looks at his empiric life objectively and realistically without any of the coloring cast by hope.

38. Endless resistance is the
Universe of experience; the agony of crucifixion.

Frustration is of the very essence of objective existence. That the consciousness of embodied man is not wholly frustrated is due to the fact that actual ordinary consciousness is not *wholly* objective. Glimmerings from the Roots do arise from time to time, and they cast transient sheaths of joyousness over the objective field. But generally, the source of these glimmerings is not known for what it is, and so the objective field is credited with value which of itself, taken in abstraction, it does not possess. The purely objective is a binder or restricter that denies or inhibits the aspiration of the soul. The creative drive from within can find room within the objective only by the rending of constricting form. Hence it is that the fresh manifestation of Spirit is always at the price of crucifixion. The birth of the Christ within man is ever at the price of rending apart the old man of the world.

39. Ceaseless creativeness is Nirvana,
the Bliss beyond all human conceiving.

Creativeness, taken in isolation from the created effect, is unalloyed Bliss. A Nirvanic State that is taken in complete isolation is pure Bliss, quite beyond the conception of ordinary consciousness. But this is a partial consciousness, standing as the counterpart of isolated objective consciousness. It is not the final or synthetic State, and thus is not the final Goal of the mystic Path. But it is a possible abiding place, and it is possible for the mystic to arrive in, and be enclosed by, the Nirvanic State in a sense analogous to the ordinary binding within objective consciousness. There is a sense in which we may speak of a bondage to Bliss as well as a bondage to pain. It is, unquestionably, a far more desirable kind of bondage than that in the dark field of the object, but the bound Nirvani is not yet a full Master. To be sure, he has conquered one kind of bondage, and thus realized some of the powers of mastery, but an even greater problem of self-mastery remains unresolved.

The attainment of Nirvana implies the successful meeting of all the dark trials of the Path. The struggle with personal egoism has resulted in a successful issue; the clinging to objects has been dissolved; the battle with temptations and threatening shadows along the Path has been successfully fought; and resolution has been maintained firmly; but there still remains the task of rising superior to Glory. The little appreciated fact is that the Goal of aspiration may become a possessor of the Self, and something like spiritual egoism may replace the old personal egoism.

It is easy for many to understand that dark tendencies in the soul should be overcome, for with many the light of conscience at least glows in the consciousness. These may, and generally do, find it difficult to overcome the dark tendencies. Quite commonly, we find ourselves doing that which we would not do and leaving undone that which we unquestionably feel we should do. The undesirability of such tendencies we recognize, but find difficulty in knowing how to deal with them. The better part of our innate moral sense certainly supports the discipline of the Way that leads to Nirvana. Yet beyond this there lies an unsuspected and inherently more difficult problem.

We may think of Nirvana as the State in which all of highest excellence or value is realized, and in a form that is not alloyed with any dross. It is, indeed, the Divine Presence of the Christian mystic. It is quite natural to conceive of this as the Ultimate, beyond which there is nothing more. But there is a defect. For here is a State that I enjoy and to which I tend to cling, and thus it involves a kind of selfishness, though it is a spiritual kind of selfishness. Thus I am possessed, even though possessed by That to which I give highest value and honor.

After all, Bliss is a valued modification of consciousness. But where there is valuation, there is still duality—a difference between that which is valued and that which is depreciated. The highest State transcends even the possibility of valuation, and its complementary depreciation. The Highest Perfection finds no distinction whatsoever. This is the State in which there is no Self of any sort, whether personal or spiritual, and where there is no embodiment of Supreme Values or God. It is the Vast Solitude, the Teeming Desert.

To turn one's back upon the best of everything is intrinsically more difficult than to turn away from those things and qualities that one's moral judgment and best feeling condemn readily enough. But it is not enough to arrive at the Place beyond evil; it is also necessary to transcend the Good. This is a dark saying, hard to understand, yet it is so. But he who has found Nirvana is safe.

*40. But for Consciousness-without-an-object,
there is neither creativeness nor resistance.*

One might say that IT is both creativeness and resistance, but in the last analysis this is a distortion of the Reality. To be sure, IT supports both possibilities, but as directly realized IT is a Consciousness so utterly different from anything that can be conceived by the relative consciousness that only negations can be predicated of IT. As it were, the creating and the creation are simply annulled. From that standpoint it is equally true to say that the universe is and yet it is not and never has been, nor ever will be. And equally, it would have to be said that there is not, never has been, nor ever would be, any creativeness. It is quite useless to try to conceive this, since there is no substitute for the Direct Realization.

*41. Ever-becoming and ever-ceasing-to-be
are endless action.*

That ever-becoming and ever-ceasing to be are action is self-evident. But the aphorism implies more than this. It defines the nature of action. Action is not merely a moving from here to there; it is a dying of a "here" together with a birth of a "there." To act is to destroy and beget. To act is to lose that which has been, though it replaces the old with something new.

*42. When ever-becoming cancels the
ever-ceasing-to-be, then Rest is realized.*

This seems self-evident, as Rest is clearly the other of all action, whether in the positive or negative sense. But one might draw the erroneous conclusion that Rest and Action exist exclusively in discrete portions of time. Actually, Rest and Action may be realized at the same time. At a sufficiently profound level of realization, ceaseless Action leaves the eternal Rest inviolate. The disjunction of these two complementaries is valid only for partial consciousness.

43. Ceaseless Action is the Universe.

The Universe or Cosmos is the active phase or mode of THAT of which neither Action nor Rest may be predicated, when conceived as a totality.

44. Unending Rest is Nirvana.

Since Nirvana, as here understood, is ever the complementary other of the Universe, it is that which the Universe is not. Hence, with respect to Action, Nirvana has the value of Rest.

It should be clearly understood that with respect to the present aphorisms the conception of Nirvana is not necessarily identical with the definitions of the oriental usage of the term, though there is at least a considerable degree of agreement in the meanings. The term is here used to represent meanings born out of a direct Realization that may not be *wholly* identical with any other that has been formulated.

45. But Consciousness-without-an-object is neither Action nor Rest.

Both Action and Rest are rooted in THAT, but of THAT as a whole neither Action nor Rest can be predicated. THAT is all embracing but unconditioned. Thus, since any positive predication is a conditioning because it defines, and gives, to that extent, a delineation of nature or character, thereby implying an Other that is different, it follows that no such predication can be valid. On the other hand, negative predication is valid if it is clearly understood that it is a restriction that is denied, and not a Power.

46. When consciousness is attached to objects, it is restricted through the forms imposed by the world-containing Space, by Time, and by Law.

Space, Time, and Law condition the contents of consciousness, but not the consciousness itself. And when any center of consciousness is attached to, and thus identified with, contents or objects, it seems to be likewise conditioned. Thus to the extent man is so attached, he is not free but is determined. The doctrine of determinism, therefore, does express a part truth, i.e., a truth that has pragmatic but not transcendental validity. So he who feels himself wholly conditioned is highly attached. But the concrete consciousness may be in a state that is anything from slightly to highly detached, and thus have a corresponding experience of freedom, which we may view as determination through the Subject, rather than conditioning through the Object or environment. Mankind as a whole knows little genuine freedom, but lives conditioned in part by the objective environment and in part by psychical factors, which are none the less objective because of being subtle. But authentic freedom is possible.

47. When consciousness is disengaged from objects, Liberation from the forms of the world-containing Space, of Time, and of Law is attained.

Disengagement or detachment from objects does not necessarily imply the noncognition of objects. But it does imply the break of involvement in the sense of a false identification with objects. It is possible to act upon and with objects and yet remain so detached that the individual is unbound. Thus, action is not incompatible with Liberation. One who attains and maintains this state of consciousness can achieve an authentically willed action.

48. Attachment to objects is consciousness bound within the Universe.

The meaning here with respect to consciousness is to be understood in the sense of an individual center of consciousness, not consciousness in the abstract or universal sense. Further, it is not stated that attachment to objects produces the Universe, but simply that consciousness—in the sense of individual center of consciousness—is bound within the Universe. Thus, this aphorism does not lead to the implication that the Universe, as such, is necessarily an illusion devoid of all reality value, but rather affirms that attachment produces a phase of bondage with respect to individual consciousness. Undoubtedly this does result in a state of delusion, but this may be no more than a mode of the individual consciousness, with respect to which the judgment that the Universe, as such, is unreal would be an unjustified extrapolation.

49. Liberation from such attachment is the State of unlimited Nirvanic Freedom.

That the Nirvanic State of Consciousness is one of Liberation or Freedom has long been the traditional teaching. The aphorism accentuates the fact that this Freedom depends upon detachment from the object, but does not imply that such detachment is the whole meaning of the Nirvanic Freedom. It does imply that, while realization of the Nirvanic State is dependent upon detachment from the object, it is not dependent upon noncognition of the Object. For simple cognition of the Object does not necessitate attachment to it. Thus realization of Nirvana is, in principle, compatible with continued cognition of the World, provided there is nonattachment to it.

The Nirvanic State of Consciousness when realized in its purity does imply noncognition as well as detachment from the Universe of Objects. Possibly this is the more frequent form of the realization, and there exists the view that this is the only possible form of the realization. But this is an error. If this were the truth, then Nirvana could only be a realization in a full trance of objective consciousness, or after physical death. But a more integral realization is possible, such that the Nirvanic State may be known together with cognition of, and even action in, the world, provided there is detachment. Confirmation of this may be found in several of the northern Buddhistic Sutras and in the writings of Sri Aurobindo.

Detachment is a negative condition of the realization, but positively more is required in order that the realization may reach into the relative consciousness. A new power of cognition must also be actuated, else the realization is incomplete. This new power is born spontaneously, though there may be a time lag in the adjustment of the relative consciousness. However, the aphoristic statement is not concerned with psychological detail of this sort, no matter how great may be its human importance. Actually, the aphorisms are a sort of spiritual mathematic dealing with essential relationship, rather than with the more humanistic factors.

50. But Consciousness-without-an-object is neither bondage nor Freedom.

First of all, this is true for the general reason that pure Consciousness is not conditioned or determined by either or both members of any pair of opposites. But without the pure Consciousness, there could be neither bondage nor Liberation. Only because of the experience of bondage is it possible to realize Liberation; likewise, without knowledge of Freedom there could be no cognition of a state of bondage. Movement, development, or process appear to our relative consciousness as either determined by law or a manifestation of free spontaneity, but these are only alternatives of the relative consciousness and not ontological forms. To any given center of consciousness, Being may appear either as absolutely conditioned or as a freely playing spontaneity, but the fact that it so appears to such a center tells us something about the individual psychology of the latter, and does not reveal to us the nature of the Ultimate as it is in itself.

> 51. *Consciousness-without-an-object*
> *may be symbolized by a SPACE that is*
> *unaffected by the presence or absence of objects,*
> *for which there is neither Time nor Timelessness;*
> *neither a world-containing Space nor a Spatial Void;*
> *neither Tension nor Equilibrium;*
> *neither Resistance nor Creativeness;*
> *neither Agony nor Bliss; neither Action nor Rest;*
> *neither Restriction nor Freedom.*

This, together with the following aphorisms, introduces an alternative symbol for Consciousness-without-an-object, i.e., the symbol of SPACE. No form, either conceptual or aesthetic, can possibly be an adequate representation of the all-containing Ultimate Reality, since such form is a comprehended or contained entity. But a form may serve as a pointer to a meaning beyond itself and thus fulfill an office in the human consciousness in the sense of orienting the latter beyond itself. The effective symbol must possess the dual character (*a*) of being in some measure comprehensible by the human consciousness, and (*b*) of reaching beyond the possibility of human comprehension. In the literature dealing with Realization, many symbols may be found that have served this office. But in time, symbols tend to lose their power as the evolving human consciousness approaches a comprehensive understanding of them. Then new and more profound symbols must be found to replace the old. Consciousness-without-an-object is such a symbol for the more subjective orientation of human consciousness, while SPACE is a corresponding symbol for the more objective orientation. The notion of "Void" or "Emptiness" has been used, but has the weakness of suggesting to many minds complete annihilation, hence the more positive symbols of Consciousness-without-an-object and SPACE are used here.

"Space" is a symbol that has been used before, and one of the best explanations of it is to be found in *Tibetan Yoga and Secret Doctrines*. Thus:

> The "Parent" Space is the eternal, ever-present Cause of all—the incomprehensible Deity, whose "Invisible Robes" are the mystic Root of all Matter, and of the Universe. Space is the one eternal thing that we can most easily imagine, immovable in its abstraction and uninfluenced by either the presence or absence in it of an objective Universe. It is without dimension, in every sense, and self-existent. Spirit is the first differentiation from "THAT," the Causeless Cause of both Spirit and Matter. As taught in the Esoteric Catechism, it is neither "limitless void," nor "conditioned fullness," but both. It was and ever will be.[8]

"Space," as used for the symbol, is not to be identified with any of our perceptual or conceptual spaces that are conceived as having specific properties, such as three dimensional, "curved," and so on. The notion must be understood in the most abstract sense possible, as the root or base of every specifically conceivable space. Nor is it to be conceived as either "fullness" or as "voidness," but rather as embracing both conceptions. It thus is a better symbol than either "voidness" or "plenum."

But while the interpretation of THAT as either voidness or plenum is not ultimately valid, yet relative to the needs of different types of human consciousness the symbol is most effective when taken in one or the other of these two aspects. When the approach is predominantly negative with respect to relative consciousness, naturally the symbol is conceived under the form of the Voidness, as in the case of Shunya Buddhism. But in this work the accentuation is positive, and thus "SPACE" or "Consciousness-without-an-object" is conceived provisionally as substantive, with the acknowledgement that this orientation is not ultimately valid.

As the distinction between these two aspects or emphases is of considerable importance, some discussion of them may be valuable. Technically, the distinction has been given the form of Substantialism versus Nonsubstantialism. Thus, quoting from Hamilton: "Philosophers, as they affirm or deny the authority of consciousness in guaranteeing a substratum or substance to the manifestations of the Ego and Non-Ego, are divided into Realists or Substantialists and into Nihilists or Non-Substantialists."[9] It is easy to see that under the class of Non-substantialism also belong the philosophies classed as Positivism, Phenomenalism, Agnosticism, and Aestheticism.[10] As examples of the substantialistic philosophical orientation, particular attention may be drawn to the philosophies of Spinoza and Sri Aurobindo Ghose[11]; while as examples of non-substantialistic philosophies, we may cite those of August Compte and the Taoist, and most of the Buddhist, particularly Zen Buddhism.

One fact that stands out is that the contrasting views, while quite understandably exemplified in various speculative philosophies, are also to be found among philosophies based upon realization. This may strike one with the force of considerable surprise. For, if realization is an authentic insight into Truth, should it not lead to fundamental agreement when manifested as philosophic symbols? Offhand, one may quite reasonably expect such to be the case, yet a fairly wide acquaintance with the literature reveals divergencies sufficiently wide as to appear like contradictions. Since this can be a stumbling block for the seeker, it is probably well to give the question some consideration.

One reaction to this apparent contradiction, on the part of the seeker who has attained some degree of realization, is to view those formulations that are most consonant with his own insight as revealing an authentic Enlightenment, while the incompatible statements are regarded as in essential error and thus not the expression from the matrix of a genuine Enlightenment. As a result, we may have the development of a considerable degree of separative intolerance at a relatively high level. While all this may be quite understandable as a subjective phenomenon and may serve certain psychological needs, nonetheless, objectively considered, it is less than an integral view. Or, even if the seeker does not take so extreme a position, he may view his own expression and those of similar form as necessarily the more comprehensive, while viewing opposed expressions as inferior insights. In general, such attitudes are simply not sound, for even a considerable degree of Enlightenment is compatible with a failure to transcend one's own individual psychology. Indeed, the Transcendental Consciousness as it is on its own level is inevitably stepped down and modified by the psychological temperament of the sadakha,[12] and if the individual has not become cognizant of the relativity of his own psychology, he can very easily fall into the error of projecting his own attitude as an objective universal. Actually, opposed interpretations may be just as valid, and even more valid, and in any case, an Enlightenment that is sufficiently profound will find a relative or partial truth in all authentic formulations.

The philosophic expressions, whether Substantialistic or non-substantialistic, are, in any case, but partial statements, expressions of one or another facet, and are valid as long as taken in a provisional sense. One may know this and acknowledge it and then proceed with the development that accords the better with his Vision. Then there need not be any fundamental conflict with counter-, yet essentially complementary, views. Of necessity, any formulation must be partial and incomplete, however wide its integration.

> 52. *As the GREAT SPACE is not to be*
> *identified with the Universe,*
> *so neither is It to be identified with any Self.*

The SPACE of the symbol is here called the GREAT SPACE to emphasize the fact that it is to be understood as space in the ultimate or generic sense, in contradistinction to the special spaces of perception and conception. Further, IT is neither an objective nor a subjective space and hence may not be designated as either the Self or the Universe.

> 53. *The GREAT SPACE is not God,*
> *but the comprehender of all Gods,*
> *as well as of all lesser creatures.*

The GREAT SPACE transcends and embraces all entities, even the greatest. There is a sense in which we may validly speak of the Divine Person, but, underlying, overlaying, and enveloping even This, is THAT, symbolized by the GREAT SPACE.

> 54. *The GREAT SPACE, or*
> *Consciousness-without-an-object, is the*
> *Sole Reality upon which all objects*
> *and all selves depend and derive their existence.*

The essential additional affirmation of this aphorism is that the GREAT SPACE is the *sole* Reality. What this means seems evident enough until one stops to think about it, and then at once difficulties appear in both the notions "sole" and "reality." First of all, "sole" suggests the meaning of "one," which is clearly abstracted from a matrix that also embraces the notions of "many" and "plurality." In this sense, a sole reality would exclude the possibility of multiplicity, and we would still find ourselves within the dualistic field. Actually THAT must be conceived as both not many and not one, when speaking in the strictly metaphysical sense, but unless we would abandon the effort to build a thinkable and psychologically positive symbol, we must go further than purely negative definition. Actually, the symbol is a psychological value that serves the orientation of individual consciousness and thus is something less than metaphysical truth. Therefore, the accentuation of soleness or oneness is to be conceived as a corrective to the states of consciousness that lie in bondage to the sense of manyness. It is thus not an ultimate conception. However, soleness may be conceived in a sense having a higher, as well as in a sense having a lower, relative validity. So we should think of the soleness as having a unity more like that possessed by the mathematical continuum than that of the bare number "one." For the continuum is a notion of a unity of a totality composed of infinite multiciplicity but not involving relationships between discrete entities. This appears to me the best positive conception as yet possible for suggesting the Reality underlying the negative definition of "not one and not many."

With respect to the notion of "Reality," we have even greater difficulties, for whether used in the philosophic or the pragmatic senses it has had, historically, several meanings. Most commonly, at least in western thought, this notion has been employed in relation to supposed objective existences, and this is obviously not the sense that could apply to the GREAT SPACE, which is neither objective nor subjective. We must, therefore, undertake some effort to derive the meaning that is valid for the aphorism.

Ordinarily, we think of "reality" as in contrast to the notion of "illusion," but this hardly leads to a clear understanding, since each notion becomes negatively defined by the other, and we are little, if at all, advanced to a true conception of what we *feel* in relation to these notions.[13] Pragmatically, we generally have little difficulty in differentiating between many illusions and relative realities, such as a mirage lake and a real lake, but this is not enough to define for us what we mean when these terms are extended to a metaphysical usage. For clearly, as a bare, visual, sense-impression, the mirage lake is as authentic as a real lake. We might say that as aesthetic modification of consciousness the one is as real as the other, but the distinction of reality versus illusion arises when some judgment is added to the pure aesthetic modification. But a judgment does not give reality; it gives either truth or error. If the judgment produces an error, then we are obsessed by an illusion; otherwise there is no illusion.

It would appear that this identification of illusion and error leads to the conclusion that the other of illusion is not reality but truth, and this opens a door for analysis that is much more fruitful. In support of this view, attention is called to the following quotation from Immanuel Kant: "Still less can appearance and illusion be taken as identical. For truth or illusion is not to be found in the objects of intuition, but in the judgments upon them, so far as they are thought. It is therefore quite right to say that the senses never err, not because they always judge rightly, but because they do not judge at all."[14]

If the other of truth is illusion, then it at once becomes evident that the other of reality is appearance, the latter notion not implying illusion unless an erroneous judgment has been made concerning it and in that case, the illusion has been produced by the mistaken judgment and is not a property of the appearance as such. We can now derive a meaning for "reality" that is valid with respect to the usage of the aphorism. "Reality" becomes identical with "Noumenon," and its other, "appearance," with "phenomenon." With this, the distinction becomes epistemologically defined and acquires a certain clarity of meaning.

In the history of western thought, the most important development of the contrasting conceptions of "Noumenon" and "phenomenon" has been in the Greek philosophies and the philosophy of Immanuel Kant. The meanings given in these two usages, while fundamentally related, are not identical; a result growing out of the critical thinking of later times. With Plato, in particular, the noumenon designates the intelligible, or the things of thought, but which are not objects for sensibility. The latter are phenomena and are of an inferior and even undivine order. With Kant, the noumenon is generally equivalent to the thing-in-itself as it is in abstraction from the intuition of the senses, while the phenomenon remains, as it was with the Greeks, the sensibly given object. But unlike the Greeks, Kant did not view the noumenon as an existence given through the pure reason. Pure thought might find it a necessary or useful conception but did not, by itself, give it existence. What Kant has to say here is quite valuable as pointing to a conception that is of fundamental importance in the present work, and accordingly, the following quotation is worthy of special attention.

> In the Critique he says: If I admit things which are objects of the understanding only, and nevertheless can be given as objects of an intuition, though not of sensuous intuition . . .

such things would be called Noumena. . . . Unless, therefore, we are to move in a constant circle, we must admit that the very word phenomena indicates a relation to something the immediate representation of which is no doubt sensuous, but which nevertheless, even without this qualification of our sensibility (on which the form of our intuition is founded), must be something by itself, that is, an object independent of our sensibility. Hence arises the concept of a noumenon, which, however, is not positive, nor a definite knowledge of anything, but which implies only the thinking of something without taking any account of the form of sensuous intuition. But, in order that a noumenon may signify a real object that can be distinguished from all phenomena, *it is not enough that I should free my thought of all conditions of sensuous intuition, but I must besides have some reason for admitting another kind of intuition besides the sensuous*, in which such an object can be given, otherwise my thought would be empty, however free it may be from contradictions.[15]

Kant's significant addition to the Greek conception is the statement that if the noumenon is to be realized as real, and thus more than a formal conception, there must be an intuition of it other than sensuous intuition. This is clearly the intellectual intuition of Schelling and other subsequent philosophers. In the present system, such a function is affirmed but has been called "introception," for reasons to be discussed in a future volume.

At last we are in a position to define "Reality" as the noumenon that is immediately cognized by Introception, or Knowledge through Identity, while "phenomenon" means the sensuous appearance. A third form of cognition would be conceptual representation that occupies a position intermediate between the phenomenon and the noumenon. But we must take a further step, since the Subject or Self, neglected by the Greeks and treated as a constant by Kant, becomes for us a component that is constant and primary only in relation to the object, but in relation to Pure Consciousness is derivative. We might view this Subject as a sort of transcendental phenomenon, i.e., transcendental with respect to the object but standing in something like a phenomenal relationship to Pure Consciousness.

*55. The GREAT SPACE comprehends both the
Path of the Universe and the Path of Nirvana.*

Essentially this aphorism is a reassertion of previous formulations in terms of Consciousness-without-an-object. The two Ways of the Subjective and the Objective are embraced in the one Way of the universal and transcendental comprehender. A consciousness that is sufficiently awakened would find Nirvana and the Universe to be coexistences capable of simultaneous realization.

*56. BESIDE THE GREAT SPACE
THERE IS NONE OTHER.*

Notes to Chapter 6

1. The Subject or Self occupies a position analogous to that of the parameter in mathematics. In simple and general terms, the parameter may be thought of as a local invariant that varies when considered over a larger domain. With respect to a specific case of a given curve, it stands as the invariant element, but in the generation of a whole family of curves of a given type, it is a variable. The ultimate invariant is the plane or space in which the curves lie. This supplies us with a thinkable analogue.

With respect to a specific entity, the invariable identity is the Self, but with respect to all creatures and all modes of consciousness, the Self becomes a parameter that varies. Behind and supporting this parameter is the ultimate invariant, Pure Consciousness Itself. Herein we have a key for the reconciliation of the Atmic doctrine of Shankara and the anatmic doctrine of Buddha. Esotericism states that the Atmic doctrine was a "stepped down" formulation of the Buddha's doctrine and thus was more easily assimilated by relative consciousness, whereas the pure Buddhist doctrine was well-nigh completely incomprehensible without a preliminary reorientation of human consciousness.

2. These are the plus and minus signs.

3. Anyone who has read any considerable amount of mystical literature can hardly fail to be impressed with the frequent affirmations and denials of the same predicate. Often an assertion made is immediately denied, or a counter assertion is made that logically implies the negation of the first. The effect is naturally confusing and can, quite understandably, lead the reader to question the sanity of the writer. But the fact is that the mystic is seeking a formulation that is true with respect to his realization, and he finds that his first statement, while partly true, is also a falsification. The denial or counter assertion is then offered as a correction. Too often the reader is offered no rational explanation and is left to

draw his own conclusions, which are all too likely to be unfavorable to the mystic and to mysticism as such. And, indeed, what is the good of a statement if one cannot depend upon it so as to draw valid conclusions that can be different from other ideas that are not true to the meaning intended? Or, if the credibility of the mystic is not questioned, then it may be concluded that the reality the mystic is reporting is a sort of irrational chaos, something quite incompatible with the notions of harmony, order, and equilibrium—a somewhat that not only defeats all possible knowing, but is quite untrustworthy as well.

Now the fact is, the Gnostic Reality is not a disorderly chaos but is of such a nature that a valid representation cannot be given in our ordinary conceptual forms. These ordinary forms come within the framework of the logic of identity, or otherwise stated, the logic of contradiction. The primary principle here is classification in the form of the dichotomy, i.e., all things are either A or not-A. There is implied the exclusion of all that is neither A nor not-A, or is both A and not-A. This is known in logic as the principle of the "excluded middle," and is employed considerably in reasoning with respect to finite classes. But this is by no means our sole logical principle employed in scientific thought. Thus, mathematics requires the use of logical forms that cannot be reduced to the logic of identity, nor is this adequate for problems dealing with processes of becoming, as in organic evolution. As a consequence, there are logicians who seriously question the universal validity of the principle of the excluded middle. Thus it appears to be unsound when applied to infinite classes, as in the case of the transfinite numbers. As a consequence, then, the mystic may well be justified in his effort to get around the excluded middle, without there being any implication of defect of sanity on his part or lack of orderliness in the Reality he is trying to represent.

Actually, it is not hard to see how the logical dichotomy falls short of being all embracing. Thus, the two classes of A and not-A, which are supposed to embrace all that is, actually do not embrace the thinker who is forming the classification. This is true even when the two classes consist of the Self and the not-Self. The Self in the classification is a projected Self, and therefore an object, and thus is not the actual cognizing witness. The latter embraces both classes, but is not contained privatively in either one. Therefore, it can lie only in the excluded middle.

4. The reality of God as the Supreme Value is not questioned here. The Supreme Value exists in the human soul and may be realized directly. It is the Other that completes the lonely self. The Supreme Value is the Presence in mystic realization. The error of many unphilosophical mystics lies in interpreting the Presence as an existence *in re*, that is, as an objective thing. In the true understanding of the real nature of God, Meister Eckhart reveals himself as one of the clearest seeing of all mystics. For Eckhart, God is the other of the self, and

these two stand in a relation of mutual dependence. Hence, God is not a non-relative primal principle. This primal principle Eckhart called the God-head, a notion that is used by him in a sense analogous to the Buddhistic Shunyata.

5. That mystical insight is a source of knowledge is a primary thesis of the present work. The correctness of this thesis may be, and has been, challenged both on epistemological and psychological grounds. The justification of the thesis thus consists of two parts: (*a*) justification as against philosophic criticism; and (*b*) justification as against psychological criticism. The justification as against philosophical criticism is dealt with in various places throughout this work. The second justification is not needed on the level of Recognition itself, but only for the strictly relative type of consciousness.

6. See Chapter 60, "The Symbol of the Fourth Dimension," in *Pathways Through to Space*, pp. 128–133.

7. This alteration of the location of apparent activity is illustrated by the familiar experience of seemingly seeing surrounding objects move when one looks forth from a train that is starting to leave a station.

8. *Tibetan Yoga and Secret Doctrines*, 3rd Ed., p. 67.

9. Quoted from Baldwin's *Dictionary of Philosophy and Psychology*, Vol. 11, p. 614.

10. For an able discussion of Aestheticism as the predominant form of oriental philosophy, see F. S. C. Northrop's *The Meeting of East and West*.

11. See *The Life Divine* by Sri Aurobindo, Chapter IX, "The Pure Existent," p. 68.

12. The seeker or one who is practicing Yoga.

13. For an illuminating discussion of illusionism, see *The Life Divine* by Sri Aurobindo, Book 11, Chapters V and Vl.

14. *Critique of Pure Reason*. Max Muller translation, p. 293.

15. *Critique of Pure Reason*. Max Muller translation, pp. 217, 219. Italics mine.

Glossary

Note: (Sk) after an entry means that the word is Sanskrit.

Advaita (Sk). A term applied to a Vedantist sect founded by Shankara. The literal meaning is "non-dual." Generally, the system of thought developed by Shankara is regarded as the most thoroughly monistic of all philosophies. However, in the strict sense, the inner core of this philosophy is neither monistic nor non-monistic. Hence, to call it non-dualistic is more correct.

Ambrosia. In the Greek mythology, a celestial substance capable of imparting immortality. (The word means "immortal, undying.") Often thought of as food or a drink. The Sanskrit equivalent is "Amrita." In the most common usage, this term is employed in a figurative sense. Such, however, is not the case as the term is used in this book. The Ambrosia is an actual Substance and at the same time a Force and a Transcendent Consciousness wherein the subject and the object are blended. Any real depth of penetration into the Transcendent Consciousness will bring the individual into an immediate blending with this Ambrosia. It has a quality which is recognizably substantial and at the same time fluidic. But It is fluidic in somewhat the sense that electricity is fluidic, more than in the sense that an ordinary gas or liquid is fluidic. It is quite easy to see how the experience of the Ambrosia should have suggested "wine," and then, the "cup," the "chalice," the "caldron," and the "Holy Grail," as symbols representing It. Thus the search for the Holy Grail is the search for Immortal Life. The "Blood" or the "Royal Blood" is another symbol carrying the same meaning. Here the meaning indicated is "Life" which, in the sense of the Royal Blood, is clearly Immortal Life. The symbolism of the Lord's Supper refers directly to the Ambrosia. The "Bread" represents the substantiality and the "Wine" or "Blood," the fluidic, life-giving quality. To enter Cosmic Consciousness is to partake of the Ambrosia, and this bestows Immortality, though this is by no means all of Its significance. Further, this is not simply the primary immortality in which all things share, but a self-conscious and therefore individual immortality. This immortality is achieved by man and not merely inherited automatically. In this book, the Ambrosia is often referred to as the "Current."

In the "Analytic Psychology" of Dr. C. G. Jung, the term "Libido" acquires, in its most refined development, a meaning that comes close to that of the Ambrosia. Thus it becomes possible to speak of the Libido as Divine.

Ananda (Sk). The literal meaning is "Bliss," "Joy," "Felicity," "Happiness." It is an aspect of the Ambrosia. Hence, the expressions, "Current of Joy," "Current of Bliss," etc. One of the outstanding characteristics of the Higher Consciousness lies in the fact that the different qualities under which It manifests to subject-object consciousness are not definitely separated but are blended. Bliss, Immortal Life, and Knowledge, in the higher sense, are not three separate facts but, rather, three aspects of one fact, or Reality. Ananda, however, lies closer to the affections than to cognition. Hence, Transcendence attained primarily through the affections manifests more as Bliss than as Knowledge, but the division here is not absolute.

Atman (Sk). The "Self," the "I," the "I AM" and the "subjective moment of consciousness." In the highest sense this is the Universal Spirit or the Supreme Soul of the Universe. When this higher meaning is emphasized the term "Paramatman" is commonly employed. The Atman is sometimes used in the sense of the "Divine Monad" and the seventh or highest principle in man. There is, however, a lower usage in which this term is applied to the personal ego. The anatman doctrine of Gautama Buddha, in the more comprehensible sense, refers to the personal ego, and amounts to a denial of the self-existence of this ego. However, there is a higher and more metaphysical application of the doctrine of anatman which constitutes one of the most difficult and profound ideas in all metaphysical thought. Superficially, it would seem that the anatman of Buddha and the Atmavidya, or Knowledge of the Self, of Shankara involve a contradiction. However, such is not the case as it is a matter of difference of emphasis and also of approach to the same Transcendent Reality. The Atman of Shankara is here spelled with a capital "A" while that of Buddha is spelled with a small "a." This affords a key to the reconciliation of the two doctrines. However, the inner Core of Buddha's Teaching is more profound even than that of Shankara, but it is more difficult to understand.

Avidya (Sk). Ignorance or the opposite of Real Knowledge. This is not "ignorance" in the familiar sense of "lack of information." All consciousness or knowledge, however highly developed, so long as it is restricted to the subject-object manifold is Avidya. Only Those who have Awakened to the Higher Consciousness have transcended Avidya or Ignorance. Avidya is the real cause of human suffering, bondage, and evil. Likewise, these are destroyed when Ignorance is destroyed.

Bhagavad-gita (Sk). One of the best known of the Hindu religious scriptures. It is almost wholly in the form of a dialogue between Krishna, who represents the SELF, the Atman, or Cosmic Consciousness, and Arjuna, who symbolizes the egoistic man of action. It gives a brief resume of the Roads by which Union or Yoga may be attained. This is one of the most important manuals that point the Way to Cosmic Consciousness.

Buddha (Sk). Lit., "The Enlightened." This enlightenment is Transcendental Knowledge in the highest sense. It is the State of Knowledge wherein the Real Self is known for what it is. It is the Consciousness that is detached from all that is evanescent and finite or merely phenomenal. The State of Buddhahood is the Supreme State of Holiness.

It is a Custom within the Buddhist community to call a man who has attained Enlightenment a Buddha. Most commonly, Gautama, a Prince of Kapilavastu, is known as *the* Buddha, after His attainment, but there were Buddhas before Him, and others have attained Enlightenment since His time. But He who was born Gautama is the greatest of the Buddhas who have appeared within historic times.

"Buddhism" is the name given to the religious movement that had its origin in the life and teachings of the great Buddha. But, more strictly, "Buddhism" means the unchanging Doctrine or Dharma which underlies all that is evanescent.

Buddhi (Sk). In the microcosmic sense, this is the Spiritual Soul of man and the vehicle of Atman or the Spiritual Self. Buddhi may also be thought of as disembodied Intelligence, the Basis of Discernment, discrimination, and the apprehension of pure Meaning. It is also Compassion, in the highest sense, the very Soul of the Law of Harmony or Equilibrium. In the macrocosmic sense, It is the Universal Soul.

Chit (Sk). Abstract Consciousness; pure Consciousness which is not consciousness of an object.

Chela (Sk). A disciple. The relationship of a Chela to his Guru is far closer than than of a pupil to his teacher. In fact, this relationship is the closest of all human relationships. While a Chela generally receives more or less instruction, the essential function of a Guru is to effect a Transformation in the consciousness of the Chela so that what we have called "Cosmic Consciousness" may awaken in the latter.

Consciousness. In its most immediate sense, the state of "being aware." In the broad, though common, sense, consciousness is the state we are in when not in the state of dreamless sleep. Quite often this term is used in the sense that should be restricted to self-consciousness, or the consciousness of being conscious. Consciousness that is not self-conscious is very often regarded as unconsciousness. The whole question of what consciousness is becomes a very subtle matter, once an individual goes beneath the surface of meaning.

Consciousness of the Self. This is consciousness of the subject to all consciousness, but, in the highest sense, this is not consciousness of the subject regarded as an object. It may be called "consciousness turned toward its source or the positive pole of consciousness." It is extremely difficult to attain this consciousness, for very easily it reduces to consciousness of a subtle object. To attain consciousness of the Self in its purity is to Awaken to Cosmic or Transcendent Consciousness. Sometimes the foregoing is the meaning implied when the term "self-consciousness" is used, but more commonly the latter means "consciousness of being conscious."

Cosmic Consciousness. In the strict sense, this is Consciousness on the level of some Cosmic Plane of Being and so is not a consciousness of form or phenomena. However, the term is employed in this work in a somewhat looser sense, more closely approximating that given by Dr. Bucke in "Cosmic Consciousness." In the latter sense, any consciousness attained by awakening out of crystallized subject-object consciousness is called "Cosmic Consciousness." It thus covers a zone intermediate between subject-object consciousness and Cosmic Consciousness in the strictest sense. See "Transcendent Consciousness."

Current of Bliss or Joy. See "Ambrosia."

Dharma (Sk). The Sacred Law or Doctrine; often used in a sense somewhat analogous to that of "duty." But this latter interpretation is deceptive. It rather carries the meaning of true alignment with Essential Being or Reality in thought, feeling, and action.

Dhyana (Sk). The Door to, or Vehicle of Prajna or Transcendental Wisdom. It may be thought of as a higher function of consciousness, not within the range of study of Current western psychologic methodology. Often translated "meditation," but this is deceptive as most meditation deals with a content, while Dhyana is a Way of Consciousness that transcends content.

Egoistic Consciousness. This is the consciousness of one's self as distinct from other selves. The feeling of "I am I and none other." It is opposed to the State of Consciousness known as Buddhahood, wherein the sense of self as distinct from other selves is destroyed. Egoistic consciousness is a fundamental barrier to Liberation or Enlightenment.

Elixir of Life. See "Ambrosia."

Emptiness which is Fullness. Transcendent Consciousness appears as though It were emptiness from the standpoint of subject-object consciousness, but when transcendentally Realized is Known to be utter Fullness.

Gautama (Sk). The sacerdotal name of the family of the great Buddha. See "Buddha."

Guru (Sk). A Spiritual Teacher. Essentially not a teacher of information, but one who guides and nurtures the Awakening of the Chela or Disciple.

Guru-current. Used in the sense of a general spiritual influence or force which tends toward the Awakening of Spiritual Consciousness in the aspirant.

Hegel. A philosopher who is the leading representative of the German Idealists. His school is also known as Absolute Idealism.

Ignorance. See "Avidya."

Kant, Immanuel. The leading German philosopher and considered by many as the greatest philosopher of the West. He is the chief representative of the critical spirit in philosophy. By this is meant the recognition that before a valid construction in terms of knowledge is possible, it is necessary to study critically the nature and limits of knowledge as such.

Karma (Sk). In the general sense, the principal of Law in action. More specifically, it is the idea of moral causality carrying a meaning which, in part, overlaps the western idea of causality and, in part, the idea of destiny.

Krishna (Sk). An Indian Saviour of about 5,000 years ago. This name appears in the Bhagavad-gita as a symbol for the Higher Self. In the latter sense, "Krishna" is a principle somewhat analogous to the mystical "Christ" of St. Paul.

Liberation. Consciousness in the State of Freedom from bondage to form. It is the same as Nirvanic Consciousness.

Loka (Sk). A field or sphere of consciousness, force, and substance subject to some principle of modification. Thus, the form of consciousness defined by Kant's "Critique of Pure Reason" would be a particular Loka of consciousness.

Consciousness cast under another form would be another Loka, etc. The Hell, the Purgatory, and the Paradise of Dante are three Lokas of consciousness. In the ultimate sense, we must regard the consciousness of every individual as a Loka. The term has both broad and narrow meanings. Liberated or Nirvanic Consciousness is not a Loka, however, as such is a pure Consciousness freed from the imposition of form.

Manas (Sk). Very commonly translated as the "mind," since this is its literal meaning. However, "mind" in western usage, particularly in philosophy, has come to have a much broader meaning than "Manas," so this translation is confusing. See the discussion in Chapter 77 on pp. 166. "Manas" also has the meaning of "Higher Ego," or the sentient reincarnating principle in man. It is Manas that makes man an intelligent and moral being. It is the prime distinguishing characterisic of man when he is contrasted to the animals and certain orders of unintelligent spiritual beings.

Mara (Sk). The personified force of evil or temptation. It is the adversary of him who seeks to enter the Path that leads to Freedom from bondage to embodied consciousness. In other words, Mara is the great barrier to Cosmic or Transcendent Consciousness.

Maya (Sk). Illusion. It is the power which renders phenomenal existence possible and, hence, is lord over the flux of becoming. The counter principle is "Reality," predicated only of that which is eternal and changeless.

Nectar. See "Ambrosia."

Nirmanakaya (Sk). A mysterious form of embodiment which may be assumed by One who has attained Enlightenment and still retains correlation with relative consciousness. This is the most objective phase of the Trikaya, the other two phases being the Sambhogakaya and the Dharmakaya. The doctrine of the Trikaya is quite involved and simply cannot be understood by the unillumined relative consciousness. In one sense, these may be viewed as the three Bodies of a Buddha, but, in another sense, they are impersonal metaphysical concepts. On this Level, there is not the sharp division between principles and entities that is characteristic of relative thinking. One view, quite current among western students, regards the three Kayas as alternative states of consciousness which may be chosen in an exclusive sense. Thus the Dharmakayas are regarded as distinct from the Nirmanakayas. But the profounder reality is, that a full Buddha is conscious on the level of all three Kayas and thus is, at once, a Dharmakaya, a Sambhogakaya, and a Nirmanakaya. An Entity who has won this triple Crown unites in himself the possibilities of the Non-Relative and relative worlds. We may conceive of an incomplete Enlightenment which reaches only to the level of the Nirmanakaya, or of another form of Enlightenment which attains the central Core of Shunyata combined with a refusal to accept any correlation with relative consciousness. In this case, we would have an exclusively Dharmakayic State. In such an instance, we do have a contrast between the Dharmakayas and the Nirmanakayas. Such Dharmakayas are incapable of affecting the destiny of relative consciousness, save through Those who have won the Triple Crown. But the latter are as much Dharmakayas as they are Nirmanakayas. Thus, in principle there is not an exclusive division between the three Kayas.

The Dharmakayic State is spiritually the highest of all but, in the humanistic sense, the Nirmanakaya is especially honored because it is through the Nirmanakaya, and only through It, that the redemption of mankind is possible. However, the Light of the Nirmanakaya is derived from the Dharmakaya and thus it is not the contrast between Dharmakaya and Nirmanakaya that is important, but rather the contrast between the pure Dharmakaya and the combined Dharmakaya, Sambhogakaya, and Nirmanakaya. It is this combination that links the Transcendent with the relative.

Nirvana (Sk). While the meaning of this term is not unambiguous as used in literature, sometimes referring to pure subjectivity and at others including Shunyata, it seems the better practice to restrict it to the former meaning. Nirvana thus stands as the opposite of objective consciousness but is comprehended by Shunyata which comprehends objective as well as subjective possibilities. Nirvana may be regarded as Consciousness-without-an-object-but-with-the-Subject while Shunyata is Consciousness-without-an-object-and-without-a-subject. Both are formless as to content. This latter fact affords a basis for uniting the two States under the notion of "blown-out," the literal meaning of Nirvana. But this leads to confusion, as the difference between pure subjectivity and Shunyata is as great as the difference between pure subjectivity and objective consciousness. To be sure, neither State can be imagined by relative consciousness, but considerable clarification is achieved by building a thinkable logical model.

We may regard Nirvana as Liberation, Shunyata as Enlightenment. Not Nirvana, but Shunyata is the *summum bonum*. There is reason to believe that the West may find Enlightenment more acceptable than Liberation. While pure subjective Liberation is peculiarly close to the religious feeling of the Hindu, it fails of being vital to the more active consciousness of the Occidental. But Enlightenment occupies a neutral position between these two. Since the central emphasis of Buddha was not Liberation so much as Enlightenment, He stands as the one genuine spiritual World Teacher that has been known in historic times. Shankara spoke to the Hindu and more especially to the Brahmin community, while Jesus was oriented to the more objective occidental spirit. Thus neither of these two are synthetic World Teachers. They stand rather as specialists. Hinduism can never be effectively transplanted into the West, nor will Christianity ever be a really effective force in India or China. But in Buddha and the Dharma of Buddha there is a common uniting ground for both the subjective and objective geniuses. Thus it is that while the Advaita Vedanta of Shankara is only slightly different from Buddhism on one side, on the other the western scientist finds much in Buddhism that sounds like his own thought. Yet, all the while there is a marked contrast between the Vedanta and the western scientific spirit. I repeat, Buddha is the only known World Teacher.

Nirvani (Sk). One who has attained Nirvana, hence, an Emancipated Soul. In general, the perfected individual becomes a Nirvani only after death of the physical body, but there are some, of whom Gautama Buddha is the great example, who attained this State while still living.

Nirvikalpa Samadhi (Sk). The highest form of ecstatic Consciousness possible to man. It may be regarded as a kind of Nirvanic Consciousness, modified by reason of the individual retaining correlation with a physical body. It is a State of Formless Consciousness. It seems to be the rule that this State is only attained in deep trance, but it is possible to attain It without trance, though in this case there is a decided dimming of the outer consciousness. While Buddha did not condemn the trance state, He did not regard it as necessary and advocated Realization without trance.

Philosopher's Stone. That principle by which the base nature is transmuted into the Spiritual and Divine. Other usage of this term exists, but the above is the profounder meaning and is the sense employed in the text.

Realization. The Awakening to the Transcendent or Cosmic Consciousness. As used in the text when this word is given this meaning, it is spelled with a capital "R." Realization is not a development of consciousness in the subject-object sense. It implies a radical event involving a shifting of the level of consciousness.

Recognition. Used in the text with essentially the same meaning as "Realization," this term emphasizes the implication that Awakening is a return to that which had been "known" but which had been forgotten, perhaps for ages. The use of this word in this sense does imply a theory of knowledge that diverges in important respects from the more current theories. It implies that

Real Knowledge is not derived from experience, but rather that experience is the occasion or the catalytic agent which arouses the Recognition of inherent Knowledge.

Relative consciousness. The ordinary kind of human consciousness involving the relationship of a knower to a known, the perceiver to a perceived, etc. It also involves knowledge of objective terms in relation to each other. It stands in radical contrast to Cosmic or Transcendental Consciousness.

Samadhi (Sk). The ecstatic state wherein the individual awakes to some more or less transcendent level. It may or may not involve the trance state. There are several degrees of Samadhi of which Nirvikalpa Samadhi is the highest. It is the means of cross-correlation between various levels of consciousness, in no two of which does consciousness manifest under the same form. The meaning of Samadhi is not sharply differentiated from that of Dhyana, save that Dhyana is the Door to Prajna or Transcendental Wisdom, while there are lesser forms of Samadhi that open doors to levels of consciousness substantially less than Transcendental Wisdom.

Samsara (Sk). A Buddhist term including the same meaning as the "world-field" used in the text. It has, however, a wider connotation as it includes all levels of consciousness in which there is an awareness of an object, combined with the delusion that the object has an existence independent of the observer. Thus, the dream-state, while not a part of the world-field in the narrower sense, is part of Sangsara. The relatively subjective realms such as the various heavenly worlds, the purgatories and the hells are also part of Sangsara. Even relatively high orders of Seership, like that of Swedenborg, penetrate no further than superior aspects of Sangsara. However, Enlightened Consciousness includes the possibility of awareness of objects, but the difference in this case lies in the fact that the dependent existence of the object is Realized. Such awareness of objects is not Sangsaric, as it does not imply bondage to the object.

So long as the independence of objects is believed in—a state that implies bondage to objects—Sangsara appears as the Adversary, i.e., Mara, Satan, etc. But just so soon as this delusion is destroyed, Sangsara in this sense vanishes. This vanishing of Sangsara applies to the past as well as to the present and future, for it ceases, not only to be, but as well ever to have been. This is a mystery to relative consciousness which is rendered intelligible only by the transformation of consciousness-base known as the Awakening.

In psychological terms, Sangsara is a detached psychical complex and thus constitutes a threat to psychical integration. Left to itself, the Sangsaric state leads to exhaustion of the life-stream and real unconsciousness. The practical function of the various racial and world-Saviours is the effecting of pragmatic interlocking of the detached complex with the Root-Source of Life and Consciousness. In the case of the Disciple, this function is a more or less conscious correlation, but with the mass of men it operates through the psychologic unconsciousness. Without the function of the Saviours, the state of most men would be quite hopeless. The Saviour-Function may be viewed as religious, philosophical, or psychological. The form of interpretation is a matter of indifference, provided it is such as to render the function acceptable to men.

Sankhya (Sk).   One of the six Indian schools of philosophy; originated by Kapila. It teaches a dualistic system in which spirit and matter are regarded as co-eternal and not simply aspects of a common and absolute base.

SAT (Sk).   This term represents Absoluteness rather than the Absolute. It is the ever-present, eternal, and unchanging Reality, THAT which is neither Being nor not-Being, but the Base of all that is. It has the same reference as Shunyata, Tao, Dharmakaya or Consciousness-without-an-object-and-without-a-subject.

Self-consciousness.   In the highest sense, this is "consciousness of the Self." More commonly, it is the consciousness of being conscious, implying the recognition that there is a perceiving subject but not, necessarily, the Recognition of the pure Consciousness of the Self. Self-consciousness distinguishes human from animal consciousness.

Shankara (Sk).   This is the name of a Brahmin philosopher who is generally regarded as the greatest of the Vedantic Sages. He is the founder of the Advaita (non-dual) philosophy. His philosophy, together with that of Buddha, is regarded as the most thoroughly monistic of any ever promulgated. At the Core, there is no difference between Buddha and Shankara, but the latter supplied a more comprehensible philosophic statement. However, Shankara attained superior comprehensibility at the price of a partial veiling of the pure Dharma. Buddha represents the superior synthesis while Shankara attained a superior expression of one wing of the Buddhist Enlightenment.

Shunyata (Sk).   Literally Voidness. It is the same as the Dharmakaya. The Voidness is such only to relative consciousness. Actually, It is the one substantial Reality. The question is often raised as to the wisdom of speaking of ultimate Fullness as Voidness, since psychologically the latter term often produces difficulties. But there is a still greater psychological difficulty, which grows out of the fact that any image of fullness which can be presented to relative consciousness suggests objective content. The result is the substitution of one Sangsaric state for another and this is not Enlightenment. Real Enlightenment implies the radical dissolution of all anchorage to the object and hence the aspiration of the student must be directed to THAT which is never an object in any sense. To relative consciousness, this can only mean polarization to seeming Voidness.

Subject-object consciousness. The same as "relative consciousness." In this term, the subject-object character of ordinary human consciousness is emphasized.

Tamas (Sk). The quality of indifference in the inferior sense. It is thus the polar opposite of the High Indifference, which is a State of perfect affective Fullness or Balance. The quality of Tamas tends toward real death or unconsciousness.

Transcendent Consciousness. In the present work, this is a very important term and requires special discussion. In the broadest sense, the Transcendent stands in radical contrast to the empirical. It is that which lies beyond experience. Hence, Transcendent Consciousness is non-experiential consciousness; and, since experience may be regarded as consciousness in the stream of becoming or under time, the form is of necessity a timeless Consciousness. The actuality of such Consciousness can never be proved directly from experience when the latter term is taken in this restricted sense. Thus, It is either a philosophic abstraction or a direct mystical Recognition. In this work, Its actuality is asserted on the basis of a direct mystical Recognition. This term is not here used as a synonym of "Cosmic Consciousness," but is reserved for pure, formless, mystic Consciousness. On the other hand, mystic Consciousness which gives a content in terms of subtle form or in terms involving any kind of multiplicity, I call "Cosmic Consciousness."

Since the appearance of the "Critique of Pure Reason," many philosophic students have maintained that Kant has definitely shown the impossibility of any Transcendent Consciousness or Knowledge. (The transcendental element in the apperceiving power of the Self is distinguished by Kant from the "Transcendent.") If we were to assume that the Kantian analysis comprehended all possible functions of consciousness, apparently the foregoing conclusion would be unavoidable. But the whole problem rests upon the actuality of the function of Dhyana, which was outside the Kantian analysis as well as beyond the reach of western psychologic methodology. Since my whole case rests upon the affirmation of the actuality of the function of Dhyana, it is not answered by a simple reference to the older criticism. On the contrary, a valid criticism, in this respect, would first have to establish the point that there is no such function as Dhyana. This could only be done by one who was in a position to prove that he was familiar with every possibility of consciousness and found no Dhyana function. Negative proof is possible only when every possibility is delimited; and, while this method is often successful in mathematics, there is always presupposed an explicit definition of the whole field of discourse under discussion. But from the standpoint of the present epistemology, this is arbitrary. A possibility is proved either by experience or Realization, but a theoretical delimitation of all possibilities is quite another matter.

I am quite well aware that the scientific imagination has shown great capacity in inventing objective interpretations of all observable phenomena. It is also an extra-logical canon of science that the presumption of truth is to be given hypotheses that do not violate established forms of interpretation. But, logically considered, this is no more than a reference to the authority of style or custom. For my part, I do not share in this superstitious reverence for style and custom and offer respect only to the logical spirit of science. But all this applies only to observable phenomena. When we consider the meaningful content of consciousness, we are definitely outside the reach of western scientific methodology, though not, therefore, beyond the range of all possible science. Now, it is only when dealing with meaningful content that it is possible to reach the realm of Dhyana.

Transcendent Knowledge. This term implies the assertion of a Knowledge the actuality of which modern empiric philosophers would deny. It is true that there is no such thing as a transcendent subject-object knowledge. But it is not in this sense that the term is used here, but rather as "Knowledge through Identity." The following question then arises: What is the difference between Transcendent Consciousness and Transcendent Knowledge? The distinction is admittedly subtle. We might say that It is the Transcendent Consciousness as reflected through the knowledge quale. Thus, a Transcendent Consciousness manifested through an affective quale would not be Transcendent Knowledge. The assertion of the Reality of this Knowledge implies that Knowledge may descend from the Transcendent to the relative domain. It does not imply that all knowledge necessarily has that source, as certainly in some sense some knowledge comes from experience. Following the Indian usage, the descending Knowledge would be Vidya, while mere empiric knowledge would be avidya.

Vedanta (Sk). This is the group of systems that form a philosophic interpretation of the Upanishads. The earliest Vedantic system originates with Vyasa, and is at least 3,300 years old. Its most systematic and philosophically adequate formulation was given by Shankara, about 2,500 years ago. The latter is known as the Advaita Vedanta, the most consistently monistic philosophy in existence. It is in the latter sense the Vedanta is referred to in this work.

The Vedanta, like the Theosophia and the Gnosis, implies descent of Real Knowledge from a Transcendent Level.

Index

Action, 401
  abstraction and, 30–31
  and affection, 128
  ascetic, 84, 160–163
  and causality, 48
  creative principle and, 27, 117, 144, 397–401, 405–408
  and discrimination, 148, 162–163
  during transcendence, 7, 77–78, 90–92, 104–105, 121–123, 142, 150–151, 278
  and idea/reference, 241–251, 320–321
  and integration, 121–123, 184–185
  and karma, 73–78, 266
  righteous/*dharmic*, 145–148, 147–148
  spontaneity and, 26, 79–80, 186
  and state of High Indifference, 186
  will and, 37, 90–92, 144, 161, 184, 278
Advaita Vedanta, 33, 415, 422
  See also Vedanta
Aestheticism, 407
Affection(s), 128–129, 169–170
  and cognition, 169
  and Realization, 166–167
  silencing of, 138
Agnosticism, 109, 407
Ahamkara (negative aspect of individuality), 174
Akasha (Sky/Space), 294
Ambition(s), transcendence of, 6
Ambrosia, Current of, 415
  breath and, 4, 6
  experience of, 15, 19–21, 29
  and external attachment(s), 15
  and immortality, 29
  and interpersonal contact, 7
  Shakti as, 42
Ananda (Bliss), 32, 416
  See also Sanskrit
Animal consciousness, 47
  affection and, 132
  and ego, 59

Animism, 113
Aphorisms, On Consciousness Without An Object, 309–314
  commentaries on, 354–414
  discussion of, 315–414
Archimedes, lever of, 44
Aristotle, 107, 111, 124, 300
  and conception/perception, 191–194
Art
  and Awakening, 132
  philosophy and, 319–320
  physical conception and, 325
Asceticism
  alternative paths and, 84, 164–166, 170
  appearance of, 20
  Awakening and, 150–151, 160
  physical body and, 9, 20
  practice of, 160–163
A Search in Secret India (Brunton), 26
Atheism, 83
  appearance of, 173
Atman, 416
  light of, 6, 25, 29
  mind/*manas* and, 167–170, 193
  recognition of Self as, 5, 25, 29, 65, 169, 257
  and space, 185, 200, 378–384
Atman-Buddhi-Manas as intellectual principle, 32–33
Attention, 26
  inferior/superior, 48
Attitude, 26
  and belief, 318–319, 320
  discipline and, 161–163, 165–166, 253–301
  extroverted/introverted, 335–336
  and Meaning, 84, 249–250
  religious, 320
  of renunciation, 184
  and subservient worship, 56–57
  toward food, 72–73
Austerity, 165–166
  See also Asceticism; Renunciation

427

Avidya, 17, 416
  See also Ignorance
Avidya (Ignorance), 178
Awakening
  barriers to, 174–182, 256–257
  basis of, 17, 24, 54–56, 79–85, 86, 100, 112–117, 119–121, 156, 162, 178, 181–182
  of *Buddhi*, 32–33
  and death, 95–98, 115, 159
  dimensionality and, 131–132, 145, 157–160, 258, 343–344
  and egoism, 70–73, 167
  and Guru, 80–85, 419
  to Knowledge, 5–6, 14, 30, 53, 64–68, 86–89, 107–117, 150–151, 159, 178, 244
  and occult powers, 59–63
  omniscience and, 39
  phenomenal universe and, 136–139, 157–160, 178, 181–182
  and religion, 78–79, 160
  and space/time, 201, 322–323, 378–384
  subjective meditation and, 12, 181–182
  See also Recognition

Bacon, Francis, 111, 125
Balzac, 112, 125
Baptism of the Spirit (St. Paul), 29
  See also Ambrosia, Current of
Beatrice, 78–79
Beauty
  cognition and, 170
  cosmic vs. transcendental, 14, 55
  love and, 129
  physical conception and, 325
  Self and, 42–43
  woman and, 41
Being
  and Beauty, 42–43
  and becoming, 393–394, 401–402, 425–426
  and creative principle, 397–401
  false predication and, 177–178, 179–180
  and idea/reference, 241–251, 329–330
  and non-Being, 135, 328–329
  Point-I/Space-I, 186–189, 322–323, 378–384
  and Sanskrit designations, 31–32
Benevolence, 271
Bhagavad Gita, 417
  quotation(s), 22
  Recognition and, 25–26, 73, 258

Birth
  Awakening and, 78–79, 87, 150–151, 157–160
  and becoming, 393–394
  and death, 94–98, 150, 159, 271, 393–396
  and Great Mother Unconscious, 293
  spatial void and, 380
Blavatsky, H. P., 112
Blessing(s)
  and High Indifference, 99–106
  and karma/causality, 76–78
Bliss, 16, 418
  Ananda, 32
  creative principle and, 64, 396, 397–401, 405–408
  current of, 19–21, 37
  and fire of consciousness, 37
  heavenly worlds and, 95
  and karma/causality, 76–78
  of *Nirvana*, 27
  and state of High Indifference, 186, 340–341
  unbroken concentration and, 8
  See also Ambrosia, Current of
Bodhi tree, 140
Body, physical
  asceticism and, 9, 150–151
  and Awakening, 34, 157–160
  and current of bliss, 20–21, 27, 42, 57–59, 72–73, 269
  and death, 93–98, 151, 271
  and electro-magnetic force, 36–37, 54, 122, 183, 270
  fire of consciousness and, 35, 36, 225, 270
  of Guru, 81–82
  and karma, 73–78
  lifeforce of, 10, 34, 272, 277
  out-of-, experience, 36–37
  purification of, 7, 72–73, 75–78
  Siva/Shakti and, 42
  and soul, 200–201
  sustaining power of, 133–139, 157, 183, 330
Boehme, Jacob, 19, 112
Bondage
  of action, 30, 75
  and false predication, 176–177, 400
  illusion and, 137–138, 364–365
  and karma/causality, 73–78, 266
  Sangsara and, 341–342
  and sleep/dream states, 93–98
  and space/time, 197–208, 378–384, 402–403
  theological orthodoxy and, 83
  thought and, 307, 322
  and truth, 88, 89

Brahman, 16
  Atman as, 32
  indivisibility of, 200
Brahmanism, 19
Brahmasutras, 3
Breath
  Ambrosia of, 4, 6
  contemplation and, 3–4
Brunton, Paul, 26
Bucke, Dr. R. M., 12, 23
  and Immanuel Kant, 33–34
  transcendental consciousness and, 14, 69
Buddha, 111, 155, 169, 193, 241, 417, 422
  combined paths of, 33, 275
  form/formlessness and, 13–14
  predicament of, 140–142
  and space/time, 199, 207
  teachings of, 73, 151, 340
  thought vs. feeling and, 45
Buddhi, 193, 417
  and intellect, 32–33
  manas and, 169
  See also Sanskrit
Buddhism, 19, 83, 252, 305, 407
  and *Anatma/Nastikata*, 220, 353, 412
  Tibetan, 221, 224
Buddhist Bible (Goddard), 220, 221, 228
Bushmen, of Australia, 59

Caesar-power, 200–203, 283
  and space power, 207
Calmness, 267
Causality
  absence of, 347
  and consciousness without an object, 360–361
  and false predication, 176–177, 333
  Guru and, 80–85
  isolation of, 11
  and karma, 73–78
  Self and, 22
  selfishness and, 48
  soul and, 30
  and state of High Indifference, 186
  transcendence of, 6, 16, 29, 265–266
Certainty
  egoism and, 70–73
  Knowledge and, 40, 86, 110–117
Changelessness, 16, 27, 177
  change and, 247
  and consciousness without an object, 365–366

Charm, 41
Chela (disciple), 417
Chinese philosophy, 230–231
Chit (Consciousness), 32, 417
  mind/*manas* and, 168–170
  and Recognition, 170
  See also Sanskrit
Choice, bliss of freedom and, 12
Chosen Race, 47
Christ, Jesus, 111, 241
  form/formlessness and, 14
  immaculate conception of, 42
  and Kingdom of Heaven, 141, 169
  as mystic, 19, 193
  and Nicodemus, 293
  occult powers and, 62–63
  and Saint Paul, 80
  and space/time, 199, 200, 200–201
  subject/object consciousness and, 18–19
  theological superstitions and, 82–83
  and Water of Life, 29
  works/words of, 82, 295
Christian orthodoxy
  and concept of evil, 55
  crucifixion and, 157–160
  and Holy Ghost, 64
  theological superstitions and, 82–83
Cogito ergo sum (Descartes), 112
Cognition, 129
  and conception/perception, 191–194, 258–259, 354–355, 367–368, 371–372
  and equality, 140
  language and, 194–197, 208, 321–322, 354–355
  lifeforce and, 272
  mind/*manas* and, 169, 371–372
  and sensation, 130, 169
Communion, 19
  and equality, 53
  experience of, 152, 208–212
  and presence of Realization, 69–70
  totality of, 92
  worship and, 56–57
Compassion
  Buddha and, 33
  and desire for wisdom, 53, 104
  during transcendence, 106
  and karma/causality, 77–78
  Sherifa and, 212–213
  transformation and, 89, 156, 170, 232
  world of form and, 14

Compte, August, 407
Conation, 128
Conception, 191–194, 267–268, 319–320,
    341–342
  and consciousness without an object,
    360–361, 399–401
  expression of, 211–212, 315–414
  and interpretation, 352
  and space/time, 197–208, 376, 378–384
  and transcendental symbols, 245, 291, 295
  universal energy and, 324–327
Conceptualists, 191–192
Conduct, right, 145–148
Confidence, 170
Consciousness, 418
  action and, 7, 16, 37, 54–56, 73–78, 90–92,
    144–145, 150–151, 167, 186, 278,
    401–402, 405–408
  Awakening of, 8, 12, 14, 32–33, 54–56,
    64–68, 78–79, 84, 86–89, 119–121,
    150–151, 156, 159
  barriers of, 174–182, 256–257, 327
  of Buddha, 14, 33, 45, 114, 140–142, 169
  Chit, 32, 168–170
  contemplation and, 3–5, 6, 26, 46–48,
    167–168, 208–212, 253–301, 315–414
  cosmic/transcendent, 12–14, 47–49, 71,
    76–78, 85–89, 102–106, 119–121, 125,
    127, 131, 150–151, 157–160, 163, 167,
    179–180, 197–208, 209, 241–251,
    425–426
  and creative principle, 64, 73–78, 84,
    397–401
  dimensionality of, 128–133, 144–145, 157,
    258, 343–344, 368
  and evidential proof, 107–117, 149, 159,
    177, 318, 331
  of Jesus Christ, 14, 19, 34, 42, 62–63, 78–79,
    114, 131, 169, 200
  mystical, 12–14, 19, 38–41, 46–48, 107–117,
    148, 193, 252–301
  and occult powers, 59–63, 167–168
  omniscient, 38–41
  open-eyed meditation and, 9
  relative, 6, 8, 12, 13, 16–17, 54–56, 62,
    64–69, 70–73, 74–78, 86–89, 107–117,
    135–139, 140–141, 150–151, 157–160,
    167, 174–182, 191–194, 319–320,
    341–342, 423
  of Self, 13–14, 29, 46–48, 73, 76–78, 92,
    99–106, 131, 144–145, 150–151,
    208–212, 252–301

self-, and egoism, 13, 16–17, 23, 39, 42,
    63–64, 70–73, 74–78, 93–98, 119–121,
    140–141, 167, 174–182, 319–320,
    341–342
  superior/inferior, 59–60, 63–64, 70, 87, 89,
    104, 114, 120, 132, 159, 163, 305–309
  transformation of, 5, 21, 25–26, 32–33,
    54–56, 64–68, 70, 76–78, 80–85, 84,
    86–89, 93–98, 99–106, 119–121, 131,
    150–151, 157–160, 163, 170, 186–189,
    208–212, 241–251, 252–301, 341–342
  unlimited Power of, 16, 42, 46–48, 84,
    144–145, 178, 285–288, 354–414
  See also Transcendent being/consciousness
Contemplation, 3
  Aphorisms of, On Consciousness Without
    An Object, 315–414
  and joy, 51–52
  mind/*manas* and, 168
  on That, 6, 118–119
  Sage teachings and, 26
Copernicus, 88–89, 298
Cosmic Consciousness, 12–14, 47–49, 243,
    418
  and Awakening, 78–79, 89, 157–160, 163
  barriers to, 174–182, 256–257
  dimensionality and, 131, 145, 157–160, 258,
    343–344
  Guru and, 417
  and knowledge, 85–89, 107–117, 125, 131,
    179–180, 209, 425–426
  and solar/planetary recognition, 56–57
  and space/time, 197–208, 378–384
  See also Consciousness; Transcendent
    Being/Consciousness
Cosmic Consciousness (Bucke), 12, 31, 49, 224
Courage, and responsibility, 166
Craving
  joy and, 20
  See also Desire(s)
Creative Will
  and absence of evil, 144
  Ananda, 32
  attitude and, 26–27
  and bliss, 399–401
  conscious awakening and, 8, 117, 143
  and consciousness without an object,
    360–361, 397–401
  and false predication, 181
  and illusion, 180–182
  inspiration and, 10
  and religion, 63–64

space and, 405–408
woman and, 41–42
Crest-Jewel (Shankara), 37
Critique of Pure Reason (Kant), 169, 242, 251, 317, 374, 410–411, 425–426
Crucifixion, 34
  resistance and, 399
  transformation and, 157–160
Current of Ambrosia. *See* Ambrosia, Current of; Bliss; Joy
Cycle of Necessity, 24

Dance of Life (Havelock), 319
Dante, 112, 125
Darkness
  and compassion, 156
  crucifixion and, 34
  experience of, 29
  relative consciousness and, 6, 72, 327
  Self and, 13, 39, 72
Darshan, 84–85
Darwin, 247–248
Death, 34
  absence of, 50, 271, 396–397
  Awakening and, 78–79, 115, 150–151, 159, 294
  during transcendence, 106, 159
  relativity of, 151, 393–396
  sleep and, 93–98
Democracy, 97
  and equality, 139–140
  inefficiencies of, 153–156
Democritus, 191
Descartes, 111, 255
Desire(s)
  asceticism and, 160–163
  as barrier to Self, 174–182, 256–257
  and compassion, 104
  current of bliss and, 20
  for death, 93
  energy of, 47, 270
  for knowledge, 24, 30, 53, 64–68, 271
  mind and, 306
  raja of, 168
  and Recognition, 28, 79–85, 170, 174, 175–176
  transcendence of, 6, 105, 106, 161–163, 255–256
Detachment
  and asceticism, 160, 161–163
  and discipline, 166, 253–301
  and indifference, 99–106, 124–126, 181

  and Recognition, 88, 170
  and silencing of affections, 138
Determinism, 402–404
Deussen, Paul, 3, 263
Dharmakaya (voidness), 230, 424–425
Dharma (Righteousness), 145–148, 418
  absence of, 153–155
Dhyana (Door, to Wisdom), 229, 231, 243, 275, 418, 425–426
  discipline of, 234
Dialectic materialsim, 200–201
Differentiation, lack of, 16
Dimensionality
  subject/object consciousness and, 128–133, 143, 144, 145, 343–344
  transformation and, 157–160, 258
Dirac, 136
Direct Realization (Shankara), 8
Discipline(s)
  alternative paths of, 32–33, 55, 66–69, 72, 82, 164–166, 170, 233, 252–301
  asceticism and, 150–151, 160–163
  Christian, 232
  dispassion as, 170, 253–301
  monastic, 164–166
  morality and, 54–56
  and sleep/dream states, 96, 97–98
  of thought vs. feeling, 45–46, 66, 275, 305–309
  See also Dhyana
Discrimination
  Awakening and, 40–41, 181–182, 322–323
  dharmic action and, 147–148
  heavenly worlds and, 95
  illusion and, 179, 181
  and Liberation, 182
  and Meaning, 84, 332
  Point-I/Space-I, 186–189, 322–323, 378–384
Divinity
  and creative principle, 397–401
  Guru and, 22, 81–85
  and karma/causality, 77–78
  knowledge and, 65, 110, 182, 329, 346
  recognition of, 7, 40–41, 62, 77–78, 182, 187–188
  of Self, 46–48, 346
  and space/time, 200–208, 378–384
  and state of High Indifference, 106, 181, 283
  superstition and, 63
  and Will, 165
Doubt, absence of, 92

Dreaming, 9–10, 330
  and death, 95–98
  illusion and, 179
  transformation and, 293
  universe and, 178
Drug-induced states, 114–115
Duality
  and absence of evil, 144
  end of, 104–105, 106, 144–145, 415
  freedom from (*nirdvandva*), 298
  and *Sangsara/Maya*, 119–121
  worship and, 56–57
Duty, 145–148
  See also Dharma

Eckhart, Meister, 299, 413–414
Economic power, 155, 159, 203–205
Ecstasy, 41, 275, 297
  and physical body, 57–58
Efficiency, 153
Effort. *See* Self-effort
Egoism, 13, 256, 419
  and absence of equality, 53
  Awakening and, 78–79, 86–89, 157–160, 170
  and consciousness, 47, 53–56, 59–63, 69, 92, 141, 341–342
  and death/sleep, 93–98, 151
  and economic/political power, 153–155
  happiness and, 68
  and karma/causality, 73–78
  and knowledge, 64–69, 89, 91, 142, 147–148, 149, 168, 254–301, 299, 321–322, 348–349, 365–366
  language and, 23, 65, 127, 141, 194–197, 321–322
  mastery of, 24, 40
  and mind, 167, 168
  and occult power, 61
  and Recognition, 70–73, 92, 99–106, 142, 149, 150–151, 170, 174–175, 254–301, 319–320
  and *Sangsara/Maya*, 119–121, 341–342
  self-determinism and, 165, 175
  See also Self-consciousness
Einstein, Albert, 197
Electro-magnetic field, 36–37, 54, 122, 183
  dynamics, 246–247, 269
Elixir of Life, 29
  See also Ambrosia, Current of
Emerson, Ralph Waldo, 69, 112

Empiricists, 191
Emptiness, 419
  Beauty and, 43
  experience of, 29, 261
  fullness of, 13, 43
  knowledge and, 65, 261
  meditation on, 15
  metaphysics and, 4–5, 136–139
  Self and, 39
  and transcendental symbols, 405–408
Enantiodromia, Law of, 388–389
Energy
  Aphorisms of, 324–325
  of Guru, 84
  and High Indifference, 102–106, 144–145, 181, 184–185
  and integration, 121–123, 183, 185, 320–321
  and karma/causality, 75–78
  and momentum, 352
  of phenomenal world, 133–139, 269, 323–324
  physics and, 88, 248–249, 323–324
  and silence, 167
  and transmutation, 161–163, 323–324
Enlightenment
  and Awakening, 78–79
  and compassion, 232
  and Recognition, 169
  and *Shunyata*, 424–425
  and traditional disciplines, 233, 407
Epistemology, 85
  Awakening and, 179
  and death, 94
  and idea/reference, 243–251
Equality, 53, 139–140
Equilibrium, Law of, 384–389, 413
  and *Nirvana*, 390–393
  space and, 405–408
Eros, 193, 232
Ethics
  and *dharmic* action, 147–148
  and Immanuel Kant, 33–34
  pragmatism and, 335
Ethics (Spinoza), 68
Evans-Wentz, Walter Y., 220
Evil
  absence of, 21, 144, 182
  creative principle and, 64, 144
  and death, 95–98, 96–98
  and detachment, 75
  and ignorance, 55, 75

morality and, 54–56
power of, 47
and suffering, 56
Evolution
  Darwin and, 247–248
  and equilibrium, 384–389
  and extinction, 249–250
  ignorance and, 181–182, 249
  and karma/causality, 77–78
  and occult powers, 59–63
  omniscience and, 38–41
  and space/time, 197–208, 378–384
  transcendence of self-consciousness and,
    16–17, 157–160, 182, 327–328
Exhalation, joyfullness and, 4
  See also Breath
Expectation(s), 6
Experience(s)
  and Awakening, 79–85, 160–163
  breath and, 3–4
  of communion, 152, 208–212
  and fire of consciousness, 35–38, 225
  of High Indifference, 99–106, 181
  and idea/reference, 241–251, 316–318, 330
  ordinary, as divine, 16
  and phenomenal world, 133–139, 399–401
  of Power, 16, 17–18, 183
  and proof, 108–117, 149, 159, 177, 318,
    331, 353
  psychic, 274–275
  silence and, 167
  vs. Recognition, 5, 15–16, 87, 129, 149,
    316, 425–426

Faith, 170
False predication, 174, 176–177, 333, 412–413
  and ignorance, 181–182
  philosophy and, 406–407, 410–411
  science and, 250, 353
Fear
  of death, 93–98
  and state of High Indifference, 186
  superstition and, 63
Fechner, Gustav Theodor, 66, 112
Feeling
  desire and, 80
  dharmic action and, 145–148
  and High Indifference, 185
  knowledge and, 66, 85–89, 115, 128–129,
    275, 297
  mind/manas and, 167–170

and prayer, 68
and thought, 45, 354–355
Felicity, 268
Fire/Flame, of Self
  experience of, 36–38, 270
  Guru and, 22, 84
  induction of, 84
  and knowledge, 70
  and physical body, 34–35, 37, 270
  Siva/Shakti and, 42
  transformation and, 295
Food, and Recognition, 72–73, 269
Formlessness, 13
  and creative principle, 27, 397–401
  evolution and, 16–17, 181–182
  and Law, 385–389
  and manifestation, 24, 133–139, 327–328
  Recognition of, 17–18, 30–31, 99–106
Fourth Dimension, 128–133
  continuum of, 343–344
  and unnumbered dimensions, 145
  See also Dimensionality
Freedom, 266
  See also Liberation

Gandhi, Mahatma, 82–83
Gautama, 140, 151, 193, 419
  See also Buddha
Genius, 98–99, 113–114
Gethsemane, agony of, 34
Ghose, Sri Aurobindo, 301, 309, 404, 407
Glorious Transition, 29
  See also Recognition(s)
Goddard, Dwight, 228
God(s)
  ambrosia of, 29
  and compassion, 104–105, 156
  and creative principle, 397
  desire and, 80
  -intoxication, 27
  knowledge and, 65, 110, 266–267, 299,
    413–414
  as object of worship, 18–19, 56–57
  and prayer, 68
  presence of, 106
  superstition and, 63
  and transcendental symbols, 245, 328–329,
    405–408
Gospel of Buddha, 140
Government, problem of, 153–156
  and Facism, 200

and temporal power, 200–204
and totalitarianism, 200–201
See also Democracy
Grace, 22
See also Self, spontaneity of
Gratitude, 33
Great Mother Unconscious, 293
Guilt, freedom from, 266, 296
Guru, 3, 419
   Atlantean Sage, 171–172
   and compassion, 104–105
   current of, 419
   devotion to, 83–84
   -disciple relationship, 5, 80, 84, 417
   divinity of, 22, 346
   as requirement of Awakening, 81–85
   See also Sage(s)/Compassionate Ones; Shankara

Hallucination(s), 331, 339, 367
Happiness
   Awakening and, 182
   breath and, 3–4
   discipline and, 162–163
   knowledge and, 85–89, 144
Hate, 55
   See also Love
Havelock, Ellis, 319
Heaven, Kingdom of, 78–79, 141
   Recognition and, 169
   and subject/object consciousness, 142–143
Hegel, 19, 66, 107, 108, 158, 300, 386, 419
   awakening and, 33
   and conception/perception, 192, 211, 299
Hell, 141
   illusion and, 181
High Indifference, 99–106, 119–121, 124–126, 281
   and compassion, 156
   and illusion, 180–181
   periods of, 218–222
   renunciation and, 143, 184–185
   and unity, 144–145, 340–341
Holy Ghost, 64
Humanity, 30
   cognition and, 132, 272
   consciousness and, 47, 59–63, 94–98, 125, 138
   and economic/political power, 153–155, 159
   and evil, 64
   and false predication, 177

and illusion/*Maya*, 137–139
inferior/superior, 48
and karma/causality, 76–78
and natural environment, 241
and occult powers, 61–62
somnambulism of, 93–98, 174, 175, 179
superstition and, 63
Hume, David, 109, 256, 333
Humility, 47
   and economic/political power, 155
   and egoism, 70–73
Hypnotic state, 97, 275, 367
   and Awakening, 181–182
   and bondage, 322, 379
   drug-induced, 114–115
   somnambulism and, 179
Hysteria, 275

I AM THAT
   alternative paths to, 32–33, 45–46, 66–69, 72, 82, 164–166, 170, 252–301
   and Beauty, 43
   intellect and, 38
   metaphysical "we" and, 24–25, 25, 49
   mind/*manas* and, 167–170
   Nirvana and, 26, 29, 186–189, 259
   Recognition of, 6, 8, 17–18, 29, 65, 71, 92, 110, 150–151, 183, 185, 257, 264–265
Idealism, 148, 149, 336, 349
   and conception/perception, 192
   and subjective consciousness, 349
Ideation, 124
   and attitude, 319–320
   illusion and, 181
   reference and, 241–251, 315, 329–330
Identity
   Aphorisms of, 315–414
   and death, 95–98
   and formlessness, 13, 144–145
   and High Indifference, 99–106, 181, 230
   and karma/causality, 73–78
   knowledge and, 23, 55, 64–68, 71, 110, 142, 159, 259, 263, 272–273, 371–372
   pain and, 35, 322
   recognition of *Atman*/Self/God and, 5–6, 13, 14, 25, 65, 73, 82, 110, 182, 257, 270, 346–347
   Siva/Shakti and, 42, 263
   Space-I/Point-I, 186–189, 378–384, 408–409
   and unity, 18–19, 144–145

Ignorance, 17, 98
  Chosen Race and, 47
  evil as, 55
  and evolution, 181–182, 249–250
  false predication and, 178, 181
  illusion and, 181
  and karma/causality, 77–78
  mind and, 306
  sin as, 161
Illness, 115
  and false predication, 178
  and religion, 182
Illumination, inner
  metaphysics and, 4–5
Illusion, 119–121, 300
  and bondage, 137–138
  and evolution, 181–182
  false predication and, 178, 301
  perception and, 179, 331, 409–410
Immaculate Conception, 42
Immortality
  ambrosia of, 29, 38
  creative principle and, 27, 64, 397–401
  and death, 94–98, 140, 150–151, 394–396
  divinity and, 346–347
  and space/time, 197–208, 255, 378–384
Incarnation, 77–78
India
  and concept of mind, 168
  and enjoyment, 268, 275, 298
  and Hindu literature, 340
  and Oriental Philosophy, 168–169, 231, 293
  Realism and, 135
  sage(s) of, 26, 82–83, 117, 125, 268–269, 294, 422, 424
  See also Sanskrit; Shankara; Vedanta
Infinity, 103, 120
  barriers to, 174–182, 256–257
  Recognition and, 149
  two/three-fold of, 130–131
Initiation, 143
Insanity, 109, 129, 297
  referential, 331
  suffering and, 301
Insight, 66
  and Buddhist *anatman*, 259
  and detachment, 88
  and idea/reference, 241–251, 374–375
  and integration, 180, 185, 320–321
  and mysticism, 252–301, 376, 414
  and proof, 107–117, 149, 159, 177, 193, 318, 331

Inspiration, 10, 124
  and attitude, 319–320
  and worship, 57
Integration of the Personality (Jung), 295, 299
Intellect
  as barrier to Self, 174–182, 256–257
  Buddhi and, 32–33, 169
  consciousness and, 47, 107–117, 167, 170, 174–182
  and dreamstate, 98
  and feeling, 45–46
  and Immanuel Kant, 33–34
  knowledge and, 65, 66, 85–89, 107–117, 260, 347–348
  mind/*manas* and, 167–170
  Recognition and, 26, 82, 85–89, 174–182, 260, 289
  transcendence and, 21, 90–92, 245, 260
  and unlearning, 88
  will and, 37, 167–170
Intuition, 110, 117
  cognition and, 272
  conception and, 410–411
  equilibrium and, 385–386
  language and, 196, 321–322
  manas and, 169–170

James, William, 65, 149, 270, 300
  and Hegel, 66
  and science of religion, 173
Joy
  and cognition, 170, 208–212, 268, 272
  and compassion, 156
  experience of, 3–4, 15, 20–21, 29, 115, 208–212, 261, 269
  fire of transformation and, 35
  relative consciousness and, 25
  Siva/Shakti and, 42
  unrevealed, during Recognition, 31
Jung, Dr. C. G., 225, 231, 251
  and transcendental symbols, 245, 291
  and transformative process, 292, 295, 299
  See also Psychology, analytic
Justice, 153

Kama manas (Wishfulness), 306
Kant, Immanuel, 107, 109, 343, 373, 384–385, 410, 419
  and *a priori* knowledge, 191
  and Awakening of others, 14, 86
  and *Critique of Pure Reason*, 169, 242, 251, 317, 374, 410–411, 425–426

and *Manas*, 33, 169
  pure apperception of, 10, 13, 33, 67, 86, 92
  thought vs. feeling and, 45
Karma, 419
  and Recognition, 73–78
  transcendence of, 6, 266
Kepler, Johannes, 112
Khan, Inayat, 19
Knowledge
  a priori/a posteriori, 191–192, 365, 373
  and conception/perception, 191–194, 241–251, 267–268, 331, 371–372, 376, 380, 413–414
  desire for, 24, 30, 79–85
  experiential, 5, 16, 108–117, 133–139, 208–212, 241–251, 331, 425–426
  extension of, to others, 30, 48, 50, 51, 58, 59–63, 65–69, 84–85, 111, 127, 141–142
  and fire of consciousness, 36–38, 84–85
  and humility, 47
  and idea/reference, 241–251, 331
  identification with, 23, 64–68, 142, 159, 182, 263, 272–273, 371–372
  and meaning of substance, 68–69
  objective content of, 21, 73–78, 144, 249–250, 315–414
  omniscient, 38–41
  and Recognition, 5–6, 30, 33, 55, 73–78, 85–89, 99–106, 108–117, 124, 133–139, 150–151, 167, 252–301, 371–372, 413–414
  transcendental, 45, 73–78, 85–89, 102–106, 124, 148–149, 150–151, 168, 194–197, 199–208, 241–251, 315–414, 425–426
  and unlearning, 87
Krishna, 111, 419
  quotation(s), 22

Language
  of Aphorisms, 315, 321–322
  Awakening and, 78–79
  and conception/perception, 191–194, 205, 233, 291, 343
  cosmic sense and, 49–50, 194–197
  and creativity, 27
  ego and, 23, 65
  Recognition and, 29, 127, 141, 194–197, 263
  and self-consciousness, 23, 39
  time/space and, 198, 205, 378–384
  See also Sanskrit

Lao-Tzu, 111
Law, universal, 384–389
Leaves of Grass (Whitman), 51, 82
Liberation, 419
  and Awakening, 78–79, 181–182
  barriers to, 174–182, 256–257
  death and, 93, 141
  discrimination and, 181–182
  and expression, 8–9, 51, 65, 82, 86, 127, 141
  initiation and, 143
  and karma/causality, 77–78
  meditation and, 6
  Nirvana and, 340
  pure apperception of, 10, 33, 67
  Recognition and, 182, 266
  and space/time, 199–208, 207, 378–384, 404–405
Libido, 225, 291
Life Divine, The (Ghose), 301, 309
Lifeforce, 272, 274, 277
  variability of, 10
Light
  alternative paths to, 33, 45–46, 66–69, 72, 82, 164–166, 170, 252–301
  of *Atman*, 6, 25, 29, 257
  and Awakening, 80–85
  and Beauty, 42–43
  and compassion, 156
  of consciousness, 29, 51, 66, 69–70, 84, 124–126, 261, 274–275, 324–325, 327, 341, 388
  crucifixion and, 34
  induction of, 84, 98
  photisms and, 274
  and Siva/Shakti, 42
  See also Fire/Flame, of Self
Logic, 109, 136, 315
  Aristotelian, 300
  and evidential proof, 177, 318, 331
  Hegelian, 299, 386
  and mathematics, 351
  and mind-action, 167
  and space/time, 197–198, 378–384
  spontaneity and, 294
  subject/object consciousness and, 141–142, 159, 179, 333, 374
Logos, 193, 232
Loka (World, of consciousness), 178, 419–420
Love
  all-pervasiveness of, 22
  Ananda, 32

and consciousness, 47, 55, 129, 143, 170, 232
Guru and, 80–85
identification with, 18, 55
and karma/causality, 77–78
and *Manas*, 32

Mahanirvana Tantra, 294–295
Mahaparanirvana, 187–188
Manas (intellectual principle), 32, 193, 420
levels of, 167–170, 176, 309
and mind, 167–170, 176
sensuality and, 176
See also Sanskrit
Mara, 51, 420
and morality, 54–56
Marx, Karl, 108
Mass. *See* Matter-energy
Mata (Opinion), 168–169
Mathematics, 351, 367, 370
space and, 379, 412
Matter-energy
and being, 4–5, 157–160, 225, 269, 326
and death, 150–151
and equality, 139–140
and inertia, 136–137, 326
and karma/causality, 75–78
nature of, 133–139, 144–145, 248–249, 323–324
physics and, 88, 248–249, 323–324
and *Sangsara/Maya*, 119–121
See also Body, physical; Substance; Universe
Maya (Illusion), 119–121
false predication and, 178
perception and, 137–139, 179
Meaning
of Aphorisms, On Consciousness Without An Object, 315–414
cosmic sense and, 49–50, 92, 136, 207–208, 344
discipline and, 162–163
egoism and, 71
Guru and, 83–84
infinity and, 131
mind and, 167–170
referential, 249–250, 318
soul and, 40–41, 108–110
of substance, 68–69
symbols and, 328, 405–408
theological dogma and, 82
Meditation
aphorisms and, 315

dhyana and, 229
open-eyed, 9
Recognition and, 6
technique, 11–12, 15
Mercy, 41
Metaphysics
and contemplation of THAT, 6
of death, 150–151
empty space and, 4–5
enjoyment and, 20
fire of consciousness and, 35
form/formlessness and, 13, 133–139
of God, 106
and illusion, 180
relative unconsciousness and, 136, 318–319
of *Sat-Chit-Ananda*, 32–33
of science, 328
and space/time, 207–208, 378–384
Mind
and Awakening, 79–85, 87–89, 166–170
and conception/perception, 191–194, 208–212, 267–268, 331, 341–342, 371–372
contemplation and, 3
and Divine Will, 165–166
division of, 305
and egoism, 167
and expression of thoughts, 8–9, 127, 141, 208–212, 258–259
and knowledge, 5, 64–68, 87–89, 208–212, 267–268, 291, 331, 354–355, 371–372
manas and, 168–170
and occult powers, 59–63
and sleep/dream states, 93–98
unlearning and, 87–88
Miracle(s)
supernatural powers and, 62–63
Mohammed, 111
mystical insight of, 14
Moksha (Liberation/Freedom), 78–79, 340
Monasticism, 164–166
Monism, 200, 301, 415
Morality
Awakening and, 54–56, 132
discipline and, 166
and Immanuel Kant, 33–34
love and, 129
politics and, 154
Moses, 111
Motion, Absolute Ceaseless
action and, 401–402

Ananda, 32
and energy, 352
and state of High Indifference, 186
witness state and, 343
Mysticism
and death, 150–151
experience of, 12–14, 111–112, 150–151, 252
Jesus Christ and, 19
and mind, 167–170
and omniscience, 38–41
and psychosis, 332
reason and, 23, 169, 193, 317
and transcendental symbols, 245, 291, 321, 405–408
understanding and, 49–50, 148, 250–251, 349, 376, 414
unfoldment of, 252–301

Namelessness, 31, 182–183, 230
God and, 245
See also High Indifference; Sanskrit
Naturalism, 134, 148, 158–159, 251, 335, 348
Nature, and Beauty, 42–43
Nectar, 29, 420
See also Ambrosia, Current of
Negation. *See* Subject-Object Consciousness, and negation
Neo-realism, 134, 158–159, 335, 348, 349
Newton, Sir Isaac, 112, 202, 246, 331
and law of inertia, 137
Nicodemus, 293
Nietzsche, 201
Nihilists, 406–407
Nirdvandva (freed from pairs of opposites), 298, 299
Nirmanakayas (Those who made the Great Renunciation), 104, 420
and compassion, 143
Nirvana, 421–422
and Aphorisms, On Consciousness Without An Object, 315–414
and Awakening, 78–79, 323
bliss of, 27, 190–191
dimensional Profundity and, 131, 145, 343–344
and equilibrium, 390–393, 396–397
I AM of, 29, 186–189, 259, 368–369, 380–384
and karma/causality, 75–78

perception and, 5, 26, 104, 344, 368–369
recognition of formlessness and, 13, 103, 141, 357
and space/time, 186–189, 199–208, 377–378, 379–384, 404, 412
and subject/object consciousness, 142–143, 168–170, 186–189, 323, 330, 344, 368–369
Nirvani, 422
Nirvikalpa Samadhi, 14, 422
western culture and, 14
Nonsubstantialists, 406–407
Nothingness, 136–139
and consciousness without an object, 362–363, 380–384
knowledge of, 263
sensuality and, 176
Noumenal World/Consciousness, 13
Buddha and, 14
Walt Whitman and, 14

Obedience, 164–166
Occultism, 59–63, 193
and mind, 167–170
Omniscience, 38–41
OM TAT SAT, 213, 314
Oneness
Beauty and, 43
consciousness and, 47–49, 350
I AM and, 18–19, 49
spirit and, 144–145
"we" of, 24–25, 49

Pain
and death, 96
identification and, 35
transcendence and, 7
Paracelsus, 112
Paranirvana, 13
Point-I/Space-I, 187–188
Paul, Saint, 19, 111
and Awakening, 80
and concept of evil, 55
and opposition, 51
Peace, 183, 267
Perception
conception and, 191–194, 267–268, 319–320, 331, 341–342, 344, 354–355, 364–414
and death, 93–98

false predication and, 177–178
and Kant's pure apperception, 10, 92
and knowledge, 86–89, 267–268, 331, 359
language and, 194–197, 321–322, 354–355
and recognition of Atman/Self, 5, 92, 169–170, 267–268
seeming emptiness and, 4–5, 137–139
and space/time, 197–198, 376, 378–384
Perfection, 401
Personality
bliss and, 8
death and, 93–98
of God-conscious men, 147–148, 149, 151
and the High Indifference, 106, 180–181
and renunciation, 184
sensibility and, 6–7
Phenomenalism, 407
Philosopher's Stone, 422
Philosophy
and Aphorisms, On Consciousness Without An Object, 315–414
and Awakening, 33, 78–79, 132, 158–159, 384–385
and conception/perception, 191–194, 252, 305–306, 334, 406–407, 410–411
and false predication, 176–177, 181, 333, 406–407
and idea/reference, 241–251, 316, 319–320, 333–334
India and, 135, 231
knowledge and, 65–66, 86, 90–92, 108–117, 148–149, 193, 252, 347–348
and meaning of substance, 68–69, 133–139, 333
and mind, 167–170
and proof, 107–117, 149, 159, 177, 193, 318, 331, 334
and space/time, 197–208, 378–384
See also Recognition, and western culture
Physics
and causality, 11, 48
and energy transformations, 323–324
metaphysics and, 4–5, 36, 87, 248–249
and thermodynamics, 248–249
Plato, 107, 111, 112, 126, 158, 277, 410
and conception/perception, 191–194
Plotinus, 209
Pluralistic Universe (James), 300

Poetry
as contemplation, 118–119
cosmic sense and, 49–50, 193
language and, 196, 294, 321–322
opposition to, 51
See also Aphorisms, On Consciousness Without An Object
Political power, 200–206
See also Government
Positivism, 407
Poverty, 164–166
Power(s), 338
barriers to, 174–182, 256–257
economic/political, 153–155, 159, 200–205
experience of, 16, 183
and Guru, 80–85
and language, 205, 321–322
occult, 59–63
and opposition, 51
silence and, 20, 167
space/time, 200–208, 378–384
woman and, 41–42
Pragmatism, 149, 158–159, 221, 335, 348, 402–403
Nirvana and, 340
Prajna, 243, 423
Prayer, 68
Pride, spiritual, 165
Profundity, 131, 232
consciousness without an object and, 320–321
and monasticism, 164–166
Psyche, 335
and law of enantiodromia, 388–389
organ of, 357–358
Psychic phenomena, 274–275
Psychological Types (Jung), 251, 300
Psychology, analytic, 231, 233, 291, 333
and interpretation, 249–250, 348, 374–375
and semi-esoterica, 305
Psychosis, 332
Purification
and asceticism, 161–163
identification and, 55
of physical body, 7

Rama Tirtha, 19
Rationalists, 191, 348

Realism, 135
Reality, 16, 300
 and conception/perception, 191–194, 318, 331, 349, 361, 410–411
 nonderivative, 362–363
 and *Sangsara/Maya*, 119–121
 and space/time, 197–208, 378–384, 408–409
Reason
 mind/*manas* and, 169
 mysticism and, 23, 252–301, 317
Recognition(s), 422–423
 alternative paths to, 32–33, 45–46, 66–69, 72, 82, 160–163, 165–166, 170, 181–182, 252–301
 Aphorisms of, On Consciousness Without An Object, 315–414
 barriers to, 173–182, 256–257
 conditions/propositions of, 79–85, 110, 112–117, 149, 167, 170, 173–174, 181–182, 184–185, 206–208, 273–301, 357
 consequences of, 25–26, 28, 51, 75, 76–78, 111, 182, 185, 186–189, 208–212, 346, 370–371, 375–376
 and egoism, 70–73, 75, 76–78, 119–121, 147–148, 165, 167
 expression of, 10, 15–16, 23, 25–27, 28, 29, 43–44, 51, 51–52, 65, 70–73, 82, 86, 90–92, 99–106, 116–117, 121, 127, 133, 141, 151, 160, 183, 194–197, 208–212, 222, 252–301, 413–414
 of formlessness, 13, 17–18
 Glorious Transition of, 29
 and Guru, 80–85, 346
 and incarnation(s), 5, 77–78
 and karma/causality, 73–78, 266
 meditation and, 6
 object of, 6, 39, 65–69, 70–73, 128–133, 169, 175–176, 181–182, 191–194, 305–414
 science and, 30, 31, 107–117, 129, 132, 246–247, 262, 318–319, 426
 of Self, 13–14, 17–18, 55–56, 61, 65, 67, 77–78, 85–89, 92, 150–151, 167, 169, 170, 185, 186–189, 208–212, 357
 solar and planetary, 56–57
 and space/time, 197–208, 322–323, 378–384
 superstition and, 63, 83
 western culture and, 14, 33, 82, 107–117, 135–139, 167–168, 179, 191–194, 223, 241–251, 252, 305, 335–336, 410–411
Reincarnation, 5

Relative consciousness, 423
 Awakening and, 78–79, 86–89, 119, 150–151
 as bridge for others, 24, 53–56, 58, 66–69, 77–78, 86, 89, 99–106, 107–117, 126, 127, 191–194
 and death, 93–98, 150–151
 evolution and, 16–17, 59–63, 157–160, 181–182, 197–208
 and karma/causality, 73–78
 and light of *Atman*/Self, 25, 66, 70–73, 257, 264
 and mind-action, 167, 167–170, 191–194, 331, 341–342, 354–355, 357–367
 phenomenal world and, 13, 62, 87, 119–121, 133–139, 153–155, 165, 179, 318, 348–349, 376, 397–401
 and Point-I/Space-I, 186–189, 322–323, 378–384
 and Self, 39, 64–69, 70–73, 92, 99–106, 254–301
 and unconsciousness, 136
 See also Egoism
Religion
 asceticism and, 160
 and attitude, 320
 and Awakening, 78–79, 96, 132, 266
 creative principle and, 63–64
 energy degradation and, 249–250
 God-Realized Men and, 111, 113, 173–174
 intellect and, 90–92
 and sick souls, 182
 theological orthodoxy and, 83–84
 union and, 42
 William James and, 66, 160, 173
 worship of I AM and, 19
Renunciation
 and austerity, 165–166
 compassion and, 104–105, 143, 170
 discipline of, 160–163, 164, 184, 253–301
 dispassion as, 170, 255–256
 and karma/causality, 77–78
 of *Nirvana*, 323
Revelation, 17–18
Russell, Bertrand, 86, 107, 108

Sacrifice
 asceticism and, 160–161
 and karma/causality, 77–78
 nonduality and, 91–92, 151
 will and, 184
Sacrilege, 42

Sage(s)/Compassionate Ones, 104–105, 155, 424
  Atlantean, 171–172
  conversing with a, 5
  encounters with, 5, 26, 111, 254, 291
  opposition to, 51
  works of, 37, 65, 81, 82, 111, 294, 340
  See also Guru; India; Shankara
Samadhi, 275, 297, 367, 422, 423
  western culture and, 14, 243
Samadhindriya, 357–358
Samsara (world-field), 423–424
Samshaya, 168–169
Sangsara (Subject/Object consciousness), 81, 119–121, 189–190, 338–339, 423–424
  Buddha and, 199
  mind/*manas* and, 168–169
  See also Maya (Illusion); Sanskrit
Sankhya, 144–145, 424
  See also Duality
Sanskrit
  and metapsychology, 357–358
  and mind as concept, 168
  and science of namelessness, 31
  and transcendent expression, 194–197
  translation of, 231, 298
Sat-Chit-Ananda (Being, Consciousness, Bliss), 32
  See also Sanskrit
Sat (THAT), 31, 193, 424
  See also Sanskrit
Saul of Tarsus, 80
  See also Paul, Saint
Scheffler, Johannn, 299
Schopenhauer, 241
Schwegler, Albert, 68
Science
  attitude and, 318–319
  and Awakening, 132
  and critical self-consciousness, 179, 225, 250, 426
  empiric, 246, 334–335
  and false predication, 176–177, 250, 353
  metaphysics of, 328
  and philosophy, 136, 262, 334, 337, 348
  Recognition and, 30, 31, 107–117, 129, 132, 223, 305–306
  and space/time, 199–200, 202, 378–384
  and technology, 203–204, 205
Secret Doctrines (Blavatsky), 37, 112, 228, 406
Secret of the Golden Flower, 296
Seeking, act of, 22–23

Self, 418
  and Beauty, 42–43
  and false predication, 176–177, 410–411
  formlessness of, 13, 17–18
  and karma/causality, 73–78
  language and, 23, 65, 127, 141, 194–197, 321–322, 329
  Nirvana and, 26
  and occultism, 61
  omniscience and, 39–41
  open-eyed meditation and, 9
  and perfection, 401
  Recognition of, 13–14, 17–18, 29, 55–56, 65, 67, 73, 77–78, 80–85, 80–89, 92, 99–106, 150–151, 167, 169, 185, 186–189, 208–212, 252–301, 346, 408–409
  spontaneity of, 21, 22, 186
  See also I AM THAT
Self-consciousness, 13, 424
  and death, 93–98, 165
  evolution and, 16–17, 59–63, 157–160, 181–182
  and false predication, 176–177, 181–182
  and karma/causality, 73–78
  language and, 23, 39, 127, 141, 194–197, 321–322
  Nirvana and, 339–340
  and Point-I/Space-I, 186–189, 322–323, 378–384
  Siva/Shakti and, 42
  vs. consciousness of Self, 13, 47, 64–68, 167, 174–180, 181–182, 267–268, 285, 327, 339–340
  See also Egoism
Self-determinism, 166, 175
  end of, 294
  mind and, 306
Self-effort
  and asceticism, 160–163
  and Awakening, 84–85
  and death, 95–98
  expression of, 208–212
  and God, 80–85
  and power, 63
  understanding and, 5, 97–98, 107–117, 253–301, 294
Selfishness
  absence of joy and, 48
  and morality, 54–56
  and Recognition, 91
Self-righteousness, 165

Sensation
  as barrier to Self, 175–176, 256–257
  and Beauty, 42–43
  and cognition, 130, 169, 348
  and current of bliss, 20–21
  and evolution, 17, 157–160, 181–182
  fire of consciousness and, 35, 167
  and intuition, 410–411
  knowledge and, 66, 87, 142, 348
  meditation and, 11, 12
  open-eyed meditation and, 9
  and phenomenal world, 133–139, 174, 175–176
  and substance, 4–5, 44, 129
Senses
  knowledge and, 5
  and perception of emptiness, 4–5
Seraphita, 78–79
Serenity, 267
Shakespeare, 112
Shakti
  as embodiment of light, 42
  See also Siva
Shankara, 3, 8, 28, 111, 193, 422, 424
  and absence of evil, 55
  and Awakening of others, 14, 57, 254
  and destruction of universe, 136
  and *Dhyana*, 231
  duality and, 119
  quotations, 16
  and Recognition, 13, 33, 169, 254
  and space/time, 199, 200, 412
  thought vs. feeling and, 45
  works by, 37, 66, 73
Shiva principle. *See* Siva
Short Treatise (Spinoza), 68
Shunyata (voidness), 414, 424–425
Sickness. *See* Illness
Silence
  cosmic sense and, 49–50
  current of bliss and, 19–21
  experience of, 29, 30–31, 40, 288
  and manifestation, 24, 40
  of Self, 13, 23, 39, 106
  Tathagata and, 140–142
  and thought, 45, 138, 167
Silesius, Angelus, 299
Simplicity, 21
Sin, 64
  carnal, 161
  and karma, 73–78

prayer and, 68
See also Christian orthodoxy
Siva, 42
Sleep
  and breakthough period(s), 291
  and death, 93–98
  and dreaming, 9–10, 95, 96, 330
  meditation and, 9
  and waking, 96
Socrates, 111
Solitude, 43–44
Soma, 29
See also Ambrosia, Current of
Soul(s)
  and cognizance, 136, 169
  and creative principle, 397
  and greatness, 53
  and meaning, 39
  religion and, 182
  and responsibility, 165–166
  somnambulism of, 96, 174, 175
  and space/time, 200–201, 378–384
  transformation of, 157–160
  will and, 30, 168
  yearning of, 78–79, 109
Sound
  essence of, 19
  silence and, 167
  See also Silence
Space
  dimensionality of, 128–133, 145, 157–160, 258, 272, 343–344, 379–384
  and the High Indifference, 106, 180–181, 185, 230, 283
  I-, and point-I, 186–189, 378–384
  and illusory perception, 137–139, 175–182, 379
  and karma/causality, 73–78
  and realization of Self, 22, 29, 71, 230
  and time, 197–208, 250, 378–379, 402–404, 405
  transcendence of, 6, 71, 314, 342–343, 378–384, 405, 408–409
Specialism, 78–79, 131, 243
Spengler, 192, 197, 207
  and time, 198
Spinoza, 19, 68, 111
Spirit
  and death, 94–98
  and equality, 140
  flame of, 22

Index

Guru and, 80–85
and matter, 144–145, 328–329
and sensuality, 175–176
and space/time, 200–201, 378–384
totality of, 144–145
Stillness, 26
Subject-object consciousness, 13, 47, 425
and absence of evil, 144
and adept world, 142–143
and Aphorisms, On Consciousness Without An Object, 315–414
and Awakening, 87, 174–182
as barrier, 174–182, 256–257
and Beauty, 42–43, 87
cosmic sense and, 49–50, 107–117, 193
and death, 95, 159–160
dimensionality of, 128–133, 143, 144, 145, 157–160, 258, 343–344
and egoism, 70–73, 91, 141, 147–148, 153–155, 174
evolution and, 17, 59–63, 157–160, 181–182
and indifference, 99–106, 143, 144–145, 180–181, 185
and integration, 121–123, 180, 185, 320–321
and karma/causality, 73–78
and knowledge, 69, 85–89, 91, 142–143, 150–151, 179, 191–194, 254–301, 426
language and, 23, 65, 127, 141, 194–197, 321–322
mind/*manas* and, 167–170, 267–268, 305–309
negation and, 141–142, 146–147, 174, 200–203, 327–328, 398–401
nirvana and, 104, 142, 168–170
and *Sangsara/Maya*, 119–121, 168–170, 339, 341–342
and Self, 39, 77–78, 92
and soul, 109, 168–170
and space/time, 197–208, 322–323, 378–384
See also Egoism
Substance
and karma/causality, 75–78
knowledge and, 65, 66, 262
meaning of, 68–69
sensation and, 4–5, 44
Substantialists, 406–407
Suffering, 416
belief in, 286
and compassion, 156
crucifixion and, 34–35
delusion and, 301

Equilibrium and, 396–397
evil and, 56
and karma/causality, 77–78
Sangsara and, 341–342
seeming emptiness and, 137–139
thought and, 322
Supernatural powers, 62
See also Occult powers
Superstition(s), 62–63
theology and, 82–83
System of the Vedanta, The (Desusen), 3

Tamasic [negative] indifference, 103, 425
Tao, 230, 407
Tathagata, Wisdom of, 83, 140–142
Technology, 203–204, 205
See also Science
Temptation, 14
discipline and, 166
and economic/political power, 153–155
Tenderness, 41
That
as consciousness without and object, 350, 370–471
and creative principle, 397–401
identification with, 6, 234, 355, 383, 408–409
See also I AM THAT
Theosophia, 25, 252, 305, 426
and alternative paths, 82, 165–166, 170
Thought
absence of, 30, 45, 167
clarity of, 10
during transcendence, 7, 30, 106, 208–212, 267–268
expression of, and liberation, 8–9, 30, 51, 98–99, 127, 141
and illusory perception, 137–139, 322
levels of, 305–309, 354–355
meditation and, 11
obscuration and, 28, 167, 306, 322
and Recognition, 25–26, 29–30, 231, 258–259, 267–268
satanic, 171
scientific/philosophic, 11, 348–349
Yoga and, 322
Tibetan Book of the Dead (Evan-Wentz), 228
Tibetan Yoga, 37, 228, 406
Tibetan Yoga and Secret Doctrines (Evans-Wentz), 11

Time
  and consciousness without an object, 360–361, 371–372, 378–379, 405
  domains of, 61–62, 198–199, 316, 376
  and karma/causality, 73–78
  and realization of Self, 22, 29, 378–379
  space and, 197–208, 250, 378–384, 402–404, 405
  transcendence of, 6, 255, 264, 316, 377–378, 405
Trance, 275
Transcendentalism, 78–79
Transcendent Being/Consciousness, 425–426
  barriers to, 174–182, 256–257
  Buddha and, 14, 199
  egoism and, 70–73, 74–78, 90–92, 147–148, 157–160, 174–175
  and expression, 127, 141, 194–197, 316–414
  and knowledge, 45, 73, 85–89, 142, 149, 157–160, 168, 179–180, 243, 264, 331, 357–358, 417
  and physical matter, 4–5, 73–78, 144–145
  Recognition and, 150–151, 262, 264, 316–414
  and space/time, 199–208, 264, 377–378, 379–384
  vs. cosmic consciousness, 12–14, 131, 157, 179–180
  See also Consciousness
Truth
  and Aphorisms, On Consciousness Without An Object, 315–414
  cognition and, 170, 257–258, 272
  experience of, 17–18, 82, 149
  and illusion, 409–410
  invulnerability of, 88
  language and, 65, 127, 141, 194–197, 321–322, 354–355

Unconsciousness, relative, 136
Understanding
  cognition and, 129, 169, 272, 375–376
  language and, 194–197, 245, 321–322
  liberation and, 9, 408–409
  mind/*manas* and, 169
  philosophic reconciliations and, 148–149
  referential interpretation and, 250–251
  unlearning and, 87–88, 182
Unity
  I AM and, 18–19, 49, 65, 110
  Kant's pure apperception of, 33, 67
  Siva/Shakti and, 42
  totality of, 92, 144–145, 321–322

Universe
  apperceptive consciousness and, 13, 67, 136
  and Awakening, 136–139, 157–160, 179
  and creative principle, 397–401
  dream and, 178
  energy transformation and, 323–324
  and equality, 139–140
  and equilibrium, 389
  fire of consciousness and, 35
  and karma/causality, 73–78
  Knowledge/Meaning and, 40–41, 64–68, 321–322
  and Law, 384–389
  and *Sangsara*/*Maya*, 119–121
  secondary, and illusion, 180–181
  and space/time, 197–208, 230, 378–384, 408–409
  and subject/object consciousness, 142–143, 177, 179, 181, 321–322, 367–368, 376
  sustaining power of, 16, 29, 71, 133–139, 178, 295, 338–339, 397–401

Varieties of Religious Experience (James), 160, 224
  and science of religion, 173
Vedanta, 3, 305, 426
  Advaita, 33, 415, 422
  and *Ahamkara*, 174
  and *Avidya*, 178
  and *Dhyana*, 231
  error of, 180
  and *Maya*, 119
  meditative readings of, 28
  and subjective consciousness, 349
Vidya (knowledge), 426
Violence, 18
Virgin, Celestial, 42, 64
Voice of the Silence, 73, 167
Void[ness], 327, 353, 356, 369
  and creative principle, 397–401
  and *Shunyata*, 424–425
  spatial, 342–343, 380–384, 405–408
  von Hartmann, 356
Voodoo, 63, 249

Waking state
  and consciousness without an object, 363
  open-eyed meditation and, 9
  space and, 379
Water of Life, 29
  and fire of consciousness, 37
  See also Ambrosia, Current of
Weierstrass, 343

Well-being, 3–4
Whitman, Walt, 14, 19, 82, 112, 124–125, 210
  life of, 152
  opposition to, 51
Will
  and absence of evil, 144
  balance and, 44, 175, 282
  battle of, 161
  causality and, 16, 30
  and creative principle, 397–401
  and destruction of universe, 136, 178
  Divine, 165
  dream-state and, 97
  to live, 9, 34, 35, 186, 278
  mind and, 167–170
  out-of-body experience and, 37
  self-, 165, 175
  soul and, 30, 168
  womanhood and, 41–42, 175
Wisdom, 423
  barriers to, 174–182, 256–257
  and economic/political power, 155
  and genius, 98–99
  and High Indifference, 99–106, 180–181
  and karma/causality, 77–78
  opposition to, 51
  and path(s) of knowledge, 33, 53, 64–68, 72, 82, 107–117
  of Thathagata, 83
  thought vs. feelings and, 45–46, 66
Witness state, 225, 343
  dreaming and, 9–10
  and the High Indifference, 106, 181
  silence of mind and, 167
Wolff, Sherifa, 5, 25
  gratitude and, 25
Woman, 41–42
Worship
  and attitude of otherness, 56–57
  and creative principle, 63–64, 397–401
  God as object of, 18–19
  and identity, 182
  and prayer, 68

Yepes, John, 152
Yoga, 321–322
  culmination of, 323–324
Yutang, Lin, 231

Zen Buddhism, 407